Understanding Inequality

Understanding Inequality

The Intersection of Race/ Ethnicity, Class, and Gender

Second Edition

Edited by
Barbara A. Arrighi

ROWMAN & LITTLEFIELD PUBLISHERS, INC.
Lanham • Boulder • New York • Toronto • Plymouth, UK

ROWMAN & LITTLEFIELD PUBLISHERS, INC.

Published in the United States of America
by Rowman & Littlefield Publishers, Inc.
A wholly owned subsidary of The Rowman & Littlefield Publishing Group, Inc.
4501 Forbes Boulevard, Suite 200, Lanham, Maryland 20706
www.rowmanlittlefield.com

Estover Road
Plymouth PL6 7PY
United Kingdom

Copyright © 2007 by Rowman & Littlefield Publishers, Inc.

British Library Cataloguing in Publication Information Available

Library of Congress Cataloging-in-Publication Data

Understanding inequality : the intersection of race/ethnicity, class, and gender /
edited by Barbara A. Arrighi. — 2nd ed.
    p. cm.
  Includes bibliographical references and index.
  ISBN-13: 978-0-7425-4678-3 (cloth : alk. paper)
  ISBN-13: 978-0-7425-4679-0 (pbk. : alk. paper)
  ISBN-10: 0-7425-4678-0 (cloth : alk. paper)
  ISBN-10: 0-7425-4679-9 (pbk. : alk. paper)
  1. Equality—United States. 2. United States—Social conditions. 3. Minorities—
United States—Social conditions. 4. Social classes—United States. 5. Sex role—
United States. I. Arrighi, Barbara.
  HN90.S6U53 2006
  305.0973—dc22   2006019621

Printed in the United States of America

♾™ The paper used in this publication meets the minimum requirements of
American National Standard for Information Sciences—Permanence of Paper
for Printed Library Materials, ANSI/NISO Z39.48-1992.

For
My family

Contents

Preface

My primary goal in editing this text was to create a reader that would encourage students to think in new ways about old issues. In order to achieve that goal, I knew it was imperative to include a mixture of scholarly, research-oriented readings and essays that would elicit classroom discussion. As a writer and researcher, the highest praise I can offer my colleagues whose work is included here is that I wish I had been the author of the fine writing assembled in this reader.

The selections have been excerpted to a digestible length and degree of difficulty suitable for undergraduate courses. I think readability has been achieved without jeopardizing the integrity of the writing or intent of the authors. Having said that, it is my sincere hope the selections will whet your appetite so that you will read the original sources in their entirety. You will not be disappointed.

Acknowledgments

Many people have influenced the writing of this text. First and foremost, I pay tribute to the students in my classes from whom I continue to gain an understanding about difference, tolerance, patience, humor, humility, teaching, and learning.

My heartfelt appreciation is extended to the contributors for granting permission to have their writing included in this text. It speaks to the high value these scholars place on the continued discourse about race/ethnicity, class, and gender. I am grateful, too, for the helpful comments of anonymous reviewers who assisted me in thinking outside of the box, both in terms of content and context. Many ongoing discussions and debates with numerous colleagues from varied disciplines have influenced my thinking about the issues raised in these pages. I am grateful to Joan Ferrante's undergraduate social research class for completing the data collection for the "Mating, Marriage, and the Marketplace: A Survey of College Students' Attitudes and Expectations" article. I regret the acknowledgment of their contribution was inadvertently omitted in the first edition. I want to thank colleagues J. Robert Lilly and Sharlotte Neely who suggested readings to me. I wish to acknowledge Okera Nsombi, a former student, who has become a mentor. Okera's observations about race/ethnicity have been invaluable to me as is his gentle way of facilitating student learning. Thanks to Alan McClare, executive editor, at Rowman & Littlefield, for his assistance in this process and his openness to the addition of editor's notes for this edition. I am appreciative of Terry Pence, department chair, for creating a supportive environment for faculty research and to the administration of Northern Kentucky University for granting me the time to complete the second edition of this text. A special note of appreciation to Peter Kivisto, Lauren Kane, and Terri Teleen for their important contribution to this text.

I acknowledge and appreciate the patience, tolerance, and support of my family who continue to be the impetus for what I do.

The following credit lines are presented in the order in which the chapters appear.

Charles Lemert, "Mysterious Power on Social Structures," from *Social Things: An Introduction to the Sociological Life*, by Charles Lemert (Lanham, MD: Rowman & Littlefield Publishers, 1997), pp. 124–135, 152. Reprinted with permission.

Stephen Worchel, "'They' Are All the Same, but Each Member of My Group is Unique," from *Written in Blood: Ethnic Identity and the Struggle for Human Harmony*, by Stephen Worchel (New York: Worth Publishers, 1999). Used with permission.

bell hooks, "Women and Feminism," from *Talking Back: Thinking Feminist, Thinking Black*, by bell hooks (Boston: South End Press, 1989), pp. 177–83. Reprinted with permission.

Derrick Bell, "Divining Our Racial Themes," from *Faces at the Bottom of the Well*, by Derrick Bell (New York: Basic Books, Inc., 1992). Reprinted by permission of Basic Books, a member of Perseus Books, L.L.C.

Fatema Mernissi, "Size 6: The Western Women's Harem," from *Scheherazade Goes West*, by Fatema Mernissi, copyright © 2001 by Fatema Mernissi. Abridged by permission of Atria Books, an imprint of Simon & Schuster Adult Publishing Group.

Arturo Madrid, "Diversity and Its Discontents." The original version of this essay was delivered as the Tomás Rivera lecture at the 1988 meeting of the American Association for Higher Education. Reprinted from *Academe* (November–December l990) by kind permission of the author.

Billie Wright Dziech, "Coping With the Alienation of White, Male Students," from *Chronicle of Higher Education* (13 January 1995). Washington, D.C. Reprinted with permission.

Simone de Beauvoir, "The Second Sex," from *The Second Sex*, by Simone de Beauvoir, trans. H. M. Parshley (New York: Alfred A. Knopf, Inc., 1952, 1980). Reprinted by permission of Alfred A. Knopf, a Division of Random House, Inc.

Diane Reay, "The Double-Bind of the 'Working-Class,' Feminist Academic: The Success of Failure or the Failure of Success?" from *Class Matters*, edited by Pat

Mahoney and Christine Zmroczek (New York: Taylor & Francis, 1997), pp. 18–29. Reproduced by permission of Taylor & Francis.

Michelle Fine, Lois Weis, Judi Addelston, and Julia Marusza, "(In) Secure Times: Constructing White Working-Class Masculinities in the Late Twentieth Century," from "(In) Secure Times" in *Gender & Society* 11 (1997): 52–68. Reprinted by permission of Sage Publications, Inc.

Michael Kimmel, "A Black Woman Took My Job," from "A Black Woman Took My Job," by Michael S. Kimmel in *New Internationalist* (November 2004). Toronto: New Internationalist. Reprinted with permission.

Haya Stier and Marta Tienda, "Are Men Marginal to the Family? Insights from Chicago's Inner City," from *Men, Work and Family*, edited by Jane C. Hood (Thousand Oaks, CA: Sage Publications, 1993), pp. 24–43. Reprinted by permission of Sage Publications, Inc.

William J. Chambliss, "Policing the Ghetto Underclass: The Politics of Law and Law Enforcement," from *Social Problems* 41, no. 2 (May 1994): 177–94. Reprinted by permission.

Leslie Marmon Silko, "America's Iron Curtain: The Border Patrol State," from *Yellow Woman and a Beauty of the Spirit: Essays on Native American Life Today*, by Leslie Marmon Silko, copyright © 1995 by Leslie Marmon Silko. (Originally appeared in *The Nation Magazine*.) Reprinted with permission of Simon & Schuster Adult Publishing Group.

Marc Cooper, "The Heartland's Raw Deal: How Meatpacking Is Creating a New Immigrant Underclass," from "The Heartland's Raw Deal: How Meatpacking Is Creating a New Immigrant Underclass," by Marc Cooper in *The Nation* (3 March 1997): 10–12, 14–17. Reprinted with permission.

Judith Butler, "Bodies that Matter: On the Discursive Limits of 'Sex,'" from *Bodies That Matter*, by Judith Butler, copyright © 1993. Reproduced by permission of Routledge/Taylor & Francis Group, LLC.

Judith Lorber, "Believing Is Seeing: Biology as Ideology," from "Believing Is Seeing," by Judith Lorber in *Gender & Society* (1993): 568–81. Reprinted by permission of Sage Publications, Inc.

Laureen Snider, "Towards Safer Societies: Punishment, Masculinities, and Violence against Women," from "Towards Safer Societies," by Laureen Snider in *The British Journal of Criminology* 38 (1998): 1–39. Reprinted by permission of Oxford University Press.

Barbara A. Arrighi, "Tomboys Yes, Janegirls Never." By permission of the author.

Anne Fausto-Sterling, "Hormonal Hurricanes: Menstruation and Female Behavior," from *Myths of Gender*, by Anne Fausto-Sterling. Copyright © 1986 by Basic Books, Inc. Reprinted by permission of Basic Books, a member of Perseus Books, L.L.C.

Deborah Tannen, "Talking from 9 to 5: How Women's and Men's Conversational Styles Affect Who Gets Heard, Who Gets Credit, and What Gets Done at Work," from *Talking From 9 to 5*, by Deborah Tannen. Copyright © 1994 by Deborah Tannen. Reprinted by permission of HarperCollins Publishers.

Richard L. Zweigenhaft and G. William Domhoff, "Women in the Power Elite," from *Diversity in the Power Elite*. Reprinted by permission of the authors and Rowman & Littlefield.

Sally Ann Davies-Netzley, "Women above the Glass Ceiling: Perspectives on Corporate Mobility and Strategies for Success," from *Gender & Society* 12: 340–53, copyright 1998 by Sage Publications. Reprinted by permission of Sage Publications.

Katha Pollitt, "Invisible Women." By permission of the author.

Jane Jerome Camhi, "Women against Women: American Antisuffragism, 1880–1920."

Susan J. Douglas, "Where the Girls Are: Growing Up Female with the Mass Media," from *Where the Girls Are*, by Susan J. Douglas, copyright © 1994 by Susan J. Douglas. Used by permission of Times Books, a division of Random House, Inc.

Barbara A. Arrighi, "Mating, Marriage, and the Marketplace: A Survey of College Students' Attitudes and Expectations." By permission of the author.

Kathleen Rowe, "The Unruly Woman: Gender and the Genres of Laughter," from *The Unruly Woman: Gender and the Genres of Laughter*, by Kathleen Rowe, copyright © 1995. Courtesy of the University of Texas Press.

Lawrence Otis Graham, "Black Man with a Nose Job: How We Defend Ethnic Beauty," from *Member of the Club*, by Lawrence Otis Graham (New York: HarperCollins, 1995), pp. 223–31. Copyright © 1995 by Lawrence Otis Graham. Reprinted by permission of HarperCollins Publishers, Inc.

Timonth Nonn, "Hitting Bottom: Homelessness, Poverty, and Masculinity." Reprinted with permission of the author.

Edward H. Thompson, "Older Men as Invisible Men in Contemporary Society," from *Older Men's Lives* by Edward H. Thompson, pp. 15–17, 18–21. Copyright © 1994. Reprinted by permission of Sage Publications

John Stuart Mill, "The Subjection of Women." 1869.

Susan Estrich, "Real Rape," from *Real Rape: How the Legal System Victimizes Women Who Say No*, by Susan Estrich, pp. 1, 3–9, 11–15, 29–32, 36–41, 43, 97–98, 102–4. Cambridge, MA: Harvard University Press, copyright © 1987 by the President and Fellows of Harvard College. Reprinted by permission of the publisher.

Mary F. Rogers, "Clarence Thomas, Patriarchal Discourse, and Public/Private Spheres," from *Sociological Quarterly* 39, no. 2 (1998): 289–308. Reprinted with permission of Blackwell Publishing, Inc.

Karen Blumenthal, "How Harvard Helped Curb Title IX's Role in Admitting Women," from *WSJ*, 3/02/05.

Walda Katz-Fishman, "Downsizing Higher Education: Confronting the New Realities of the High-Tech Information Age Global Economy," from *Understanding Inequality*, 1st ed. Reprinted with permission of the author.

Introduction

In the introduction of the first edition of this text, I told of a young black male who was dragged to his death because his skin color was darker than the white man's who killed him. I wish that as I write the second edition, I could report that significant progress has been made in the way we think about one another and act toward each other. I wish I could write that the color of one's skin, the texture of one's hair, the shape of one's skin never intrudes on our treatment of one another. Instead, it seems that as a society we lurch along in a nonlinear manner in the quest for greater equality, too often committed to denying the -isms—racism, classism, sexism, ethnocentrism—rather than confronting them.

As I write the introduction for the second edition, it is ironic that recently another man was tied to a pickup truck and dragged to his death—dragged for more than a mile. He was left to die in the middle of a busy intersection of Gallup, New Mexico. Only this time the dark-skinned man was of Mexican heritage. The officials in Gallup maintained that it had nothing to do with race/ethnicity.[1] Their reaction is not unique. There have been other "nonracial" incidents. For example, in Sparta, Tennessee, this summer, officials denied that race was a factor in the burning—in one night—of two black churches and five vacant houses in one block.[2]

The creator of a board game called Ghettopoly denied racism was a factor in a Monopoly-like game he marketed that uses racial stereotypes including: "murderous, thieving, dope-dealing, carjacking degenerates." Instead of the usual monopoly pieces, Ghettopoly players move pimps, machine guns, and rocks of crack around the board.[3]

The principal of Stratford High School in Goose Creek, South Carolina, and the police denied racism as they planned and executed a 6:45 A.M. drug

1

raid of the school, a time when most of the students in attendance would be
black—students who represent only one-quarter of the student population.[4]
The principal approved of police hiding in stairwells and closets. With guns
drawn and attack dogs at the ready, police jumped out, yelling at students to
kneel down and face the wall. Black students made up two-thirds of those
handcuffed and questioned at gunpoint. No drugs were found.[5]

Feeling humiliated and let down by those in authority, students reported
that initially they thought something had happened at the school and the police were there to protect them, not arrest them. The disquieting photo published in *The New York Times* showing students kneeling and handcuffed, surrounded by police and lunging dogs, is reminiscent of scenes played across
television screens and newspapers over forty years ago.

Some officials in Cincinnati, Ohio, deny racism has any bearing on the fact
that at least nine of the city's firehouses are either 90 percent black or 90 percent white. Further, firehouses with black firefighters have no black personnel
in command positions, whereas, firehouses with white firefighters have white
personnel in command positions. Black firefighters make up no more than
one-fourth of the department's officers.[6]

While some argue it is not about racism, recently resigned city manager
Valerie Lemming (who is black) views it as "emblematic of deeper
divides—in the city, at City Hall, and in the Fire Department."[7] There are some
tensions between white and black firefighters that remain due to the mishan-
dling of civil disobedience that erupted in the city in 2001 after police shot
and killed an unarmed black male. In protest, black firefighters resigned from
the firefighters' union. Strained relations between union firefighters (mostly
white) and nonunion (mostly black) continues today.

While we deny that racism is a problem, the FBI confirms that more than
half of the nation's 7,400 reported hate crimes in 2003 were the result of racial
prejudice.[8] And the Southern Poverty Law Center listed 762 hate groups in existence in the United States. Despite the reports, the Department of Homeland
Security and the FBI acknowledge their attention is focused on foreign threats,
not domestic terrorists. White supremacist groups failed to get even a mention
in a recent internal assessment report.[9]

We insist that racism is nonexistent and segregation has been outlawed for
decades, yet only 19 percent of white children have contact with peers from
other ethnic groups on a daily basis—even though according to the census,
40 percent of children are nonwhite. Two-thirds of black children report living in neighborhoods and attending schools that are for the most part segregated.[10] Indeed, recently in Richmond, Virginia, a black couple expressed
interest in a home that was for sale. The owner told the couple the home
could be sold to whites only. Although the owner's 1944 deed did contain a
restrictive covenant—a vestige of the structure of racist property laws and
practice—it was ruled unconstitutional in 1948, and outlawed by the Fair

Housing Act of 1968.[11] Yet the homeowner hadn't moved beyond the 1940s in his thinking.

We deny racism and classism exist, despite the faces on our televisions recently of distraught, dispossessed blacks and Latino people, left to fend for themselves for five days after Hurricane Katrina. An emergency plan had been established and emergency exercises took place in New Orleans just weeks before the catastrophic hurricane and aftermath, yet no official (at any level of government) heeded warnings from a variety of scientists about the number of casualties there would be if the city were flooded. As a result, those who have suffered the most deleterious effects are those in New Orleans that lived at or near the poverty level (the majority of whom are members of minority groups). Few had cars or funding to allow them to escape from the rapidly flooding of the city. Thus, the wrath of Katrina played out on national television the intersection of race/ethnicity and class, the problem white America continues to deny.

Some students complain—not you, of course—because they *have* to take a race and gender course as part of their undergraduate degree. In their minds, they don't discriminate against anyone so why should they *have to listen to this stuff*? If prejudice and discrimination aren't coming from you or me, then from where, whom, what?

WHAT'S OLD? WHAT'S NEW?

I have retained a majority of the readings from the first edition. I concur with one anonymous reviewer's phrase: some of the articles "kick-ass." No seismic paradigm shift has occurred in the structure of society or our institutions that would call for a substantial change in the readings. What is new in the second edition are editor's notes following some of the readings. Connecting the scholarly with praxis broadens the sociological analyses beyond the text, beyond the classroom because the sociological is everywhere in our lives.

For the editor's notes I relied upon what is happening around us in the daily news. I did so for two reasons: First, daily news articles act as an effective barometer of the social, political, and economic milieu and second, news clips are an effective pedagogical tool to facilitate students' understanding of the complex relationship of race/ethnicity, class, and gender. There is something in the news every day that relates to the subject matter of this text.

The introduction of the first edition opened with a quote from Charles Lemert: "In . . . America, it was the well-off white boys who counted most. Their girls ran a far second. Few others counted, and some who didn't were told so in so many words. . . . The big social things affect us, often, in silence, but affect us and produce us they do."[12]

Lemert was referring to what things were like when he was growing up, in the 1950s when white privilege reigned supreme, when whites didn't have to be bothered to think about color and men didn't have to think about women as possible competitors. The institutions of society were structured to support the privilege of a few. Then, in 1964, the Civil Rights Act, a federal mandate, was put in place to rid institutions of overt discrimination and segregation. The consequences of that mandate continue to reverberate throughout our society. Laws regulate behavior (action) that the social deem unacceptable or, in some cases, desirable; however, laws do not legislate attitudes (feelings). The task now is to rid institutions of the vestiges of the, often covert, discrimination that remain. The underlying attitudes supporting discriminatory behavior get changed from one person to the next—mothers and fathers to sons and daughters, teachers to pupils, pupil to pupil, employer to employee, employee to employee, and so on.

As you read this text, it is my hope that you will think about how similar people are, not their differences. After all, the evidence indicates that all humans migrated out of Africa. Some geneticists argue that the first migration occurred during the Ice Age, a period when Europe would not have been fit for habitation.[13] Archaeologists maintain that a second migration out of Africa, to what is now Europe, occurred much later. If this is so, if we have a common ancestry, why do we expend so much energy denying it?

No matter the outer trappings of folks—the shade of one's skin, the shape of one's skin, the nap of one's hair—people want to live a comfortable life: obtain a good job, own a nice home, raise a healthy family, go on vacations. The convergence of people's life goals and values is worth focusing on, not the differences of our exterior facade. Despite the superficial differences, women and men, blacks and whites are more alike than different. There are many questions to consider as you survey the readings. Why do we as a society persist in translating physical differences into social and political differences in our everyday lives?

If we all want much the same things in life, how do we get divided, segregated, subordinated, dominated? If we are more alike on the interior—the part of us that is supposed to matter—why is it so easy to settle for behavior that is about dividing, segregating, dominating? Is there some payoff for engaging in discriminatory behavior—behavior that is inconsistent with the notion of equality, one of the values that we say we hold dear? Part of the reason—which you will find in the readings—is that some groups in society control more of the resources (wealth) so there is less for the majority to divvy up.

Understanding inequality requires examining the pattern of distribution of resources and opportunities in a society. Who gets what? Do certain groups consistently have greater access to society's most desirable resources? If so, at whose expense? If distribution is structured—built into our system—what does that mean for individual effort? Put another way, what is one's chance of getting a piece of the pie? What factors determine the size of the piece? Is the deck stacked in favor of some and against others?

RACE/ETHNICITY, CLASS, AND GENDER

The "isms" are interrelated. What does that mean? It means it is difficult to examine the issue of race/ethnicity without including social class in the analysis. The same is true for gender and class. I have designated sections for each -ism in the text, but it is intended to simplify the discussion. The -isms don't occur in isolation, there is an interaction—as I noted in the discussion of the poor and the people of color left uncared for in New Orleans after Hurricane Katrina. Even if a discussion focuses on gender and/or race/ethnicity, social class is in the equation, whether explicitly stated or implied. Keep in mind what was stated about *patterns*. There is a pattern—a structure—to the distribution of material resources in this society that consistently places the majority of women and other minorities in lower income groups than white males.

For example, in reviewing 2003 census data for median earnings of full-time, year-round workers (median earnings means that half of those in each group earn above and half earn below): white men's earnings were $41,211; black men's earnings were $32,241; white women's earnings were $31,169; black women's earnings were $26,965; Hispanic men's earnings were $26,083; Hispanic women's earnings were $22,363.[14] The earnings' discrepancy among the groups represents a pattern, a structure of income inequality that has persisted for decades, despite civil rights legislation of 1964, despite affirmative action. The disparity persists even if the occupations are the same. The disparity persists even if the analysis controls for education.

WHAT'S MISSING?

One thing is certain: The pathway to equality for women and other minorities will falter if it excludes white men. Gender doesn't mean females, but too often, scholarly literature either excises white males from the discourse or excoriates them as the group that bears the blame. Am I denying the existence of patriarchy as a system of domination? Of course not! However, when one group is discarded in order to include other groups, we employ zero sum tactics. And when we summarily censure or scapegoat a group, one possible consequence is the intensification of intergroup conflict whether it is blacks against whites or men against women. Using marginalization or exclusion as a form of social control grants arbitrary dismissal of others. By limiting the input of a select few we demonstrate only that the oppressors' strategies have been internalized. The consequence: pre-Enlightenment—partial knowledge, not a full debate on any subject. Excluding or denigrating all white males because women and other minorities have been denied full participation in matters of intellect and policy does little to advance equality in society.

NEW SCAPEGOATS: WHITE MALES

While at first glimpse it might seem justifiable as well as expeditious to attribute all things negative to white males, I ask that you consider two factors. First, excluding males ignores the disparate economic and/or social conditions of men, many of whom are in desperate economic circumstances. Second, if equalizing opportunity and reducing intergroup conflict are desirable societal goals, then understanding the status of white males vis-à-vis other groups is paramount. The inclusion of white males in the discussion increases understanding of the complexities of issues surrounding race/ethnicity, gender, and class. It then becomes possible to think of men not as a monolithic group of elite oppressors but as a heterogeneous group—fulfilling rather narrow societal gender/class/race/ethnicity roles just as women do. Through the inclusion of white males, intergroup commonalities can become evident.

THE ROLE OF PATRIARCHY

While calling for the inclusion of white males in the discussion, it is necessary to acknowledge that patriarchy exists. The definition of patriarchy is that of a system of domination by a few men over *all* others, including children, women, and men. By definition then, women and most men are subordinated in some form. That is not to deny that in a patriarchal system women rank only slightly above children (if that). However, finding the connections that women and men have as well as the divisions will provide a greater understanding than will simplify focusing on the latter.

EQUALITY ELUDES US

There is no question that the road to equality on the basis of sex and race/ethnicity is long and arduous. Since the passage of the Civil Rights Act, additional laws have been enacted and existing laws have been modified to ameliorate inequality. Scholarly tomes and research, which previously ignored or marginalized minority voices, have slowly begun to integrate the thinking of the *other* into the sociological center. For example, the writings of scholars such as W. E. B. DuBois and Frances Gilman Perkins, whose works were once dismissed by sociological gatekeepers, are now included in many theory texts. Yet, after decades of legislation and heightened debate, patriarchy persists and full equality remains elusive.

More than a few selections in this volume call attention to the embeddedness of patriarchy, meaning that it permeates societal institutions; that it is built into the political and economic system. Other readings demonstrate how those attempting to overcome the matrix of domination *learn* their place.

Some resist, many do not. For too many, the oppressed unwittingly become complicit in their subordination.

IMPORTANT CONCEPTUAL TOOLS

Colonization is a term that can facilitate understanding the status of minority groups in society. It means control by a dominant force over a dependent people. Aime Cesare summarized the crippling effect of colonization on indigenous populations as "millions of men in whom fear has been cunningly instilled, who have been taught to have an inferiority complex, to tremble, kneel, despair."[15] How does the colonized throw off the colonizer? Frantz Fanon wrote: "In decolonization, there is therefore the need of a complete calling in question of the colonial situation."[16] In other words, one must question embedded societal constraints. The decolonized person thinks and acts *outside the box*. Martin Luther King Jr. acted outside of the box. Rosa Parks acted outside of the box. Suffragettes acted outside of the box. Charles Lemert (one of the authors in this text) suggests, "Parents and teachers could be said to be the colonizers of the minds of children."[17]

There are other terms that will be useful in guiding you through the readings. For example, in the first reading, Lemert introduces the concept of social structure—the patterned constraints, opportunities, and invisible but powerful forces in our everyday lives that sort us out, and work on us as we play, sleep, and work—pushing and pulling us as we go about the business of living. We never think about social structure unless it doesn't work for us, but it is always there bearing down on us. *Social structure*, an abstract-sounding term, too often makes people's eyes glaze over, but Lemert brings the term to life with down-to-earth examples, such as the social and economic conditions of the Lakota and the Hallway Hangers.

Stephen Worchel's reading is a short, cogent explanation about stereotyping and goes a long way to enlighten readers about the process by which we tend to pigeonhole members of various groups with our preconceived ideas about them. Some classic stereotypes include: red heads have tempers, Latino men are macho, Asians are math wizards, people who receive food stamps drive expensive cars. Worchel makes us aware of the consequences of making judgments about others based on stereotypes.

EMBEDDED IDEOLOGY:
RACISM/ETHNOCENTRISM AND SEXISM

Consider the similarities between systems of racism and sexism. Both constrain the social and/or physical mobility of minorities, either overtly or covertly. Are blacks and women always aware of the constraints? If not, why not? If a man says something sexually demeaning to a woman, does the woman immediately connect the remark with a system of sexism or does she see it happening to her only? If a white woman uses a racial slur against a black man, does the man *hear* the remark within a context of a system of racism? Charles Lemert maintains that people who lack privilege are more likely to understand the structural aspects because it is integral to their survival.[18] The less privileged have to be street smart, to learn how to "duck the muck" that can be flung from above.

The excerpt by bell hooks examines how the vestiges of racism and sexism have worked to keep black women and white women from forming an effective alliance to dismantle the -isms. The period of enslavement created a divide that continues today in gender- and race-segregated jobs and workplaces; where corporate competition between women can be fierce as both groups vie for the few token positions available, and most hit the glass ceiling. Following hooks is Derrick Bell's treatise on racism, in which he argues that if racist behavior is to change so too must racist ideology. As you read hooks' and Bell's essays, think of other ways in which racism and sexism are embedded within society.

Since 11 September 2001 there has been expanded media coverage of the repressive conditions women endure in other parts of the world. An insightful comparison of one aspect of the constraints placed on women in both the West and the East is presented by Fatima Mernissi. Sometimes it takes a view from "without" to see the absurdity of that which exists "within." The editor's note offers a recent news account that supports Mernissi's argument.

THE *OTHER* WEARS MANY FACES

Arturo Madrid addresses the issue of *otherness*—being alienated, isolated, invisible, and/or excluded. Madrid who is an American of Mexican heritage, poignantly describes what it feels like to be excluded, to be made to feel like the *other* in the United States, a country in which Madrid's ancestors predate the earliest European immigrants. Recall your grade school social studies or American history when much of the southwest belonged to Mexico before the Europeans arrived. Imagine how you would feel if part of the United States were taken from us now. When you are reading Madrid's words, think of a time when you were made to feel like the other. Perhaps the discomfort was only fleeting, like being the new person among old friends. Perhaps it was permanent—being the only black employee in a company of one hundred employees. Imagine if that discomfort was imposed wherever you went. Is there a pattern, a structure, to otherness?

In a twist, Billie Wright Dziech addresses the *otherness* of white males, a group rarely thought of as being excluded or alienated. Dziech emphasizes the importance of finding common ground and the need to balance the needs of all students if positive change is to occur. Dziech's piece responds to white, male college students' complaints of feeling marginalized. She argues that no student should be made to feel excluded or attacked in the classroom.

The excerpt from Simone de Beauvoir's book, *The Second Sex*, explains how she thinks men have defined woman as the *other*. However, de Beauvoir maintains that, unlike members of other minority groups who avoid their oppressors, women gravitate to theirs, forming intimate relationships with men. Rather than flee, women cling to their oppressors, and de Beauvoir explains why. How do today's women fit with de Beauvoir's thinking?

SOCIAL CLASS: THE DIRTY LITTLE SECRET

Since the social and political upheaval of the 1960s and 1970s, social class, a central tenet of the inequality literature, has vied with race/ethnicity and gender for scholarly attention. In the United States, our embedded ideology promotes individualism and upward mobility, and contributes to an almost universal denial of social class barriers.

Although there is a specific section of the text dedicated to the discussion of social class, as noted, class cannot be considered without its connection to gender and race/ethnicity. I encourage you to think outside of the box; consider the aspects of social class that can be uncovered in the articles that are not included under the class heading. From whose perspective is the article written? What clues do you have about the author's social class? What is the research question or essay thesis? What is the social class of those being researched or discussed? Because social class intersects with race/ethnicity and gender and does not stand alone, it will be one of your tasks to uncover the clues about class in each article, even when not explicit, and determine what the pattern is.

Remember as a child how you would find the hidden pictures in a *Highlights* magazine? Take a similar tack in those articles in which the author is not explicitly addressing social class; instead it is there waiting for you to extract it. Sociologists look beneath the surface to determine what each layer means and you are entreated to do the same. For example, a reading about cosmetic surgery implies monetary resources and discretionary time beyond the reach of people scrounging for the necessities of life. The role social class plays in shaping us is something we are not conscious of in our daily life, especially if we are of the privileged class. The folks left behind in Hurricane Katrina were made painfully aware of how the class and race/ethnicity structure failed them. Class is there, embedded, working in tandem with gender and/or race/ethnicity.

STRUCTURED INEQUALITY— THE INVISIBLE IRON CAGE OF CLASS

The readings in the section addressing social class are meant to give readers an inkling that the role class plays in sorting out women and men in society.

Diane Reay's selection demonstrates that members of the working class are marked and constrained by their class position. In recounting her struggle to belong in academia, first as a working-class student and then as a faculty member, Reay reports the persistence of *otherness*—not belonging, an interloper. She wonders, too, about the ramifications of joining the middle class rather than dismantling it as Karl Marx sought.

Like Reay's work, the research by Michelle Fine, Lois Weis, Judi Addelston, and Julia Marusza is jarring in that it reminds us of some of the prevailing attitudes among poor and working-class men—men who feel their unfulfilled privileges are being undermined by the *other*—women and blacks. The article is a reminder that white male privilege is not equally distributed and the anger of those who feel betrayed by that inequality. To what extent do you think the attitudes revealed in the selection are prevalent in the United States today?

STRUCTURED INEQUALITY—RACE/ETHNICITY

"A Black Woman Took My Job" is an analysis of how males have learned their roles only to have things change. In the reading, Michael Kimmel refers to the "invisibility of masculinity" and that making it visible is a necessary component to embracing healthier manhood.

In Haya Stier and Marta Tienda's reading, the researchers conclude that, even in the face of dire economic conditions, lower-class fathers attempt to support their families. The authors' findings counter stereotypes of black and Latino fathers as absent, irresponsible, and/or disengaged. Note the interaction of race/ethnicity and social class in the reading.

The excerpt by William J. Chambliss is chilling. He found that the metropolitan police in Washington, D.C., stopped young black male drivers an average of every twenty minutes during a shift. Research such as Chambliss's gave rise to the term Driving While Black (DWB). What is disturbing is that Chambliss's findings were not an aberration. The editor's note following the Chambliss chapter summarizes statistics that were aired on *Dateline*, a television show, on 4 April 2004, that reveal updated but similar actions taken by police against minorities in several cities across the country. What does it mean when a pattern of this kind of behavior becomes evident? Is it structured inequality?

The analysis shifts to other minority groups. Leslie Marmon Silko's reading is a telling glimpse at the tactics of the border patrol that are strikingly similar to Chambliss's, only the location and the minority group are different. The editor's note that follows the Silko essay reveals a significant disparity between the surveillance of the Mexican border and the Canadian border, despite the fact that thousands and thousands of vehicles and people cross between the United States and Canada on a daily basis, with only random stops or searches. Why the heavier surveillance of Mexico's border? Remember to look beneath the surface.

The purported collusion between corporations and the Immigration and Naturalization Service (INS) is the subject of Marc Cooper's reading. Cooper charges that legal as well as illegal workers are exploited by the meat-packing industry. Illegal workers are desirable because they are more docile, more accepting of on-the-job injuries that are common in meat packing. The editor's note points to news accounts that reveal the hazards for Mexican workers in the United States.

STRUCTURED INEQUALITY—ACQUIRING GENDER

A number of readings in the text are within the social construction of gender perspective, which means that gender, rather than fixed and inherent, is fluid and acquired. Scholars like Don H. Zimmerman and Candace West maintain that "Gender . . . is not a set of traits, not a variable, nor a role, but the product of social doings of some sort."[19] And Myra Marx Ferree argues that although gender is relational and nonessential, it is presented as an essential, natural, innate, and interactional process.[20] In Judith Butler's reading, however, she critiques the notion of gender as performance. Butler asks: If gender is constructed, who does the constructing? When does it occur, and how does it occur? Does our acceptance of gender as inherent stifle our questions?

Judith Lorber is a fitting follow-up to Butler. Lorber argues that becoming women and men in Western society has more to do with ideology and power than physical characteristics. Using sports and technological competence to illustrate her argument, Lorber maintains that social practices, not biology, fit individuals into a gender category. The editor's note following Lorber addresses some of the gains that women have made in sports since Title IX was legislated. Similar to Lorber, Anne Fausto-Sterling's focus is on how the biological and ideological become entwined. She examines numerous studies about premenstrual syndrome and finds that long-held biases and beliefs about women continue to inform and often misinform research on the topic. If bias about women affects the quality of research, how does that, in turn, influence women's views about their biology? The editor's note also raises questions about our thinking about men's biology.

Writing from a criminological perspective, the excerpt from Laureen Snider's comprehensive essay about building safer societies addresses the violence that permeates culturally appropriate masculine socialization. Snider discusses men's loss of traditional prerogatives due to economic restructuring as well as women's changing roles. While finding fault with a patriarchal system of domination, Snider does not let women entirely off the hook in instilling machismo in boy children. The editor's note addresses the psychic violence imposed by growing economic inequality, especially for maintaining the male provider role and the growing disparity between the haves and the have nots.

Barbara A. Arrighi's essay is an essential follow-up to Snider. While acknowledging that girl children have narrow gender performance parameters, she argues that the expectations for boys are as limiting and become entrenched at an earlier age. She maintains that to some extent everyone has a hand in ensuring boys don't become janegirls, including mothers, dads, teachers, and peers.

CORPORATE GATEKEEPING: FITTING IN

The excerpt from Deborah Tannen's book introduces the reader to the catch-22 for women in the corporate world: females who use forceful communication at work are negatively sanctioned as *masculine* women, and women whose communication styles are perceived as *feminine* are labeled as ineffective. Tannen's work suggests the fine line women must walk to gain leadership positions. The editor's note supports and expounds on Tannen's argument about women's struggles to fit in the corporate world.

Richard L. Zweigenhaft and G. William Domhoff's work builds on Tannen's. The authors present a sobering picture of women's slow rise to the director level of the corporate world, and why women continue to be tokens at the top. The irony is that female corporate board women have more in common with corporate men at the top than not. What is at work here? The editor's note tells what research found in Canada.

A fitting follow-up to Zweigenhaft and Domhoff is Sally Ann Davis-Netzley's research. Davis-Netzley interviewed female and male executives, and, though she found some overlap in their responses, she detected a gendered pattern to their perceptions. The editor's note reports why women can be important to corporations. In another part of the corporate world—the print media—Katha Pollitt's chapter calls attention to the paucity of women writers represented on op-ed pages. She takes umbrage at the arguments from women and men that it's difficult to find women ready, willing, and able to take on the job. Pollitt suggests editors (like directors on corporate boards) should open their eyes.

WOMEN'S EQUALITY: PROGRESS AND RESISTANCE

Women's pursuit of equality has been an uneven process that has proceeded, too often, in the face of women's disunity. The patriarchal structure of institutions works to constrain women, and part of that structure is the acquiescence of some women who then censure and impede the progress of women who resist the constraints. After all, women, like men, do not have a unified perspective. White women of privilege who support the status quo—the dominance of elite men, do so, whether wittingly or unwittingly, at an economic and social cost to other women. Therefore, we cannot say *all* women. Why is it that some women have advocated for change, while other women have defended the status quo? Women's social position is based on the interaction of class and race.

Three selections provide a context within which to understand the slow progress toward gender equality. An excerpt from Jane Jerome Camhi's book is apropos. Camhi's work is evocative of Marx—economic position influences ideas. She recounts the concerted effort of anti-suffragettes in the early part of the century to block women's right to vote. Camhi's work demonstrates how elite women often worked against women whom they viewed as defective, morally and socially—women who were poor, women of color, and immigrant women—in order to protect their privileged social position.

Susan J. Douglas fast-forwards us to the late 1960s and finds that resistance to women's equality continued from those who were entrenched in places and positions of power: in the legislature, the economy, and the media. However, resistance came, too, from women in positions to influence public opinion at the time. Your task is to analyze why, from a structural perspective, women of influence resisted other women's push for equality. The editor's note could be titled: The more things change, the more they stay the same.

Then a late 1990s survey of college-student attitudes and expectations concerning mating, marriage, and the marketplace by Barbara A. Arrighi provides some expected findings and some unexpected. The results indicate that while young women and men have egalitarian expectations and attitudes concerning home, neither group appears to be annoyed by gender-segregated workplaces. It would be interesting to determine to what extent your class deviates from the findings of my survey.

THE PRICE OF DEVIANCE

What happens to those who act out of the box, refuse to conform to gender or race/ethnicity stereotyped behavior? Kathleen Rowe considers the fate of *unruly women*—women like Roseanne Arnold, women who do not fit the scripted feminine model. Unruly women include women who are loud/not quiet, overweight/not underweight, women who take up too much space. Are such women less accepted by other women or men? The editor's note cites others who ask why "deviant" women get so much flak?

Cosmetic surgery has become commonplace among women but increasingly men are having elective procedures done to enhance their appearance. However, Lawrence Otis Graham's provocative essay reveals how his decision to have a "nose job" raised questions about his commitment to his heritage. Then, too, his excerpt is a reminder of the norm of conforming to an arbitrary societal standard of attractiveness. Graham's experience shows the unique dimension that race/ethnicity brings to the issue. Is the standard of attractiveness a "white" standard? If so, what social forces will influence change?

Timothy Nonn's research about men who live in the Tenderloin district of San Francisco reveals the jeopardy of deviant men. Men who are down and out rather than self-sufficient, men who are gay rather than heterosexual, men who are Latino or black rather than white—all these men pay a price. Nonn reports the strategies of the men to bolster their image to bolster their survival: looking mean, looking aggressive, and putting on the cool pose.

It might seem implausible to place an article about aging men in a section on deviance. However, Edward H. Thompson's essay points out the emasculating process that occurs as men age. The quintessential masculine male is strong, tough, independent, but if men live long enough, they eventually become weak and dependent, characteristics associated with being female. Thus, by simply aging, men deviate from the macho image of the younger male.

PATRIARCHY AND ITS CONSEQUENCES

John Stuart Mill's essay questioning the subordination of women is as timely today as it was when he first presented it. What courage Mill displayed by writing such a controversial piece more than one hundred years ago! Is Mill correct? Do men want a willing slave in a woman today as Mill states or do men want an equal partner?

Susan Estrich knows about rape because she is a lawyer and because she was a victim of rape. Estrich's reading shows the relationship between rape and a system of patriarchy within which the laws deciding what *is and isn't* rape have been established by those of privilege. The editor's note ties Estrich's reading to the recent revelations concerning a deceased U.S. senator and to the experience of a young woman thousands of miles away.

The reading about the Anita Hill–Clarence Thomas Senate hearings by Mary R. Rogers crafts an intricate analysis of the unusual circumstances in which white elite males expanded their patriarchal cloak to Thomas during his nomination hearing for the Supreme Court. The teamwork of the senators and Thomas worked in tandem to discredit Hill, a law professor, who had accused Thomas of sexual harassment during the time Thomas was her boss.

EDUCATION: THE EQUALIZER?

Harvard University's president, Larry Summers, set off a firestorm in 2005 because he suggested that the reasons why women continue to lag behind men in so many ways has to do, in part, with innate differences. When he made his remarks some women faculty walked out of the room. There was plenty of criticism to go around. Women were accused of overreacting and Mr. Summers was criticized for being insensitive. Karen Blumenthal's reading provides a context for the reaction of the women. The editor's note elaborates on Blumenthal's reading.

Walda Katz-Fishman offers a comprehensive treatise of the status of higher education. She reports facts and figures that present education as a purveyor of inequality. It is an appropriate ending to our discussion, as Katz-Fishman dispels the traditionally held view that education is the universal elixir for equality. The editor's note finds continuing deterioration of the status of higher education in the United States, as well as early education.

NOTES

1. Joseph Kolb, "Suspect Arrested in Dragging of Immigrant in New Mexico," *The New York Times*, 2 April 2005, p. A8.

2. Gary Tanner, "Two Black Churches Torched in Tennessee," *The Cincinnati Enquirer*, 9 July 2005, p. A7.

3. Bob Herbert, "An Ugly Game," *The New York Times*, 17 October 2003, p. A27.

4. Tamar Lewin, "Raid at High School Leads to Racial Divide, Not Drugs," *The New York Times*, 9 December 2003, p. A16.

5. Ibid.

6. Gregory Korte, "Firefighters Lead Lives of Quiet Separation," *The Cincinnati Enquirer*, 20 May 2005, pp. 1, A14.

7. Ibid.

8. Curt Anderson, "Racial Bias Behind Majority of Hate Crimes," *The Cincinnati Enquirer*, 23 November 2004, p. 23.

9. Lois Romano, "Where Have All the Militias Gone?" *The Washington Post National Weekly*, 25 April–1 May 2005, p. 30.

10. Mirian Jordan, "Ethnic Diversity Doesn't Blend in Kids" Lives," *Wall Street Journal*, 18 June 2004, p. B1.

11. Motoko Rich, "Restrictive Covenants Stubbornly Stay on the Books," *The New York Times*, 21 April 2005, p. D1.

12. Charles Lemert, *Social Things: An Introduction the Sociological Life* (Lanham, MD: Rowman & Littlefield Publishers, 1997), p. 97.

13. Nicholas Wade, "DNA Study Yields Clues on Early Human's First Migration," *The New York Times*, 13 May 2005, p. A7.

14. Census data.

15. Aime Cesare, *Discourse on Colonialism* (1955), excerpt translated by Joan Pinkham, (New York: Monthly Review Press, 1972), pp. 20–25.

16. Frantz Fanon, *The Damned*, trans. Constance Farrington (Paris: Presence Africanina, 1963), pp. 20–25.

17. Charles Lemert, *Social Things: An Introduction to the Social Life* (Lanham, MD: Rowman & Littlefield, 1997), p. 97.

18. Ibid.

19. Candace West and Don H. Zimmerman, "Doing Gender," *Gender and Society* 1 (1987): 125–51.

20. Myra Marx Ferree, "Beyond Separate Spheres: Feminism and Family Research," *Journal of Marriage and the Family* 38 (1990): 473–832.

I

HELPFUL CONCEPTUAL TOOLS

1

Mysterious Power of Social Structures

Charles Lemert

Today, if you are born poor, you will grow up to be poor. There are exceptions, of course, but the exceptions are rare when measured against the ideals of social progress in which [modern democratic] societies believe. In the mid-1980s, shortly after Frankie and the Hangers[1] entered adult life, the wealthiest 40 percent of all Americans gained 67 percent of the country's total income, while the poorest 40 percent received only 15 percent. The United States is one of the modern societies most honorably committed to the ideals of equal opportunity and social progress. Yet the gap between the income and wealth of the richest Americans has remained in roughly this range for most of the last two centuries. By the 1990s, the gap had grown into a canyon. In 1994, the wealthiest 20 percent of the population raked in 56 percent of the total income, while the poorest 20 percent eked out but 4 percent of all that was earned that year. Or, worse yet, the richest 5 percent of the population earned 18 percent of all income, more than four times that earned by the poorest 20 percent. Some who are poor better their situation, but most do not. The problem is getting worse, not better.

Though the facts of social inequality raise many questions, three are the most important for a sociologist: (1) What goes on in the larger structures of society to produce the reality with which Frankie and millions of others must live? (2) How do people, whether poor or not, live with the effects of those structures that so obviously shape their thinking about whether or not, as Frankie put it, they are going to fuck up? And (3) how do individuals measure their own social chances in comparison with whatever opportunities their world provides? Simply put, these are questions of social *structures*, of the individual *subjects* who must live with them, and of the social *differences* these structures create. Hardly a person alive does not face these questions one way or another, even if only in the crude but astute way Frankie did. All, sociologies, practical and professional, must address them.

It would be nice if the answers were as straightforward as the questions, but they are not. One (but only one) of the reasons the answers are so hard to come by is that there is a good deal of mystery surrounding the stark facts Frankie knew so well. This chapter . . . will consider . . . most difficult of all— the mysterious power of social structures.

What, after all, is a structure? We use the word often, but, as with many common terms in our daily speech, we seldom examine it.

We may speak, for example, of doghouses, apartments, caves, nests, rocks, or even subway grates as structures within, under, or upon which a creature sleeps or, even, "lives." We recognize that most living things are themselves well-enough structured. Flowers have stems, trees have roots, beetles have shells, other bugs have wings; on it goes. An animal's body, for example, is structured around or within skeletons of some kind, just as most plants can be said to be structured with respect to a system of trunks and roots. Rising a bit higher in the food chain, it is not uncommon to speak of the structure of one's marriage, the structure of one's work organization or school, or the structure of professional sports, network television, or the American family. We seem to recognize that things are structured in certain ways, as if by nature.

Even children who are poor—or those, poor or not, who are deprived of parental attentions—make their rooms, or their beds, or a corner of a closet into some little structure that, for a time, shelters their emotional lives, allowing them as best they can to organize their understanding of the world about.

Perhaps, to begin, we can agree that structures, including social ones, have at least two defining characteristics: (1) They make *order* out of some set of things—cells, stars, bodies, sleeping places, playrooms, imaginations, sex, and the like. (2) They do this work because they *endure* for a time, even if a very short time. In other words, structures organize some set of things because they lend them at least a minor degree of permanence. The set of things may eventually decay, come apart, or fade away, as did that stack of fallen trees and the fanciful experiments of my late childhood. But while they remain, they remain because some hard-to-define structure holds them together.

This fascination with structures is especially remarkable among the social sciences. Economists study *markets* (a name for the structures within which economic transactions take place, fixing prices and values of other kinds). Political scientists study the structure of *political systems* (a name for the systematic, if not always fair, methods by which social groups decide who gets what among scarce resources). Cultural anthropologists, and many students of literature and the arts, study the varieties of culture (a name for the structures whereby societies organize myths, legends, stories, and other representations of what they value, hate, or wish to repress).

Sociology, it has been said, studies all of the above; it studies, that is, the structure of *social worlds* or, it is sometimes said, of *societies*. Unfortunately, though we often think we know what structures are, this confidence does not bear up under attempts to say with compelling precision just what realities terms like "social world" or "society" are meant to name. Social structures, somehow, are even less definite than others. A social world obviously includes everything that constitutes the collective life of groups of people, up to and including societies—their economics, their politics, their shared mental lives, their cultures, and more. Even when the social world is very small, like Frankie's hallway in Clarendon Heights, reference is made to some coherent order of social life that encompasses the economic, political, and cultural life of its members.

However uncertain social worlds may be, we know that social structures are real because differences among societies are easily spotted. Any particular enduring organization of an ongoing *social world* of people like the [Native Americans,] the Russians, or the British is, simply, a *society*. The ongoing social worlds of members of a recognizable society can, therefore, be said to be structured such that their economic, political, and cultural practices, including any number of peculiar customs and manners, are as a whole distinct. Of this, illustrations are everywhere. Though the practices and structural forces of American society assault the Lakota society, still the social world of Lakota society is different and unlike any other. When we recognize differences of this kind, we understand that the very existence of a variety of social worlds is evidence of the powerful work of structures.

Still, structures appear to people in the course of daily life as through a mysterious fog. As I've said, it is very hard to say with precision exactly what a social structure is. Yet we must, if only because the practical sociologies by which people live and move are constantly drawn toward attempts to explain how and why structures so inexorably determine what individuals can and cannot do, even who they are. Behind the swagger, Frankie was bemoaning the structured destiny of his pals to be fuck-ups with few real options in life. Others, who might have been luckily born among the wealthiest 20 percent, have many more options than the Hallway Hangers, or for that matter the Lakota people. The privileged enjoy many more options than they need. But they, too, are who they are, and they do what they do, because of the mysterious work of social structures.

Power is the means by which social structures do this not-exactly-fair work of sorting people according to the few or many life-chances they get. Power may simply, if incompletely, be defined as the social energy of structures. Power is the determining force that causes some people to get less and some more of whatever is considered desirable in a social world.

It is power that accounts for the most important difference between social and other kinds of structures. In the structure of the universe, some stars die, while others burn on for eons. Yet no one but a poet would consider the uneven fates of stellar bodies far into darkest space a matter of unfairness. Still, strictly speaking, the death of some stars and the eternal spinning of others are the effects of cosmic energy empowering the shape of the universe into a definite structure. Though one can say that the extinction of some species of animal life is a tragedy, even this sad fate is normally felt to be a far lesser injustice than the suffering of colonized people or, even, of the urban poor like Frankie. It is only in relation to social things, to life in social worlds, that the question of power becomes a matter of binding moral intrigue.

Perhaps the reason that is so is that power comes into serious consideration only when scarcity affects the moral as well as physical well-being of living creatures. All living beings, we know very well, are subject to the effects of scarcity, but these effects are different when the loss of life, or life's chances, is found to be a consequence of one group's theft of that to which another has a preexisting claim, perhaps a prior right of possession or ownership.

The great herds of buffalo that possessed the American plains before the white people came died as much because their home grazing lands were divided artificially by the railroad as by the voracious stupidity of hunters for sport. When their natural access to food was diminished, the buffalo began to die. This was one scarcity effect. But also, as the buffalo herds disappeared, the people native to the plains, including the Lakota, suffered a scarcity of meat upon which their way of life depended. Scarcity injured the buffalo as it did the Plains Indians. But its effect on the human societies can more reasonably be viewed as a sociologically interesting effect of social power. The white settlers and corporate bosses who took the plains for their use made life marginal for both the buffalo and the Indian. Only the moral confusion that did, indeed, prevail in the period of pioneer settlement could treat the danger to animals and people with equal indifference. What the Lakota lost was a direct and unequivocal result of the social power of the American society forming itself by a greedy grasp of the vast continental lands. That the whites viewed the theft of land and life as a right of their god's providence only masks the harsh reality. The current social structure of American society, based on its absolute control of a resource-rich continental landmass, was built and energized by social power taking a vast, but ultimately scarce, land from a weaker people.

When power works in these ways, it is relatively easy to see its effects in the structures that arise from the struggle for scarce but desirable goods like food, land, water, and much else. The sociological imagination would not be as demanding as it is if power always worked so openly. Sometimes it does; sometimes not. It is one thing, for example, to see the powerful effects of slavery on slaves and of colonization on the colonized, but quite another to see the effects of social power in the lives of people such as Frankie. Compare, for example, Frankie's complaint at the beginning of this chapter to the reflections of Black Elk, an Oglala Lakota holy man, on the massacre at Wounded Knee:

> I did not know then how much was ended. When I took back now from this high hill of my old age, I can still see the butchered women and children lying heaped and scattered all along the crooked gulch as plain as when I saw them with eyes still young. And I can see that something else died there in the bloody mud, and was buried in the blizzard. A people's dream died there. It was a beautiful dream.[2]

Black Elk saw clearly that what had happened to his people by the force of American power was devastating to the structures of his Lakota world. He was a holy man, a visionary. But this alone does not account for the greater clarity of Black Elk's understanding. Frankie's complaint is much more uncertain in that he places the responsibility (and blame) on himself and his fellow Hallway Hangers. Their plight was, he felt, a result of their own fuckings up.

It is true that poor people, including the Lakota, are perfectly capable of screwing up their own lives. But it is just as true that the energizing power of modern social structures does not very often do its work openly as it did at Wounded Knee and, thus, may be a powerful, but hidden, cause of trouble for many. This is the difference. The Lakota knew beyond any reasonable doubt that the land was theirs to use and respect and that the slaughter at Wounded Knee was a result of terrifyingly direct power. But Frankie did not so clearly see the wider powers of American social structures, even though it was these structures, every bit as much as the boys themselves, that caused their social failure.

Why could not Frankie see as clearly as Black Elk? This question leads to a still finer aspect of the mysterious workings of structuring power.

In most modern societies, most (but not all) of the time, people encounter powerful structures, not directly, but indirectly by the effects those structures cause, such as the ways teachers treated the Hallway Hangers as the losers they came to believe they were. Power may even sometimes work in the events that structures cause not to happen, as in Frankie's slim prospects for a good life. Either way, as bad as the consequences were for the Hallway Hangers, these effects of power are a far cry from the slaughter at Wounded Knee or the overt cruelty of slavery. The discouragement of the Hallway Hangers is one of the sneaky effects of powerful structures, an effect that challenges the sociological imagination.

One generic form of the sneaky epiphanies of power appears in the structures of *prestige*, that is, in the remarkable and systematic consistency with which nearly everyone in a society seems to agree that some persons ought to be respected highly, others less so, and some not at all. The way a society structures the distribution of prestige assigns to some people—certain championship prizefighters, for example—an incomprehensibly high status from which they usually become wealthy. At the same time, the prestige structure prevents others—most kindergarten teachers, for example—from achieving either status or wealth even though the worth of their work is certifiably more valuable than the entertainment value of public beatings rendered for pay and pleasure by boxers. We never see the actual structure of a status or prestige system, but schoolteachers (and their pupils) and boxers (and their excitable fans) experience it in all kinds of ways.

We know social structures more often by their consequences than by seeing them as such. In this sense, social structures are less like trees than stars. Trees we see. We can, as a consequence, well imagine their structures, that is why they are so often the subjects of photography, painting, art, poetry, and music. Distant stellar worlds, on the other hand, we never see. The thrill we get from those distant stars is always light-years away, long gone by the time we see it. Whatever may be the structure of the universe, its "reality" to astronomers, or lovers on a summer night, is at best a well-informed conjecture about something no one will ever see.

Most of us, for example, have distant relatives living in social worlds far from our own. They constitute the structure of our family (or kin) relations, and they make a difference. Not long ago my uncle Edwin, a quite famous professional sociologist, died after a long and productive life. At the funeral in California, I met a cousin I had not seen for half a century—when he was two and I was five. As he and his sisters and I and my brother shared our stories of their father, my father's brother, I felt a surprising (to use the correct term) *kinship* with them. Though differently, we were all shaped by many of the same family forces. In such ways, it is possible to catch an occasional glimpse of the social structures we otherwise experience by their effects, without ever seeing them all at once. After the funeral stories were told, we Lemerts had learned a great deal more about the particular, not-to-be-exaggerated prestige our fathers and uncles, their mothers and fathers, and each of us had come to possess, for better or worse. We understood, that is, a little more about how and why we each came to be who we are because of our kinship in this one structure among the many that influence us. Prestige bestows on individuals a sense of their status, whether high or low, in the structure of social things. This too is power, as anyone assigned an inferior status like Frankie's knows most painfully.

Alongside its sly workings in the structure of prestige, power also works through the structure of *authority*—the rules and regulations that assign to some people a limited right to tell others what they can and cannot do. Erving Goffman—the same Goffman who said "universal human nature is not a very human thing"—was one of sociology's most astute observers of the hidden effects of social structures like authority. In an intriguing footnote in one of his books, Goffman told a story of an event in the 1960s when the authority structures were very much in turmoil.

The event took place at Columbia University in the late spring of 1968 in the office of the university's president, Grayson Kirk. Rebel students, protesting the injustices of American society as they saw them in their own university, had taken over President Kirk's office and, quite literally, trashed it. This was not an uncommon form of student protest in those days, often inspiring outrage on the part of the authorities, including Mr. Kirk. Goffman begins his footnote by quoting a long paragraph from a book about the Columbia office trashing, then provides his own observation:

> One and a half hours after the President's suite had been cleared of student demonstrators, Grayson Kirk stood in the center of his private office looking at the blankets, cigarette butts and orange peels that covered his rug. Turning to A. M. Rosenthal of the *New York Times* and several other reporters who had come into the office with him he murmured, "My God, how could human beings do a thing like this?" . . .
>
> The great sociological question, of course, is not how could it be that human beings would do a thing like this, but rather how is it that human beings do this sort of thing so rarely. How come persons in authority have been so over-

whelmingly successful in conning those beneath them into keeping the hell out of their offices?[3]

This is indeed the great sociological question. Just more than fifty years before President Kirk's office was trashed, Max Weber, a more sober commentator than Goffman, had asked the same question: "Why do men obey?" Why, indeed, do people obey authorities and their rules? It may be that no question comes closer than this one to opening up the hidden workings of power. We may be drawn to people of high prestige for the magic they sometimes seem to possess. But respect for authority is more complicated by far, thus more intriguing.

The remarkable fact that people tend to keep the hell out of the offices of the authorities, and otherwise respect the rules and regulations, even those nowhere written down, is perhaps the most impressive general evidence for the power of social structures in ordinary life. While there are many kinds of social structures, those that stand behind obedience to authority—norms, customs, rules, etiquettes, and the like—are among the more telling ones. When they work in our favor, we seldom notice. When they work against us, we notice the pain of punishment or exclusion. And, in the case of President Kirk and other authorities astonished by the actions of rebels, when authoritative structures fail to work any longer, such an occurrence is the subject of widespread interest.

Hence another curious feature of social structures: They tend to be invisible to those who enjoy their benefits until such time as they fail to deliver. But, even then, when workers and students, journalists, sociologists, and other rebels exercise their sociological imaginations to account for their failures in life, the collapsed social structure can only be reconstructed, *after the fact*. And, like the structure of prestige, it is never a totally present entity upon which hands can be laid. . . .

Social structures are salient enough to organize the small deeds of social worlds because they endure, for better or worse. Their duration, like that of mountains bearing the fossils and relics of life long gone, can only be the carrying forth of effects of the deep past. The class structure that, if you are young, may be at this very moment sorting you for a good chance at life, even as it assigns others lesser chances, did not spring up all at once like the dinosaurs of *Jurassic Park*. Structures are working on you as you read or nap, but their working is the slow-moving, leading edge of a social mountain, long enduring, not soon to tumble. The sociological imagination must always look up to the far peaks that define the dark valleys or pleasant streams where people live.

Mysteries abound. But it is not all that eerie to suppose that structures, like voices from the grave, press upon us out of the deep past of lost, but still powerful, worlds. Their weight may be deadly for many, or inspiring for those more privileged, but they are dead in the sense that structures do not, ever, have the same vital force as the actions individuals are generally able to take. Where the mystery persists is in how it happens that dead and invisible structures send forth so much power. Such a situation confounds the more common experience that the actions of social life rise up, instead, from individuals clustered in their many and different, but local, groups.

NOTES

1. Frankie and the Hallway Hangers were students who lived in Clarendon Heights, a public housing project for the poor. The Hangers, whose families were broken either by death or by separation, were on the verge of social and criminal trouble.—Ed.

2. *Black Elk Speaks: Being the Life Story of a Holy Man of the Oglala Sioux As Told through John C. Neihardt (Flaming Rainbow)* (New York: W. W. Morrow, 1932); reprint (University of Nebraska Press, 1974), p. 270.

3. Erving Goffman, *Relations in Public* (New York: Harper Torchbooks, 1971), p. 288.

EDITOR'S NOTE

Charles Lemert's reading is meant to illustrate the long-lasting impact of social structure on peoples' lives, like the Lakota. The continued suffering of the Lakota, a result of the structure of white power, cannot be dismissed with a glib, "Well, that was then, this is now." For the Lakota *then is now*.

Europeans' past human rights violations and the United States's broken promises underlie the current situation of the Lakota. Native Americans are owed over $1 billion from the United States for leasing reservation land for oil, mining, and timber. A class-action suit was filed on behalf of Native Americans eight years ago, without reaching a settlement.[1] A treaty signed over one hundred years ago was to provide quality health care for Native Americans; however, the government spends less than $2,000 a year per Native American.[2]

Even the promise of education has been hellish for Native Americans. A series of lawsuits have been filed on behalf of members of the Lakota and other tribes who allege they were abused at Catholic boarding schools in the 1970s. The petitioners maintain that physical abuse was part of daily existence and sexual abuse was widespread. Not only did the abuse come from nuns and priests, but former students argue that older students were forced to hit younger children, students were locked in closets, made to eat lye soap, and even thrown down laundry chutes. According to the former students, the ideology of the school was to "kill the Indian, and save the man."[3]

If you were a Native American, how would you feel about the U.S. government?

NOTES

1. Evelyn Nieves, "A String of Broken Promises," *The Washington Post National Weekly Edition*, 1–7 November 2004, pp. 14–15.

2. Ibid.

3. Sharon Waxman, "Discipline, or Mistreatment?" *The Washington Post National Weekly Edition*, 9–15 June 2003, pp. 30–31.

2

"They" Are All the Same, but Each Member of My Group is Unique

Stephen Worchel

Some years ago, I took my first trip to China. During my visit, I probably interacted with twenty to thirty Chinese for any length of time. Upon returning, I encountered a Chinese colleague, and during our conversation I proclaimed that I finally had a good picture of the Chinese people: "They are bright, hard-working, happy, and friendly." My colleague smiled and asked me to describe Americans. I was taken aback, but after considerable thought I politely informed him that Americans are so diverse that it is really impossible to describe them in a few words. He never stopped smiling as he reminded me that there are over one billion people in China, including twenty-eight distinct minority groups, yet I had no trouble describing "Chinese people" after meeting only twenty to thirty of them.

There is considerable evidence that we often view out-groups as homogeneous, while we see considerable diversity within our own group. For example, Quattrone and Jones (1980) asked students at Princeton and Rutgers universities to describe the student body at their own and the other university. In both cases, the students perceived considerably more variability within the student body at their own university. Linville, Fischer, and Salavoy (1989) found that residents of an elderly people's home and a student group rated the other age group as more homogenous than their own group. There are some exceptions to this tendency. For example, people in minority groups often see their group as more homogeneous than the majority group (Simon and Brown, 1987), and members of new groups see their groups as more homogeneous than out-groups (Worchel, Coutant-Sassic, and Grossman, 1992). However, the inclination to see homogeneity in an out-group is very pervasive.

It has been argued that this effect occurs because we generally have more information from a greater variety of experiences with members of our own group than with members of out-groups. I've interacted with thousands of Americans in work, social, and religious settings, but my interactions with the Chinese were limited to professional situations in which we were strangers to each other. I failed to take this difference into account when forming my mental image of the Chinese. Another possibility is that because our in-group is more important to us and we have a higher motivation to perceive it correctly, we develop a more varied picture of it (Park, Judd, and Ryan, 1991).

But whatever the basis, consider the implications of this process. First, if I believe that members of other ethnic groups are similar, I will quickly form an impression of the whole group after meeting only a few of its members: "Know one, know them all." Second, I can justify limiting my interaction with an out-group because I'll know about the group and its members after only a few contacts. This reduced contact will ensure that my representation of the group is rarely challenged. I felt little need to return to China or meet other Chinese, because I now had a "good" picture of the group. I was ready to expand my growing knowledge of the world's people by taking a week's trip to Brazil.

MORE THAN A PICTURE: THE INFLUENCE OF STEREOTYPES

At a benign level, stereotypes help order our world and keep us from becoming overwhelmed by information. But this benefit comes at a cost. By putting people into categories, we tend to overlook differences between people in a category. And we tend to hold on to a stereotype as if it were our last friend on earth. Indeed, we humans have employed an elaborate array of mental activities to maintain our views.

First, we employ *selective attention*. Our stereotypes guide us to pay attention to certain details of a situation and ignore the rest (Schaller and Maass, 1989). For example, if my stereotype of your group includes the trait clumsiness, I will be quick to notice when you trip over a fold in the carpet. Without that component in the stereotype, I would most likely overlook this behavior. When I guide my attention to certain behaviors (and ignore others), my chance of finding support for my stereotype increases dramatically.

But we don't stop there. Next, our stereotypes induce selective interpretation of events, especially ambiguous events. In an early study, white participants watched either a black or a white person interacting with a white person (Duncan, 1976). During an animated conversation, the first person gave the second an "ambiguous shove." When the observers were asked about the shove, they viewed it as playing around or emphasizing a point when it came from a white actor. However, when the actor was black, the shove was interpreted as hostile and aggressive. Other research has shown that we are most likely to interpret events in line with our stereotypes when we are busy and have little time to pay close attention to actions that are unfolding (Gilbert and Hixon, 1991). The point is that our stereotypes prime us to interpret events in ways that confirm our expectations. This tendency not only causes us to interpret actions at times but also helps our stereotypes resist pressure to change.

Stereotypes also affect our memory of events: we often recall details and situations that support our stereotypes. When I was a college student, a group of Brazilians lived next door. That year, I had attended Mardi Gras and came home with the impression that Brazilians were great party animals. Three years later I saw one of my former neighbors in medical school. I was quite surprised because all I remembered of him was the parties he and his roommates had during the year he lived next to me. I couldn't recall that he had ever studied or that there had been any moments of silence in his apartment. In an interesting demonstration of selective memory, C. Cohen (1981) showed people a video of a woman having a birthday dinner with her husband. When the viewers were told that the woman was a waitress, they recalled that she had a television set and drank beer. But when they were told that she was a librarian, they remembered that she wore glasses and listened to classical music during the dinner. All of the points recalled were correct, but the expectations of the perceivers influenced which points they remembered.

Not only do stereotypes affect how we store and interpret information, they guide our attitudes and behaviors. Because many stereotypes involve outgroups and we are motivated to enhance the image of our own group, many, if not most, stereotypes are relatively negative. On the basis of negative information, we are apt to develop *prejudice* toward individuals from these outgroups. *Prejudice* is "a negative attitude toward, or evaluation of, a person based on his or her membership in a group other than one's own" (Worchel, Cooper, and Goethals, 1991, p. 360). In other words, we dislike an individual because he or she belongs to a different ethnic group, religion, sex, or nation. Our dislike is based not on the individual's behavior but on his or her group. From this base of prejudice, discrimination is likely to follow. *Discrimination* is action taken to harm a group, or a member of a group, on the basis of membership in the group. In its extreme form, the combination of prejudice and discrimination can lead to *delegitimization* of a target group (Bar-Tal, 1988), determining that it does not deserve fair treatment according to a code of norms calling for proper and decent behavior. This view opens the door for the exploitation of the target group and even justifies resorting to violence.

REFERENCES

Bar-Tal, D. 1988. Delegitimizing Relations between Israeli Jews and Palestinians: A Social-Psychological Analysis. In *Arab-Jewish Relations in Israel: A Quest for Human Understanding*, ed. J. Hoffman. Bristol, IN: Wyndham Hall Press.

Cohen, C. 1981. Person Categories and Social Perception: Testing Some Boundaries of the Processing Effects of Prior Knowledge. *Journal of Personality and Social Psychology* 40: 441–52.

Duncan, D. 1976. Differential Social Perception and Attribution of Intergroup Violence: Testing the Lower Limits of Stereotyping of Blacks. *Journal of Personality and Social Psychology* 34: 590–98.

Gilbert, D., and J. Hixon. 1991. The Trouble of Thinking: Activation and Application of Journal of Stereotypic Beliefs. *Journal of Personality and Social Psychology* 50: 509–17.

Linville, P., P. G. Fisher, and P. Salavoy. 1989. Perceived Distributions of the Characteristics of In-group and Out-group Members: Empirical Evidence and a Computer Simulation. *Journal of Personality and Social Psychology* 57: 165–88.

Park, B., C. Judd, and C. Ryan. 1991. Social Categorization and the Representation of Variability Information. In *European Review of Social Psychology*, vol. 2., edited by W. Stroeber and M. Hewstone. London: Wiley.

Quattrone, G., and E. Jones. 1980. The Perception of Variability Within In-groups and Out-groups. Implications for the Law of Small Numbers. *Journal of Personality and Social Psychology* 31: 141–52.

Schaller, M., and A. Maass. 1989. Illusory Correlations and Social Categorization: Toward an Integration of Motivational and Cognitive Factors in Stereotype Formation. *Journal of Personality and Social Psychology* 56: 709–21.

Simon, B., and R. Brown. 1987. Perceived Intragroup Homogeneity in Minority-Majority Contexts. *Journal of Personality and Social Psychology* 53: 703–11.

Worchel, S., J. Cooper, and G. Goethals. 1991. *Understanding Social Psychology*, 5th ed. Pacific Grove, CA: Brookes Cole.

Worchel, S., D. Coutant-Sassic, and M. Grossman. 1992. A Developmental Approach to Group Dynamics: A Model and Illustrative Research. In *Group Process and Productivity*, edited by S. Worchel, W. Wood, and J. Simpson. Newbury Park, CA: Sage.

EDITOR'S NOTE

Stephen Worchel's reading provides excellent examples of how we use stereotypes in everyday life—how we designate the *other*—the one whom we determine is not part of our group. Once we take that action, we can then heap on the stereotypes; each stereotype works to dehumanize the *other* a little more. Enough stereotypes and we can then simply eliminate the *other* from our radar, either attitudinally through prejudice or physically through discrimination. Prejudice affects the psyche, discrimination (action) affects the *other*'s physical survival—prevents the *other* from going to school, getting a job, living in a neighborhood, belonging to a club—but takes a psychological toll as well. Several recent examples complement Worchel's reading.

First, in 2004, there were at least 1,500 cases of harassment and anti-Muslim violence incidents reported by the Council on American-Islamic Relations. That represents a 50 percent increase over the previous year.[1] It is believed that the number is higher than that reported but many don't file a complaint, fearful of drawing attention to themselves. Arabs and Asians worry they could be put on the "wrong" list—being seen as the *other*. Their concern is not without warrant. One-fourth of the incidents reported focused on issues about law enforcement, including detentions, searches, and unreasonable arrests.[2]

The "all Muslims are terrorists stereotype" is evident in the report from Memphis, Tennessee, where Muslims wanted to use a five-acre plot of land for a cemetery.[3] The complaints from the angry neighbors ranged from not wanting "a staging ground for terrorists" to "We don't need bin Laden's cousins in our neighborhood."[4]

Precedence exists in the United States for the treatment of those officially designated the *other*—genocide of Native Americans, enslavement of African Americans, imprisonment of Japanese Americans during World War II. All suffered from official labels that were institutionalized within the political system, the legal system, the educational system, the military, as well as the economy.

Today, there is a new *other* and unfortunately a new form of discrimination: The Department of Homeland Security has created a database of all Arab-American populations by city and ZIP code.[5] Once the government has city and ZIP code, what might be the next step against those who are currently stamped the *other*?

NOTES

1. Andrea Elliott, "Muslims Report 50% Increase in Bias Crimes," *The New York Times*, 12 May 2005, p. A24.

2. Ibid.

3. Woody Baird, "Muslims' Plans for Cemetery Face Foes," *The Enquirer*, 26 December 2004, p. A 6.

4. Ibid.

5. Eric Lipton, "Panel Says Census Move on Arab-Americans Recalls World War II Internment, *The New York Times*, 10 November 2004, p. A17.

II

EMBEDDED IDEOLOGY

Racism/Ethnocentrism and Sexism

3

Black Women and Feminism

bell hooks

Toward the end of 1987 I spoke at Tufts University at an annual dinner for black women. My topic was "Black Women in Predominantly White Institutions." I was excited by the idea of talking with so many young black women but surprised when these women suggested that sexism was not a political issue of concern to black women, that the serious issue was racism. I've heard this response many times, yet somehow I did not expect that I would need to prove over and over that sexism means that many black females will be exploited and victimized. Confronted by these young black women to whom sexism was not important, I felt that feminism had failed to develop a politics that addresses black women. Particularly, I felt that black women active in black liberation struggles in the 1960s and early 1970s, who had spoken and written on sexism (remember the anthology *The Black Woman*, edited by Toni Cade Bambara?) had let our younger sisters down by not making more of a sustained political effort so that black women (and black people) would have greater understanding of the impact of sexist oppression on our lives.

When I began to share my own experiences of racism and sexism, pointing to incidents (particularly in relationships with black men), a veil was lifted. Suddenly the group acknowledged what had been previously denied—the ways sexism wounds us as black women. I had talked earlier about the way many black women students in predominantly white institutions keep silent in classes, stating emphatically that our progress in such places requires us to have a voice, to not remain silent. In the ensuing discussion, women commented on black fathers who had told their daughters "nobody wants a loud-talking black woman." The group expressed ambivalent feelings about speaking, particularly on political issues in classroom settings where they were often attacked or unsupported by other black women students.

Their earlier reluctance to acknowledge sexism reminded me of previous arguments with other groups of women about both the book and the film *The Color Purple*. Our discussions focused almost solely on whether portraying brutal sexist domination of a black female by a black male had any basis in reality. I was struck by the extent to which folks will go to argue that sexism in black communities has not promoted the abuse and subjugation of black women by black men. This fierce denial has its roots in the history of black people's response to racism and white supremacy. Traditionally it has been important for black people to assert that slavery, apartheid, and continued discrimination have not undermined the humanity of black people, that not only has the race been preserved but that the survival of black families and communities are the living testimony of our victory. To acknowledge, then, that our families and communities have been undermined by sexism would not only require an acknowledgement that racism is not the only form of domination and oppression that affects us as a people; it would mean critically challenging the assumption that our survival as a people depends on creating a cultural climate in which black men can achieve manhood within paradigms constructed by white patriarchy.

Often the history of our struggle as black people is made synonymous with the efforts of black males to have patriarchal power and privilege. As one black woman college student put it, "In order to redeem the race we have to redeem black manhood." If such redemption means creating a society in which black men assume the stereotypical male role of provider and head of household, then sexism is seen not as destructive but as essential to the promotion and maintenance of the black family. Tragically, it has been our acceptance of this model that has prevented us from acknowledging that black male sexist domination has *not* enhanced or enriched black family life. The seemingly positive aspects of the patriarchy (caretaker and provider) have been the most difficult for masses of black men to realize, and the negative aspects (maintaining control through psychological or physical violence) are practiced daily. Until black people redefine in a nonsexist revolutionary way the terms of our liberation, black women and men will always be confronted with the issue of whether supporting feminist efforts to end sexism is inimical to our interests as a people.

In her insightful essay, "Considering Feminism as a Model for Social Change," Sheila Radford-Hill makes the useful critique that black women producing feminist theory, myself included, focus more on the racism of white women within the feminist movement, and on the importance of racial difference, than on the ways feminist struggle could strengthen and help black communities. In part, the direction of our work was shaped by the nature of our experience. Not only were there very few black women writing feminist theory, but most of us were not living in or working with black communities. The aim of *Ain't I a Woman* was not to focus on the racism of white women. Its primary purpose was to establish that sexism greatly determines the social status and experience of black women. I did not try to examine the ways that struggling to end sexism would benefit black people, but this is my current concern.

Many black women insist that they do not join the feminist movement because they cannot bond with white women who are racist. If one argues that there really are some white women who are resisting and challenging racism, who are genuinely committed to ending white supremacy, one is accused of being naive, of not acknowledging history. Most black women, rich and poor, have contact with white women, usually in work settings. In such settings black women cooperate with white women despite racism. Yet black women are reluctant to express solidarity with white feminists. Black women's consciousness is shaped by internalized racism and by reactionary white women's concerns as they are expressed in popular culture, such as day-time soap operas or in the world of white fashion and cosmetic products, which massess of black women consume without rejecting this racist propaganda and devaluing of black women.

Emulating white women or bonding with them in these "apolitical" areas is not consistently questioned or challenged. Yet I do not know a single black woman advocate of feminist politics who is not bombarded by ongoing interrogations by other black people about linking with racist white women (as though we lack the political acumen to determine whether white women are racists, or when it is in our interest to act in solidarity with them).

At times, the insistence that feminism is really "a white female thing that has nothing to do with black women" masks black female rage toward white women, a rage rooted in the historical servant-served relationship where white women have used power to dominate, exploit, and oppress. Many black women share this animosity, and it is evoked again and again when white women attempt to assert control over us. This resistance to white female domination must be separated from a black female refusal to bond with white women engaged in feminist struggle. This refusal is often rooted as well in traditional sexist models: women learn to see one another as enemies, as threats, as competitors. Viewing white women as competitors for jobs, for companions, for valuation in a culture that only values select groups of women, often serves as a barrier to bonding, even in settings where radical white women are not acting in a dominating manner. In some settings it has become a way of one-upping white women for black women to trivialize feminism.

Black women must separate feminism as a political agenda from white women or we will never be able to focus on the issue of sexism as it affects black communities. Even though there are a few black women (I am one) who assert that we empower ourselves by using the term "feminism," by addressing our concerns as black women as well as our concern with the welfare of the human community globally, we have had little impact. Small groups of black feminist theorists and activists who use the term "black feminism" (the Combahee River Collective is one example) have not had much success in organizing large groups of black women, or stimulating widespread interest in the feminist movement.

Their statement of purpose and plans for action focus exclusively on black women acknowledging the need for forms of separatism. Here the argument that black women do not collectively advocate feminism because of an unwillingness to bond with racist white women appears most problematic. Key concerns that serve as barriers to black women advocating feminist politics are heterosexism, the fear that one will be seen as betraying black men or promoting hatred of men and as a consequence becoming less desirable to male companions; homophobia (often I am told by black people that all feminists are lesbians); and deeply ingrained misogynist attitudes toward one another, perpetuating sexist thinking and sexist competition.

Recently, I spoke with a number of black women about why they are not more involved in feminist thinking and feminist movement. Many of them talked about harsh treatment by other black women, about being socially ostracized or talked about in negative and contemptuous ways at all-female gatherings or at conferences on gender issues. A few people committed to feminist politics described times when they found support from white women and resistance from black women peers. A black woman scheduled on a panel arrived late and couldn't find a seat in the room. When she entered and had been standing for a while, I greeted her warmly from the podium and encouraged her to join me as there were seats in front. Not only did she choose to stand, during the break she said to me, "How dare you embarrass me by asking me to come up front." Her tone was quite hostile. I was disturbed that she saw this gesture as an attempt to embarrass her rather than as a gesture of recognition. This is not an isolated case. There are many occasions when we witness the failure of black women to trust one another, when we approach one another with suspicion.

Years ago I attended a small conference with about twenty black women. We were to organize a national conference on black feminism. We came from various positions, politics, and sexual preferences. A well-known black woman scholar at a prestigious institution, whose feminist thinking was not deemed appropriately advanced, was treated with contempt and hostility. It was a disturbing time. A number of the black women present had white women companions and lovers. Yet concerning the issue of whether white women should be allowed to attend the conference, they were adamant that it should be for black women only, that white women all too often control us.

It is our collective responsibility as individual black women committed to feminist movement to work at making space where black women who are just beginning to explore feminist issues can do so without fear of hostile treatment, quick judgments, dismissals, etc.

I find more black women than ever before are appearing on panels that focus on gender. Yet I have observed, and other black women thinkers have shared as well, that often these women see gender as a subject for discourse or for increased professional visibility, not for political action. Often professional black women with academic degrees are quite conservative politically. Their perspectives differ greatly from our foremothers who were politically astute, assertive, and radical in their work for social change.

Feminist praxis is greatly shaped by academic women and men. Since there are not many academic black women committed to radical politics, especially with a gender focus, there is no collective base in the academy for forging a feminist politics that addresses masses of black women. There is much more work by black women on gender and sexism emerging from scholars who do literary criticism and from creative fiction and drama writers than from women in history, sociology, and political science. While it does not negate commitment to radical politics, in literature it is much easier to separate academic work and political concerns. Concurrently, if black women academics are not committed to feminist ethics, to feminist consciousness-raising, they end up organizing conferences in which social interactions mirror sexist norms, including ways black women regard one another. For the uninitiated coming to see and learn what feminism centered on black women might be like, this can be quite disillusioning.

Often in these settings the word "feminism" is evoked in negative terms, even though sexism and gender issues are discussed. I hear black women academics laying claim to the term "womanist" while rejecting "feminist." I do not think Alice Walker intended this term to deflect from feminist commitment, yet this is often how it is evoked. Walker defines womanist as black feminist or feminist of color. When I hear black women using the term "womanist," it is in opposition to the term "feminist"; it is viewed as constituting something separate from feminist politics shaped by white women. For me, the term "womanist" is not sufficiently linked to a tradition of radical political commitment to struggle and change. What would a womanist politic look like? If it is a term for black feminist, then why do those who embrace it reject the other?

I believe that women should think less in terms of feminism as an identity and more in terms of "advocating feminism"; to move from emphasis on personal lifestyle issues toward creating political paradigms and racial models of social change that emphasize collective as well as individual change. For this reason I do not call myself a black feminist. Black women must continue to insist on our right to participate in shaping feminist issues. Current feminist scholarship can be useful to black women in formulating critical analyses of gender issues about black people, particularly feminist work on parenting. (When I first read Dorothy Dinnerstein, it was interesting to think about her work in terms of black mother-son relationships.)

Black women need to construct a model of feminist theorizing and scholarship that is inclusive, that widens our options, that enhances our understanding of black experience and gender. Significantly, the most basic task confronting black feminists (irrespective of the terms we use to identify ourselves) is to educate one another and black people about sexism, about the ways resisting sexism can empower black women, a process which makes sharing feminist vision more difficult.

Black women must identify ways feminist thought and practice can aid in our process of self-recovery and share that knowledge with out sisters. This is the base on which to build political solidarity. When that grounding exists, black women will be fully engaged in feminist movement that transforms self, community, and society.

EDITOR'S NOTE

"[B]lond white chicks who go missing get covered, poor, black, Hispanic, or other people of color who go missing do not get covered." The quote is from Tom Rosenstiel, director of the Washington-based Project for Excellence in Journalism.[1] "Rosenstiel also said: "You're more likely to get coverage if you're attractive than if you're not."[2] Those two statements are frothing with meaning and fit with bell hooks's reading on many levels.

More than one thousand people are profiled on The National Center for Missing Adults website, but few get media attention because most are just average people—young, old, well-heeled, poor, and all ethnic backgrounds, but it is the blond white women that get the media attention.[3] What is the message to those of us who are not young, blonde, white chicks?

NOTES

1. Erin Texeira, "Missing Minorities Get Less TV Attention," *The Cincinnati Enquirer*, 16 June 2005, p. A8.
2. Ibid.
3. Ibid.

4

Divining Our Racial Themes

Derrick Bell

The fact of slavery refuses to fade, along with the deeply embedded personal attitudes and public policy assumptions that supported it for so long. Indeed, the racism that made slavery feasible is far from dead in the last decade of twentieth-century America; and the civil rights gains, so hard won, are being steadily eroded. Despite undeniable progress for many, no African Americans are insulated from incidents of racial discrimination. Our careers, even our lives, are threatened because of our color. Even the most successful of us are haunted by the plight of our less fortunate brethren who struggle for what some social scientists call the "underclass." Burdened with life-long poverty and soul-devastating despair, they live beyond the pale of the American Dream. What we designate as "racial progress" is not a solution to that problem. It is a regeneration of the problem in a particularly perverse form.

According to data compiled in 1990 for basic measures of poverty, unemployment, and income, the slow advances African Americans made during the 1960s and 1970s have definitely been reversed. The unemployment rate for blacks is 2.5 times the rate for whites. Black per-capita income is not even two-thirds of the income for whites; and blacks, most of whom own little wealth or business property, are three times more likely to have income below the poverty level than whites.[1] If trends of the last two decades are allowed to continue, readers can safely—and sadly—assume that the current figures are worse than those cited here.[2]

Statistics cannot, however, begin to express the havoc caused by joblessness and poverty: broken homes, anarchy in communities, futility in the public schools. All are the bitter harvest of race-determined unemployment in a society where work provides sustenance, status, and the all-important sense of self-worth. What we now call the "inner city" is, in fact, the American equivalent of the South African homelands. Poverty is less the source than the status of men and women who, despised because of their race, seek refuge in self-rejection. Drug-related crime, teenaged parenthood, and disrupted and disrupting family life all are manifestations of a despair that feeds on self. That despair is bred anew each day by the images on ever-playing television sets, images confirming that theirs is the disgraceful form of living, not the only way people live.

Few whites are able to identify with blacks as a group—the essential prerequisite for feeling empathy with, rather than aversion from, blacks' self-inflicted suffering. . . . Unable or unwilling to perceive that "there but for the grace of God, go I," few whites are ready to actively promote civil rights for blacks. Because of an irrational but easily roused fear that any social reform will unjustly benefit blacks, whites fail to support the programs this country desperately needs to address the ever-widening gap between the rich and the poor, both black and white.

Lulled by comforting racial stereotypes, fearful that blacks will unfairly get ahead of them, all too many whites respond to even the most dire reports of race-based disadvantage with either a sympathetic headshake or victim-blaming rationalizations. Both responses lead easily to the conclusion that contemporary complaints of racial discrimination are simply excuses put forward by people who are unable or unwilling to compete on an equal basis in a competitive society.

For white people who both deny racism and see a heavy dose of the Horatio Alger myth as the answer to blacks' problems, how sweet it must be when a black person stands in a public place and condemns as slothful and unambitious those blacks who are not making it. Whites eagerly embrace black conservatives' homilies to self-help, however grossly unrealistic such messages are in an economy where millions, white as well as black, are unemployed and, more important, in one where racial discrimination in the workplace is as vicious (if less obvious) than it was when employers posted signs "no negras need apply."

Whatever the relief from responsibility such thinking provides those who embrace it, more than a decade of civil rights setbacks in the White House, in the courts, and in the critical realm of media-nurtured public opinion has forced retrenchment in the tattered civil rights ranks. We must reassess our cause and our approach to it, but repetition of time-worn slogans simply will not do. As a popular colloquialism puts it, it is time to "get real" about rate and the persistence of racism in America.

To make such an assessment—to plan for the future by reviewing the experiences of the past—we must ask whether the formidable hurdles we now face in the elusive quest for racial equality are simply a challenge to our commitment, whether they are the latest variation of the old hymn "One More River to Cross." Or, as we once again gear up to meet the challenges posed by these unexpected new setbacks, are we ignoring a current message with implications for the future which history has already taught us about the past?

Such assessment is hard to make. On the one hand, contemporary color barriers are certainly less visible as a result of our successful effort to strip the law's endorsement from the hated Jim Crow signs. Today one can travel for thousands of miles across this country and never see a public facility designated as "Colored" or "White." Indeed, the very absence of visible signs of discrimination creates an atmosphere of racial neutrality and encourages whites to believe that racism is a thing of the past. On the other hand, the general use of so-called neutral standards to continue exclusionary practices reduces the effectiveness of traditional civil rights laws, while rendering discriminatory actions more oppressive than ever. Racial bias in the pre-*Brown* era was stark, open, unalloyed with hypocrisy and blank-faced lies. We black, when rejected, knew who our enemies were. They were not us! Today, because bias is masked in unofficial practiced and "neutral" standards, we must wrestle with the question whether race or some individual failing has cost us the job, denied us the promotion, or prompted our being rejected as tenants for an apartment. Either conclusion breeds frustration and alienation—and a rage we dare not show to others or admit to ourselves.

Modern discrimination is, moreover, not practiced indiscriminately. Whites, ready and willing applaud, even idolize black athletes and entertainers, refuse to hire, or balk at working with, blacks. Whites who number individual blacks among their closest friends approve, or do not oppose, practices that bar selling or renting homes or apartments in their neighborhoods to blacks they don't know. Employers, not wanting "too many of them," are willing to hire one or two black people, but will reject those who apply later. Most hotels and restaurants who offer black patrons courteous—even deferential—treatment, uniformly reject black job applicants, except perhaps for the most menial jobs. When did you last see a black waiter in a really good restaurant?

Racial schizophrenia is not limited to hotels and restaurants. As a result, neither professional status nor relatively high income protects even accomplished blacks from capricious acts of discrimination that may reflect either individual "preference" or an institution's bias. The motivations for bias vary; the disadvantage to black victims is the same.

Careful examination reveals a pattern to these seemingly arbitrary racial actions. When whites perceive that it will be profitable or at least cost-free to serve, hire, admit, or otherwise deal with blacks on a nondiscriminatory basis, they do so. When they fear—accurately or not—that there may be a loss, inconvenience, or upset to themselves or other whites, discriminatory conduct usually follows. Selections and rejections reflect preference as much as prejudice. A preference for whites makes it harder to prove the discrimination outlawed by civil rights laws. This difficulty, when combined with lackluster enforcement, explains why discrimination in employment and in the housing market continues to prevail more than two decades after enactment of the Equal Employment Opportunity Act of 1965[3] and the Fair Housing Act of 1968.[4]

Racial policy is the culmination of thousands of these individual practices. Black people, then, are caught in a double bind. We are, as I have said, disadvantaged unless whites perceive that nondiscriminatory treatment for us will be a benefit for them. In addition, even when nonracist practices might bring a benefit, whites may rely on discrimination against blacks as a unifying factor and a safety valve for frustrations during economic hard times.

Almost always, the injustices that dramatically diminish the rights of blacks are linked to the serious economic disadvantage suffered by many whites who lack money and power. Whites, rather than acknowledge the similarity of their disadvantage, particularly when compared with that of better-off whites, are easily detoured into protecting their sense of entitlement vis-à-vis blacks for all things of value. Evidently, this racial preference expectation is hypnotic. It is this compulsive fascination that seems to prevent most whites from even seeing—much less resenting—the far more sizable gap between their status and those who occupy the lofty levels at the top of our society.

Race consciousness of this character, as Professor Kimberlè Crenshaw suggested in 1988 in a pathbreaking *Harvard Law Review* article, makes it difficult for whites "to imagine the world differently. It also creates the desire for identification with privileged elites. By focusing on a distinct, subordinate 'other,' whites include themselves in the dominant circle—an arena in which most hold no real power, but only their privileged racial identity."[5]

The critically important stabilizing role that blacks play in this society constitutes a major barrier in the way of achieving racial equality. Throughout history, politicians have used blacks as scapegoats for failed economic or political policies. Before the Civil War, rich slave owners persuaded the white working class to stand with them against the danger of slave revolts—even though the existence of slavery condemned white workers to a life of economic privation.[6] After the Civil War, poor whites fought social reforms and settled for segregation rather than see formerly enslaved blacks get ahead.[7] Most labor unions preferred to allow plant owners to break strikes with black scab labor rather than allow blacks to join their ranks.[8] The "them against us" racial ploy—always a potent force in economic bad times—is working again: today whites, as disadvantaged by high-status entrance requirements as blacks, fight to end affirmative action policies that, by eliminating class-based entrance requirements and requiring widespread advertising of jobs, have likely helped far more whites than blacks. And in the 1990s, as through much of the 1980s, millions of Americans—white as well as black—face steadily worsening conditions: unemployment, inaccessible health care, inadequate housing, mediocre education, and pollution of the environment. The gap in national incomes is approaching a crisis as those in the top fifth now earn more than their counterparts in the bottom four-fifths combined. The conservative guru Kevin Phillips used a different but no less disturbing comparison: the top 2 million income earners in this country earn more than the next 100 million.[9]

Shocking. And yet conservative white politicians are able to gain and hold even the highest office despite their failure to address seriously any of these issues. They rely instead on time-tested formula of getting needy whites to identify on the basis of their shared skin color, and suggest with little or no subtlety that white people must stand together against the Willie Hortons, or against racial quotas, or against affirmative action. The code words differ. The message is the same. Whites are rallied on the basis of racial pride and patriotism to accept their often lowly lot in life, and encouraged to vent their frustration by opposing any serious advancement by blacks. Crucial to this situation is the unstated understanding by the mass of whites that they will accept large disparities in economic opportunity in respect to other whites as long as they have a priority over blacks and other people of color for access to the few opportunities available.

This "racial bonding" by whites[10] means that black rights and interests are always vulnerable to diminishment if not to outright destruction. The willingness of whites over time to respond to this racial rallying cry explains—far more than does the failure of liberal democratic practices (re black rights) to coincide with liberal democratic theory—blacks' continuing subordinate status. This is, of course, contrary to the philosophy of Gunnar Myrdal's massive midcentury study *The American Dilemma*. Myrdal and two generations of civil rights advocates accepted the idea of racism as merely an odious holdover from slavery, "a terrible and inexplicable anomaly struck in the middle of our liberal democratic ethos."[11] No one doubted that the standard American policy making was adequate to the task of abolishing racism. White America, it was assumed, *wanted* to abolish racism.[12]

Forty years later, in *The New American Dilemma*, Professor Jennifer Hochschild examined what she called Myrdal's "anomaly thesis," and concluded that it simply cannot explain the persistence of racial discrimination.[13] Rather, the continued viability of racism demonstrates "that racism is not simply an excrescence on a fundamentally healthy liberal democratic body, but is part of what shapes and energizes the body."[14] Under this view, "liberal democracy and racism in the United States are historically, even inherently, reinforcing; American society as we know it exists only because of its foundation in racially based slavery, and it thrives only because racial discrimination continues. The apparent anomaly is an actual symbiosis."[15]

The permanence of this "symbiosis" ensures that civil rights gains will be temporary and setbacks inevitable. Consider: In this last decade of the twentieth century, color determines the social and economic status of all African Americans, both those who have been highly successful and their poverty-bound brethren whose lives are grounded in misery and despair. We rise and fall less as a result of our efforts than in response to the needs of a white society that condemns all blacks to quasi citizenship as surely as it segregated our parents and enslaved their forebears. The fact is that, despite what we designate as progress wrought through struggle over many generations, we remain what we were in the beginning: a dark and foreign presence, always the designated "other." Tolerated in good times, despised when things go wrong, as a people we are scapegoated and sacrificed as distraction or catalyst for compromise to facilitate resolution of political differences or relieve economic adversity.

We are now, as were our forebears when they were brought to the New World, objects of barter for those who, while profiting from our existence, deny our humanity. It is in the light of this fact that we must consider the haunting questions about slavery and exploitation contained in Professor Linda Myers's *Understanding an Afrocentric World View: Introduction to an Optimal Psychology*, questions that serve as their own answers.[16]

We simply cannot prepare realistically for our future without assessing honestly our past. It seems cold, accusatory, but we must try to fathom with her "the mentality of a people that could continue for over three hundred years to kidnap an estimated 50 million youth and young adults from Africa, transport them across the Atlantic with about half dying unable to withstand the inhumanity of the passage, and enslave them as animals."[17]

As Professor Myers reminds us, blacks were not the only, and certainly not America's most, persecuted people. Appropriate, she asks about the mindset of European Americans to Native Americans. After all, those in possession of the land were basically friendly to the newcomers. And yet the European Americans proceeded to annihilate almost the entire race, ultimately forcing the survivors onto reservations after stealing their land. Far from acknowledging and atoning for the atrocities, American history portrays whites as the heroes, the Indian victims as savage villains. "What," she wonders, "can be understood about the world view of a people who claim to be building a democracy with freedom and justice for all, and at the same time own slaves and deny others basic human rights?"[18]

Of course, Americans did not invent slavery. The practice has existed throughout recorded history, and Professor Orlando Patterson, a respected scholar, argues impressively that American slavery was no worse than that practiced in other parts of the world.[19] But it is not comparative slavery policies that concern me. Slavery is, as an example of what white America has done, a constant reminder of what white America might do.

We must see this country's history of slavery, not as an insuperable racial barrier to blacks, but as a legacy of enlightenment from our enslaved forebears reminding us that if they survived the ultimate form of racism, we and those whites who stand with us can at least view racial oppression in its many contemporary forms without underestimating its critical importance and likely permanent status in this country.

To initiate the reconsideration, I want to set forth this proposition, which will be easier to reject than refute: *Black people will never gain equality in this country. Even those Herculean efforts we hail as successful will produce no more than temporary "peaks of progress," short-lived victories that slide into irrelevance as racial patterns adapt in ways that maintain white dominance. This is a hard-to-accept fact that all history verifies. We must acknowledge it, not as a sign of submission, but as an act of ultimate defiance.*

We identify with and hail as hero the man or woman willing to face even death without flinching.[20] Why? Because, while no one escapes death, those who conquer their dread of it are freed to live more fully. In similar fashion, African Americans must confront and conquer the otherwise deadening reality of our permanent subordinate status. Only in this way can we prevent ourselves from being dragged down by society's racial hostility. Beyond survival lies the potential to perceive more clearly both a reason and the means for further struggle.

I realize that even with the challenge to rethinking these stories pose, many people will find it difficult to embrace my assumption that racism is a permanent component of American life. Mesmerized by the racial equality syndrome, they are too easily reassured by simple admonitions to "stay on course," which come far too easily from those—black and white—who are not on the deprived end of the economic chasm between blacks and whites.

The goal of racial equality is, while comforting to many whites, more illusionary than real for blacks. For too long, we have worked for substantive reform, then settled for weakly worded and poorly enforced legislation, indeterminate judicial decisions, token government positions, even holidays. I repeat. If we are to seek new goals for our struggles, we must first reassess the worth of the racial assumptions on which, without careful thought, we have presumed too much and relied on too long.

Let's begin.

NOTES

1. David Swinton, "The Economic Status of African Americans: 'Permanent' Poverty and Inequality," in *The State of Black America* (New York: National Urban League, 1991), 25.

2. Not all the data are bleak. While the median family income for black families declined in the 1970s and 1980s, the proportion of African-American families with incomes of $35,000 to $50,000 increased from 23.3 to 27.5 percent. The proportion with incomes above $50,000 increased by 38 percent, from 10.0 to 13.8 percent. The overall median income for blacks declined, though: while the top quarter made progress, the bottom half was sliding backward, and the proportion of blacks receiving very low income (less than $5,000) actually increased. Swinton, 36–37.

3. Act of 2 July 1964, P.L. 88-352, 42 U.S.C.A. 2000e–2000e–17.

4. Fair Housing Act of 1968 (1970) (as amended 1988 in 13(a) of Pub. L. 100–430, short title "Fair Housing Amendments Act of 1988").

5. Kimberlè Crenshaw, "Race, Reform, and Retrenchment: Transformation and Legitimation in Antidiscrimination Law," *Harvard Law Review* 101 (1988): 1331, 1380–81.

6. Edmund Morgan, *American Slavery, American Freedom* (New York: Norton, 1975), 8.

7. Derrick Bell, 'The Racial Imperative in American Law," in *The Age of Segregation: Race Relations in the South, 1890–1945* (Jackson: University Press of Mississippi, 1978).

8. Herbert Hill, *Black Labor and the American Legal System* (Washington, D.C.: Bureau of National Affairs, 1977); William Gould, *Black Workers and White Unions* (Ithaca, NY: Cornell University Press, 1977).

9. Kevin Phillips, *Politics of Rich and Poor* (New York: Random House, 1990).

10. bell hooks, *Feminist Theory from Margin to Center* (Cambridge: South End Press, 1984), 54.

11. Gunnar Myrdal, *An American Dilemma* (New York: Harper and Bros., 1944), xix.

12. According to Myrdal, the "Negro problem in America represents a moral lag in the development of the nation and a study of it must record nearly everything which is bad and wrong in America. . . . However, . . . not since Reconstruction has there been more reason to anticipate fundamental changes in American race relations, changes which will involve a development toward the American ideals." Ibid.

13. Jennifer Hochschild, *The New American Dilemma* (New Haven, CT: Yale University Press, 1984), 203.

14. Ibid., 5.

15. Ibid.

16. Linda Myers, *Understanding an Afrocentric World View: Introduction to an Optimal Psychology* (Dubuque: Kendall/Hunt, 1988), 8.

17. Ibid.

18. Ibid.

19. He suggests, "The dishonor of slavery . . . came in the primal act of submission. It was the most immediate human expression of the inability to defend oneself or to secure one's livelihood. . . . The dishonor the slave was compelled to experience sprang instead from that raw, human sense of debasement in having no being except as an expression of another's being." Patterson, *Slavery and Social Death* (Cambridge: Harvard University Press, 1982), 76.

20. Ernest Becker, *The Denial of Death* (New York: Free Press, 1973), 11–12.

EDITOR'S NOTE

Perhaps the reason the "fact of slavery refuses to fade" as Derrick Bell put it, is that we put a lid on the issue, but occasionally the lid blows off (like it did in New Orleans due to Hurricane Katrina) or the issue gets swept under the rug until the carpet is so high it trips us. Then white folks shake their heads and say: "What more do you black folks want?" When blacks call attention to their lack of opportunity, whites say: "Get over it." How can blacks get over it, if it permeates everything in their lives? If you doubt there are two different perspectives, read on: A CNN/Gallup Poll was taken in 2002 and found that 68 percent of blacks favor an apology from the federal government for its role in enslavement while 62 percent of whites do not.[1] Ninety percent of white respondents think the government should not pay reparations for underwriting enslavement and 50 percent of blacks think it should.[2]

Why the disparate perspectives? Steinhorn and Diggs-Brown's study of television and minorities helps explain whites' belief about race. The researchers maintain that television has provided whites with the feeling that they interact with black people without actually doing it.[3] By watching entertainers like Oprah, Will Smith, Halle Berry, or Denzel Washington on television, as well as black sports heroes, whites believe they have a relationship with blacks, that they accept blacks. Thus, although they live in segregated neighborhoods, attend segregated schools, lead segregated social lives, attend segregated churches, whites don't see themselves as participating in a racist system. The researchers argue that the number of black characters on the television show *ER* alone exceeds the number of blacks most Americans will interact with during any given week.[4]

A noteworthy change that has received scant attention is the state and/or local ordinances enacted requiring businesses to disclose any historical connection to enslavement.[5] Cities, like Chicago, are ordering corporations that have historically built their businesses and profits on the backs of enslaved people to ante up, to make restitution in some way for their part in the institution of enslavement. Because the ordinances affect corporations and do not directly affect whites, little resentment has been forthcoming from whites, but at some point a backlash could occur. Until then, the apologies and reparations might ameliorate some of the anger and pain over the mistreatment African Americans have endured.

J. P. Morgan, for one, has established a $5 million scholarship fund for black students in Louisiana as an attempt to make restitution for Morgan's business practices that relied on enslavement.[6] A search of Morgan's records found that between 1834 and 1861, the company held more than 13,000 people as collateral for mortgages and at one point, had financial rights over more than 1,200 enslaved people due to property foreclosures.[7] Wachovia is another corporation that issued an apology for having put enslaved workers on the railroad and for using others as collateral on defaulted loans in the 1800s. Still other companies have stonewalled. For example Lehman Brothers Holdings Inc., Brown Bothers Harriman, Lloyds of London, R. J. Reynolds Tobacco Holdings, Brown & Williamson Tobacco Corporation, and Liggett Group Inc. have refused to apologize.[8] If corporations have been slow to issue an apology, perhaps it is because the government has not rushed to do so.

The U.S. Senate had not even considered the issue of reparation for enslavement, but after decades of failing to make lynching a federal offense, the Senate took a small step by issuing an apology for their failure to codify the offense into federal law. Although the legislation had been passed by the House several times in the early twentieth century, the Senate never did. However, recently, eighty-five senators sponsored the resolution of apology while fifteen senators (including Trent Lott) refused to do so. The Majority Whip, Bill Frist, insisted that no vote be recorded for fear of embarrassing the fifteen senators.[9]

How would Derrick Bell respond?

NOTES

1. Darryl Fears, "More Than Apologies," *The Washington Post National Weekly Edition*, 27 June–10 July 2005, p. 30.

2. Ibid.

3. Paul Farhl, *The Washington Post National Weekly Edition*, 21 February 2000, p. 23.

4. Ibid.

5. Robin Sidel, "A Historian's Quest Links J. P. Morgan to Slave Ownership," *The Wall Street Journal*, 10 May 2005, pp. 1, A8.

6. Ibid.

7. Ibid.

8. Darryl Fears, "More Than Apologies."

9. Tom Teepen, "Frist Leads Dodgers of Lynching Apology," *The Cincinnati Enquirer*, 17 June 2005, p. B7.

5

Size 6

The Western Women's Harem

Fatema Mernissi

It was during my unsuccessful attempt to buy a cotton skirt in an American department store that I was told my hips were too large to fit into a size 6. That distressing experience made me realize how the image of beauty in the West can hurt and humiliate a woman as much as the veil does when enforced by the state police in extremist nations such as Iran, Afghanistan, or Saudi Arabia. Yes, that day I stumbled onto one of the keys to the enigma of passive beauty in Western harem fantasies. The elegant saleslady in the American store looked at me without moving from her desk and said that she had no skirt my size. "In this whole big store, there is no skirt for me?" I said. "You are joking." I felt very suspicious and thought that she just might be too tired to help me. I could understand that. But then the saleswoman added a condescending judgment, which sounded to me like an Imam's *fatwa*. It left no room for discussion:

"You are too big!" she said.

"I am too big compared to what?" I asked, looking at her intently, because I realized that I was facing a critical cultural gap here.

"Compared to a size 6," came the saleslady's reply.

Her voice had a clear-cut edge to it that is typical of those who enforce religious laws. "Size 4 and 6 are the norm," she went on, encouraged by my bewildered look. "Deviant sizes such as the one you need can be bought in special stores."

That was the first time that I had ever heard such nonsense about my size. In the Moroccan streets, men's flattering comments regarding my particularly generous hips have for decades led me to believe that the entire planet shared their convictions.

In any case, when it comes to beauty and compliments, nothing is too serious or definite in the medina, where everything can be negotiated. But things seemed to be different in that American department store. In fact, I have to confess that I lost my usual self-confidence in that New York environment. Not that I am always sure of myself, but I don't walk around the Moroccan streets or down the university corridors wondering what people are thinking about me. Of course, when I hear a compliment, my ego expands like a cheese soufflé, but on the whole, I don't expect to hear much from others. Some mornings, I feel ugly because I am sick or tired; others, I feel wonderful because it is sunny out or I have written a good paragraph. But suddenly, in that peaceful American store that I had entered so triumphantly, as a sovereign consumer ready to spend money, I felt savagely attacked. My hips, until then the sign of a relaxed and uninhibited maturity, were suddenly being condemned as a deformity.

"And who decides the norm?" I asked the saleslady, in an attempt to regain some self-confidence by challenging the established rules. I never let others evaluate me, if only because I remember my childhood too well. In ancient Fez, which valued round-faced plump adolescents, I was repeatedly told that I was too tall, too skinny, my cheekbones were too high, my eyes were too slanted. My mother often complained that I would never find a husband and urged me to study and learn all that I could, from storytelling to embroidery, in order to survive. But I often retorted that since "Allah had created me the way I am, how could he be so wrong, Mother?" That would silence the poor woman for a while, because if she contradicted me, she would be attacking God himself. And this tactic of glorifying my strange looks as a divine gift not only helped me to survive in my stuffy city, but also caused me to start believing the story myself. I became almost self-confident. I say almost, because I realized early on that self-confidence is not a tangible and stable thing like a silver bracelet that never changes over the years. Self-confidence is like a tiny fragile light, which goes off and on. You have to replenish it constantly.

"And who says that everyone must be a size 6?" I joked to the saleslady that day, deliberately neglecting to mention size 4, which is the size of my skinny twelve-year-old niece.

At that point, the saleslady suddenly gave me an anxious took. "The norm is everywhere, my dear," she said. "It's all over, in the magazines, on television, in the ads. You can't escape it. . . ." She paused and then concluded, "If they sold size 14 or 16, which is probably what you need, they would go bankrupt."

She stopped for a minute and then stared at me, intrigued. "Where on earth do you come from? I am sorry I can't help you. Really, I am." And she looked it too. She seemed, all of a sudden, interested, and brushed off another woman who was seeking her attention with a cutting, "Get someone else to help you, I'm busy." Only then did I notice that she was probably my age, in her late fifties. But unlike me, she had the thin body of an adolescent girl. Her knee-length, navy blue, Chanel dress had a white silk collar reminiscent of the subdued elegance of aristocratic French Catholic schoolgirls at the turn of the century. A pearl-studded belt emphasized the slimness of her waist. With her meticulously styled short hair and sophisticated makeup, she looked half my age at first glance.

"I come from a country where there is no size for women's clothes," I told her. "I buy my own material and the neighborhood seamstress or craftsman makes me the silk or leather skirt I want. They just take my measurements each time I see them. Neither the seamstress nor I know exactly what size my new skirt is. We discover it together in the making. No one cares about my size in Morocco as long as I pay taxes on time. Actually, I don't know what my size is, to tell you the truth."

The saleswoman laughed merrily and said that I should advertise my country as a paradise for stressed working women. "You mean you don't watch your weight?" she inquired, with a tinge of disbelief in her voice. And then, after a brief moment of silence, she added in a lower register, as if talking to herself. "Many women working in highly paid fashion-related jobs could lose their positions if they didn't keep to a strict diet."

Her words sounded so simple, but the threat they implied was so cruel that I realized for the first time that maybe "size 6" is a more violent restriction imposed on women than is the Muslim veil. Quickly I said good-bye so as not to make any more demands on the saleslady's time or involve her in any more unwelcome, confidential exchanges about age-discriminating salary cuts. A surveillance camera was probably watching us both.

Yes, I thought as I wandered off, I have finally found the answer to my harem enigma. Unlike the Muslim man, who uses space to establish male domination by excluding women from the public arena, the Western man manipulates time and light. He declares that in order to be beautiful, a woman must look fourteen years old. If she dares to look fifty, or worse, sixty, she is beyond the pale. By putting the spotlight on the female child and framing her as the ideal of beauty, he condemns the mature woman to invisibility. In fact, the modern Western man enforces Immanuel Kant's nineteenth-century theories: To be beautiful, women have to appear childish and brainless. When a woman looks mature and self-assertive, or allows her hips to expand, she is condemned as ugly. Thus, the walls of the European harem separate youthful beauty from ugly maturity.

These Western attitudes, I thought, are even more dangerous and cunning than the Muslim ones because the weapon used against women is time. Time is less visible, more fluid than space. The Western man uses images and spotlights to freeze female beauty within an idealized childhood, and forces women to perceive aging—that normal unfolding of the years—as a shameful devaluation. "Here I am, transformed into a dinosaur," I caught myself saying aloud as I went up and down the rows of skirts in the store, hoping to prove the saleslady wrong—to no avail. This Western time-defined veil is even crazier than the space-defined one enforced by the Ayatollahs.

The violence embodied in the Western harem is less visible than in the Eastern harem because aging is not attacked directly, but rather masked as an aesthetic choice. Yes, I suddenly felt not only very ugly but also quite useless in that store, where, if you had big hips, you were simply out of the picture. You drifted into the fringes of nothingness. By putting the spotlight on the prepubescent female, the Western man veils the older, more mature woman, wrapping her in shrouds of ugliness. This idea gives me the chills because it tattoos the invisible harem directly onto a woman's skin. Chinese foot-binding worked the same way: Men declared beautiful only those women who had small, childlike feet. Chinese men did not force women to band-age their feet to keep them from developing normally—all they did was to define the beauty ideal. In feudal China, a beautiful woman was the one who voluntarily sacrificed her right to unhindered physical movement by mutilating her own feet, and thereby proving that her main goal in life was to please men. Similarly, in the Western world, I was expected to shrink my hips into a size 6 if I wanted to find a decent skirt tailored for a beautiful woman. We Muslim women have only one month of fasting, Ramadan, but the poor Western woman who diets has to fast twelve months out of the year. "*Quelle horreur,*" I kept repeating to myself, while looking around at the American women shopping. All those my age looked like youthful teenagers.

According to the writer Naomi Wolf, the ideal size for American models de-creased sharply in the 1990s. "A generation ago, the average model weighed 8 percent less than the average American woman, whereas today she weighs 23 percent less. . . . The weight of Miss America plummeted, and the average weight of *Playboy* playmates dropped from 11 percent below the national av-erage in 1970 to 17 percent below it in eight years."[1] The shrinking of the ideal size, according to Wolf, is one of the primary reasons for anorexia and other health-related problems: "Eating disorders rose exponentially, and a mass of neurosis was promoted that used food and weight to strip women of . . . a sense of control."[2]

Now, at last, the mystery of my Western harem made sense. Framing youth as beauty and condemning maturity is the weapon used against women in the West just as limiting access to public space is the weapon used in the East. The objective remains identical in both cultures: to make women feel unwelcome, inadequate, and ugly.

The power of the Western man resides in dictating what women should wear and how they should look. He controls the whole fashion industry, from cos-metics to underwear. The West, I realized, was the only part of the world where women's fashion is a man's business. In places like Morocco, where you de-sign your own clothes and discuss them with craftsmen and women, fashion is your own business. Not so in the West. As Naomi Wolf explains in *The Beauty Myth*, men have engineered a prodigious amount of fetish-like, fashion-related paraphernalia: "Powerful industries—the $33-billion-a-year diet in-dustry, the $20-billion cosmetic industry, the $300-billion cosmetic surgery industry, and the $7-billion pornography industry—have arisen from the cap-ital made out of unconscious anxieties, and are in turn able, through their influence on mass culture, to use, stimulate, and reinforce the hallucination in a rising economic spiral."[3]

But how does the system function? I wondered. Why do women accept it?

Of all the possible explanations, I like that of the French sociologist, Pierre Bourdieu, the best. In his latest book, *La Domination Masculine*, he proposes something he calls *"la violence symbolique"*: "Symbolic violence is a form of power which is hammered directly on the body, and as if by magic, without any apparent physical constraint. But this magic operates only because it activates the codes pounded in the deepest layers of the body."[4] Reading Bourdieu, I had the impression that I finally understood Western man's psyche better. The cosmetic and fashion industries are only the tip of the iceberg, he states, which is why women are so ready to adhere to their dictates. Something else is going on [at] a far deeper level. Otherwise, why would women belittle themselves spontaneously? Why, argues Bourdieu, would women make their lives more difficult, for example, by preferring men who are taller or older than they are? "The majority of French women wish to have a husband who is older and also, which seems consistent, bigger as far as size is concerned," writes Bourdieu.[5] Caught in the enchanted submission characteristic of the symbolic violence inscribed in the mysterious layers of the flesh, women relinquish what he calls "les signes ordinaires de la hiérarchie sexuelle," the ordinary signs of sexual hierarchy, such as old age and a larger body. By so doing, explains Bourdieu, women spontaneously accept the subservient position. It is this spontaneity Bourdieu describes as magic enchantment.[6]

Once I understood how this magic submission worked, I became very happy that the conservative Ayatollahs do not know about it yet. If they did, they would readily switch to its sophisticated methods, because they are so much more effective. To deprive me of food is definitely the best way to paralyze my thinking capabilities.

Both Naomi Wolf and Pierre Bourdieu come to the conclusion that insidious "body codes" paralyze Western women's abilities to compete for power, even though access to education and professional opportunities seem wide open, because the rules of the game are so different according to gender. Women enter the power game with so much of their energy deflected to their physical appearance that one hesitates to say the playing field is level. "A cultural fixation on female thinness is not an obsession about female beauty," explains Wolf. It is "an obsession about female obedience. Dieting is the most potent political sedative in women's history; a quietly mad population is a tractable one."[7] Research, she contends, "confirmed what most women know too well—that concern with weight leads to a 'virtual collapse of self-esteem and sense of effectiveness' and that . . . 'prolonged and periodic caloric restriction' resulted in a distinctive personality whose traits are passivity, anxiety, and emotionality."[8] Similarly, Bourdieu, who focuses more on how this myth hammers its inscriptions onto the flesh itself, recognizes that constantly reminding women of their physical appearance destabilizes them emotionally because it reduces them to exhibited objects. "By confining women to the status of symbolical objects to be seen and perceived by the other, masculine domination . . . puts women in a state of constant physical insecurity. . . . They have to strive ceaselessly to be engaging, attractive, and available."[9] Being frozen into the passive position of an object whose very existence depends on the eye of its beholder turns the educated modern Western woman into a harem slave.

"I thank you, Allah, for sparing me the tyranny of the 'size 6 harem,'" I repeatedly said to myself while seated on the Paris-Casablanca flight, on my way back home at last. "I am so happy that the conservative male elite does not know about it. Imagine the fundamentalists switching from the veil to forcing women to fit size 6."

How can you stage a credible political demonstration and shout in the streets that your human rights have been violated when you cannot find the right skirt?

NOTES

1. Naomi Wolf, *The Beauty Myth: How Images of Beauty Are Used Against Women* (New York: Anchor Books, Doubleday, 1992), p. 185.

2. Ibid., p. ii.

3. Ibid., p. 17.

4. Pierre Bourdieu: "La force symbolique est une forme de pouvoir qui s'exerce sur les corps, directement, et comme par magie, en dehors de toute contraine physique, mais cette magie n'opère qu'en s'appuyant sur des dispositions déposées, tel des ressorts, au plus profond des corps." In *La Domination Masculine* (Paris: Editions du Seuil, i998), op. cit. p. 44.

Here I would like to thank my French editor, Claire Delannoy, who kept me informed of the latest debates on women's issues in Paris by sending me Bourdieu's book and many others. Delannoy has been reading this manuscript since its inception in 1996 (a first version was published in Casablanca by Edition Le Fennec in 1998 as "tes-Vous Vacciné Contre le Harem").

5. Ibid., p. 41.

6. Ibid., p. 42.

7. Wolf, op. cit., p. 187.

8. Wolf, quoting research carried out by S. C. Woolly and W. W. Woolly, op. cit., pp. 187–88.

9. Bourdieu, *La Domination Masculine*, p. 73.

EDITOR'S NOTE

Many are likely to dismiss Fatema Mernissi's reading as not reality based. Most like to think they are not enslaved to fashion: that they wear what they want, when they want. But then there are those fashion-police reminders that come along and ensure that we conform to a strict gendered dress code. For example, consider the recent headlines: "Flip-flop horror at White House: Mini scandal: Lacrosse teams' footwear."[1]

Northwestern University women's lacrosse team won the NCAA championship, a notable feat, but unfortunately the media chose to focus on the women's feet. As part of their victory celebration, the young female champions were invited to the White House for a photo opportunity with the president. But, horror of horrors, four of the nine women in the front row of the photo with the president wore flip-flops![2]

One mother said: "Don't ask me about the flip-flops. . . . It mortified me." After all, at the Bush White House, "women are instructed to be 'appropriately dressed.'"[3] Fashion expert Ellen Goldstein stated: "It's a fine line. . . . If it were you or me or any of the rest of the public who were meeting the president— it's inappropriate. . . . But there was nobody there in torn clothes and ratty T-shirts."[4] There's that fine line again!

Does Mernissi have a point? Why, with such a spectacular victory, was the focus on fashion and not on the outstanding athleticism of the young women? How do mothers and peers contribute to women's stringent adherence to a gendered code of dress?

NOTES

1. Tim Whitmire, "Flip-flop horror at White House," *The Cincinnati Enquirer*, 23 July 2005, p. A8.
2. Ibid.
3. Ibid.
4. Ibid.

III

THE *OTHER* WEARS MANY FACES

6

Diversity and Its Discontents

Arturo Madrid

My name is Arturo Madrid. I am a citizen of the United States, as are my parents and as were my grandparents and my great-grandparents. My ancestors' presence in what is now the United States antedates Plymouth Rock, even without taking into account any American Indian heritage I might have.

I do not, however, fit those mental sets that define America and Americans. My physical appearance, my speech patterns, my name, my profession (a professor of Spanish) create a text that confuses the reader. My normal experience is to be asked, "And where are *you* from?" My response depends on my mood. Passive-aggressive, I answer, "From here." Aggressive-passive, I ask, "Do you mean where I am originally from?" But ultimately my answer to those follow-up questions that will ask about origins will be that we have always been from here.

Overcoming my resentment I try to educate, knowing that nine times out of ten my words fall on inattentive ears. I have spent most of my adult life explaining who I am not. I am exotic, but—as Richard Rodriguez of *Hunger of Memory* fame so painfully found out—not exotic enough . . . not Peruvian, or Pakistani, or whatever. I am, however, very clearly the *other*, if only your everyday, garden-variety, domestic *other*. I will share with you another phenomenon that I have been a part of, that of being a missing person, and how I came late to that awareness. But I've always known that I was the *other*, even before I knew the vocabulary or understood the significance of otherness.

I grew up in an isolated and historically marginal part of the United States, a small mountain village in the state of New Mexico, the eldest child of parents native to that region, whose ancestors had always lived there. In those vast and empty spaces people who look like me, speak as I do, and have names like mine predominate. But the *americanos* lived among us: the descendants of those nineteenth-century immigrants who dispossessed us of our lands; missionaries who came to convert us and stayed to live among us; artists who became enchanted with our land and humanscape and went native; refugees from unhealthy climes, crowded spaces, unpleasant circumstances; and, of course, the inhabitants of Los Alamos, whose socio-cultural distance from us was accentuated by the fact that they occupied a space removed from and proscribed to us. More importantly, however, they—*los americanos*—were omnipresent (and almost exclusively so) in newspapers, newsmagazines, books, on radio, in movies, and, ultimately, on television.

Despite the operating myth of the day, school did not erase my otherness. It did try to deny it, and in doing so only accentuated it. To this day what takes place in schools is more socialization than education, but when I was in elementary school—and given where I was—socialization was everything. School was where one became an American, because there was a pervasive and systematic denial by the society that surrounded us that we were Americans. That denial was both explicit and implicit.

Quite beyond saluting the flag and pledging allegiance to it (a very intense and meaningful action, given that the United States was involved in a war and our brothers, cousins, uncles, and fathers were on the frontlines), becoming American was learning English, and its corollary: not speaking Spanish. Until very recently ours was a proscribed language, either de jure—by rule, by policy, by law—or de facto—by practice, implicitly if not explicitly, through social and political and economic pressure. I do not argue that learning English was not appropriate. On the contrary. Like it or not, and we had no basis to make any judgments on that matter, we were Americans by virtue of having been born Americans and English was the common language of Americans. And there was a myth, a pervasive myth, to the effect that if only we learned to speak English well—and particularly without an accent—we would be welcomed into the American fellowship.

The true text was not our speech, but rather our names and our appearance, for we would always have an accent, however perfect our pronunciation, however excellent our enunciation, however divine our diction. That accent would be heard in our pigmentation, our physiognomy, our names. We were, in short, the *other*.

Being the *other* involves contradictory phenomena. On the one hand being the *other* frequently means being invisible. Ralph Ellison wrote eloquently about that experience in his magisterial novel, *Invisible Man*. On the other hand, being the *other* sometimes involves sticking out like a sore thumb. What is she/he doing here?

For some of us being the *other* is only annoying; for others it is debilitating; for still others it is damning. Many try to flee otherness by taking on protective colorations that provide invisibility, whether of dress or speech or manner or name. Only a fortunate few succeed. For the majority of us otherness is permanently sealed by physical appearance. For the rest, otherness is betrayed by ways of being, speaking, or doing.

The first half of my life I spent downplaying the significance and consequences of otherness. The second half has seen me wrestling to understand its complex and deeply ingrained realities; striving to fathom why otherness denies us a voice or visibility or validity in American society and its institutions; struggling to make otherness familiar, reasonable, even normal to my fellow Americans.

I spoke earlier of another phenomenon that I am a part of: that of being a missing person. Growing up in northern New Mexico I had only a slight sense of us being missing persons. *Hispanos*, as we called (and call) ourselves in New Mexico, were very much a part of the fabric of the society, and there were *hispano* professionals everywhere about me: doctors, lawyers, schoolteachers, and administrators. My people owned businesses, ran organizations, and were both appointed and elected public officials.

My awareness of our absence from the larger institutional life of the society became sharper when I went off to college, but even then it was attenuated by the circumstances of history and geography. The demography of Albuquerque still strongly reflected its historical and cultural origins, despite the influx of Midwesterners and Easterners. Moreover, many of my classmates at the University of New Mexico were *hispanos*, and even some of my professors. I thought that would obtain at UCLA, where I began graduate studies in 1960. Los Angeles had a very large Mexican population and that population was visible even in and around Westwood and on the campus. Many of the groundskeepers and food-service personnel at UCLA were Mexican. But Mexican-American students were few and mostly invisible, and I do not recall seeing or knowing a single Mexican-American (or, for that matter, African American, Asian, or American Indian) professional on the staff or faculty of that institution during the five years I was there. Needless to say, people like me were not present in any capacity at Dartmouth College, the site of my first teaching appointment, and of course were not even part of the institutional or individual mindset. I knew then that we—a we that had come to encompass American Indians, Asian Americans, African Americans, Puerto Ricans, and women—were truly missing persons in American institutional life.

Over the past three decades the de jure and de facto types of segregation that have historically characterized American institutions have been under assault. As a consequence, minorities and women have become part of American institutional life. Although there are still many areas where we are not to be found, the missing persons phenomenon is not as pervasive as it once was. However, the presence of the *other*, particularly minorities, in institutions and in institutional life resembles what we call in Spanish *a flor de tierra* (a surface phenomenon): we are spare plants whose roots do not go deep, vulnerable to inclemencies of an economic, or political, or social, nature.

Our entrance into and our status in institutional life are not unlike a scenario set forth by my grandmother's pastor when she informed him that she and her family were leaving their mountain village to relocate to the Rio

Grande Valley. When he asked her to promise that she would remain true to the faith and continue to involve herself in it, she asked why he thought she would do otherwise. "Doña Trinidad," he told her, "in the Valley there is no Spanish church. There is only an American church." "But," she protested, "I read and speak English and would be able to worship there." The pastor responded, "It is possible that they will not admit you, and even if they do, they might not accept you. And that is why I want you to promise me that you are going to go to church. Because if they don't let you in through the front door, I want you to go in through the back door. And if you can't get in through the back door, go in the side door. And if you are unable to enter through the side door I want you to go in through the window. What is important is that you enter and stay."

Some of us entered institutional life through the front door; others through the back door; and still others through the side doors. Many, if not most of us, came in through windows, and continue to come in through windows. Of those who entered through the front door, some never made it past the lobby; others were ushered into corners and niches. Those who entered through back and side doors inevitably have remained in back and side rooms. And those who entered through windows found enclosures built around them. For, despite the lip service given to the goal of the integration of minorities into institutional life, what has frequently occurred instead is ghettoization, marginalization, isolation.

Not only have the entry points been limited, but in addition the dynamics have been singularly conflictive. Gaining entry and its corollary, gaining space, have frequently come as a consequence of demands made on institutions and institutional officers. Rather than entering institutions more or less passively, minorities have of necessity entered them actively, even aggressively. Rather than waiting to receive, they have demanded. Institutional relations have thus been adversarial, infused with specific and generalized tensions.

The nature of the entrance and the nature of the space occupied have greatly influenced the view and attitude of the majority population within those institutions. All of us are put into the same box; that is, no matter what the individual reality, the assessment of the individual is inevitably conditioned by a perception that is held of the class. Whatever our history, whatever our record, whatever our validations, whatever our accomplishments, by and large we are perceived unidimensionally and dealt with accordingly. I remember an experience I had in this regard, atypical only in its explicitness. A few years ago I allowed myself to be persuaded to seek the presidency of a well-known state university. I was invited for an interview and presented myself before the selection committee, which included members of the board of trustees. The opening question of that brief but memorable interview was directed at me by a member of that august body. "Dr. Madrid," he asked, why does a one-dimensional person like you think he can be the president of a multidimensional institution like ours?"

Over the past four decades America's demography has undergone significant changes. Since 1965 the principal demographic growth we have experienced in the United States has been of peoples whose national origins are non-European. This population growth has occurred both through birth and through immigration. A few years ago discussion of the national birthrate had a scare dimension: the high—"inordinately high"—birthrate of the Hispanic population. The popular discourse was informed by words such as "breeding." Several years later, as a consequence of careful tracking by government agencies, we now know that what has happened is that the birthrate of the majority population has decreased. When viewed historically and comparatively, the minority populations (for the most part) have also had a decline in birthrate, but not one as great as that of the majority.

Prior to the Immigration Act of 1965, 69 percent of immigration was from Europe. By far the largest number of immigrants to the United States since 1965 have been from the Americas and from Asia: 34 percent are from Asia; another 34 percent are from Central and South America; 16 percent are from Europe; 10 percent are from the Caribbean; the remaining 6 percent are from other continents and Canada. As was the case with previous immigration waves, the current one consists principally of young people: 60 percent are between the ages of sixteen and forty-four. Thus, for the next few decades, we will continue to see a growth in the percentage of non-European-origin Americans as compared to European Americans.

To sum up, we now live in one of the most demographically diverse nations in the world, and one that is increasingly more so.

We live in an age of continuous and intense change, a world in which what held true yesterday does not today, and certainly will not tomorrow. What change does, moreover, is bring about even more change. The only constant we have at this point in our national development is change. And change is threatening. The older we get the more likely we are to be anxious about change, and the greater our desire to maintain the status quo.

Evident in our public life is a fear of change, whether economic or moral. Some who fear change are responsive to the call of economic protectionism, others to the message of moral protectionism. Parenthetically, I have referred to the movement to require more of students without in turn giving them more as academic protectionism. . . . Much more serious, however, is the dark side of the populism which underlies this ongoing protectionism—the resentment of the *other*. An excellent and fascinating example of that aspect of populism is the cry for linguistic protectionism—for making English the official language of the United States. And who among us is unaware of the tensions that underlie immigration reform, of the underside of demographic protectionism?

A matter of increasing concern is whether this new protectionism, and the mistrust of the *other* which accompanies it, is not making more significant inroads than we have supposed in higher education. Specifically, I wish to discuss the question of whether a goal (quality) and a reality (demographic diversity) have been erroneously placed in conflict, and, if so, what problems this perception of conflict might present.

We consider quality to be finite; that is, it is limited with respect to quantity; it has very few manifestations; it is not widely distributed. I have it and you have it, but they don't. We associate quality with homogeneity, with uniformity, with standardization, with order, regularity, neatness. All too often we equate it with smoothness, glibness, slickness, elegance. Certainly it is always expensive. We tend to identify it with those who lead, with the rich and famous. And, when you come right down to it, it's inherent. Either you've got it or you ain't.

Diversity, from the Latin *divertere*, meaning to turn aside, to go different ways, to differ, is the condition of being different or having differences, is an instance of being different. Its companion word, diverse, means differing, unlike, distinct; having or capable of having various forms; composed of unlike or distinct elements. Diversity is lack of standardization, of regularity, of orderliness, homogeneity, conformity, uniformity. Diversity introduces complications, is difficult to organize, is troublesome to manage, is problematical. Diversity is irregular, disorderly, uneven, rough. The way we use the word diversity gives us away. Something is too diverse, is extremely diverse. We want a little diversity.

When we talk about diversity, we are talking about the *other*, whatever that other might be: someone of a different gender, race, class, national origin; somebody at a greater or lesser distance from the norm; someone outside the set; someone who possesses a different set of characteristics, features, or attributes; someone who does not fall within the taxonomies we use daily and with which we are comfortable; someone who does not fit into the mental configurations that give our lives order and meaning.

In short, diversity is desirable only in principle, not in practice. Long live diversity . . . as long as it conforms to my standards, my mind set, my view of life, my sense of order. We desire, we like, we admire diversity, not unlike the way the French (and others) appreciate women; that is, *Vive la différence!*—as long as it stays in its place.

What I find paradoxical about and lacking in this debate is that diversity is the natural order of things. Evolution produces diversity. Margaret Visser, writing about food in her latest book, *Much Depends on Dinner*, makes an eloquent statement in this regard:

> Machines like, demand, and produce uniformity. But nature loathes it: her strength lies in multiplicity and in differences. Sameness in biology means fewer possibilities and therefore weakness.

The United States, by its very nature, by its very development, is the essence of diversity. It is diverse in its geography, population, institutions, technology;

its social, cultural, and intellectual modes. It is a society that at its best does not consider quality to be monolithic in form or finite in quantity, or to be inherent in class. Quality in our society proceeds in large measure out of the stimulus of diverse modes of thinking and acting; out of the creativity made possible by the different ways in which we approach things; out of diversion from paths or modes hallowed by tradition.

One of the principal strengths of our society is its ability to address, on a continuing and substantive basis, the real economic, political, and social problems that have faced and continue to face us. What makes the United States so attractive to immigrants is the protections and opportunities it offers; what keeps our society together is tolerance for cultural, religious, social, political, and even linguistic difference; what makes us a unique, dynamic, and extraordinary nation is the power and creativity of our diversity.

The true history of the United States is one of struggle against intolerance, against oppression, against xenophobia, against those forces that have prohibited persons from participating in the larger life of the society on the basis of their race, their gender, their religion, their national origin, their linguistic and cultural background. These phenomena are not consigned to the past. They remain with us and frequently take on virulent dimensions.

If you believe, as I do, that the well-being of a society is directly related to the degree and extent to which all of its citizens participate in its institutions, then you will have to agree that we have a challenge before us. In view of the extraordinary changes that are taking place in our society we need to take up the struggle again, irritating, grating, troublesome, unfashionable, unpleasant as it is. As educated and educator members of this society we have a special responsibility for ensuring that all American institutions, not just our elementary and secondary schools, our juvenile halls, or our jails, reflect the diversity of our society. Not to do so is to risk greater alienation on the part of a growing segment of our society; is to risk increased social tension in an already conflictive world; and, ultimately, is to risk the survival of a range of institutions that, for all their defects and deficiencies, provide us the opportunity and the freedom to improve our individual and collective lot.

Because diversity—the *other*—is among us, will define and determine our lives in ways that we still do not fully appreciate, whether that *other* is women (no longer bound by tradition, house, and family); or Asians, African Americans, Indians, and Hispanics (no longer invisible, regional, or marginal); or our newest immigrants (no longer distant, exotic, alien). Given the changing profile of America, will we come to terms with diversity in our personal and professional lives? Will we begin to recognize the diverse forms that quality can take? If so, we will thus initiate the process of making quality limitless in its manifestations, infinite in quantity, unrestricted with respect to its origins, and more importantly, virulently contagious.

I hope we will. And that we will further join together to expand—not to close—the circle.

EDITOR'S NOTE

Madrid's words are powerful: "[D]iversity is desirable only in principle, not in practice . . . our history one of struggle against intolerance . . . not consigned to the past." His family's history in this country predates the arrival of the Europeans, yet he is still treated as the foreigner. How would you react to such treatment?

Charles Krauthammer, columnist for the *Washington Post*, expresses a view many Americans hold. He says: "The cure for excessive immigration is successful assimilation." And the "first task . . . should be abolishing bilingual education everywhere."[1] What happened when Mr. Krauthammer's ancestors came to this continent and took land from the Native Americans and Mexican people (Professor Madrid's ancestors)? Did the Europeans assimilate to the cultures and customs that were already established on this continent prior to their arrival or did they impose their own?

While Krauthammer seeks the status quo, Latino power is ascending. Now that Latinos are officially the largest minority group in the United States, they are beginning to flex their muscle. Some are becoming more vocal about how they are identified and many are rejecting the term *Hispanic*. A Mexican-American poet and novelist, Sandra Cisneros, says the name sounds "like a slave name."[2] On the 2000 census 42 percent of Latino respondents marked the box "some other race." Forty-eight percent identified themselves as white.[3] One person noted: "White means privilege and black means obstacles to overcome."[4] Like Madrid argues, they are not a monolithic group.

Once stereotypes become codified into a nation's political and legal institutions, reversing it is almost insurmountable. Even when a nation's constitution bans discrimination, people, especially those who reap privileges from discriminatory laws and practices, are reluctant to change. For example, though the 3,000-year-old caste system has been dismantled by India's constitution, those at the bottom of the old caste system—the untouchables—continue to be discriminated against, especially in rural areas.[5] When the tsunami of 2004 indiscriminately wound a path of destruction, the aid, in some areas, was doled out on the basis of caste. As a result, less relief went to the poorest victims. They reported receiving food only after the other "castes" were satisfied. The more affluent received stable shelter while the poorest were given tents, if anything, far away from the other castes.[6]

Taking a very different approach to the issue of divisiveness and separation, a country in Africa that has been in the news in the last few years for its massacre of the *other* is Rwanda. Not generally held up as a model for tolerance of the *other*, now, after almost a million Tutsi have been annihilated by the Hutu, the official Rwandan stance is: "There is no ethnicity here. We are all Rwandan."[7] Re-education camps have been set up with the idea that if "ethnic differences can be learned, so can the idea that ethnicity does not exist."[8] Will the efforts succeed?

NOTES

1. Charles Krauthammer, "Blending in Crucial for Immigrants," *The Cincinnati Enquirer*, 17 June 2005, p. B7.

2. Darryl Fears, "The Power of a Label," *The Washington Post National Weekly Edition*, 1–7 September 2003, p. 29.

3. Mireya Navarro, "Census Reflects Hispanic Identity That is Hardly Black and White," *The New York Times*, 9 November 2003, pp. 1, 21.

4. Ibid.

5. Rama Lakshmi, "Fault Lines in the Old Caste System, *The* Washington *Post National Weekly Edition*, 24–30 January 2005, p. 16.

6. Ibid.

7. Marc Lacey, "A Decade After Massacres, Rwanda Outlaws Ethnicity," *The New York Times*, 9 April 2004, p. A3.

8. Ibid.

7

Coping With the Alienation of White, Male Students

Billie Wright Dziech

Beyond noting a sharp shift toward the Republican Party among white male voters in November, most post-election analyses devoted comparatively little consideration to the reasons for their political preference. Higher education, however, cannot afford to ignore the resentment expressed by some of those voters, who complained in exit polls that minority groups and other "special interests" were dominating the concerns of policy makers. Whether we like it or not, we must consider the possibility that higher education is one of the sectors of society at which their message was directed.

Frustration and anger have been cited as partial causes of the rightward trend that led 63 percent of white male voters to cast ballots for Republicans and only 37 percent for Democrats. Even more significant for colleges is one finding of a recent MTV poll: "The shift toward Republican affiliation is most evident among white men aged 23 to 29."

Obviously more than one factor affects voting behavior. But if young white men do, in fact, prefer the political party that questions affirmative action and multiculturalism, higher education must do some self-assessment. Support for both concepts has become almost universal at colleges and universities, albeit, in the case of affirmative action, only after initial pressure from the federal government.

I do not intend to debate the merits and limitations of multiculturalism and affirmative action here. Instead, I want to suggest that if we are to achieve the equality, civility, and mutual respect that we seek on campus, we must consider the possibility that our policies not only have failed to achieve their goals but also may have succeeded in alienating many young white men.

Those of us familiar with white male students know that a slow but inexorable process has been at work among them while the attention of campus leaders largely has been focused on other groups. As I have traveled across the country during the past several years speaking about sexual harassment—generally regarded as a "female" issue—I have at the same time learned a lot about male students. For example:

- A student—the first in his family to attend college—working his way through a small private college told me: "You know what affirmative action means to me? It means that even with a 3.9, I have less chance of getting into med school than someone with a 3.4 who's lucky enough to be a 'victim'—whatever that means."
- Hundreds of miles away at a huge urban university, another white male student explained his hostility to his institution this way: "I guess you could say I'm mad. All they ever do around here is lecture me about how I have to care about people who would blow my brains out if they could get away with it. Nobody gives a damn about me."
- Yet another such student confided: "I'm sick of being blamed for everyone else's problems. I just want to be left alone so I can finish school and get on with my life."

It is easy to ascribe such remarks to the arrogant indifference of the empowered and to maintain that they are resisting change and refusing to acknowledge the predicament of women and members of minority groups. It is more difficult, more painful to consider that in responding to students from historically oppressed groups, we may have overlooked and alienated others to whom we have equal responsibility. The revised curricula and the educational programs and support services that we have designed to bring civility and justice to our campuses apparently have made many mainstream students feel ostracized and castigated for conditions over which they have no control.

They have heard exhortations and sermons about the white male, racist, Eurocentric hold on American history, but they have not always responded as we hoped they would. Outside of class, when they talk to parents, peers, and faculty members whom they trust, many of them say that they believe they are being forced to pay for history they had no part in and that they feel weary, angry, and alienated.

"We are always coming up with the emphatic facts of history in our private experience and verifying them here," Emerson once wrote. "All history becomes subjective; in other words there is no history, only biography. Every mind must know the whole lesson for itself—must go over the whole ground. What it does not see, what it does not live, it will not know."

What academe has forgotten is that the "whole ground" and the "emphatic facts of history" for an eighteen-year-old living in the last decade of the twentieth century differ radically from those that shaped many of his professors. . . . While one cannot deny that generations of women and members of minority groups suffered deprivation and degradation at the hands of a power structure dominated by white men, today's white male student generally has had little personal experience to help him appreciate the struggles of the groups that now appear to be favored.

He sees no academic departments equivalent to women's or African-American studies that address *his* history. . . . Justifiably or not, the most authentic, the most vivid lesson that he may draw from his experience is that he is expected to pay for the transgressions of his ancestors and that the truly disadvantaged are people like himself, not those whose stories of victimization dominate the headlines.

There are no simple ways to alter such a perception. Even as I write, I feel trepidation at the prospect of having my words misinterpreted or exaggerated, despite my long-standing commitment to women's concerns. But it is this commitment to inclusion that should motivate us to address the complex challenge confronting us. At this point, it is impossible to say definitely how— or even whether—equitable remedies can be found for the frustration and resentment some white men feel, but we can take some steps in that direction.

Colleges must begin by acknowledging that the resentment felt by some white male students represents a legitimate concern. Then we must initiate genuinely open discussion about its causes and about ways to defuse it. This will be an arduous process, because of the new wounds and enmities that have developed along with the positive changes of the last two decades. We must undertake passionate, informed debate about how to balance our obligations to all of our constituencies—females, males, minorities, heterosexuals, and homosexuals. . . . Our intent should be not to prove that the claims of one interest group are superior to another's but rather to discover ways of honoring differences among students without appearing to favor some at the expense of others. The task will require considerably more honesty than we have exhibited in the past.

Symposia, lectures, and discussions addressing white-male experience would show colleges' commitment to increased understanding of all campus constituencies. We need to talk about how white men were viewed in the past and are viewed today and about how both men and women have been burdened by stereotypes. Furthermore, if existing institutional grievance procedures do not adequately respond to white men who complain about sexual harassment or racial discrimination, we must devise procedures that do.

In addition, we should review the class activities, extracurricular groups, educational programs, and institutional policies intended to teach tolerance, which typically are designed and controlled by faculty or staff members. Despite our good intentions, we sometimes act simplistically and autocratically in our efforts to encourage sensitivity. Perhaps we should talk less and listen more, guide rather than direct. Our students are, after all, only one step removed from the "real world" during their sojourn on campus. Tomorrow we will not be there to instruct or harangue them about their behavior toward one another. A wide spectrum of students, not just typical student-government types, should be enlisted to explore the issues of respect and civility. Students must be genuinely engaged if they are to be moved to examine their attitudes and perhaps modify their perspectives. That engagement is less likely to occur when someone who is not a student invents and controls the process.

Whether affirmative action is discriminatory, whether multiculturalism dilutes the college curriculum, whether remedying social injustice is an appropriate role for higher education—these are important but debatable points. Less ambiguous and far more significant is the need for Americans to accept a collective history, distinguished by both its failures and its successes, and to get on with the task of building a more equitable and moral society.

White men will be a part of that endeavor. Rightly or wrongly, many white male students feet ignored and maligned as they, like all students, struggle for respect, opportunity, and support on our campuses. Dismissing and denigrating their perceptions of how they are being treated have led only to increased misunderstanding and intolerance, as they carry their frustrations and anger from the campuses to their workplaces and communities. Old wounds will not be healed by inflicting new ones. Our task now is to use wisely the time we have with all of our students, so that when they leave us they will understand not only their country's weaknesses and the sources of its divisions but also its strengths and the bonds that unite people and give them hope for the future.

8

The Second Sex

Simone de Beauvoir

For a long time I have hesitated to write a book on women. The subject is irritating, especially to women; and it is not new. Enough ink has been spilled in the quarreling over feminism, now practically over, and perhaps we should say no more about it. It is still talked about, however, for the voluminous nonsense uttered during the last century seems to have done little to illuminate the problem. After all, is there a problem? And if so, what is it? Are there women, really? Most assuredly the theory of the eternal feminine still has its adherents who will whisper in your ear: "Even in Russia women still *are women*"; and other erudite persons—sometimes the very same—say with a sigh: "Woman is losing her way, woman is lost." One wonders if women still exist, if they will always exist, whether or not it is desirable that they should, what place they occupy in this world, what their place should be. "What has become of women?" was asked recently in an ephemeral magazine. . . .[1]

If her functioning as a female is not enough to define woman, if we decline also to explain her through "the eternal feminine," and if nevertheless we admit, provisionally, that women do exist, then we must face the question: what is a woman?

To state the question is, to me, to suggest, at once, a preliminary answer. The fact that I ask it is in itself significant. A man would never get the notion of writing a book on the peculiar situation of the human male.[2] But if I wish to define myself, I must first of all say: "I am a woman"; on this truth must be based all further discussion. A man never begins by presenting himself as an individual of a certain sex; it goes without saying that he is a man. The terms *masculine* and *feminine* are used symmetrically only as a matter of form, as on legal papers. In actuality the relation of the two sexes is not quite like that of two electrical poles, for man represents both the positive and the neutral, as is indicated by the common use of *man* to designate human beings in general;

whereas woman represents only the negative, defined by limiting criteria, without reciprocity. In the midst of an abstract discussion it is vexing to hear a man say: "You think thus and so because you are a woman"; but I know that my only defense is to reply: "I think thus and so because it is true," thereby removing my subjective self from the argument. It would be out of the question to reply: "And you think the contrary because you are a man," for it is understood that the fact of being a man is no peculiarity. A man is in the right in being a man; it is the woman who is in the wrong. It amounts to this: just as for the ancients there was an absolute vertical with reference to which the oblique was defined, so there is an absolute human type, the masculine. Woman has ovaries, a uterus; these peculiarities imprison her in her subjectivity, circumscribe her within the limits of her own nature. It is often said that she thinks with her glands. Man superbly ignores the fact that his anatomy also includes glands, such as the testicles, and that they secrete hormones. He thinks of his body as a direct and normal connection with the world, which he believes he apprehends objectively, whereas he regards the body of a woman as a hindrance, a prison, weighed down by everything peculiar to it. "The female is a female by virtue of a certain *lack* of qualities," said Aristotle; "we should regard the female nature as afflicted with a natural defectiveness." And St. Thomas for his part pronounced woman to be an "imperfect man," an "incidental" being. This is symbolized in Genesis where Eve is depicted as made from what Boussuet called "a supernumerary bone" of Adam.

Thus humanity is male and man defines woman not in herself but as relative to him; she is not regarded as an autonomous being. Michelet writes: "Woman, the relative being." And Benda is most positive in his *Rapport d'Uriel*: "The body of man makes sense in itself quite apart from that of woman, whereas the latter seems wanting in significance by itself. . . . Man can think of himself without woman. She cannot think of herself without man." And she is simply what man decrees; thus she is called "the sex," by which is meant that she appears essentially to the male as a sexual being. For him she is sex—absolute sex, no less. She is defined and differentiated with reference to man and not he with reference to her; she is the incidental, the inessential as opposed to the essential. He is the Subject, he is the Absolute—she is the Other.[3]

The category of the *Other* is as primordial as consciousness itself. In the most primitive societies, in the most ancient mythologies, one finds the expression of a duality—that of the Self and the Other. This duality was not originally attached to the division of the sexes; it was not dependent upon any empirical facts. It is revealed in such works as that of Granet on Chinese thought and those of Dumézil on the East Indies and Rome. The feminine element was at first no more involved in such pairs as Varuna-Mitra, Uranus-Zeus, Sun-Moon, and Day-Night than it was in the contrasts between Good and Evil, lucky and unlucky auspices, right and left, God and Lucifer. Otherness is a fundamental category of human thought.

Thus it is that no group ever sets itself up as the One without at once setting up the Other over against itself. If three travelers chance to occupy the same compartment, that is enough to make vaguely hostile "others" out of all the rest of the passengers on the train. In small-town eyes all persons not belonging to the village are "strangers" and suspect; to the native of a country all who inhabit other countries are "foreigners"; Jews are "different" for the anti-Semite, Negroes are "inferior" for American racists, aborigines are "natives" for colonists, proletarians are the "lower class" for the privileged.

But the other consciousness, the other ego, sets up a reciprocal claim. The native traveling abroad is shocked to find himself in turn regarded as a "stranger" by the natives of neighboring countries. As a matter of fact, wars, festivals, trading, treaties, and contests among tribes, nations, and classes tend to deprive the concept *Other* of its absolute sense and to make manifest its relativity; willy-nilly, individuals and groups are forced to realize the reciprocity of their relations. How is it, then, that this reciprocity has not been recognized between the sexes, that one of the contrasting terms is set up as the sole essential, denying any relativity in regard to its correlative and defining the latter as pure otherness? Why is it that women do not dispute male sovereignty? No subject will readily volunteer to become the object, the inessential; it is not the Other who, in defining himself as the Other, establishes the One. The Other is posed as such by the One in defining himself as the One. But if the Other is not to regain the status of being the One, he must be submissive enough to accept this alien point of view. Whence comes this submission in the case of woman?

There are, to be sure, other cases in which a certain category has been able to dominate another completely for a time. Very often this privilege depends upon inequality of numbers—the majority imposes its rule upon the minority or persecutes it. But women are not a minority, like the American Negroes or the Jews; there are as many women as men on earth. Again, the two groups concerned have often been originally independent; they may have been formerly unaware of each other's existence, or perhaps they recognized each other's autonomy. But a historical event has resulted in the subjugation of the weaker by the stronger. The scattering of the Jews, the introduction of slavery into America, the conquests of imperialism are examples in point. In these cases the oppressed retained at least the memory of former days; they possessed in common a past, a tradition, sometimes a religion or a culture.

The parallel drawn by Bebel between women and the proletariat is valid in that neither ever formed a minority or a separate collective unit of mankind. And instead of a single historical event it is in both cases a historical development that explains their status as a class and accounts for the membership of *particular individuals* in that class. But proletarians have not always existed, whereas there have always been women. They are women in virtue of their anatomy and physiology. Throughout history they have always been subordinated to men, [4] and hence their dependency is not the result of a historical event or a social change—it was not something that *occurred*. The reason why otherness in this case seems to be an absolute is in part that it lacks the contingent or incidental nature of historical facts. A condition brought about at a certain time can be abolished at some other time, as the Negroes of Haiti and others have proved, but it might seem that a natural condition is beyond the possibility of change. In truth, however, the nature of things is no more immutably given, once for all, than is historical reality. If woman seems to be the inessential which never becomes the essential, it is because she herself fails to bring about this change. Proletarians say "We"; Negroes also. Regarding themselves as subjects, they transform the bourgeois, the whites, into "others." But women do not say "We," except at some congress of feminists or similar formal demonstration; men say women, and women use the same word in referring to themselves. They do not authentically assume a subjective attitude. The proletarians have accomplished the revolution in Russia, the Negroes in Haiti, the Indo-Chinese are battling for it in Indo-China; but the women's effort has never been anything more than a symbolic aviation. They have gained only what men have been willing to grant; they have taken nothing, they have only received.[5]

The reason for this is that women lack concrete means for organizing themselves into a unit which can stand face to face with the correlative unit. They have no past, no history, no religion of their own; and they have no such solidarity of work and interest as that of the proletariat. They are not even promiscuously herded together in the way that creates community feeling among the American Negroes, the ghetto Jews, the workers of Saint-Denis, or the factory hands of Renault. They live dispersed among the males, attached through residence, housework, economic condition, and social standing to certain men—fathers or husbands—more firmly than they are to other women. If they belong to the bourgeoisie, they feet solidarity with men of that class, not with proletarian women; if they are white, their allegiance is to white men, not to Negro women. The proletariat can propose to massacre the ruling class, and a sufficiently fanatical Jew or Negro might dream of getting sole possession of the atomic bomb and making humanity wholly Jewish or black; but woman cannot even dream of exterminating the males. The bond that unites her to her oppressors is not comparable to any other. The division of the sexes is a biological fact, not an event in human history. Male and female stand opposed within a primordial *Mitsein*, and woman has not broken it. The couple is a fundamental unity with its two halves riveted together, and the cleavage of society along the line of sex is impossible.

Master and slave, also, are united by a reciprocal need, in this case economic, which does not liberate the slave. In the relation of master to slave the master does not make a point of the need that he has for the other; he has in his grasp the power of satisfying this need through his own action; whereas the slave, in his dependent condition, his hope and fear, is quite conscious of the need he has for his master. Even if the need is at bottom equally urgent for both, it always works in favor of the oppressor and against the oppressed. That is why the liberation of the working class, for example, has been slow.

Now, woman has always been man's dependent, if not his slave; the two sexes have never shared the world in equality. And even today woman is heavily handicapped, though her situation is beginning to change. Almost nowhere is her legal status the same as man's,[6] and frequently it is much to her disadvantage. Even when her rights are legally recognized in the abstract, long-standing custom prevents their full expression in the mores. In the economic sphere men and women can almost be said to make up two castes; other things being equal, the former hold the better jobs, get higher wages, and have more opportunity for success than their new competitors. In industry and politics men have a great many more positions and they monopolize the most important posts. In addition to all this, they enjoy a traditional prestige that the education of children tends in every way to support, for the present enshrines the past—and in the past all history has been made by men. At the present time, when women are beginning to take part in the affairs of the world, it is still a world that belongs to men—they have no doubt of it at all and women have scarcely any. To decline to be the Other, to refuse to be a party to the deal—this would be for women to renounce all the advantages conferred upon them by their alliance with the superior caste. Man-the-sovereign will provide woman-the-liege with material protection and will undertake the moral justification of her existence; thus she can evade at once both economic risk and the metaphysical risk of a liberty in which ends and aims must be contrived without assistance. Indeed, along with the ethical urge of each individual to affirm his subjective existence, there is also the temptation to forgo liberty and become a thing. This is an inauspicious road, for he who takes it—passive, lost, ruined—becomes henceforth the creature of another's will, frustrated in his transcendence and deprived of every value. But it is an easy road; on it one avoids the strain involved in undertaking an authentic existence. When man makes of woman the Other, he may, then, expect her to manifest deep-seated tendencies toward complicity. Thus, woman may fail to lay claim to the status of subject because she lacks definite resources, because she feels the necessary bond that ties her to man regardless of reciprocity, and because she is, often very well pleased with her role as the Other.

But the very fact that woman is the Other tends to cast suspicion upon all the justifications that men have ever been able to provide for it. These have all too evidently been dictated by men's interest. A little known feminist of the seventeenth century, Poulain de la Barre, put it this way: "All that has been written about women by men should be suspect, for the men are at once judge and party to the lawsuit." Everywhere, at all times, the males have displayed their satisfaction in feeling that they are the lords of creation. "Blessed be God . . . that He did not make me a woman," say the Jews in their morning prayers, while their wives pray on a note of resignation: "Blessed be the Lord, who created me according to His will." The first among the blessings for which Plato thanked the gods was that he had been created free, not enslaved; the second, a man, not a woman. But the males could not enjoy this privilege fully unless they believed it to be founded on the absolute and the eternal; they sought to make the fact of their supremacy into a right. "Being men, those who have made and compiled the laws have favored their own sex, and jurists have elevated these laws into principles," to quote Poulain de la Barre once more.

Legislators, priests, philosophers, writers, and scientists have striven to show that the subordinate position of woman is willed in heaven and advantageous on earth. The religions invented by men reflect this wish for domination. In the legends of Eve and Pandora men have taken up arms against women. They have made use of philosophy and theology, as the quotations from Aristotle and St. Thomas have shown. Since ancient times satirists and moralists have delighted in showing up the weaknesses of women. We are familiar with the savage indictments hurled against women throughout French literature. Montherlant, for example, follows the tradition of Jean de Meung, though with less gusto. This hostility may at times be well founded, often it is gratuitous; but in truth it more or less successfully conceals a desire for self-justification. As Montaigne says, "It is easier to accuse one sex than to excuse the other." Sometimes what is going on is clear enough. For instance, the Roman law limiting the rights of woman cited "the imbecility, the instability of the sex" just when the weakening of family ties seemed to threaten the interests of male heirs. And in the effort to keep the married woman under guardianship, appeal was made in the sixteenth century to the authority of St. Augustine, who declared that "woman is a creature neither decisive nor constant," at a time when the single woman was thought capable of managing her property. Montaigne understood clearly how arbitrary and unjust was woman's appointed lot: "Women are not in the wrong when they decline to accept the rules laid down for them, since the men make these rules without consulting them. No wonder intrigue and strife abound." But he did not go so far as to champion their cause.

It was only later, in the eighteenth century, that genuinely democratic men began to view the matter objectively. Diderot, among others, strove to show that woman is, like man, a human being. Later John Stuart Mill came fervently to her defense. But these philosophers displayed unusual impartiality. In the nineteenth century the feminist quarrel became again a quarrel of partisans. One of the consequences of the industrial revolution was the entrance of women into productive labor, and it was just here that the claims of the feminists emerged from the realm of theory and acquired an economic basis, while their opponents became the more aggressive. Although landed property lost power to some extent, the bourgeoisie clung to the old morality that found the guarantee of private property in the solidity of the family. Woman was ordered back into the home the more harshly as her emancipation became a real menace. Even within the working class the men endeavored to restrain woman's liberation, because they began to see the women as dangerous competitors— the more so because they were accustomed to work for lower wages.[7]

In proving woman's inferiority, the antifeminists then began to draw not only upon religion, philosophy, and theology, as before, but also upon science-biology, experimental psychology, etc. At most they were willing to grant "equality in difference" to the *other sex*. That profitable formula is most significant; it is precisely like the "equal but separate" formula of the Jim Crow laws aimed at the North American Negroes. As is well known, this so-called equalitarian segregation has resulted only in the most extreme discrimination. The similarity just noted is no way due to chance, for whether it is a race, a caste, a class, or a sex that is reduced to a position of inferiority, the methods of justification are the same. "The eternal feminine" corresponds to "the black soul" and to "the Jewish character." True, the Jewish problem is on the whole very different from the other two—to the anti-Semite the Jew is not so much an inferior as he is an enemy for whom there is to be granted no place on earth, for whom annihilation is the fate desired. But there are deep similarities between the situation of woman and that of the Negro. Both are being emancipated today from a like paternalism, and the former master class wishes to "keep them in their place"—that is, the place chosen for them. In both cases the former masters lavish more or less sincere eulogies, either on the virtues of "the good Negro" with his dormant, childish, merry soul—the submissive Negro—or on the merits of the woman who is "truly feminine"—that is, frivolous, infantile, irresponsible—the submissive woman. In both cases the dominant class bases its argument on a state of affairs that it has itself created. As George Bernard Shaw puts it, in substance, "The American white relegates the black to the rank of shoeshine boy; and he concludes from this that the black is good for nothing but shining shoes." This vicious circle is met with in all analogous circumstances; when an individual (or a group of individuals) is kept in a situation of inferiority, the fact is that he is inferior. But the significance of the verb *to be* must be rightly understood here; it is in bad faith to give it a static value when it really has the dynamic Hegelian sense of "to have become." Yes, women on the whole *are* today inferior to men; that is, their situation affords them fewer possibilities. The question is: should that state of affairs continue?

Many men hope that it will continue; not all have given up the battle. The conservative bourgeoisie still see in the emancipation of women a menace to their morality and their interests. Some men dread feminine competition. Recently a male student wrote in the *Hebdo-Latin*: "Every woman student who goes into medicine or law robs us of a job." He never questioned his rights in this world. And economic interests are not the only ones concerned.

So it is that many men will affirm as if in good faith that women are the equals of man and that they have nothing to clamor for, while at the same time they will say that women can never be the equals of man and that their demands are in vain. It is, in point of fact, a difficult matter for man to realize the extreme importance of social discriminations which seem outwardly insignificant but which produce in woman moral and intellectual effects so profound that they appear to spring from her original nature. The most sympathetic of men never fully comprehend woman's concrete situation. And there is no reason to put much trust in the men when they rush to the defense of privileges whose full extent they can hardly measure. We shall not, then, permit ourselves to be intimidated by the number and violence of the attacks launched against women, nor to be entrapped by the self-seeking eulogies bestowed on the "true woman," nor to profit by the enthusiasm for woman's destiny manifested by men who would not for the world have any part of it.

We should consider the arguments of the feminists with no less suspicion, however, for very often their controversial aim deprives them of all real value. If the "woman question" seems trivial, it is because masculine arrogance has made of it a "quarrel"; and when quarreling one no longer reasons well. People have tirelessly sought to prove that woman is superior, inferior, or equal to man. Some say that, having been created after Adam, she is evidently a secondary being; others say on the contrary that Adam was only a rough draft and that God succeeded in producing the human being in perfection when He created Eve. Woman's brain is smaller; yes, but it is relatively larger. Christ was made a man; yes, but perhaps for his greater humility. Each argument at once suggests its opposite, and both are often fallacious. If we are to gain understanding, we must get out of these ruts; we must discard the vague notions of superiority, inferiority, equality which have hitherto corrupted every discussion of the subject and start afresh.

NOTES

1. *Franchise*, dead today.

2. The Kinsey Report [Alfred C. Kinsey et al.: *Sexual Behavior in the Human Male* (Philadelphia: W. B. Saunders Co., 1948)] is no exception, for it is limited to describing the sexual characteristics of American men which is quite a different matter.

3. E. Lévinas expresses this idea most explicitly in his essay *Temps et l'Autre*. "Is there not a case in which otherness, alterity [*altérité*], unquestionably marks the nature of a being, as its essence, an instance of otherness not consisting purely and simply in the opposition of two species of the same genus? I think that the feminine represents the contrary in its absolute sense, this contrariness being in no wise affected by any relation between it and its correlative and thus remaining absolutely other. Sex is not a certain specific difference . . . no more is the sexual difference a mere contradiction. . . . Nor does this difference lie in the duality of two complementary terms, for two complementary terms imply a pre-existing whole. . . . Otherness reaches its full flowering in the feminine, a term of the same rank as consciousness but of opposite meaning."

I suppose that Lévinas does not forget that woman, too, is aware of her own consciousness, or ego. But it is striking that he deliberately takes a man's point of view, disregarding the reciprocity of subject and object. When he writes that woman is mystery, he implies that she is mystery for man. Thus his description, which is intended to be objective, is in fact an assertion of masculine privilege.

4. With rare exceptions, perhaps, like certain matriarchal rulers, queens, and the like.—Tr.

5. See *The Second Sex*, Part II, ch. viii.

6. At the moment an "equal rights" amendment to the Constitution of the United States is before Congress.—Tr.

7. See *The Second Sex*, part II, pp. 115–17.

IV

STRUCTURED INEQUALITY— THE INVISIBLE IRON CAGE OF CLASS

9

The Double-Bind of the "Working-Class," Feminist Academic

The Success of Failure or the Failure of Success?

Diane Reay

Academia has rarely developed complex understandings of working-class people. Even celebrated studies like that of Paul Willis (1977) can be read as an indictment of the working class; they are so stupid that they invest time and energy into ensuring their own oppression. However, the biggest oversight for feminist academics from working-class backgrounds is the primacy the vast majority of academic studies have given to male experience. From quantitative surveys of socioeconomic categorization (Goldthorpe, 1980, 1983; Lockwood, 1986) to ethnographies like that of Willis, women are invisible. In my own writing about the working classes I want to recognize what is problematic about working-class communities. Although many individuals within them challenge and combat discrimination and prejudice, they are sexist; racism, and homophobia are endemic and women have to negotiate narrow, constricting versions of femininity. That is not the same as asserting that middle-class groupings in society are more enlightened. Rather sexism, racism, and homophobia are hidden and denied among the middle classes, but equally prevalent (Reay, 1995a).

Currently, even mentioning social class in academia feels "out-of-place," naively old-fashioned. The invidious influence of the 1990s academic preoccupation with postmodern identities has resulted in the relegation of social class to an intellectual backwater. Class may be mentioned on the dust jacket in books on education but once inside the text the experiences of working-class pupils are often marginalized or subsumed within understandings of middle-class experience as normative (see, for example, Evans, 1991).

The early 1990s was a period when much of the media focus seemed to be on the middle classes. Either we were all middle class now or else the middle classes were variously viewed as under siege, in crisis, or losing their privileges (for example, see Gray, 1994; Phillips, 1995). The processes impacting on working-class life have been reduced either to declarations about the disappearance of "the working class" or to continuing pathologizations which neither of the working-class academic perspectives attempt to address. Modifying, reworking, updating theoretical understandings of the "working classes" to match changing realities is rarely on the academic agenda.

The female academic from a working-class background is the end product of very different processes to those of social reproduction. She is caught up in change and social transformation. However, the positive connotations invested in terms such as transformation and change mask an inherent negativity often overlooked in discussions of meritocracy.

The contradictory positioning of the once working-class female academic juxtapose radical potentialities with confirmation of revisionist policies. There is an inherent paradox. While we bring with us insider knowledge of class inequalities, at the same time the academic from a working-class background represents a justification of right-wing rhetoric. We are the tokenistic edge of elitist policies: "the inner-city kid with the right parents, the right teachers and the right brain." We stand for a triumph of individualism over community; proof that equal opportunities work.

Why did we work so hard in the first place? It seems incontrovertible to me that the educationally successful working-class girl has to work very hard indeed; at learning a totally new language, at undoing the silences of her childhood (Bourdieu, 1984; Borkowski, 1992); at transforming key aspects around female embodiment. Janet Zandy writes about the physicality of class difference:

> Working-class people practice a language of the body that eludes theoretical textual studies. Working-class people do not have the quiet hands or the neutral faces of the privileged classes—especially when they are within their own communities. (Zandy, 1995, p. 5)

Survival in middle-class contexts for working-class women often requires developing a decorum and reserve that fits in with middle-class standards of acceptable female sexuality (Walkerdine, 1995). It also demands a voice to replace the one that has so often been silenced in educational contexts.

How do we understand the desires and fears that accompanied such a difficult transition out of one class and into another? Kelly and Nihlen (1982) point out the gap in theories of social and cultural reproduction; the inability to explain "the ones who got away." Educational theorists fail to even engage with the overt psychological processes entailed in upward social mobility, let alone look beneath at the more hidden layers of compromise and compromising. However, the white working-class girl who becomes middle class is implicated in what often feels like a treacherous process; one of shedding at least part, if not all, of her earlier class identity (Lynch and O'Neill, 1994). We have utilized one system of meritocratic individualism, the school system, in order to attain a place within another, that of higher education. How then to reconcile the working-class culture we started out with?

I suggest the female academic from a working-class background is unlikely ever to feel at home in academia. For many, socialization, at least within the family, was into collective and community-based understandings of the social world, not the competitive individuals we now face in which social networks are about instrumentalism, not connection. However, this is not to valorize working-class pasts.

We worked so hard at school not primarily to be acceptable to the middle classes, who were always the enemy, but to redeem our parents, to prove our family was "just as good." And yet when I see any documentary about miners I am overwhelmed, suffused with powerful feelings of belonging, along with a sense of outrage about their treatment. The irony is now there is no real community of coalminers, however internally divided, to belong to. There is a further irony for me as a feminist academic in that I can see my father's hand guiding my conceptions of community. It is all about his version and very little about my mother's. In spite of my aim of painting an ambivalent, tentative picture highlighting complexities of interpretation and motivation, he is the hero of my fantasy of community; this man who never really belonged to the community he valorized.

While my parents' rage propelled me through the educational system, dealing with it subsequently in middle-class contexts has proved problematic. I regularly get angry about middle-class privilege and then guilty because I am now implicated in it. However, I have come to see that sense of unfairness as one of the most valuable things I possess.

If you have grown up working class you know that the solution to class inequalities does not lie in making the working classes middle-class but in working at dismantling and sharing out the economic, social, and cultural capital which go with middle-class status. I would suggest that the permeation of new middle-class values within the working classes has been disastrous. Collectivist understandings of self and social group have been increasingly displaced by individualistic notions premised on the self as consumer. The prevailing culture of individualism and competitiveness has given free rein to an end-of-millennium capitalism which seems increasingly out of control and unaccountable. The social groups who have had to pay the highest price for these developments are the traditional and the new working classes—the poor, manual workers, the unemployed, the low-paid in the service sectors and lone-mother families. Competition and individualism are all about hierarchy and pecking order in which the individual rather than her circumstances are judged. The working classes are no longer entitled to a sense of unfairness because everything from their financial situation and the state of their health to their children's schooling has been repackaged under late capitalism as the responsibility of the individual alone.

The answer is not to further empower ourselves within academic hierarchies but to listen to, and learn from, the still-working-class woman so that there is an erosion of status hierarchies based on educational qualifications and/or wealth. Only through work that centers class injustice, as well as the injustices of "race" and gender, can we keep at bay "the alienation of advantage" (Hennessy, 1993). However, therein lies the double-bind.

As James G. Ladwig and Jennifer M. Gore assert, any discussion of social privilege and power needs to pay attention to "questions of *academic* privilege, and power, competition, and contestation" (1994, p. 236; authors' emphasis). I am now in a position of inevitable complicity. Any success in promoting issues that center social justice has become inextricably entangled with self-promotion and struggles for power within academic fields. Daphne Patai remarks that what she entitles "tiresome self-reflexivity" would be inconceivable "in a setting in which material want was an incontrovertible fact of life" (1994, p. 66). We academics, despite our incessant moaning about overwork and intolerable conditions, are in a luxurious situation compared to the growing ranks of the poor (Hutton, 1995). Inevitably, my rage has been diluted with guilt. I try to see myself through my mother's eyes because then I can see just how privileged I have become.

> The fact is that those of us whose medium is words do occupy privileged positions, and we hardly give up those positions when we engage in endless self-scrutiny and anxious self-identification. (Patai, 1994, p. 67)

There are other things at issue for academics who were once working class; questions around loyalty and disloyalty, belonging and not belonging. We have to live with the paradox that a defining part of our identity is turning into a chimera, our "working classness" is a fantasy that often we alone are still engaging in. My own experience of growing up working class has left vivid memories of the heritage and history of my social origins imprinted on my consciousness. However, that consciousness, rooted in working-class affiliation, appears increasingly to be a misfit; a sense of self both out of place and out of time.

Kathleen Casey writes that for the black child to become educated is "to contradict the whole system of racist signification" (1993, p. 123). In the same way to become educated as a working-class person is to refute the whole system of class signification. However, as Scates asserts, it is a far more contradictory and compromising process. Casey writes that "to succeed at studying 'white' knowledge is to undo the system itself, to refute its (re)production of black inferiority materially and symbolically." I would suggest a further version in which studying middle-class knowledge presents the individual from a working-class background with a dilemma. Far from undoing the system it can represent a collusion with it and act to reproduce rather than refute the (re)production of working-class inferiority. If we are the tokenistic proof of meritocracy then our academic success serves to underscore the unworthiness of those who fail. All too often when the pervading sense of inferiority which comes with growing up working class meets a degree of academic success and recognition, we are seduced into seeing ourselves as special and more worthy, rather than more fortunate than those we left behind. Of course the middle classes, and here we are talking of the vast majority of academics, have a vested interest in overlooking the classed nature of society. To view the world through a class lens would be to focus on their position of relative privilege.

Prevailing academic discourses construct hierarchies of oppression that have nothing to do with the world outside but are all about vying for attention within academic circles. Middle class, white feminists who focus on their oppression to the exclusion of their privilege, the eminent white, male academics who are still "just working-class lads," just as much as middle-class males academics from public school backgrounds who are reinventing their schooling as a source of oppression, are buying into the narcissistic competitiveness of academia. A male academic suggested that I wrote about my working-class background because I wanted to compete in the academic game of being the most oppressed. However, it is not that straightforward. There is also a sense of impossibility; the psychic refusal of becoming middle class. It is no longer an issue of not making a good enough job of passing because the process of completing three degrees has ensured that I do. Rather, it is the sense of treachery and accedence to institutionalized and socially endemic inequalities the middle-class label holds that I continue to struggle with, while needing to recognize that I am now seen as middle class.

The experiences of the working classes get left out because they have no constituency in academia. This is not to be cynical but to acknowledge that academia is primarily a self-seeking culture premised on competition where class is often conscripted as a means to academic career promotion. As bell hooks points out,

> When those of us in the academy who are working-class or from working-class backgrounds share our perspectives, we subvert the tendency to focus only on the thoughts, attitudes and experiences of those who are materially privileged. (hooks, 1994, p. 185)

Feminist academics from working-class backgrounds never escape those processes of compromise and compromising I described earlier. I realize that my own centering of class is part of a continuing project of reconciling what I have become with what I was, while simultaneously trying to carve out a self that I can feel at ease with.

REFERENCES

Borkowski, B. (1992). "Ausbruch and Aufbruch dutch Bildung aus Milieu-und Geschlechtsrollen-Begrenzungen" ["Breaking Out and Up Through Education from Milieu and Gender Constraints"], in Schuluter, A. (ed.) *Arbeitertochter und ihr sozialer Aufstieg. Zum Verhaltnis von Kllase, Geschlecht und soziater Mobilität [Upwardly socially mobile working-class girls. On the relationship between class, gender and social mobility]*. Weinheim: Deutscher Studien Verlag.

Bourdieu, Pierre. (1984). *Distinction*. London: Routledge and Kegan Paul, Ltd.

Casey, Kathleen. (1993). *I Answer with My Life: Life Histories of Women Teachers Working for Social Change*. New York: Routledge.

Evans, Mary. (1991). *A Good School: Life at a Girls' Grammar School in the 1950s*. London: The Women's Press.

Goldthorpe, J. H. (1980). *Social Mobility and Class Structure in Modern Britain*. Oxford: Clarendon.

Goldthorpe, J. H. (1983). "Women and Class Analysis," *Sociology* 17, 4: 465–88.

Gray, John. (1994). "Into the Abyss?" *The Sunday Times*, 30 October.

Hennessy, Rosemary. (1993). *Materialist Feminism and the Politics of Discourse*. New York: Routledge, Chapman & Hall.

hooks, bell. (1994). *Teaching to Transgress: Education as the Practice of Freedom*. London: Routledge.

Hutton, Will. (1995). *The State We're In*. London: Cape.

Kelly, G. P., and A. S. Nihlen. (1982). "Schooling and the Reproduction of Patriarchy: Unequal Workloads, Unequal Rewards," in Michael Apple (ed.), *Cultural and Economic Reproduction in Education*. London: Routledge and Kegan Paul.

Ladwig, James G., and Jennifer M. Gore. (1994)."Extending Power and Specifying Method Within the Discourse of Activist Research," in Andrew Gitlin (ed.), *Power and Method: Political Activism and Educational Research*. London: Routledge.

Lockwood, D. (1986). "Class, Status and Gender," in R. Crompton and M. Mann (eds.), *Gender and Stratification*. Cambridge: Polity.

Lynch, Kathleen, and Cathleen O'Neill. (1994). "The Colonisation of Social Class in Education," *British Journal of Sociology of Education* 15, 3: 307–24.

Patai, Daphne. (1994). "When Method Becomes Power," in Andrew Gitlin (ed.), *Power and Method: Political Activism and Educational Research*. London: Routledge.

Phillips, Melanie. (1995). "Threatened, Lost, Self-Hating, Angry, Taxed, Envied and Insecure; Whatever Happened to the Middle-Classes?" *The Observer*, 2 July.

Reay, Diane. (1995a). "'They Employ Cleaners to Do That': Habitus in the Primary Classroom," *British Journal of Sociology of Education* 10, 5: 353–71.

Scates, Maxine. (1995). "Leaving it All Behind?" in Janet Zandy (ed.), *Liberating Memory. Our Work and Our Working-Class Consciousness*. New Brunswick: Rutgers University Press.

Walkerdine, Valerie. (1995). "Subject to Change Without Notice: Psychology, Postmodernity and the Popular," in Steve Pile and Nigel Thrift (eds.), *Mapping the Subject: Geographies of Cultural Transformation*. London: Routledge.

Willis, Paul. (1997). *Learning to Labour: How Working Class Kids Get Working Class Jobs*. Farnborough: Saxon House.

Zandy, Janet (ed.). (1995). *Liberating Memory: Our Work and Our Working-Class Consciousness*. New Brunswick: Rutgers University Press.

EDITOR'S NOTE

Diane Reay uses the sociological imagination to connect her personal troubles—her lower-class status as a child—to public issues. Thus, she understands how her "unique" situation is not unique after all, but in common with millions of others in her social class. She argues that class stamps people for life, even if they experience social mobility as adults. Two recent observations support Reay's reading.

Tamar Lewin, writing in *The New York Times*, reports on the middle-age/second marriage of a wealthy woman whose grandfather had butlers, homes in Florida, and drove a Rolls Royce to a man who dropped out of school in the eighth grade. The husband has difficulty communicating with his wife's family and friends. In fact, he was fired from a job at a prep school because his communication was too direct. He hadn't learned the style and subtleties of upper-class folks. He "sometimes finds himself back in class bewilderment, feeling again that he does not get the nuances."[1] He finds his wife's family so "well bred and very nice" that "it's hard to tell whether it's sincere, whether they really like you."[2]

The couple has children from previous marriages—really from two different worlds. The wife's sons have never had to worry about paying for college or, for that matter, anything. One of the sons took a semester off to attend massage school and travel, to find himself. On the other hand, the husband's daughters have never had time off to travel. One works three jobs while attending law school and will owe over a $100,000 dollars when she graduates. Both daughters admit to trying to hide their background being "careful about their manners, their plans, their clothes."[3] It is telling that the young women are acutely aware how different their childhood has been from their stepbrothers, but the young men seem unaware and have met few of their stepsisters' cousins. Although the daughters' experience would seem a private matter, unique to them, it bears a structural pattern: the privileged have the luxury of knowing little to nothing of the poor while "knowing" the wealthy can mean survival for the poor.

Lewin interviews another young woman, a lawyer, with "humble" beginnings, who struggles with the contradictions between her social class of origin and her life now as an attorney. Della Mae Justice was a child living in foster care in Pikeville, Kentucky, when she was rescued by her cousin and his wife. Although she went on to finish fifth in her law school class, she, like Reay, recalls difficulty fitting into middle-class and upper middle-class lifestyles. She believes that "If your goal is to become, on a national scale, a very important person, you can't start way back on the continuum, because you have too much to make up in one lifetime."[4]

Justice recounts the awkward time at dinner with her school group when she didn't know what to do with the toothpicks on a club sandwich. She didn't eat. She remembers not having enough general knowledge of the world to play Trivial Pursuit. Her world was simply too limited.[5]

Justice's life has come full circle. She left a lucrative law practice in Lexington, Kentucky, and moved back to Pikeville to take custody of her halfbrother's two children. Although Justice maintains that the move back to Pikeville was so the children could have contact with their mother and father,

one wonders what other motives there might be.[6] Meanwhile, Justice has begun the process of introducing the children to their new social class; she is determined their place on the continuum is not as far back as hers was.

Reay, Justice, and the newly married mixed-class couple all can relate their
social class experiences with Lemert's discussion of the structure of social class.
Can you?

NOTES

1. Tamar Lewin, "A Marriage of Unequals," *The New York Times*, 19 May 2005, pp. 1,
A19.
   2. Ibid.
   3. Ibid.
   4. Ibid.
   5. Ibid.
   6. Ibid.

10

(In) Secure Times

Constructing White Working-Class Masculinities in the Late Twentieth Century

Michelle Fine, Lois Weis, Judi Addelston, and Julia Marusza

The poor and working-class white boys and men in this article belong to a continuum of white working-class men who, up until recently in U.S. history, have been relatively privileged. These men, however, do not articulate a sense of themselves inside that history. In current economic and social relations that felt sense of privilege is tenuous at best. Since the 1970s, the U.S. steel industry has been in rapid decline as have other areas of manufacturing and production, followed by the downward spiral of businesses that sprung up around larger industry (Bluestone and Harrison 1982). In the span of a few decades, foreign investment, corporate flight, downsizing, and automation have suddenly left members of the working class without a steady family wage, which, compounded with the dissipation of labor unions, has left many white working-class men feeling emasculated and angry (Weis, 1990; Weis, Proweller, and Centrie 1996). It seems that overnight, the ability to work hard and provide disappeared. White working-class men, of course, are not more racist or sexist than middle-class and upper-class white men. In this analysis, however, we offer data that demonstrate how white working-class male anger takes on virulent forms as it is displaced in a climate of reaction against global economic change.

As they search for someone who has stolen their presumed privilege, we begin to understand ways in which white poor and working-class men in the 1980s and 1990s manage to maintain a sense of self in the midst of rising feminism, affirmative action, and gay/lesbian rights. . . . As scholars of the dominant culture begin to recognize that "white is a color" (Roman 1993; Wong 1994), our work makes visible the borders, strategies, and fragilities of white working-class male culture, in insecure times, at a moment in history when many feel that this identity is under siege.

93

ON WHITENESS

In the United States, the hierarchies of race, gender, and class are embodied in the contemporary "struggle" of working-class white men. As their stories reveal, these boys and men are trying to sustain a *place* within this hierarchy and secure the very *hierarchies* that assure their place. Among the varied demographic categories that spill out of this race/gender hierarchy, white men are the only ones who have a vested interest in maintaining both their position and their hierarchy—even, ironically, working-class boys and men who enjoy little of the privilege accrued to their gender/race status.

Scholars of colonial thought have highlighted the ways in which notions about non-Western "Others" are produced simultaneously with the production of discourse about the Western white "self," and these works become relevant to our analyses of race/gender domination.

One continuing effect of colonial discourse is the production of an unnamed, unmarked white/Western self against which all others can be named and judged. It is the unmarked self that must be deconstructed, named, and marked (Frankenberg 1993). This article takes up this challenge. As we will argue here, white working-class male identity is parasitically coproduced as these men name and mark others, largely African Americans and white women. Their identity would not exist in its present form (and perhaps not at all) if these simultaneous productions were not taking place. At a moment of economic crisis in which white working-class men are being squeezed, the disparaging constructions of others proliferate.

HIGH SCHOOL STUDENTS:
RACISM AND THE CONSTRUCTION OF THE "OTHER"

This is an exploration of white working-class high school students in a deindustrializing urban area called "Freeway." Data were collected in the classrooms, study halls, during extracurricular activities, and through in-depth interviews with over sixty juniors, most of their teachers, the vice-principal, social workers, guidance counselors, and others over the course of an academic year.

While there are several facets to the production of the boys' identity, we focus on the ways in which young white boys coproduce African American male identities and their own identities. For the most part, these young white boys narrate a sense of self grounded in the sphere of sexuality, in which they script themselves as the protectors of white women whom they feel are in danger of what they regard as a deviant African American male sexuality. Not only are these young working-class boys unable to see themselves as belonging to a tradition of privilege in their being white and male, their felt loss of that historic status in a restructuring economy leaves them searching in their school, their neighborhood, and surrounding communities for those responsible.

Freeway is a divided city and a small number of Arabs and Hispanics live among African Americans largely on one side of the "tracks," and whites on the other, although there are whites living in one section of Freeway just adjacent to the steel mill, which is in the area populated by people of color. Virtually no people of color live in the white area, unlike many large cities in the United States, where there are pockets of considerable mix.

Among these white adolescent men, people of color are used consistently as a foil against which acceptable moral, and particularly sexual, standards are established. The goodness of white is always contrasted with the badness of black—blacks are involved with drugs, blacks are unacceptable sexually, black men attempt to "invade" white sexual space by talking with white women, black women are simply filthy. The binary translates in ways that complement white boys. As described by Jim, there is a virtual denial of anything at all good being identified with blackness and of anything bad identified with whiteness:[1]

> The minorities are really bad into drugs. You're talking everything. Anything you want, you get from them. A prime example, the —— ward of Freeway; about twenty years ago, the —— ward was predominantly white, my grandfather used to live there. Then Italians, Polish, the Irish people, everything was fine. The houses were maintained; there was a good standard of living. . . . The blacks brought drugs. I'm not saying white people didn't have drugs; they had drugs, but to a certain extent. But drugs were like a social thing. But now you go down to the —— ward; it's amazing; it's a ghetto.

Much expressed racism centers on white men's entitled access to white women, thus serving the dual purpose of fixing blacks and white women on a ladder of social relations.

These young white men construct white women as if they were in need of their protection. The young men fight for these young women. Their complaints are communicated through a language of property rights, Black boys intruding onto *white property*. It is the fact that *black* men are invading *white* women, the property of *white* men, that is at issue here.

The black female disparaged; the black male avenged. The elevation of white womanhood, in fact, has been irreducibly linked to the debasement of both black women and men (Davis 1990). By this A. Davis asserts that in the historic positioning of black females as unfeminine and black males as predators, the notion of what is feminine has become an idealized version of white womanhood. It is most interesting that not one white female in this study ever discussed young black men as a "problem." This is not to say that white women were not racist, but this discursive rendering of black men was quite noticeably the terrain of white men.

The word "nigger" flows freely from the lips of white men and they treat black women far worse than they say black men treat white women. During a conversation at the lunch table, for example, Mike says that Yolanda [a black female] should go to "Niggeria" [Nigeria]. In another conversation about Martin Luther King Day, Dave says, "I have a wet dream—about little white boys and little black girls." On another occasion, when two African American women walk into the cafeteria, Peter comments, "Black people . . . they're yecch. They smell funny and they [got] hair under their arms." The white boys at this table follow up this sentiment by making noises to denote disgust.

YOUNG ADULTS: WHITE POOR AND WORKING-CLASS MEN IN AN ECONOMIC STRANGLEHOLD

As with Freeway boys, we hear from these somewhat older men a set of identities that are carved explicitly out of territory bordered by African Americans and white women. Similar to the Freeway study, these groups are targeted by the young while adult men as they search their communities, work sites, and even the local social service office for those who are responsible for stealing their presumed privilege. While most of these men narrate hostile comparison with "Others," some offer sympathetic, but still bordered, views. Like cartographers working with different tools on the same geopolitical space, all these men—from western New York and northern New Jersey—sculpt their identities as if they were discernibly framed by, and contrasted through, race, gender, and sexuality.

As with the teens, the critique by young adult white men declares the boundaries of acceptable behavior at themselves. The white male critique is, by and large, a critique of the actions/behaviors taken by African Americans, particularly men. This circles around three interrelationship points: "not working," welfare abuse or "cheats," and affirmative action.

Because many, if not most, of the white men interviewed have themselves been out of work and/or received welfare benefits and food stamps, their critique serves to denigrate African Americans.[2] It also draws the limits of what constitutes "deserving" circumstances for not working, receiving welfare, and relying on government-sponsored programs at themselves.

By young adulthood, the target site for this white male critique shifts from sexuality to work but remains grounded *against* men of color.

The white male critique of affirmative action is that it is not "fair." It privileges blacks, Hispanics, and at times white women, above white men. According to these men, white men are today being set up as the "new minority," which contradicts their notions of equal opportunity. Nowhere in these narrative is there any recognition that white men as a group have historically been privileged, irrespective of individual merit. The assertions about affirmative action offer white men a way of "Othering" African Americans, in particular.

Many of the white men who have been out of work, or are now in a precarious economic state, speak with a strong disdain for African American men and, if less so, for white women as well. Others, however, narrate positions relative to white women and people of color within a discourse of concern and connection. This more liberal discourse is typically spoken by working-class men who occupy positions of relative economic security. But even here the borders of their identity nevertheless fall along the same fault lines of race and gender (Roediger 1994).

The white working-class firefighters interviewed in our study narrate somewhat similar views. Joe, for instance, works in a fire department in Jersey City. He, like so many of our informants, insists that he is "not a racist," but he vehemently feels that "civil rights has [*sic*] gone far enough." As we discovered, the fire and police departments in Jersey City have historically garnered a disproportionate share of the city's public sector investment and growth over the last decade, and they employ a disproportionate share of white men. We began to hear these departments as the last public sector spaces in which white working-class men could at once exercise identities as white, working, and men.

Mark is another white firefighter. Echoing much of what Joe has said, Mark portrays the firehouse as a relatively protected and defended space for whiteness. By extension, the firehouse represents the civic goodness of [white] public institutions. In both Joe's and Mark's interviews, there is a self-consciousness about "not sounding racist," yet both consistently link any mention of people of color and the mention of social problems—be it child neglect, violence, or vandalism. Whiteness preserves the collective good, whereas people of color periodically threaten the collective good.

CONCLUSION

Jobs that once served to secure the lives and identities of many working-class people are swiftly becoming a thing of the past. The corrosion of white working-class male felt privilege—as experienced by the boys and men in this analysis—has also been paralleled by the dissipation of labor unions, which are being washed away as quickly as industry. Even though capital has traditionally used fundamental cleavages such as racism and sexism as tools to fracture a working-class consciousness from forming, labor unions have typically played a strong role in U.S. history in creating a space for some workers to organize against capital for change (Roediger 1994). Historical ties to white working-class union activity are fading fast, particularly among young white working-class men, whose fathers, uncles, and older brothers no longer have a union tradition to pass on to the next generation. With the erosion of union culture and no formal space left to develop and refine meaningful critique, some white working-class men, instead, scramble to reassert their assumed place of privilege on a race/gender hierarchy in an economy that has ironically devalued all workers. Our data indicate that white working-class boys and men, unorganized and angry, consistently displace their rage toward histori-cally and locally available groups.

We have offered two scenes in which white men in various stages of adult-hood, poor and working-class, are constructing identities on the backs of people of color and white women. Clearly this is not only the case for white working-class men, nor is it generalizable to *all* white working-class men, but these men are among the best narrators of virulent oppositional hostil-ity. It is important that the boys and young adult men in both studies in dif-ferent geographic locations exhibit similar sentiments. These white men are a race/class/gender group that has been dramatically squeezed relative to their prior positions. Meanwhile, the fantasies and stereotypes of "Others" continue to be promoted, and these delicate, oppositional identities con-stantly require "steroids" of denigration to be maintained. As the Freeway data suggest, white working-class men also virulently construct notions of identity around another historically available "Other"—gays. Many studies, such as that by M. Messner and D. Sabo (1994), evidence how homophobia is used as a profound foil around which to forge aggressive forms of hetero-sexuality. Heteromasculinity, for the working class in the United States, may indeed be endangered.

As these white boys and men comment on their sense of mistreatment, we reflect, ironically, on their stone-faced fragility. The 1980s and 1990s have marked a time when the women they associate with got independent, their jobs got scarce, their unions got weak, and their privileged access to public in-stitutions was compromised by the success of equal rights and affirmative ac-tion. Traditional bases of white male material power—head of the family, pro-ductive worker, and exclusive access to "good" public sector and/or unionized jobs—eroded rapidly. Sold out by elites, they are in panic and despair. Their reassertions of status reveal a profound fragility masked by the protection of "their women," their fight for "fairness" in the workplace, and their demand for "diversity" among (but not within) educational institutions. As they nar-rate a precarious white heteromasculinity, perhaps they speak for a narrow slice of men sitting at the white working-class nexus. More likely, they speak for a gendered and raced group whose privilege has been rattled and whose wrath is boiling over. Their focus, almost fetishisticaly, is on themselves as vic-tims and "Others" as perpetrators. . . . Comforted by Howard Stern and Rush Limbaugh, these men are on a treacherous course for self, "Others," and the possibilities for broad-based social change.

The responsibility of educators, researchers, and citizens committed to dem-ocratic practice is not simply to watch passively or interrupt responsively when these boys/men get "out of hand." We must embark on serious social change efforts aimed at both understanding and transforming what we uncover here. Spaces must be located in which men/boys are working together to affirm

white masculinity that does not rest on the construction of the viral "other."
. . . Schools, churches, and work sites all offer enormous potential for such
transformative cultural activity.

NOTES

1. We must point out that although we focus on only the white boys' construction
of blacks, we do not mean to imply that they authored the race script in its entirety nor
that they wrote the meaning of Black for the African American students. We are, for
present purposes, simply focusing on the ways in which young white men discursively
construct the "Other."

2. We include men of different ages and statuses to represent an array of voices that
are white, male, and working-class.

REFERENCES

Bluestone, B., and B. Harrison. 1982. *The deindustrialization of America*. New York: Basic
    Books.
Davis, A. 1990. *Women, culture, and politics*. New York: Vintage.
Frankenberg, R. 1993. *The social construction of whiteness: White women, race matters*.
    Minneapolis: University of Minnesota Press.
Janoff-Bulman, R. 1979. Characterological versus behavioral self blame: Inquiries into
    depression and rape. *Journal of Social Psychology* 37:1798–1809.
Messner, M., and D. Sabo. 1994. *Sex, violence, and power in sports: Rethinking masculin-
    ity*. Freedom, CA: Crossing.
Newman, K. 1993. *Declining fortunes: The withering of the American dreams*. New York:
    Basic Books.
Roediger, D. 1994. *The wages of whiteness: Race and the making of the American working
    class*. New York: Verso.
Roman, L. 1993. White is a color!: White defensiveness, postmodernism, and anti-
    racist pedagogy. In *Race, identity and representation in education*. New York: Routledge.
Weis, L. 1990. *Working class without work: High school students in a de-industrializing econ-
    omy*. New York: Routledge.
Weis, L., A. Proweller, and C. Centric. 1996. Re-examining a moment in history: Loss of
    privilege inside white, working class masculinity in the 1990s. In *Off white*, edited by
    M. Fine, L. Powell, L. Weis, and M. Wong. New York: Routledge.
Wong, L. M. 1994. Di(s)-secting and di(s)-closing whiteness: Two tales from psychol-
    ogy. *Feminism and Psychology* 4:133–53.

EDITOR'S NOTE

According to a report in the spring 2005 edition of the AAUW (Association of
American University Women) publication, in 2001 a higher proportion of
women earned master's degrees than men (59 and 41 percent, respectively).[1]

Actually, in the last few years women undergraduate students outnumber men. In fact, women make up almost half of students in medical and law school. Perhaps it is statistics such as these that have men feeling resentful toward women—like the men in the Michelle Fine et al. reading expressed.

Although men can be angry about women surpassing them in education, they have little reason to be when it comes to earnings, at least not yet. According to the AAUW, at every level of education women earn less than men do. For example, women with high school diplomas earn only 79 percent of what a male high school graduate; women with bachelor degrees earn 76 percent of what men with bachelor degrees earn, and women with advanced degrees earn 76 percent of men with advanced degrees.[2]

Incredulous as it seems, the report notes that in nearly every field, including science, math, and engineering, women with the same credentials as men almost always earn less.[3]

The economic situation of African Americans and Latino men is more unstable than white males. Their median income is lower (see the introduction), and their unemployment rate is generally double that of whites, even for college graduates.

Could it be that white men's rage is misdirected or displaced? Are women and other minorities to blame or is there something about the economy that merits closer scrutiny? For example, five of the occupations in which there is anticipated growth are some of the lowest-paying jobs.[4] Are women and other minorities the problem or is it simply safer to direct anger at those less powerful? Is it a class issue as well as a race/ethnicity and gender issue?

How might working-class women and men of all hues come together to influence policies that will make the lives of all workers better? They might look overseas. Working-class folks in other countries have better safety nets than in the United States. For one thing, workers earn a higher percentage of median wages in other countries than do U.S. workers (60 percent to 37 percent, respectively); there is not the tremendous gulf between workers' pay and executive compensation in other countries that is present in the United States. Then, too, workers in other countries receive health insurance and child care assistance, two expenses that eat up workers' paychecks in the United States.[5]

NOTES

1. Jean-Marie Navetta, "Gaps in Earning: Gains in Learning," *Outlook* 99, 1 (Spring 2005): 13.
2. Ibid.
3. Ibid.
4. Anna Quindlen, "A New Kind of Poverty," *Newsweek*, 1 December 2003, p. 76.
5. Ibid.

V

STRUCTURED INEQUALITY— RACE/ETHNICITY

11

A Black Woman Took My Job

Michael Kimmel

Over the past three generations, women's lives have been utterly and completely transformed—in politics, the military, the workplace, professions, and education. But during that time, the ideology of masculinity has remained relatively intact. The notions we have about what it means to be a man remain locked in a pattern set decades ago, when the world looked very different. The single greatest obstacle to women's equality today remains the behavior and attitudes of men.

In the mid-1970s, an American psychologist offered what he called the four basic rules of masculinity:

1. No Sissy Stuff. Masculinity is based on the relentless repudiation of the feminine.
2. Be a Big Wheel. Masculinity is measured by the size of your paycheck, and marked by wealth, power, and status. As a U.S. bumper sticker put it: "He who has the most toys when he dies, wins."
3. Be a Sturdy Oak. What makes a man a man is that he is reliable in a crisis. And what makes him reliable in a crisis is that he resembles an inanimate object. A rock, a pillar, a tree.
4. Give 'em Hell. Exude an aura of daring and aggression. Take risks; live life on the edge.

The past decade has found men bumping up against the limitations of these traditional definitions, but without much of a sense of direction about where they might look for alternatives. We chafe against the edges of traditional masculinity but seem unable or unwilling to break out of the constraints of those four rules. Hence the defensiveness, the anger, the confusion that is everywhere in evidence.

Let me pair up those four rules of manhood with the four areas of change in women's lives—gender identity, the workplace, the balance of work and family life, the sexual landscape—and suggest some of the issues I believe we are facing around the world today.

First, women made gender visible, but most men do not know they are gendered beings. Courses on gender are still populated mostly by women. Most men don't see that gender is as central to their lives as it is to women's. The privilege of privilege is that its terms are rendered invisible. It is a luxury not to have to think about race, or class, or gender. Only those marginalized by some category understand how powerful that category is when deployed against them.

The second area in which women's lives have changed is the workplace. Recall the second rule of manhood: Be a Big Wheel. Most men derive their identity as breadwinners, as family providers. Often, though, the invisibility of masculinity makes it hard to see how gender equality will actually benefit us as men. For example, while we speak of the "feminization of poverty" we rarely "see" its other side—the "masculinization of wealth." Instead of saying that U.S. women, on average, earn 70 percent of what U.S. men earn, what happens if we say that men are earning $1.30 for every $1.00 women earn? Now suddenly privilege is visible!

Recently I appeared on a television talk show opposite three "angry white males" who felt they had been the victims of workplace discrimination. The show's title was "A Black Woman Took My Job." In my comments to these men, I invited them to consider what the word "my" meant in that title: that they felt that the jobs were originally "theirs." But by what right is that "his" job? Only by his sense of entitlement, which he now perceives as threatened by the movement toward workplace gender equality.

The economic landscape has changed dramatically and those changes have not necessarily been kind to most men. The great global expansion of the 1990s affected the top 20 percent of the labor force. . . . And here come women into the workplace in unprecedented numbers. Just when men's economic breadwinner status is threatened, women appear on the scene as easy targets for men's anger—or versions of anger. Sexual harassment, for example, is a way to remind women that they are not yet equals in the workplace, that they really don't belong there.

It is also in our interests as men to begin to find a better balance of work and family life. There's a saying that "no man on his deathbed ever wished he had spent more time at the office." But remember the third rule of manhood: Be a Sturdy Oak. What has traditionally made men reliable in a crisis is also what makes us unavailable emotionally to others. We are increasingly finding that the very things that we thought would make us real men impoverish our relationships with other men and with our children. Fatherhood, friendship, partnership all require emotional resources that have been, traditionally, in short supply among men, resources such as patience, compassion, tenderness, attention to process.

In the United States, men become more active fathers by "helping out" or by "pitching in"; they spend "quality time" with their children. But it is not "quality time" that will provide the deep intimate relationships that we say we want, either with our partners or with our children. It's quantity time—putting in those long, hard hours of thankless, unnoticed drudge—that creates the foundation of intimacy.

Finally, let's examine the last rule of manhood: Give 'em Hell. What this says to men is: take risks, live dangerously. And this, of course, impacts most dramatically on our bodies, sex, health, and violence. Masculinity is the chief reason why men do not seek healthcare as often as women. Women perform self-exams, seek preventive screenings, and pay attention to diet, substance abuse, far more often than men.

Indeed. The ideas that we thought would make us "real men" are the very things that endanger our health. One researcher suggested slapping a warning label on us: Caution: Masculinity May be Hazardous to Your Health. A 1994 study of adolescent males in the United States found that adherence to traditional masculinity ideology was associated with: being suspended from school, drinking, use of street drugs, having a high number of sexual partners, not using condoms, being picked up by the police, forcing someone to have sex.[1]

These gender-conforming behaviors increase boys' risk for HIV, STDS, early death by accident, injury, or homicide. It's no exaggeration to say that the spread of HIV is driven by masculinity. HIV risk reduction requires men to take responsibility by wearing condoms. But in many cultures ignoring the health risks to one's partner, eschewing birth control, and fathering many children are signs of masculine control and power.

Finally, let me turn to what may be the single greatest public health issue of all: violence. In the United States, men and boys are responsible for 95 percent of all violent crimes. Every day twelve boys and young men commit suicide—seven times the number of girls. Every day, eighteen boys and young men die from homicide—ten times the number of girls. From an early age, boys learn that violence is not only an acceptable form of conflict resolution but one that is admired. Four times more teenage boys than girls think fighting is appropriate when someone cuts into the front of a line. Half of all teenage boys get into a physical fight each year.

Violence has been part of the meaning of manhood, part of the way men have traditionally tested, demonstrated, and proved their manhood. Without another cultural mechanism by which young boys can come to think of themselves as men, they've eagerly embraced violence as a way to become men. It would be a major undertaking to enumerate all the health consequences that result from the equation of violence and masculinity.

And just as women are saying "yes" to their own sexual desires, there's an increased awareness of the problem of rape all over the world, especially of date and acquaintance rape. In one recent U.S. study, 45 percent of all college women said that they had had some form of sexual contact against their will, and a full 25 percent had been pressed or forced to have sexual intercourse against their will. When one psychologist asked male undergraduates if they would commit rape if they were certain they could get away with it, almost 50 percent said they would. Nearly twenty years ago, anthropologist Peggy Reeves Sanday proposed a continuum of propensity to commit rape upon which all societies could be plotted—from "rape-prone" to "rape-free." (The United States was ranked as a highly rape-prone society, far more than any country in Europe; Norway and Sweden were among the most rape-free.) Sanday found that the single best predictors of rape-proneness were:

1. Whether the woman continued to own property in her own name after marriage, a measure of women's autonomy.
2. Father's involvement in child-rearing, a measure of how valued parenting is, and how valued women's work.

So women's economic autonomy is a good predictor of their safety—as is men's participation in child-rearing. If men act at home the way we say we want to act, women will be safer.

And the news gets better. A 1996 study of Swedish couples found positive health outcomes for wives, husbands, and children when the married couple adopted a partnership model in work-family balance issues. A recent study in the United States found that men who shared housework and childcare had better health, were happier in their marriages, reported fewer psychological distress symptoms, and—perhaps most important to them—had more sex! That's right, men who share housework have more sex. What could possibly be more in men's "interests" than that?

Rather than resisting the transformation of our lives that gender equality offers, I believe that we should embrace these changes, both because they offer us the possibilities of social and economic equality, and because they also offer us the possibilities of richer, fuller, happier lives with our friends, with our lovers, with our partners, and with our children. We, as men, should support gender equality, both at work and at home. Not because it's right and just—although it is those things. But because of what it will do for us, as men.

NOTES

1. J. H. Pleck, F. L. Sonenstein, and L. C. Ku, "Masculinity Ideology: Its Impact on Adolescent Males' Heterosexual Relationships." *Journal of Social Issues* 49, 3 (1993): 11–29.

12

Are Men Marginal to the Family?

Insights from Chicago's Inner City

Haya Stier and Marta Tienda

Academic and policy discussion about the linkages between family structure and poverty have generated a picture of poor, unmarried minority women abandoned by irresponsible men who shirk their parental responsibilities (e.g., Murray, 1984). In fact, many noncustodial parents either never married or never lived with their children (Furstenberg, 1991; Hannerz, 1969; Sullivan, 1989). Whereas some men actually deny their fatherhood, others who acknowledge paternity renege on obligations to provide support, despite their best intentions. A third group of noncustodial fathers marry the mother of their children, but like many men who marry before children come, lose contact with the children after subsequent separation. Thus, because of rising divorce rates and high rates of nonmarital fertility, growing numbers of children receive inadequate emotional and financial support from their biological fathers.

Do declining levels of support from noncustodial fathers mean that men, especially minority men, are becoming marginal to the family? This provocative thesis is implicit in many recent accounts about the growth of an urban underclass, but it has not been explicitly posed.[1] We explore this thesis by examining the circumstances underlying father absence for a sample of parents residing in Chicago's inner city.

THEORETICAL CONSIDERATIONS

Men's familial roles have undergone substantial changes since preindustrial times. Although all family members contributed to subsistence activities during preindustrial times, men were the dominant source of authority within the household. As family heads, men were considered to be primary providers because they were credited with their wives' and children's work. With the

relocation of economic activity outside the household that accompanied mod-
ernization, men's family roles acquired an almost exclusive concern with economic support functions (Damos, 1986). Although fathers continued involvement with their children, particularly at an emotional level, mothers
became the principals in socialization except in unusual circumstances. For example, F. F. Furstenberg (1988) noted that until the middle of the nineteenth
century, fathers usually assumed custody over the children in case of a marital
disruption. When rates of female labor force activity were low, this arrange-
ment protected children's economic well-being. The belief that children are
better off with their mother, especially during their early years of life, gradu-
ally led to changes in this practice so that by the end of the nineteenth century,
mothers usually became custodial parents in the event of marital disruption.

The "good provider" role of fathers dominated family ideology until the
1960s, when according to B. Ehrenreich (1985) and others, men began to retreat from their instrumental familial roles (Bernard, 1981; Furstenberg, 1988;
Rotundo, 1985). This retreat manifested itself in two ways: Men either *increased* their familial responsibilities by taking more active roles in child rearing and household duties, or greatly diminished their involvement in domestic and parenting roles.[2] Thus, changes in the division of labor within families
resulted in two extreme styles of modern parenthood. Whereas some fathers
have become heavily involved in child rearing and have extended their familial roles beyond that of breadwinners (Marsiglio, 1991; Pleck, 1987), other fathers deny responsibility for their children, refusing to support them altogether (Furstenberg, 1988).[3]

Many researchers have argued that men in general and minority men in particular are retreating from the family. The primary evidence for this claim de-
rives from levels of financial and emotional support provided by noncustodial
fathers. Alternative interpretations build on differences in the form and content of child support provided by men of varying economic means and ethnic
group membership. These two views of child support patterns undergird our
analysis of whether or not men are becoming marginal to the family.

The growing number of fathers who fail to provide child support for noncustodial children and who have minimal contact with them is socially
problematic because it results in both economic and emotional deprivation
(Furstenberg, Nord, Peterson, and Zill, 1983; Garfinkel and McLanahan,
1986; Weitzman, 1985). But it is unclear whether noncustodial fathers' failure to provide child support reflects their irresponsibility in dealing with familial obligations, denial of access to their children, or economic constraints. To be sure, men who lack steady incomes find it difficult to provide
regular support to their noncustodial children (Furstenberg, 1991; Furstenberg et al., 1983). Before judging men's disregard of child support as evidence of their marginality to the family, it is essential to establish why they
fail to provide child support. For example, learning that lack of access to jobs
is the reason for neglect shifts the locus of policy debate from concerns

about how to force "the scoundrels" to pay their due to concerns about the circumstances underlying their precarious labor market position (Wilson, 1987; Wilson and Neckerman, 1986). Such considerations are particularly germane to the recent debates about the growth of an urban underclass.

With the increasing rates of out-of-wedlock childbirth and divorce, absent fathers are becoming numerous. . . . One consequence of this behavior is a growing number of children, but especially minority children, being reared in poverty (Eggebeen and Lichter, 1991). To date, most empirical work on living arrangements and support patterns of noncustodial fathers has been restricted to blacks or comparisons between blacks and whites. As a result, ethnic differences in parenting styles, living arrangements, and support activities are neither well documented nor understood. In particular, relatively little is known about Hispanic men's roles as fathers and providers.

There are several compelling reasons for examining the parenting behavior of Hispanic men. First, as a group, Hispanic men are more successful in the labor market than black men, although there are marked differences between Mexican and Puerto Rican men (Tienda, 1989). If labor market standing is the key factor predicting whether fathers will provide for their noncustodial children, we would expect higher levels of support from Mexican compared to Puerto Rican men. Second, the marriage behavior of Hispanic men differs markedly from that of black men (Testa, Astone, Krogh, and Neckerman, 1989). Not only are Mexican men more likely to be married at given ages, but their rates of separation are lower than those of black men (Stier and Tienda, 1992). Puerto Rican men are somewhere between these extremes, with high proportions marrying coupled with high rates of disruption, but the patterns of child support exhibited by Puerto Rican men are virtually unknown. Finally, allegations that minority men are marginal to the family require evidence showing that at comparable income levels, men of color are less committed to providing child support than their white counterparts.

Short of this information, prevailing stereotypes about noncustodial fathers as "irresponsible scoundrels" must be interpreted as consequences of their weak market position. Our analyses, therefore, compare black, white, Mexican, and Puerto Rican fathers residing in inner-city neighborhoods where father absence is pervasive. In addition to documenting the living arrangements of inner-city fathers and their children, we examine the circumstances that undergird their support patterns.

DATA AND METHODS

Our analyses are based on the Urban Poverty and Family Life Survey of Chicago (UPFLS) conducted by National Opinion Research Center (NORC) in 1986 and 1987. These data were collected under the auspices of a multiyear study of Urban Poverty and Family Structure in the City of Chicago.[4]

The UPFLS is based on a multistage, stratified probability sample of parents aged eighteen to forty-four who resided in census tracts representing diverse socioeconomic environments.

We also used the National Survey of Families and Households (NSFH) to generate baseline tabulations against which to compare family behavior and living arrangements of the inner-city sample.[5] From this survey, which is nationally representative of persons residing in families and households, we selected all men who met the age and parent status criteria used to draw the Chicago survey. To maximize comparability between the Chicago and the national sample, we restricted the NSFH sample to fathers who resided in core cities. These sample restrictions resulted in a national sample of 947 fathers.[6]

ETHNIC DIFFERENTIALS IN FAMILY BEHAVIOR AND LIVING ARRANGEMENTS

Marriage behavior clearly differs along ethnic and racial lines. Both nationally and in Chicago, Mexican and white fathers were more likely to be married than their Puerto Rican and black counterparts. Further, black and Puerto Rican fathers were most likely to have never married, but Chicago's black fathers were more than twice as likely as their national counterparts to have never married.[7] Mexican fathers living in Chicago were over 10 percentage points more likely to be married than white fathers, but at the national level, the 7 point advantage was for whites. Although less than half of all black fathers residing in Chicago were married in 1987, the proportion of married black fathers nationally hovered around 60 percent.

Despite the considerable ethnic and geographic variation in the propensity of men to marry and stay married, there was surprisingly little diversity in the age at first marriage, which ranged between twenty-three and twenty-four years for both samples. However, there was much greater variation in the timing of fatherhood, with black men reporting younger ages at the birth of their first child (twenty-two and twenty-four years, respectively, for the Chicago and national samples). White men became fathers later than minority men, with virtually no difference between Chicago and urban men nationally.

The rate of nonmarital fatherhood in poor inner-city neighborhoods also is striking, particularly by comparison to all urban men. Black men are most likely to enter fatherhood prior to marriage; fathering children out of wedlock is particularly common among Chicago's inner-city black men, where nearly three out of four men acknowledged an out-of-wedlock child. Mexican and white men residing in Chicago's inner city were more likely than their national counterparts to father children prior to marriage, but ethnic differences were trivial. That is, among white and Mexican men, approximately 8 percent and 25 percent, respectively, of those in the national and the Chicago samples reported fathering children before they married. By contrast, nearly half of all Puerto Rican men reported fathering at least one child out of wedlock. Although several of these men eventually married the mother of their child (Testa et al., 1989; see also Sullivan, 1989), there persist marked ethnic differences in the likelihood of their doing so.

That Mexican men report the highest rates of co-residence with their own children reflects the larger share of fathers who were married at the time of the survey. Puerto Rican fathers are less likely to marry than Mexicans or whites, but nearly 80 percent of Chicago fathers reported cohabiting with their own children. The incidence of coresident between black children and their fathers was appreciably lower—less than 50 percent in Chicago and just over 60 percent nationally. In fact, as many as one-third of all black men (both in Chicago and the United States) live in households with no dependent children present. The comparable figures for all other groups are lower, especially for Mexicans.

Fathers live without children either because their offspring have already left home or because the men left their children. In most cases of divorce, and certainly most instances of out-of-wedlock births, mothers assume custody of children. Thus, half of all black and one-third of all Puerto Rican fathers have dependent children who reside elsewhere. This proportion compares with 27 percent of white fathers in Chicago, and less than 20 percent of white fathers nationally. Less than one in five Mexican-origin fathers reported having dependent children who did not live with them.[8]

As expected, 5 percent and 6 percent of currently married fathers residing in Chicago and U.S. cities, respectively, did not live with children compared to 43 percent and 55 percent of never-married fathers. At the other extreme, approximately 90 percent of currently married fathers reside with their own and other (adopted) children. Yet, between 27 percent and 30 percent of Chicago's never-married fathers reported coresiding with their own and other children, and an additional 30 percent of Chicago's never-wed fathers lived with children belonging to someone else—a mate, an older sibling, a friend. Among black men nationally, the latter pattern is typically rare, representing less than 5 percent of never-married men. However, the tendency of never-married men to reside in complex families consisting of their own and other children is more common: just over 40 percent of single fathers reported such living arrangements nationally.

These descriptive results raise two questions critical to our concern about men's marginality to the family: first, what circumstances explain the ethnic differences in men's propensity to marry in the first place? And second, what kind and how much support do absent fathers provide to their offspring? . . . Because of limited information on forms of child support in the National Survey of Families and Households, we restrict these analyses to the Chicago sample.

FATHERHOOD, MARRIAGE, AND PARENTAL OBLIGRATIONS

The previous tabulations show that married fathers are considerably more likely than unmarried fathers to coreside with their children. Although we lack information about the extent to which coresident fathers fulfill their paternal obligations, it is reasonable to assume that fathers who live with their own children provide regular emotional and material support. Further, there is ample empirical evidence showing that children residing with both parents enjoy higher economic standing than those who reside with one parent—usually the biological mother (Eggebeen and Lichter, 1991; Garfinkel and McLanahan, 1986). But in light of the high rates of out-of-wedlock fathering, a first major question is: what determines transition into marriage?

One important finding from this vast literature is that the likelihood of marriage varies directly with improvements in economic standing. Thus, the low marriage rates observed among black men, parents and nonparents alike, are attributed to their weak labor market standing, as reflected by high rates of joblessness and low earnings among those who manage to secure employment.

However, a proxy for labor market status, high school graduation also increased the (log) odds that black and Puerto Rican men would marry. Specifically, the logit coefficients indicate that black high school graduates were 2.7 times and Puerto Ricans were nearly 11 times more likely to wed than their counterparts who had not completed secondary school. The birth of a child significantly *increased* the odds of marriage for all groups of roughly a factor of two for blacks and Puerto Ricans. Among whites and Mexicans the risk of marriage increased even more when a child was born—8.7 and 3.6 times, respectively.

On balance, our results support W. J. Wilson's (1987; Wilson and Neckerman, 1986) premises about the enabling role of economic position—education or work—in raising the propensity of inner-city men to marry. That the act of fathering a child itself propels men into marriage indicates that they are inclined to accept their parental obligations when they have the means to support their children. These results also corroborate with C. B. Stack's (1974) finding that couples often do not formalize their marriage until the advent of a birth. Finally, our results show that there exist alternative pathways into adult roles in the inner city. In other words, marriage often follows rather than precedes parenting in impoverished environments. The sequencing of these two life course events differs markedly by race and Hispanic origins.

Although sample sizes have been reduced sharply for whites and Mexicans over 40 percent of Puerto Rican fathers and nearly 60 percent of black fathers reported having one or more children who did not reside with them. This means that the fathers actually recognize these children as their own.[9] Of the population of fathers who reported having nonresident children, most reported providing economic support to their offspring. There is limited ethnic variation in the practice of providing financial support, except that Mexican men, who were less likely to have nonresident children to begin with, were somewhat more likely to provide financial support—probably because they often live far away from their offspring. Puerto Ricans were the least likely to support their children financially. Although there may be limited ethnic variation in the tendency of noncustodial fathers to support their children, the nature and level of support may vary greatly both in its regularity and the amounts provided.

Most fathers also report providing in-kind support (e.g., toys, clothes) to the children. That noncustodial Mexican fathers report a lower incidence of in-kind support reflects practical difficulties: For those who left dependent children in Mexico, monetary transfers are more practical than in-kind support, which often involve services and miscellaneous goods. This interpretation is consistent with other ethnic differences in child support (e.g., the actual contact with the children discussed below).

Not only do noncustodial fathers provide economic contributions to their children, but so do their relatives. This practice is especially evident among black fathers: Nearly one in four report that their noncustodial children receive financial support from other relatives, and over half reported that other relatives provide some in-kind support. Kin-based financial support to children is less common among whites, Mexicans, and Puerto Ricans, but the frequency of in-kind support from other white and Puerto Rican relatives is comparable to that of blacks.

Economic support of any kind is more frequent than direct interaction with children. However, tabulations on visitation behavior reveal that black fathers visit their children more than any other category of men. One-third of black fathers reported daily contact with their nonresident children, whereas one-third see the child only once or twice a month, and the remainder have no contact at all. This pattern is consistent with Stack's (1974) account of father-child interaction in a poor black community. In comparison, only 18 percent of the whites, 15 percent of the Puerto Ricans, and 9 percent of Mexicans reported daily visits with the children. Half of all Puerto Ricans, three-fourths of Mexicans, and nearly half of the whites say they never see their children. On balance, and with the exception of blacks, noncustodial fathers have very limited, if any, contact with their children.

As a path to separation of fathers from their children, divorce often involves mobility of one parent, thus inhibiting frequent and regular contact with children left behind. For blacks, whose children are conceived out of wedlock at higher rates than the other groups, marriage and coresidence seem to play less decisive roles in shaping child-parent interaction. According to Stack (1974), M. L. Sullivan (1989), and U. Hannerz (1969), men (or their close relatives) are expected to take care of the children, regardless of the living arrangements or the marital relationships to the mother. Frequently these obligations are met.

Fathers who are currently employed are almost three times more likely to support their nonresident children compared to fathers who are not working. Also, high school graduates are 20 percent more likely to support their children compared to dropouts. That the ethnic differences are not statistically significant conveys an important message about the cultural underpinnings of distinct forms of support for noncustodial children. Stated differently, *ethnicity and race appear to be proxies for economic rather than family marginality*. This is not to dismiss the role of culture in shaping patterns of coresidence and the differential involvement of kin in providing for noncustodial children, but rather to stress that ethnic differences give way to indicators of fathers' economic status as determinants of material support to noncustodial children.

SUMMARY AND DISCUSSION

Are inner-city fathers marginal to their families? Our analyses documented the support roles of noncustodial inner-city fathers. That these men have diverse lifestyles is evident in their marital behavior and fulfillment of child responsibilities.

Earnings prospects (indexed by educational status) and labor market status appear to be the key determinants of child support activity for all fathers, regardless of ethnicity. Although the black fathers are more likely than white or Hispanic men to be noncustodial parents, they compensate for this loss of family responsibility through frequent contact with their offspring and by invoking the financial contributions of their kin. Similar practices, although less prevalent, are reported by white, Mexican, and Puerto Rican fathers. Thus, it appears that through their economic but especially their social relationships with other relatives, unmarried inner-city fathers provide an alternative family context for their noncustodial children.

Our analyses of inner-city fathers' child support patterns refute the idea that these men are becoming marginal to the family. Despite the severe financial constraints faced by minority men residing in Chicago's inner city, we were most struck by the relatively high proportions of men who reported providing financial and in-kind support to their noncustodial children. Unfortunately, we were unable to assess the regularity of the support provided or to consider whether it covered a reasonable share of their children's living expenses. Given the high rates of joblessness in the inner city (Tienda and Stier, 1991), it is unlikely that child support provided by inner-city fathers was adequate to cover all costs of child rearing. However, it is inappropriate to conclude that these men have retreated from the family, or that they are "irresponsible scoundrels" who neglect their children. Our results show that noncustodial fathers make great efforts to maintain ties with their children. That black fathers report the highest levels of contact with their noncustodial children corroborate Stack's (1974) interpretation about men's interactions with kin. When they lack financial resources, they contribute their own time and solicit support from other kin. We cannot determine whether or not visits compensate for income contributions but visitation is certainly important for emotional development.

More generally, our study raises questions about the origins of men's marginality in the inner city. There is widespread agreement that minority men, particularly those residing in declining inner cities, have been marginalized from the labor market (Wilson, 1987). Despite their precarious economic position, it is remarkable than inner-city fathers manage to maintain ties with their noncustodial children. However, men's economic marginality, which is clearly reflected in declining rates of labor force participation and higher rates of unemployment, does reverberate in their family roles. Poor labor market standing influences the likelihood of marrying and fathering children, and the sequencing of these major life course events (Testa et al., 1989; Wilson and Neckerman, 1986). The provider roles assumed by inner-city men may not conform to the norms of middle-class whites, but this difference should not be translated as "flight from the family."

NOTES

1. We are grateful to Joan Aldous for sharpening our thinking on this issue.

2. The latter circumstance accentuated gender inequities within the family to the extent that men's retreat from the domestic arena was accompanied by an increase in women's labor force activity (Curtis, 1986; Stier, 1991).

3. Of course, there are intermediate variants between these extremes. Our focus on the extremes serves a heuristic function in sharpening our analytic goals.

4. William J. Wilson is the principal investigator. The original design called for a sample of census tracts where at least 20 percent of families had incomes below the 1980 federal poverty line. The final sample included a broader range of socioeconomic contexts.

5. Larry Bumpass was the principal investigator. Also fielded in 1987, this national survey contains sufficient race and ethnic variation for tabular analyses of Mexican, black, and white populations, but the sample of Puerto Ricans is limited for tabular analyses.

6. Both the UPFLS and NSFH surveys were based on cross-sectional designs, but both surveys contain several retrospective sequences on life experiences, including work behavior, marriage and fertility histories, educational histories, and welfare experiences. In addition, both surveys contain information about respondents' family backgrounds and current employment status. Because the principal investigators of both surveys exchanged instruments, many questions are directly comparable. Tabular results for both surveys are weighted to approximate the universes from which they are drawn, but the sample sizes are unweighted to indicate the actual base on which statistics are computed.

7. Among Puerto Rican fathers, the share never married did not differ between the Chicago and national samples, but the national rate is subject to a high degree of sampling variability owing to the small sample size ($N = 20$).

8. Illinois is an AFCE-U state, which means that unemployed fathers are eligible for benefits. Thus, the fact that fathers are not discouraged from living with children requires other explanations for the observed differences in living arrangements.

9. We have no indication about how many of these men had children they failed to report as their own, but they would be the most marginal fathers of all.

REFERENCES

Bernard, J. (1981). The good provider role: Its rise and fall. *American Psychologist* 36 (1), 1–12.

Curtis, R. (1986, April): Family and inequality theory. *American Sociological Review* 51, 168–83.

Damos, J. (1986). *Past, present, and personal: The family and life course in American history.* New York: Oxford University Press.

Eggebeen, D., and D. T. Lichter. (1991). Race, family structure, and changing poverty among American children. *American Sociological Review* 56 (6), 801–17.

Ehrenreich, B. (1985). *The hearts of men: American dreams and the flight from family commitment.* New York: Anchor.

Furstenberg, F. F. (1988). Good dads—bad dads: Two faces of fatherhood. In A. J. Cherlin (ed.), *The changing American family and public policy* (pp. 193–218). Washington, D.C.: Urban Institute.

Furstenberg, F. F. (1991). *Daddies and fathers: Men who do for their children and men who don't.* Unpublished manuscript, University of Pennsylvania.

Furstenberg, F. F., C. W. Nord, J. L. Peterson, and N. Zill. (1983). The life course of children of divorce: Marital disruption and parental contact. *American Sociological Review* 48, 656–68.

Garfinkel, I., and S. S. McLanahan. (1986). *Single mothers and their children: A new American dilemma.* Washington, D.C.: Urban Institute.

Hannerz, U. (1969). *Soulside: Inquiring into ghetto culture and community.* New York: Columbia University Press.

Hetherington, D. E., K. A. Camara, and D. L. Featherman. (1983). Achievement and intellectual functioning of children in one-parent households. In J. Spence (ed.), *Achievement and achievement motives* (pp. 205–84). San Francisco: W. H. Freeman.

Marsiglio, W. (1991). Parental engagement activities with minor children. *Journal of Marriage and the Family* 53, 973–86.

Murray, C. (1984). *Losing ground: American social policy, 1950–1980.* New York: Basic Books.

Pleck, J. H. (1987). American fathering in historical perspective. In M. S. Kimmel (ed.), *Changing men: New directions in research on men and masculinity* (pp. 83–97). Newbury Park, CA: Sage.

Rotundo, E. A. (1985). American fatherhood: A historical perspective. *American Behavioral Scientist* 29 (1), 7–25.

Stack, C. B. (1974). *All our kin: Strategies for survival in the black community.* New York: Harper & Row.

Stier, H. (1991). Immigrant women go to work: The labor supply of immigrant wives for six Asian groups. *Social Science Quarterly* 72 (1), 67–82.

Stier, H., and M. Tienda. (1992). *Love and lifestyles: Ethnic variation in marriage behavior among inner city parents.* Unpublished manuscript, University of Chicago.

Sullivan, M. L., (1989, January). Absent fathers in the inner city. *Annals of the American Academy of Political and Social Sciences* 501, 48–58.

Testa, M., N. M. Astone, M. Krogh, and K. M. Neckerman. (1989, January). Employment and marriage among inner city fathers. *Annals of the American Academy of Political and Social Sciences* 501, 79–91.

Tienda, M. (1989, January). Puerto Ricans and the underclass debate. *Annals of the American Academy of Political and Social Sciences* 501, 105–19.

Tienda, M., and H. Stier. (1991). Joblessness and shiftlessness: Labor force activity in Chicago's inner city. In C. Jencks and P. Peterson (eds.), *The urban underclass* (pp. 135–54). Washington, D.C.: Brookings Institution.

Weitzman, L. J. (1985). *The divorce revolution: The unexpected social and economic consequences for women and children in America.* New York: Free Press.

Wilson, W. J. (1987). *The truly disadvantaged: The inner city, the underclass, and public policy.* Chicago: University of Chicago Press.

Wilson, W. J., and K. M. Neckerman. (1986). Poverty and family structure: The widening gap between evidence and public issues. In S. H. Danziger and D. H. Weinberg (eds.), *Fighting poverty: What works and what doesn't* (pp. 232–59). Cambridge, MA: Harvard University Press.

EDITOR'S NOTE

Haya Stier and Marta Tienda's reading provides evidence of the determination many of the men in their sample exhibited in eking out a living for their families. Their plight is connected to a class of workers whose jobs are at the lowest end of the occupational spectrum. And more and more families are operating without a safety net. In fact, fewer than half of families eligible for welfare receive it.[1]

The disarticulation of workers and jobs gets played out in cities across the nation. Prospective workers who live in the inner city lack the training and skills to obtain the jobs available there, nor do they have the transportation to get to the suburban areas to take the light manufacturing jobs available for which they would qualify. One recent study found that 77 percent of jobs in the inner city were held by commuters.[2]

Finding work isn't necessarily a panacea. Frequently, those in low-skilled jobs, such as janitorial work, are taken advantage of by their employer. Janitors are often engaged as independent contractors so the employer doesn't have to pay "employee taxes," nor overtime.[3] Another strategy used by corporations is to hire a contractor who subcontracts the actual work. In this way corporations can deny any knowledge of illegal workers being hired. Quite a few corporations— including Wal Mart, Target, Safeway, Albertson's, and Ralphs—have settled lawsuits in which contractors hired illegal immigrants, locked the workers in the stores, refused to pay them the first two weeks of work, failed to pay overtime, and often paid workers less than minimum wage.

Despite the economic insecurity foisted on low-income families, they continue to struggle to survive as Stier and Tienda report.

NOTES

1. Griff Witte, "Off Welfare but Back in Poverty," *The Washington Post National Weekly Edition*, 4–10 October 2004, p. 29

2. Kelly Rayburn, "Commuters Hold 77 percent of Jobs in Poor U.S. Inner-City Areas," *The Wall Street Journal*, 15 November 2004, p. A9.

3. Steven Greenhouse, "Among Janitors, Labor Violations Go With the Job," *The New York Times*, 13 July 2005, pp. 1, A19.

13

Policing the Ghetto Underclass

The Politics of Law and Law Enforcement

William J. Chambliss

For the past several years my students and I have been riding with the Rapid Deployment Unit (RDU) of the Washington, D.C., Metropolitan Police. In response to the urban riots of the 1960s, Washington, D.C., like many other cities, established specialized riot control units within the police department.[1] These units were specially trained to respond quickly and with force to the threat of riots or urban disturbances. Even in the United States, riots do not happen that often. For the police, the "war on drugs" provided a functional equivalent to riots: the crisis of inner-city drugs and violence.

In all we spent more than one hundred hours riding with members of the RDU and other police officers. These observations and discussions with police officers stimulated the reflections that follow on the state of law enforcement in U.S. cities and the impact it is having on the public's perception of crime and the lives of those most affected.

THE RAPID DEPLOYMENT UNIT

Members of the RDU are described by other police officers as the "Dirty Harrys" and "very serious bad-ass individuals." The RDU is deployed in teams of three patrol cars with two officers in each car. While each car may patrol in different areas, they are never so far from one another that they cannot be summoned on short notice to converge in one place. They patrol what Wilson (1987, 1993) calls the urban ghetto: that is, the area of the city where 40 percent of the black population lives below the poverty level.

Vehicular Stops

The RDU patrols the ghetto continuously looking for cars with young black men in them. They are especially attentive to newer-model cars, Isuzu four-wheel-drive vehicles, BMWs, and Honda Accords, based on the belief that these are the favorite cars of drug dealers. During our observations, however, the RDU officers came to the conclusion that drug dealers were leaving their fancy cars at home to avoid vehicular stops. It thus became commonplace for RDU officers to stop any car with young black men in it.

There is a nod to legality in vehicular stops in that the officers look for a violation in order to justify the stop:

> Field Notes: As we pass a new-looking BMW with two black men in it the driver of the patrol car says to his partner: "Joe, check out that car for violations." The partner says quickly: "Broken tail light, hit the horn." The siren is put on and the car pulls over.

Any minor infraction is an excuse: going through a yellow light, not stopping completely at a stop sign, or having something hanging from the rear-view mirror (a violation of which almost every car in the southeast section of the city is guilty). In addition I was told confidentially by some of the officers, though neither I nor any of my students ever observed it, that if the officers feel strongly that they should stop a car, they will stop it and break a taillight as they approach the car. According to one officer:

> This is the jungle . . . we rewrite the constitution every day down here. . . . If we pull everyone over they will eventually learn that we aren't playing games any more. We are real serious about getting the crap off the streets.

Once a car is stopped the officers radio for backup. The two other cars in the area immediately come to the scene and triangulate the suspect's car: one car comes in close behind and the two others cars form a V in front of the suspect's car.

Vehicular stops occur on an average of every twenty minutes throughout the shift. From our observations, illegal drugs, guns, weapons, or someone who is wanted by authorities are found in only 10 percent of the cars stopped. The officers themselves believe that they find serious violations in "about a third" of the vehicular stops. . . .

The RDU does not patrol the predominantly white sections of Washington, D.C. Observations of policing in this area of the city reveal an entirely different approach by the police. There are no "rips" and no vehicular stops unless there is a clear violation. Officers are not looking for cars with black drivers. If a car is stopped other cars are not called as backups, and the officer handles the infraction on his or her own.

Search Warrants

[Another] major activity is carrying out search warrants. Based on information received from informants, undercover agents, or observations a warrant is issued by the court to search an apartment or home for various reasons:

Warrants: Case No. I. Five RDU officers enter an apartment about 10:45 P.M. Before entering the officers draw their guns, break down the door and rush in. The suspect is spotted, guns are pointed at him and he is told to "lie down, NOW." The suspect is handcuffed and taken outside. An elderly woman begins screaming and crying. She tells the officers to put their guns away. An officer goes to her, his gun still drawn, and tells her to "shut up or I'll pop you in the jaw." He physically forces her to lie down on the floor face down. The officers leave the apartment, put the suspect in the car and take him to the precinct for booking.

Observations indicate police carry out warrants differently in the predominantly white section of Washington, D.C.:

Warrants: Case No. 2. A warrant is issued by the court for the arrest of a suspected drug dealer wanted for assault and attempted murder. The third district police are in an excited state over the pending arrest. An anonymous tip has provided them with information as to the suspect's whereabouts and a discussion at the station lays out a plan for making the arrest. Twelve officers are dispatched to the house where the suspect is supposedly living. Seven officers surround the house and five others approach the front door. Most, but not all, of the officers have their guns drawn. In the dark it is not possible to see all the officers, but of those observable three have guns drawn and two do not. It is a few minutes past 1:00 A.M. when the officers approach the front door. The doorbell is rung and the team leader shouts, "Police, open up." Everyone appears to be on edge. There is no response to the knock or the command. The officers break open the door. Flashlights are shining in every corner, behind furniture and into people's eyes. A terrified elderly woman stands at the top of the stairs and asks what is going on. One of the officers approaches her with calmness and no gun drawn, speaks to her in a low voice, and gently removes her from the house to be watched by the team outside. The suspect is found in the basement behind a water cooler. He is identified and handcuffed. As he is being led from the house one officer says to him, "You sure have a pretty face, buddy boy. See you at the country club."

THE CONSEQUENCES

The prison population in the United States increased by 167 percent between 1980 and 1992, with the greatest percentage increase in drug law violations. . . . The United States today incarcerates a higher percentage of its population than any country in the world: a dubious distinction formerly held by the USSR and South Africa. . . . And it is minorities, especially young African Americans and Latinos, who are disproportionately arrested, convicted, and

sentenced to prison. In 1991, African-American males between the ages of fifteen and thirty-four made up 14 percent of the population and more than 40
percent of the people in prison. White males made up 82 percent of this age
group but less than 60 percent of the prison population (Statistical Abstracts
1993). Blacks accounted for more than 40 percent of the inmates in state and
federal prisons.

In Washington, D.C., and Baltimore, Maryland, 40 to 50 percent of all
black males between the ages of eighteen and thirty-five are either in prison,
jail, on probation or parole, or there is a warrant for their arrest (Maurer
1990; Miller 1992). Arrests and convictions for drugs play an increasingly
important part as a source of criminal convictions. Nearly 30 percent of all
state and, over 55 percent of all federal prisoners in 1992 were convicted on
drug violations (Maguire, Pastore, and Flannagan 1993). Two-thirds of all
drug arrests in 1992 were for possession, and only one-third were for the sale
or manufacture of drugs. African Americans account for more than 40 percent of all drug arrests (Maguire, Pastore, and Flannagan 1993) despite the
fact that self-report surveys show that, except for crack cocaine, whites are
three to five times as likely to use drugs as blacks (Bureau of Justice Statistics
1992a). Thus, more whites than blacks use illegal drugs and more than 80
percent of the population is white. But 66 percent of the inmates in state
prisons convicted of drug offenses are black and only 33 percent are white
(Maguire, Pastore, and Flannagan 1993).

Effects on Family and Education

The intensive surveillance of black neighborhoods, and the pattern of surveillance of white neighborhoods, have the general consequence of institu-
tionalizing racism by defining the problem of crime generally, and drug use in
particular, as a problem of young black men. It further ghettoizes the African-
American community and destroys any possibility for normal family and community relations. Young African-American and Latino men are defined as a
criminal group, arrested for minor offenses over and over again, and given
criminal records that justify long prison sentences. The culture of the black
community and the black family is then blamed for high rates of illegitimate
children and crime. Crime control policies are a major contributor to the disruption of the family, the prevalence of single parent families, and children
raised without a father in the ghetto, and the "inability of people to get the
jobs still available" (Anderson 1993; Wilson 1987, 1993).

But the consequences go beyond the destruction of family and community in the ghetto. Scarce resources are transferred from desperately needed
social programs to criminal justice. For the first time in history, state and
municipal governments are spending more money in criminal justice than
education. Nationwide, expenditures on criminal justice increased by 150
percent between 1972 and 1988, while expenditures on education increased

by 46 percent. Between 1969 and 1989 per capita spending on criminal justice in U.S. cities (municipal expenditures) rose from $34 to $120 and county expenditures as a percentage of total budget rose from 10 to 15 percent between 1973 and 1989. State expenditures showed even greater increases, rising tenfold from per capita expenditures on police and corrections of $8 in 1969 to $80 in 1989. State government expenditure for building prisons increased 593 percent in actual dollars. Spending on corrections—prison building, maintenance, and parole—has more than doubled in the last ten years (Chambliss 1991; Maguire and Flannagan 1990; Maguire, Pastore, and Flannagan 1992).

WHY?

Many reasons have been proposed for the rapid increase in expenditures on criminal justice (or, in the words of Nils Christie, the growth of "the crime industry") in the United States (1993). One explanation is the alleged increase in crime. There is a general perception that crime, especially violent crime, has increased. The notion of a crime increase is a perception, apparently created by the law enforcement establishment, the media, and politicians. But this is not supported by the facts. The best available data, the findings of victim surveys conducted every year since 1973, show that the crime rate has not changed significantly in the last twenty years.

Victim surveys show also that it is very unlikely that anyone will be the victim of a crime in any given year. More than 90 percent of respondents report that neither they nor any member of their household was the victim of a criminal offense. Indeed, over a lifetime it is unlikely that most people will be the victim of a serious offense. The risk of being a victim of a violent crime in any given year is less than 3 percent (Bureau of Justice Statistics 1992b).

The 1992 Uniform Crime Report (UCR) reported a dramatic increase in the murder rate between 1988 and 1992. The FBI used the report to demonstrate a crime rate increase. What the report failed to mention was that between 1980 and 1987 the murder rate actually declined and the 1992 rate was below that of 1980. That the murder rate has shown no appreciable increase since the 1980s is particularly noteworthy given the fact that the weapons in use today are more efficient than ever before. Pistols have been replaced with rapid-firing automatic weapons that leave a victim little chance of escaping with a wound.

The Seriousness of Crime

As for people in prison, James Austin and John Irwin's survey found that more than 50 percent of the prisoners in state and federal prisons are in for offenses that opinion surveys show the general public thinks are "not very serious crimes" (1989). A recent study by the Bureau of Justice Statistics found that more than 20 percent of the inmates in federal prisons were in for drug offenses with no history of violent crime or other felonies (1994). This indicates that the growth of the crime industry is not due to the seriousness of the crimes.

Crime and Public Opinion

Another explanation for the growth of the crime industry is that lawmakers are merely responding to public opinion. In explaining the creation of President Lyndon Johnson's crime commission and the spate of anticrime legislation in the 1960s, James Q. Wilson argues that public opinion forced political action.

[However,] the Gallup Polls never showed that crime was perceived by the respondents as the most important problem facing the nation. Every year since 1935 the Gallup Poll has asked a sample of Americans "What do you think is the most important problem facing the country?" Between 1935 and 1993 crime rarely appears as one of the most important problems mentioned, and in the nearly sixty years the poll has been taken, crime is never chosen over other issues as "the most important problem facing the country." In 1989 and 1991 "drugs" or "drug abuse" is frequently mentioned but only once (April 1990) is it the most often chosen. Even when "drugs" is mentioned, crime in the April 1990 poll is seen as "the most important problem" by only 2 percent of the population (Gallup Poll 1989, 1990, 1991).

The politicization of crime by conservative politicians occurred at a time when the country was deeply divided over the Vietnam War and civil rights. In this historical context crime became a smokescreen behind which other issues could be relegated as less important. Crime served as well as legitimation for legislation designed primarily to suppress political dissent and overturn Supreme Court decisions (Chambliss and Sbarbaro 1993).

In addition to these political forces, and partly because of them, the crime control industry emerged as a powerful lobby. Law enforcement agencies control the information available about crime and, as noted above, manipulate the data to serve their purposes. In their effort to create moral panics, and thereby increase their budgets and power, law enforcement agencies are happily joined by media that are always hungry for stories that will increase their audience. Indeed, the media has become so dependent on crime news in recent years that in 1993 crime was the most frequently reported subject on television news (Media Monitor 1994). Between 1990 and 1993 the number of crime stories appearing on ABC, CBS, and NBC evening newscasts increased from 737 to 1,698.

Manipulating data, creating moral panics, and feeding the media crime stories can only go so far. Eventually arrests must be made, successful prosecutions carried out, and people sent to prison. For these symbols of effective law enforcement the large population of poor black males is the perfect bureaucratic solution. For here is a population without political clout, with few resources to successfully defend against criminal charges, and a public image as a group in which crime is endemic. Enforcing the law in the black ghetto enables the police, as one officer expressed it, to "rewrite the constitution every day."

A police officer's career and even his annual income is determined by the number of "good collars" he makes. A "good collar" is an arrest for what is defined as a serious violation of the law that culminates in a conviction. Drug arrests qualify. They are among the easiest convictions, the most difficult to defend, and often lead to the longest prison terms as a result of mandatory sentences. But they are organizationally effective only if the person arrested is relatively powerless. Arrests of white male middle-class offenders (on college campuses for example) are guaranteed to cause the organization and the arresting officers strain, as people with political influence and money hire attorneys for their defense. Arrests of poor black men, however, create only rewards for the organization and the officer as the cases are quickly processed through the courts, a guilty plea obtained, and the suspect sentenced. Organizations reward role occupants whose behavior maximizes rewards and minimizes strains for the organization. In a class society, the powerless, the poor, and those who fit the public stereotype of "the criminal" are the human resources needed by law enforcement agencies to maximize rewards and minimize strains. It is not surprising, but sociologically predictable, then, that doubling the number of police officers in the last ten years has tripled the number of people in prison and jail, filled these institutions with minor offenders, exacerbated the disproportionate imprisonment of minorities, and institutionalized racist beliefs that make being a young black man synonymous with being criminal.

SUMMARY AND CONCLUSIONS

Reversing the process will prove to be more difficult than instituting it. Political leaders will have to show the kind of courage shown by Lyndon Johnson and Hubert Humphrey who defied the conservative platform's call for more police and harsher penalties with pleas for more public spending on schools and jobs. Law enforcement agencies will have to change their reward system to emphasize community policing and rewarding officers who do not have to make arrests in their communities, rather than rewarding those who do. And the media will have to assume some responsibility for educating rather than sensationalizing. Social scientists can play a critical role by conducting studies of law enforcement in the communities most affected and communicating the results to policymakers and the public. It is unlikely, however, that any of these changes will take place so long as we continue to criminalize drugs and provide an incentive for police officers and prosecutors to entrap and arrest people for the possession or sale of small amounts of drugs. The longer it takes, the more lives will be lost and the more the United States will move toward a society permanently divided by race and class into communities that are quasi police states patrolled by RDU-type police units in search of crime, and communities where minor infractions of the law are treated, as they should be, as tolerable indiscretions.

NOTE

1. According to FBI statistics, approximately 10 percent of law enforcement personnel are now employed in specialized police units. In 1992 such specialized units accounted for 25 percent of police departments' budgets (Maguire, Pastore, and Flanagan, 1992).

REFERENCES

Anderson, Elijah. 1993. "Abolish welfare—then what?" *The Washington Post*, 13 December, A23.

Austin, James, and John Irwin. 1989. *Who Goes to Prison?* San Francisco: The National Council on Crime and Delinquency.

Bureau of Justice Statistics. 1992a. "Drugs, crime and the criminal justice system." Washington, D.C.: U.S. Department of Justice, NCJ 133652:28.

———. 1992b. "Criminal victimization in the United States: 1973–1990." Washington, D.C.: U.S. Department of Justice.

———. 1994. "Drug offenders in federal prison." Washington, D.C.: U.S. Department of Justice.

Chambliss, William J. 1991. Trading Textbooks for Prison Cells. Alexandria, VA: National Center on Institutions and Alternatives.

Chambliss, William J., and Edward Sbarbaro. 1993. "Moral panics and racial oppression." *Socio-Legal Bulletin*, Melbourne, Australia.

Christie, Nils. 1993. *Crime Control as Industry*. London: Routledge.

Cohen, Stanley. 1980. *Folk Devils and Moral Panics: The Creation of the Mods and Rockers*. New York: St. Martin's Press.

Gallup, George. 1993. *The Gallup Poll: Public Opinion, 1935-1993*. Wilmington, DE: Scholarly Resources.

Maguire, Kathleen, and Timothy J. Flanagan, eds. 1990. *Sourcebook of Criminal Justice Statistics 1990*. Washington, D.C.: Bureau of Justice Statistics.

Maguire, Kathleen, Ann Pastore, and Timothy J. Flanagan, eds. 1993. *Sourcebook of Criminal Justice Statistics*. U.S. Department of Justice, Bureau of Justice Statistics. Washington, D.C.: USGPO.

Media Monitor. 1994. 1993: *The Year in Review: TV's Leading News Topics, Reporters, and Political Jokes*. Washington, D.C.: Center for Media and Public Affairs. January/February.

Wilson, William Julius. 1987. *The Truly Disadvantaged: The Inner City, the Underclass, and Public Policy*. Chicago: University of Chicago Press.

———. 1993. *The Ghetto Underclass: Social Science Perspectives*. New York: Sage Publications.

EDITOR'S NOTE

William J. Chambliss's reading provides a systematic examination of traffic violations in the Washington, D.C., area a few years ago. One would hope that the D.C. findings were an aberration. However, statistics from an ABC *Dateline* program aired 1 April 2004 revealed that far from being rare, the Chambliss results appear to be part of a nationwide pattern of disproportionately ticketing African Americans for nonmoving violations.

Dateline conducted a study of over 4 million traffic tickets written between 1998 and 2002 in fourteen cities, including Boston, Springfield, and Worcester, Massachusetts; Houston, Texas; Minneapolis, Minnesota; Denver, Colorado; Kansas City and St. Louis, Missouri; San Diego, California; Dayton and Cincinnati, Ohio; Richmond, Virginia; Nashville, Tennessee; and Hartford, Connecticut. The research found significant differences between the number of nonmoving violations written for white and African-American drivers.[1]

The results of the study showed that in Boston, Springfield, Worcester, Cincinnati, Dayton, Richmond, and Denver, police were three times more likely to ticket African-American drivers than whites for nonmoving violations. In Kansas City, St. Louis, and San Diego, African Americans were two times as likely to be ticketed as were whites. In Houston and Minneapolis, African Americans were 50 percent more likely to be ticketed for nonmoving violations than were whites. Only in Nashville and Hartford did the study find no difference in ticketing for whites and African Americans for nonmoving violations.[2]

Dateline investigators reported that nonmoving violations are particularly problematic because the citation is not written until an officer actually stops the car. For example, a seat belt violation generally cannot be observed until the officer has already stopped a vehicle, or, if a person has an expired driver's license, an officer does not observe that until the officer has made the stop. The researchers analyzing the data concluded that police in the thirteen cities have demonstrated a pattern of discriminatory behavior that denies African-American drivers equal protection under the law.[3]

NOTES

1. *Dateline*, ABC News, New York, 1 April 2004.
2. Ibid.
3. Ibid.

14

America's Iron Curtain

The Border Patrol State

Leslie Marmon Silko

I used to travel the highways of New Mexico and Arizona with a wonderful sensation of absolute freedom as I cruised down the open road and across the vast desert plateaus. On the Laguna Pueblo reservation, where I was raised, the people were patriotic despite the way the U.S. government had treated Native Americans. As proud citizens, we grew up believing the freedom to travel was our inalienable right, a right that some Native Americans had been denied in the early twentieth century. Our cousin, old Bill Pratt, used to ride his horse three hundred miles overland from Laguna, New Mexico, to Prescott, Arizona, every summer to work as a fire lookout.

In school in the 1950s, we were taught that our right to travel from state to state without special papers or threat of detainment was a right that citizens under communist and totalitarian governments did not possess. That wide open highway told us we were U.S. citizens; we went free.

Not so long ago, my companion Gus and I were driving south from Albuquerque, returning to Tucson after a book promotion for the paperback edition of my novel *Almanac of the Dead*. I had settled back and gone to sleep while Gus drove, but I was awakened when I felt the car slowing to a stop. It was nearly midnight on New Mexico State Road 26, a dark, lonely stretch of two-lane highway between Hatch and Deming. When I sat up, I saw the headlights and emergency flashers of six vehicles—Border Patrol cars and a van were blocking both lanes of the highway. Gus stopped the car and rolled down the window to ask what was wrong. But the closest Border Patrolman and his companion did not reply; instead, the first agent ordered us to "step out of the car." Gus asked why, but his question seemed to set them off. Two more Border Patrol agents immediately approached our car, and one of them snapped, "Are you looking for trouble?" as if he would relish it.

I will never forget that night beside the highway. There was an awful feeling of menace and violence straining to break loose. It was clear that the uniformed men would be only too happy to drag us out of the car if we did not speedily comply with their request (asking a question is tantamount to resistance, it seems). So we stepped out of the car and they motioned for us to stand on the shoulder of the road. The night was very dark, and no other traffic had come down the road since we had been stopped. All I could think about was a book I had read—*Nunca Más*—the official report of a human rights commission that investigated and certified more than 12,000 "disappearances" during Argentina's "dirty war" in the late 1970s.

The weird anger of these Border Patrolmen made me think about descriptions in the report of Argentine police and military officers who became addicted to interrogation, torture, and the murder that followed. When the military and police ran out of political suspects to torture and kill, they resorted to the random abduction of citizens off the streets. I thought how easy it would be for the Border Patrol to shoot us and leave our bodies and car beside the highway, like so many bodies found in these parts and ascribed to "drug runners."

Two other Border Patrolmen stood by the white van. The one who had asked if we were looking for trouble ordered his partner to "get the dog," and from the back of the van another patrolman brought a small female German shepherd on a leash. The dog apparently did not heel well enough to suit him, and the handler jerked the leash. They opened the doors of our car and pulled the dog's head into it, but I saw immediately from the expression in her eyes that the dog hated them, and that she would not serve them. When she showed no interest in the inside of our car, they brought her around back to the trunk, near where we were standing. They half-dragged her up into the trunk, but still she did not indicate any stowed-away human beings or illegal drugs.

Their mood got uglier; the officers seemed outraged that the dog could not find any contraband, and they dragged her over to us and commanded her to sniff our legs and feet. To my relief, the strange violence the Border Patrol agents had focused on us now seemed shifted to the dog. I no longer felt so strongly that we would be murdered. We exchanged looks—the dog and I. She was afraid of what they might do, just as I was. The dog's handler jerked the leash sharply as she sniffed us, as if to make her perform better, but the dog refused to accuse us: She had an innate dignity that did not permit her to serve the murderous impulses of those men. I can't forget the expression in the dog's eyes; it was as if she were embarrassed to be associated with them. I had a small amount of medicinal marijuana in my purse that night, but she refused to expose me. I am not partial to dogs, but I will always remember the small German shepherd that night.

Unfortunately, what happened to me is an everyday occurrence here now. Since the 1980s, on top of greatly expanding border checkpoints, the Immigration and Naturalization Service (INS) and the Border Patrol have implemented policies that interfere with the rights of U.S. citizens to travel freely within our borders. INS agents now patrol all interstate highways and roads that lead to or from the U.S.-Mexico border in Texas, New Mexico, Arizona, and California. Now, when you drive east from Tucson on Interstate 10 toward El Paso, you encounter an INS check station outside Las Cruces, New Mexico. When you drive north from Las Cruces up Interstate 25, two miles north of the town of Truth or Consequences, the highway is blocked with orange emergency barriers, and all traffic is diverted into a two-lane Border Patrol checkpoint—ninety-five miles north of the U.S.-Mexico border.

I was detained once at Truth or Consequences, despite my and my companion's Arizona driver's licenses. Two men, both Chicanos, were detained at the same time, despite the fact that they too presented ID and spoke English without the thick Texas accents of the Border Patrol agents. While we were stopped, we watched as other vehicles—whose occupants were white—were waved through the checkpoint. White people traveling with brown people, however, can expect to be stopped on suspicion they work with the sanctuary movement, which shelters refugees. White people who appear to be clergy, those who wear ethnic clothing or jewelry and women with very long hair or very short hair (they could be nuns) are also frequently detained; white men with beards or men with long hair are likely to be detained, too, because Border Patrol agents have "profiles" of "those sorts" of white people who may help political refugees. (Most of the political refugees from Guatemala and El Salvador are Native American or mestizo because the indigenous people of the Americas have continued to resist efforts by invaders to displace them from their ancestral lands.) Alleged increases in illegal immigration of people of Asian ancestry means that the Border Patrol now routinely detains anyone who appears to be Asian or part Asian, as well.

Once your car is diverted from the Interstate Highway into the checkpoint area, you are under the control of the Border Patrol, which in practical terms exercises a power that no highway patrol or city patrolman possesses: They are willing to detain anyone, for no apparent reason. Other law-enforcement officers need a shred of probable cause in order to detain someone. On the books, so does the Border Patrol; but on the road, it's another matter. They'll order you to stop your car and step out; then they'll ask you to open the trunk. If you ask why or request a search warrant, you'll be told that they'll have to have a dog sniff the car before they can request a search warrant, and the dog might not get there for two or three hours. The search warrant might require an hour or two past that. They make it clear that if you force them to obtain a search warrant for the car, they will make you submit to a strip search as well.

Traveling in the open, though, the sense of violation can be even worse. Never mind high-profile cases like that of former Border Patrol agent Michael Elmer, acquitted of murder by claiming self-defense, despite admitting that as an officer he shot an "illegal" immigrant in the back and then hid the body, which remained undiscovered until another Border Patrolman reported the event. (Last month, Elmer was convicted of reckless endangerment in a separate incident, for shooting at least ten rounds from his M-16 too close to a group of immigrants as they were crossing illegally into Nogales in March 1992.) Or that in El Paso, a high school football coach driving a vanload of his players in full uniform was pulled over on the freeway and a Border Patrol agent put a cocked revolver to his head. (The football coach was Mexican-American, as were most of the players in his van; the incident eventually caused a federal judge to issue a restraining order against the Border Patrol.) We've a mountain of personal experiences like that which never make the newspapers. A history professor at U.C.L.A. told me she had been traveling by train from Los Angeles to Albuquerque twice a month doing research. On each of her trips, she'd noticed that the Border Patrol agents were at the station in Albuquerque scrutinizing the passengers. Since she is six feet tall and of Irish and German ancestry, she was not particularly concerned. Then one day when she stepped off the train in Albuquerque, two Border Patrolmen accosted her, wanting to know what she was doing, and why she was traveling between Los Angeles and Albuquerque twice a month. She presented identification and an explanation deemed "suitable" by the agents, and was allowed to go about her business.

Just the other day, I mentioned to a friend that I was writing this article and he told me about his seventy-three-year-old father, who is half Chinese and had set out alone by car from Tucson to Albuquerque the week before. His father had become confused by road construction and missed a turnoff from Interstate 10 to Interstate 25; when he turned around and circled back, he missed the turnoff a second time. But when he looped back for yet another try, Border Patrol agents stopped him and forced him to open his trunk. After they satisfied themselves the he was not smuggling Chinese immigrants, they sent him on his way. He was so rattled by the event that he had to be driven home by his daughter.

This is the police state that has developed in the southwestern United States since the 1980s. No person, no citizen, is free to travel without the scrutiny of the Border Patrol. In the city of South Tucson, where 80 percent of the respondents were Chicano or Mexicano, a joint research project by the University of Wisconsin and the University of Arizona recently concluded that one out of every five people there had been detained, mistreated verbally or nonverbally, or questioned by INS agents in the past two years.

Manifest Destiny may lack its old grandeur of theft and blood—"lock the door" is what it means now, with racism a trump card to be played again and again, shamelessly, by both major political parties. "Immigration," like "street crime" and "welfare fraud," is a political euphemism that refers to people of color. Politicians and media people talk about "illegal aliens" to dehumanize and demonize undocumented immigrants, who are for the most part people of color. Even in the days of Spanish and Mexican rule, no attempts were made to interfere with the flow of people and goods from south to north and north to south. It is the U.S. government that has continually attempted to sever contact between the tribal people north of the border and those to the south.[1]

Now that the "Iron Curtain" is gone, it is ironic that the U.S. government and its Border Patrol are constructing a steel wall ten feet high to span sections of the border with Mexico. While politicians and multinational corporations extol the virtues of NAFTA and "free trade" (in goods, not flesh), the ominous curtain is already up in a six-mile section at the border crossing at Mexicali; two miles are being erected but are not yet finished at Naco; and at Nogales, sixty miles south of Tucson, the steel wall has been all rubber-stamped and awaits construction likely to begin in March. Like the pathetic multimillion-dollar "antidrug" border surveillance balloons that were continually deflated by high winds and made only a couple of meager interceptions before they blew away, the fence along the border is a theatrical prop, a bit of pork for contractors. Border entrepreneurs have already used blowtorches to cut passageways through the fence to collect "tolls," and are doing a brisk business. Back in Washington, the INS announces a $300 million computer contract to modernize its record-keeping and Congress passes a crime bill that shunts $255 million to the INS for 1995, $181 million earmarked for border control, which is to include seven hundred new partners for the men who stopped Gus and me in our travels, and the history professor, and my friend's father, and as many as they could from South Tucson.

It is no use; borders haven't worked, and they won't work, not now, as the indigenous people of the Americas reassert their kinship and solidarity with one another. A mass migration is already under way; its roots are not simply economic. The Uto-Aztecan languages are spoken as far north as Taos Pueblo near the Colorado border, all the way south to Mexico City. Before the arrival of the Europeans, the indigenous communities throughout this region not only conducted commerce, the people shared cosmologies and oral narratives about the Maize Mother, the Twin Brothers and their Grandmother, Spider Woman, as well as Quetzalcoatl the benevolent snake. The great human migration within the Americas cannot be stopped; human beings are natural forces of the earth, just as rivers and winds are natural forces.

Deep down the issue is simple: The so-called Indian Wars from the days of Sitting Bull and Red Cloud have never really ended in the Americas. The Indian people of southern Mexico, of Guatemala, and those left in El Salvador, too, are still fighting for their lives and for their land against the "cavalry" patrols sent out by the governments of those lands. The Americas are Indian country, and the "Indian problem" is not about to go away.

One evening at sundown, we were stopped in traffic at a railroad crossing in downtown Tucson while a freight train passed us, slowly gaining speed as it headed north to Phoenix. In the twilight I saw the most amazing sight. Dozens of human beings, mostly young men, were riding the train; everywhere, on flat cars, inside open boxcars, perched on top of boxcars, hanging off ladders on tank cars and between boxcars. I couldn't count fast enough, but I saw fifty or sixty people headed north. They were dark young men, Indian and mestizo; they were smiling and a few of them waved at us in our cars. I was reminded of the ancient story of Aztlán, told by the Aztecs but known in other Uto-Aztecan communities as well. Aztlán is the beautiful land to the north, the origin place of the Aztec people. I don't remember how or why the people left Aztlán to journey farther south, but the old story says that one day, they will return.

NOTE

1. The Treaty of Guadalupe Hidalgo, signed in 1848, recognizes the right of the To-hano O'Odom (Papago) people to move freely across the U.S.-Mexico border without documents. A treaty with Canada guarantees similar rights to those of the Iroquois nation in traveling the U.S.-Canada border.

EDITOR'S NOTE

Leslie Marmon Silko's reading recounts the frustration of those who are dogged by the Border Patrol as they simply try to go about their everyday lives. Recent news accounts about the surveillance of the Mexican border raise more concerns.

Mexican workers do the agricultural work and other unpleasant work that the indigenous U.S. population refuses to do for a variety of reasons: (1) The work is generally labor intensive; (2) The work offers low compensation; and (3) The work often means unfair labor practices on the part of managers. In effect, the U.S. agricultural economy would likely grind to a halt without migrant workers (including illegal workers) from Mexico who labor under the conditions noted. The elephant in the room is the fact that the informal economy—the economy of illegal workers who are paid in cash without benefits under heinous conditions—is not separate from the formal economy as is generally portrayed; it is an integral part of it, including agribusiness, meat packing, and janitorial contractors, to name a few.

Thus, on the one hand we welcome the migrant workers and the day laborers to do the dirty work, at the same time billions are spent to stop the workers from crossing the border. Buried in this dance is the discrepancy between the monitoring of Mexico in search of illegal people vis-à-vis the monitoring of Canada.

For starters, the border between Canada and the United States is approximately 4,327 miles long and the land border between Mexico and the United States is about 1,356.[1] Although Canada's land border is longer by almost 3,000 miles, the focus of monitoring is on Mexico as the most recent statistics reveal:

The total sensors along the Canadian border number 1,271.
The total sensors along the Mexican border number 10,642.
The total cameras along the Canadian border number 59.
The total cameras along the Mexican border number 170[2]

Biometrics, another homeland security tool, relies on things like finger-prints, facial dimensions, and eye color, as well as other eye characteristics. The technology cost billions of dollars and has been used along the Mexican border. It reportedly has stopped almost 500,000 people crossing into Arizona.[3] However, there is no indication that biometrics are being used along the Canadian border.

All of these facts and figures raise questions: Why is Canada, with two and half times the length of Mexico's border, left more vulnerable than Mexico? Why, when it was through the Canadian border that a man entered in 2000 with the intent to blow up the Los Angeles airport, on New Year's, are things so lax along Canada? Why is there limited monitoring of Canada when an underground drug smuggling tunnel between Canada and the United States was discovered recently?

Why, too, if there is concern about monitoring, is there little oversight in how the funds are spent? For example, International Microwave Corporation (IMC) billed the government for fifty-nine cameras but only four were installed and, in Arizona, equipment was delivered in 2003, but no IMC workers have returned to install it. The General Services Administration filed a report indicating that millions of dollars of overcharges might have occurred and overpayment of as much as $13 million has possibly occurred.[4] This discussion doesn't even touch on the nepotism that allegedly abounds in the awarding of contracts of monitoring equipment. Do you get the picture?

NOTES

1. John Mintz, "A Closer Look at the Electronic Border Patrol," *The Washington Post National Weekly Edition*, 18–24 April 2005, pp. 29–30.

2. Ibid.

3. Eric Lipton, "Hurdles for High-Tech Efforts to Track Who Crosses Borders," *The New York Times*, 10 August 2005, pp. A1, A13.

4. Ibid.

15

The Heartland's Raw Deal

How Meatpacking is Creating a New Immigrant Underclass

Marc Cooper

In a sweeping regional arc from the Dakotas through Minnesota, Nebraska, and Iowa, and down through Kansas into northern Texas and the foothills of the Missouri Ozarks, dozens of once lily-white heartland meatpacking communities have become the new homes to tens of thousands of impoverished Third World workers.

Putting the lie to the conventional wisdom undergirding our immigration policy, the arrival of these workers en masse is neither serendipitous nor the product of cunning smugglers. Rather, it is the direct result of a conscious survival strategy; undertaken by a key U.S. industry, a plan developed and fully implemented only in the past few years.

Beef, pork, and poultry packers have been aggressively recruiting the most vulnerable of foreign workers to relocate to the U.S. plains in exchange for $6-an-hour jobs in the country's most dangerous industry. Since permanence is hardly a requirement for these jobs, the concepts of promotion and significant salary increase have as much as disappeared. That as many as half of these new immigrants lack legal residence seems no obstacle to an industry now thriving on a docile, disempowered workforce with an astronomical turnover.

Staggering illness and injury rates—thirty-six per one hundred workers in meat—and stress caused by difficult, repetitive work often means employment for just a few months before a worker quits or the company forces him or her off the job. (Government safety inspections have dropped 43 percent overall since 1994, because of budget cuts and an increasingly probusiness slant at the Occupational Safety and Health Administration.) When disabled workers and their families remain in their new homes, the social cost of their survival is then passed by the company to the public.

Less than fifty yards from Iowa Beef Processor's (IBP) shipping depot, we visit women living in a series of railroad shacks in conditions so bad that they remind me of the scavengers I once saw living in wooden huts in Seoul. Their small rooms are overwhelmed with the medicinal reek of Ben-Gay and Tiger Balm, used in industrial quantities to quench the fire in fingers and elbows pushed to their limit by work on the slaughterhouse floor.

LIFE UNDERGROUND

Unlike the Lao, who are all legal residents, something like half the Latino workers and their families here are undocumented. Several workers tell me that valid Social Security cards—that belong to others—can be purchased for $300 to $500 and that the company does no checking. Other workers contend that IBP management personnel moonlight in document-trafficking. That's a story the company denies.

IBP openly admits that many of these Latinos—legal residents and otherwise—have come here recruited by the company, which has consistently used labor brokers to comb the border areas in south Texas and California to shuttle up new recruits at as much as $300 a head. A cursory look at a birth certificate or Social Security card was enough to satisfy the broker and the personnel department that the labor draftees were legal.

"The company loves to work with illegals," says forty-five-year-old Heriberto from inside his trailer, a few yards away from the scene of the December fire. "When you are illegal you can't talk back," he adds. Heriberto brings home $300 for a six-day, forty-eight-hour week. One paycheck goes for trailer rent. Another is sent back to relatives in Mexico. "You keep your head down and follow orders. We say you can't do nothing." Switching to Spanish, he says, "*Dices nada porque la planta es del gobierno*" (You say nothing because the plant is the government). Indeed. Though Latinos make up about a quarter of the IBP workforce and have the most dangerous jobs, Latino surnames show up on less than 5 percent of the worker comp claims filed between 1987 and 1995.

There's a constant commerce of workers, relatives, and friends between Storm Lake and Santa Rita. This human conveyor belt is powered by the grueling work regimen, which generates an astonishing worker turnover rate of more than 80 percent a year—a rate common to the entire industry. "Perfect for the company," says Heriberto. "Most workers leave before six months is up and the company has to start paying health insurance."

Meanwhile, in 1995 IBP stripped off a juicy $257 million in profits on sales of $12 billion. Its CEO, Robert Peterson, made $1 million in salary and $5.2 million in bonuses that year. Storm Lake shows none of the blight that metastasized through the region after the 1980s' farm collapse. Its small and tidy downtown has no board-ups or vacancies. Four locally owned banks are thriving. The housing market is corset-tight. "You can't even rent," says Mayor Sandra Madsen. "We have two big payrolls, a stable downtown. Five years from now I think this town will realize we are all better off for the change we have gone through."

Perhaps. But for the moment, the dominant atmosphere is one of apartheid. "Race determines everything here," says an outreach worker to the Latino community. "Where you live, where you work, how much you earn, where you worship, even where you shop. . . ."

When I stop to make a phone call from the local Conoco station, two locals overhear me speaking in Spanish. "Fuckin' Mexican should learn English," one says loudly to the other. The editor of the forward-looking *Storm Lake Times*, which has been a "prodiversity" voice, jokes that the local good old boys like to call his paper "The Gook Times."

A lot of the local xenophobes had their big moment last May, when on a Friday afternoon seventeen armed Border Patrol officers—backed up by agents from the Immigration and Naturalization Service, units from local law enforcement, and surveillance planes circling over the IBP plant—staged an almost tragicomic raid on Storm Lake. In what amounted to a military occupation, agents spent two days going door to door in Little Mexico, setting up roadblocks, and rousting suspects off the street in a sweep for illegals. A U.S. attorney even showed up to take credit for an operation he had little to do with. Prodded into action by the local police chief, who along with the INS had built up a database of some six hundred suspected illegal aliens in town, the federal agents eventually arrested and deported a total of seventy-eight Latinos.

But when hundreds of other fearful workers—likely all undocumented or with false ID—failed to show up for work the next Monday and the pork began to spoil, IBP management panicked. In a story corroborated by several sources, executives started calling community workers who have the confidence of their Latino clients. "IBP told us to tell everyone to come back to work that afternoon," says a social worker. "It was O.K. now. The INS was gone and nobody was going to check anything."

Within a few weeks, say several workers, even some of those deported to Mexico were back on the job. "They just got some new ID," says one worker. "And the same gringos who turned them in hired them back like nothing had happened." After the raid was over an INS official met with the press and said IBP had cooperated in the raid and would face no employer sanctions or fines.

"YOUR TIRED, YOUR POOR"

The bitter strike at Hormel's Austin, Minnesota, plant in 1985–1986 (the subject of Barbara Kopple's Academy Award–winning documentary, *American Dream*) was the signal event in a labor counterrevolution that has convulsed and redrawn the face of U.S. meatpacking. And if you could boil that counterrevolution down into one slogan it would be: Death to Middle-Class Meatpackers!

The space now occupied by IBP was the old Hygrade plant. The workforce, unionized and virtually all white, was averaging $30,000 a year or more—some $51,000 in today's dollars. Refusing to reach agreement with its unions, Hygrade closed down in 1981.

After being enticed with $10 million in local tax subsidies, IBP reopened the plant a year later, offering $6 an hour. The pattern of deunionization and ruralization was regional. One after another, meatpacking plants moved from the big cities, where they were close to labor, into the countryside, where they were near the animals and could save on transport costs. As supermarkets took on more specialty butchers, the processing plants needed more, but less-skilled, workers. Unions became anathema. The industry's hourly pay, including benefits, peaked at $19 in 1980. By 1992 it was below 1960s levels at $12 an hour, and it has continued to fall. By 1995 unionization was half of what it was in 1963.

Where the new plants opened, labor was in relatively short supply. And even in Storm Lake, where hundreds of former Hygrade workers reapplied for the new jobs, IBP hired back only thirty. "The company wanted to bar union-experienced workers from the shop floor," says Mary Grey. With just a few companies—IBP, Cargill, Con-Agra—dominating the field, competition was, no pun intended, cutthroat. Production lines were sped up; injury rates climbed. What was once a stable workforce became frenetically mobile.

WITH A WINK AND A HANDCUFF

Since 1992 the INS has arrested more than 1,000 meatpacking workers in the Midwest. This past summer, as part of a six-week regional sweep ordered by the Clinton administration, 209 undocumented workers were detained in Iowa. The average pay for those arrested was $6.02 an hour. Now the four biggest meatpackers, including IBP and Swift, have agreed to participate in an INS program that will use computers to check IDs.

Local Latino workers laugh it all off. "Everyone knows the company and the INS are in together on all this. They never make the company pay a fine, do they?" says Javier, an IBP worker in Storm Lake who works under the ID he purchased in the name of a legal resident. "Everyone knows they are never going to arrest all of us. Who would do this shitty work for them? We know that every now and then the *migra* will come in and take a few away to keep the politicians happy. And then we won't see them again for another two years. That's how it works."

For more than a century now there's been a pattern of U.S. industries—one after another—actively recruiting Mexican labor while the rest of society turned a blind eye, says Fred Krissman, anthropologist at Washington State University. "You can go back to the 1920s and find all sorts of academic research in that period referring to Mexicans who could be brought here to work and then sent back home like homing pigeons to procreate." And there's always been that cognitive dissonance between the reality and the policy. "In 1954 during what was called Operation Wetback, a million Mexicans were randomly rounded up in the United States and deported," says Krissman. "At the same time we were bringing in 300,000 Mexicans in the Bracero program. We had trains running both ways on public money!"

The solution, he argues, is to dump current immigration policy and opt for the model of the European Union. When you have a system that frees the flow of capital across borders, you should move toward a transnationalization of labor, too. If you work in the United States you should have legal papers in the United States, and all such workers should be protected by serious enforcement of health and safety regulations on the books. This doesn't mean immigrant workers would suddenly make middle-class wages, but it would be the first step toward eliminating the employer abuses rained down on people with no legal standing. Most important, it would be a radical leap toward stabilizing these now-underground communities. At best, unions would have a better shot at organizing; at a minimum, individual workers would stand a better chance of raising their wages.

This is not a likely option when politicians from both parties struggle to outdo each other in cracking down on illegal aliens.

EDITOR'S NOTE

If we were to close the borders and deport the illegals, "crops would rot in the fields, bathrooms would stay dirty, mothers of small children would be stuck at home. America is addicted to cheap labor . . . we maintain the pretense that we don't want a docile underclass of workers coming into the United States."[1]

Marc Cooper's article resonates a hundredfold today, yet the policing intensifies, billions of dollars are being spent, and wildlife refuges are reportedly being ruined, all in the effort to stop illegal immigrants from coming to the United States to take jobs that you and I won't do. Would you like to spend your summers picking fruit twelve hours a day for less than minimum wage? Or meatpacking?

Meatpackers "perform the most dangerous factory jobs in the country. . . . Faster, faster, get the product out the door . . . the results are cuts, amputations."[2] Not only are Mexican workers cost-effective laborers for agribusiness, meatpacking, and janitorial services, they are 80 percent more likely to die on the job than are native-born workers. Ninety-five percent of the time, the death could have been prevented by compliance with industry standards. Mexican workers are hired cheap, provided little training, and no questions asked.[3] Occupational Safety and Health Administration has no data to determine speed of work in the meatpacking industry because "companies refuse to let regulators . . . measure line speed . . . examine workers' knife cutting motion or study musculoskeletal injuries from repeated hard cutting."[4] Due to their vulnerable status, illegal immigrant workers fail to file injury claims, making them the most desirable employees.

What drives these folks to risk their lives (750 "official" deaths have been documented in the Arizona desert since 2000)? One factor is NAFTA. Hailed as the savior of American and Mexican economies, it has had a negative impact on tens of thousands of small Mexican farmers who lost their livelihood because they couldn't compete with inexpensive American corn. Another factor is the loss of many of the border factories that moved to Asia in search of even cheaper labor.[5] Mothers and fathers, sisters and brothers come for survival.

In its arsenal the Border Patrol is doubling the number of agents, Black Hawk helicopters, planes, all terrain vehicles, and motorcycles all of which is slowly destroying wildlife preserves and protected areas.[6] Like tracking wild animals, agents look for fresh tracks and flattened grass as they round up unarmed, weary men and women who will work for nearly nothing, who won't complain, and who are desperate.[7]

What drives people to become Border Patrol agents? Mike McCarson liked the gun-slinging look of agents who worked without supervision. He says: "I liked to hunt and fish, and it looked more like huntin' and fishin' than working—they'd give you a vehicle and you were on your own."[8]

NOTES

1. Renee Downing, "Border Control," *The Washington Post National Weekly Edition*, 9–15 May 2005, p. 22.

2. Lance Compa and Jamie Fellner, "Meatpacking's Human Toll," *The Washington Post National Weekly Edition*, 8–14 August 2005, p. 26.

3. Justin Pritchard, "'Disposable' Employees," *The Cincinnati Enquirer*, 14 March 2004, p. A22.

4. Compa and Fellner, p. 26.

5. Downing, p. 22.

6. Ibid.

7. Jeff Tietz, "On the Border: Fine Disturbances," *The New Yorker*, 29 November 2004, pp. 90, 92, 95–98, 100–1.

8. Tietz, p. 96.

VI

STRUCTURED INEQUALITY—
ACQUIRING GENDER

16

Bodies that Matter

On the Discursive Limits of "Sex"

Judith Butler

FROM CONSTRUCTION TO MATERIALIZATION

The relation between culture and nature presupposed by some models of gender "construction" implies a culture or an agency of the social which acts upon a nature, which is itself presupposed as a passive surface, outside the social and yet its necessary counterpart. One question that feminists have raised, then, is whether the discourse which figures the action of construction as a kind of imprinting or imposition is not tacitly masculinist, whereas the figure of the passive surface, awaiting that penetrating act whereby meaning is endowed, is not tacitly or—perhaps—quite obviously feminine. Is sex to gender as feminine is to masculine?[1]

Other feminist scholars have argued that the very concept of nature needs to be rethought, for the concept of nature has a history, and the figuring of nature as the blank and lifeless page, as that which is, as it were, always already dead, is decidedly modern, linked perhaps to the emergence of technological means of domination. Indeed, some have argued that a rethinking of "nature" as a set of dynamic interrelations suits both feminist and ecological aims (and has for some produced an otherwise unlikely alliance with the work of Gilles Deleuze). This rethinking also calls into question the model of construction whereby the social unilaterally acts on the natural and invests it with its parameters and its meanings. Indeed, as much as the radical distinction between sex and gender has been crucial to the de Beauvoirian version of feminism, it has come under criticism in more recent years for degrading the natural as that which is "before" intelligibility, in need of the mark, if not the mar, of the social to signify, to be known, to acquire value. This misses the point that nature has a history, and not merely a social one, but, also, that sex

145

is positioned ambiguously in relation to that concept and its history. The concept of "sex" is itself troubled terrain, formed through a series of contestations over what ought to be decisive criteria for distinguishing between the two sexes; the concept of sex has a history that is covered over by the figure of the site or surface of inscription. Figured as such a site or surface however, the natural is construed as that which is also without value; moreover, it assumes its value at the same time that it assumes its social character, that is, at the same time that nature relinquishes itself as the natural. According to this view, then, the social construction of the natural presupposes the cancellation of the natural by the social. Insofar as it relies on this construal, the sex/ gender distinction founders along parallel lines; if gender is the social significance that sex assumes within a given culture—and for the sake of argument we will let "social" and "cultural" stand in any uneasy interchangeability— then what, if anything, is left of "sex" once it has assumed its social character as gender? At issue is the meaning of "assumption," where to be "assumed" is to be taken up into a more elevated sphere, as in "the Assumption of the Virgin." If gender consists of the social meanings that sex assumes, then sex does not *accrue* social meanings as additive properties but, rather, *is replaced* by the social meanings it takes on; sex is relinquished in the course of that assumption, and gender emerges, not as a term in a continued relationship of opposition to sex, but as the term which absorbs and displaces "sex" the mark of its full substantiation into gender or what, from a materialist point of view, might constitute a full *de*substantiation.

When the sex/gender distinction is joined with a notion of radical linguistic constructivism, the problem becomes even worse, for the "sex" which is referred to as prior to gender will itself be a postulation, a construction, offered within language, as that which is prior to language, prior to construction. But this sex posited as prior to construction will, by virtue of being posited, become the effect of that very positing, the construction of construction. If gender is the social construction of sex, and if there is no access to this "sex" except by means of its construction, then it appears not only that sex is absorbed by gender but that "sex" becomes something like a fiction, perhaps a fantasy, retroactively installed at a prelinguistic site to which there is no direct access.

But is it right to claim that "sex" vanishes altogether, that it is a fiction over and against what is true, that it is a fantasy over and against what is reality? Or do these very oppositions need to be rethought such that if "sex" is a fiction, it is one within whose necessities we live, without which life itself would be unthinkable? And if "sex" is a fantasy, is it perhaps a phantasmatic field that constitutes the very terrain of cultural intelligibility? Would such a rethinking of such conventional oppositions entail a rethinking of "constructivism" in its usual sense?

The radical constructivist position has tended to produce the premise that both refutes and confirms its own enterprise. If such a theory cannot take account of sex as the site or surface on which it acts, then it ends up presuming sex as the unconstructed, and so concedes the limits of linguistic constructivism, inadvertently circumscribing that which remains unaccountable within the terms of construction. If, on the other hand, sex is a contrived premise, a fiction, then gender does not presume a sex which it acts upon, but rather, gender produces the misnomer of a prediscursive "sex" and the meaning of construction becomes that of linguistic monism, whereby everything is only and always language. Then, what ensues is an exasperated debate that many of us have tired of hearing: Either (1) constructivism is reduced to a position of linguistic monism, whereby linguistic construction is understood to be generative and deterministic. Critics making that presumption can be heard to say, "If everything is discourse, what about the body?" or (2) when constructing is figuratively reduced to a verbal action which appears to presuppose a subject, critics working within such a presumption can be heard to say, "If gender is constructed, then who is doing the constructing?"; though, of course, (3) the most pertinent formulation of this question is the following: "If the subject is constructed, then who is constructing the subject?" In the first case, construction has taken the place of a godlike agency which not only causes but composes everything which is its object; it is the divine performative, bringing into being and exhaustively constituting that which it names, or, rather, it is that kind of transitive referring which names and inaugurates at once. For something to be constructed, according to this view of construction, is for it to be created and determined through that process.

In the second and third cases, the seductions of grammar appear to hold sway; the critic asks, Must there not be a human agent, a subject, if you will, who guides the course of construction? If the first version of constructivism presumes that construction operates deterministically, making a mockery of human agency, the second understands constructivism as presupposing a voluntarist subject who makes its gender through an instrumental action. A construction is understood in this latter case to be a kind of manipulable artifice, a conception that not only presupposes a subject, but rehabilitates precisely the voluntarist subject of humanism that constructivism has, on occasion, sought to put into question.

If gender is a construction, must there be an "I" or a "we" who enacts or performs that construction? How can there be an activity, a constructing, without presupposing an agent who precedes and performs that activity? How would we account for the motivation and direction of construction without such a subject? As a rejoinder, I would suggest that it takes a certain suspicion toward grammar to reconceive the matter in a different light. For if gender is constructed, it is not necessarily constructed by an "I" or a "we" who stands before that construction in any spatial or temporal sense of "before." Indeed, it is unclear that there can be an "I" or a "we" who has not been submitted, subjected to gender, where gendering is, among other things, the differentiating relations by which speaking subjects come into being. Subjected to gender, but subjectivated by gender, the "I" neither precedes nor follows the process of this gendering, but emerges only within and as the matrix of gender relations themselves.

This then returns us to the second objection, the one which claims that constructivism forecloses agency, preempts the agency of the subject, and finds itself presupposing the subject that it calls into question. To claim that the subject is itself produced in and as a gendered matrix of relations is not to do away with the subject, but only to ask after the conditions of its emergence and operation. The "activity" of this gendering cannot, strictly speaking, be a human act or expression, a willful appropriation, and it is certainly *not* a question of taking on a mask; it is the matrix through which all willing first becomes possible, its enabling cultural condition. In this sense, the matrix of gender relations is prior to the emergence of the "human." Consider the medical interpellation which (the recent emergence of the sonogram notwithstanding) shifts an infant from an "it" to a "she" or a "he," and in that naming, the girl is "girled," brought into the domain of language and kinship through the interpellation of gender. But that "girling" of the girl does not end there; on the contrary, that founding interpellation is reiterated by various authorities and throughout various intervals of time to reenforce or contest this naturalized effect. The naming is at once the setting of a boundary, and also the repeated inculcation of a norm.

Such attributions or interpellations contribute to that field of discourse and power that orchestrates, delimits, and sustains that which qualifies as "the human." We see this most clearly in the examples of those abjected beings who do not appear properly gendered; it is their very humanness that comes into question. Indeed, the construction of gender operates through *exclusionary* means, such that the human is not only produced over and against the inhuman, but through a set of foreclosures, radical erasures, that are, strictly speaking, refused the possibility of cultural articulation. Hence, it is not enough to claim that human subjects are constructed, for the construction of the human is a differential operation that produces the more and the less "human," the inhuman, the humanly unthinkable. These excluded sites come to bound the "human" as its constitutive outside, and to haunt those boundaries as the persistent possibility of their disruption and rearticulation.[2]

There are defenders and critics of construction, who construe that position along structuralist lines. They often claim that there are structures that construct the subject, impersonal forces, such as Culture or Discourse or Power, where these terms occupy the grammatical site of the subject after the "human" has been dislodged from its place. In such a view, the grammatical and metaphysical place of the subject is retained even as the candidate that occupies that place appears to rotate. As a result, construction is still understood as a unilateral process initiated by a prior subject, fortifying that presumption of the metaphysics of the subject that where there is activity, there lurks behind it an initiating and willful subject. On such a view, discourse or language or the social becomes personified, and in the personification the metaphysics of the subject is reconsolidated.

In this second view, construction is not an activity, but an act, one which happens once and whose effects are firmly fixed. Thus, constructivism is reduced to determinism and implies the evacuation or displacement of human agency.

And here it would be no more right to claim that the term "construction" belongs at the grammatical site of subject, for construction is neither a subject nor its act, but a process of reiteration by which both "subjects" and "acts" come to appear at all. There is no power that acts, but only a reiterated acting that is power in its persistence and instability.

What I would propose in place of these conceptions of construction is a return to the notion of matter, not as site or surface, but as *a process of materialization that stabilizes over time to produce the effect of boundary, fixity, and surface we call matter.* That matter is always materialized has, I think, to be thought in relation to the productive and, indeed, materializing effects of regulatory power in the Foucaultian sense.[3] Thus, the question is no longer, "How is gender constituted as and through a certain interpretation of sex?" (a question that leaves the "matter" of sex untheorized), but rather, "Through what regulatory norms is sex itself materialized?" And how is it that treating the materiality of sex as a given presupposes and consolidates the normative conditions of its own emergence?

Crucially, then, construction is neither a single act nor a causal process initiated by a subject and culminating in a set of fixed effects. Construction not only takes place *in* time, but is itself a temporal process which operates through the reiteration of norms; sex is both produced and destabilized in the course of this reiteration.[4] As a sedimented effect of a reiterative or ritual practice, sex acquires its naturalized effect, and yet, it is also by virtue of this reiteration that gaps and fissures are opened up as the constitutive instabilities in such constructions, as that which escapes or exceeds the norm, as that which cannot be wholly defined or fixed by the repetitive labor of that norm. This instability is the *de*constituting possibility in the very process of repetition, the power that undoes the very effects by which "sex" is stabilized, the possibility to put the consolidation of the norms of "sex" into a potentially productive crisis.[5]

To "concede" the undeniability of "sex" or its "materiality" is always to concede some version of "sex," some formation of "materiality." Is the discourse in and through which that concession occurs—and, yes, that concession invariably does occur—not itself formative of the very phenomenon that it concedes? To claim that discourse is formative is not to claim that it originates, causes, or exhaustively composes that which it concedes; rather, it is to claim that there is no reference to a pure body which is not at the same time a further formation of that body. In this sense, the linguistic capacity to refer to sexed bodies is not denied, but the very meaning of "referentiality" is altered. In philosophical terms, the constative claim is always to some degree performative.

In relation to sex, then, if one concedes the materiality of sex or of the body, does that very conceding operate—performatively—to materialize that sex?

And further, how is it that the reiterated concession of that sex—one which need not take place in speech or writing but might be "signaled" in a much more inchoate way—constitutes the sedimentation and production of that material effect?

The moderate critic might concede that *some part* of "sex" is constructed, but some other is certainly not, and then, of course, find him or herself not only under some obligation to draw the line between what is and is not constructed, but to explain how it is that "sex" comes in parts whose differentiation is not a matter of construction. But as that line of demarcation between such ostensible parts gets drawn, the "unconstructed" becomes bounded once again through a signifying practice, and the very boundary which is meant to protect some part of sex from the taint of constructivism is now defined by the anti-constructivist's own construction. Is construction something that happens to a ready-made object, a pregiven thing, and does it happen in *degree*? Or are we perhaps referring on both sides of the debate to an inevitable practice of signification, of demarcating and delimiting that to which we then "refer," such that our "references" always presuppose—and often conceal—this prior delimitation? Indeed, to "refer" naively or directly to such an extra-discursive object will always require the prior delimitation of the extra-discursive. And. insofar as the extra-discursive is delimited, it is formed by the very discourse from which it seeks to free itself. This delimitation, which often is enacted as an untheorized presupposition in any act of description, marks a boundary that includes and excludes, that decides, as it were, what will and will not be the stuff or the object to which we then refer. This marking off will have some normative force and, indeed, some violence, for it can construct only through erasing; it can bound a thing only through enforcing a certain criterion, a principle of selectivity.

What will and will not be included within the boundaries of "sex" will be set by a more or less tacit operation of exclusion. If we call into question the fixity of the structuralist law that divides and bounds the "sexes" by virtue of their dyadic differentiation within the heterosexual matrix, it will be from the exterior regions of that boundary (not from a "position," but from the discursive possibilities opened up by the constitutive outside of hegemonic positions), and it will constitute the disruptive return of the excluded from within the very logic of the heterosexual symbolic.

NOTES

1. See Sherry Ortner, "Is Female to Male as Nature is to Culture?" in *Woman, Culture, and Society*, Michele Rosaldo and Louise Lamphere (eds.) (Stanford: Stanford University Press, 1974) pp. 67–88.

2. For different but related approaches to this problematic of exclusion, abjection, and the creation of "the human," see Julia Kristeva, *Powers of Horror: An Essay on Abjec-*

tion, trans. Leon Roudiez (New York: Columbia University Press, 1982); John Fletcher and Andrew Benjamin, eds., *Abjection, Melancholia and Love: The Work of Julia Kristeva* (New York and London: Routledge, 1990); Jean-François Lyotard, *The Inhuman Reflections on Time*, trans. Geoffrey Bennington and Rachel Bowlby (Stanford: Stanford University Press, 1991).

3. Although Foucault distinguishes between juridical and productive models of power in *The History of Sexuality, Volume One*, trans. Robert Hurley (New York: Vintage, 1978), I have argued that the two models presuppose each other. The production of a subject—its subjection (*assujetissement*)—is one means of its regulation. See my "Sexual Inversions," in Domna Stanton, ed., *Discourses of Sexuality* (Ann Arbor: University of Michigan Press, 1992), pp. 344–61.

4. It is not simply a matter of construing performativity as a repetition of acts, as if "acts" remain intact and self-identical as they are repeated in time, and where "time" is understood as external to the "acts" themselves. On the contrary, an act is itself a repetition, a sedimentation, and congealment of the past that is precisely foreclosed in its act-like status. In this sense an "act" is always a provisional failure of memory. In what follows, I make use of the Lacanian notion that every act is to be construed as a repetition, the repetition of what cannot be recollected, of the irrecoverable, and is thus the haunting spectre of the subject's deconstitution. The Derridean notion of iterability, formulated in response to the theorization of speech acts by John Searle and J. L. Austin, also implies that every act is itself a recitation, the citing of a prior chain of acts which are implied in a present act and which perpetually drain any "present" act of its presentness.

5. The notion of temporality ought not to be construed as a simple succession of distinct "moments," all of which are equally distant from one another. Such a spatialized mapping of time substitutes a certain mathematical model for the kind of duration that resists such spatializing metaphors. Efforts to describe or name this temporal span tend to engage spatial mapping, as philosophers from Bergson through Heidegger have argued. Hence, it is important to underscore the effect of *sedimentation* that the temporality of construction implies. Here what are called "moments" are not distinct and equivalent units of time, for the "past" will be the accumulation and congealing of such "moments" to the point of their indistinguishability. But it will also consist of that which is refused from construction, the domains of the repressed, forgotten, and the irrecoverably foreclosed. That which is not included—exteriorized by boundary—as a phenomenal constituent of the sedimented effect called "construction" will be as crucial to its definition as that which is included; this exteriority is not distinguishable as a "moment." Indeed, the notion of the "moment" may well be nothing other than a retrospective fantasy of mathematical mastery imposed upon the interrupted durations of the past.

To argue that construction is fundamentally a matter of iteration is to make the temporal modality of "construction" into a priority. To the extent that such a theory requires a spatialization of time through the postulation of discrete and bounded moments, this temporal account of construction presupposes a spatialization of temporality itself, what one might, following Heidegger, understand as the reduction of temporality to time.

The Foucaultian emphasis on *convergent* relations of power (which might in a tentative way be contrasted with the Derridean emphasis on iterability) implies a mapping of power relations that in the course of a genealogical process form a constructed effect. The notion of convergence presupposes both motion and space; as a result, it appears to elude the paradox noted above in which the very account of temporality requires the specialization of the "moment." On the other hand, Foucault's account of convergence does not fully theorize what is at work in the "movement" by which power and discourse are said to converge. In a sense, the "mapping" of power does not fully theorize temporality.

Significantly, the Derridean analysis of testability is to be distinguished from simple repetition in which the distances between temporal "moments" are treated as uniform in their spatial extension. The "betweenness" that differentiates "moments" of time is not one that can, within Derridean terms, be spatialized or bounded as an identifiable, object. It is the monthematizable différance that erodes and contests any and all claims to discrete identity, including the discrete identity of the "moment." What differentiates moments is not a spatially extended duration, for if it were, it would also count as a "moment," and so fail to account for what falls between moments. This "entre," that which is at once "between" and "outside," is something like nonthematizable space and nonthematizable time as they converge.

Foucault's language of construction includes terms like "augmentation," "proliferation," and "convergence," all of which presume a temporal domain not explicitly theorized. Part of the problem here is that whereas Foucault appears to want his account of genealogical effects to be historically specific, he would favor an account of genealogy over a philosophical account of temporality: In "The Subject and Power" (Hubert Dreyfus and Paul Rabinow, eds., *Michel Foucault: Beyond Structuralism and Hermeneutics* [Chicago: Northwestern University Press, 1983]), Foucault refers to "the diversity of . . . logical sequence" that characterizes power relations. He would doubtless reject the apparent linearity implied by models of iterability that link them with the linearity of older models of historical sequence. And yet, we do not receive a specification of "sequence": Is it the very notion of "sequence" that varies historically, or are there configurations of sequence that vary, with sequence itself remaining invariant? The specific-social formation and figuration of temporality is in some ways unattended by both positions. Here one might consult the work of Pierre Bourdieu to understand the temporality of social construction.

17

Believing Is Seeing

Biology as Ideology

Judith Lorber

Until the eighteenth century, Western philosophers and scientists thought that there was one sex and that women's internal genitalia were the inverse of men's external genitalia: the womb and vagina were the penis and scrotum turned inside out (Laqueur 1990).

In actuality, the basic bodily material is the same for females and males, and except for procreative hormones and organs, female and male human beings have similar bodies (Naftolin and Butz 1981). Furthermore, as has been known since the middle of the nineteenth century, male and female genitalia develop from the same fetal tissue, and so infants can be born with ambiguous genitalia (Money and Ehrhardt 1972). When they are, biology is used quite arbitrarily in sex assignment. Suzanne Kessler (1990) interviewed six medical specialists in pediatric intersexuality and found that whether an infant with XY chromosomes and anomalous genitalia was categorized as a boy or girl depended on the size of the penis—if a penis was very small, the child was categorized as a girl, and sex-change surgery was used to make an artificial vagina. In the late nineteenth century, the presence or absence of ovaries was the determining criterion of gender assignment for hermaphrodites because a woman who could not procreate was not a complete woman (Kessler 1990, 20).

Yet in Western societies, we see two discrete sexes and two distinguishable genders because our society is built on two classes of people, "women" and "men." Once the gender category is given, the attributes of the person are also gendered: Whatever a "woman" is has to be "female"; whatever a "man" is has to be "male." Analyzing the social processes that construct the categories we call "female and male," "women and men," and "homosexual and heterosexual" uncovers the ideology and power differentials congealed in these categories (Foucault 1978). This article will use two familiar areas of social life—sports and technological competence—to show how myriad physiological differences are transformed into similar-appearing, gendered social bodies. My perspective goes beyond accepted feminist views that gender is a cultural overlay that modifies physiological sex differences. That perspective assumes either that there are two fairly similar sexes distorted by social practices into two genders with purposefully different characteristics or that there are two sexes whose essential differences are rendered unequal by social practices. I am arguing that bodies differ in many ways physiologically, but they are completely transformed by social practices to fit into the salient categories of a society, the most pervasive of which are "female" and "male" and "women" and "men."

Neither sex nor gender are pure categories. Combinations of incongruous genes, genitalia, and hormonal input are ignored in sex categorization, just as combinations of incongruous physiology, identity, sexuality, appearance, and behavior are ignored in the social construction of gender statuses. Menstruation, lactation, and gestation do not demarcate women from men. Only some women are pregnant and then only some of the time; some women do not have a uterus or ovaries. Some women have stopped menstruating temporarily, others have reached menopause, and some have had hysterectomies. Some women breastfeed some of the time, but some men lactate (Jaggar 1983, 165fn). Menstruation, lactation, and gestation are individual experiences of womanhood (Levesque-Lopman 1988), but not determinants of the social category "woman," or even "female." Similarly, "men are not always sperm-producers, and in fact, not all sperm producers are men. A male-to-female transsexual, prior to surgery, can be socially a woman, though still potentially (or actually) capable of spermatogenesis" (Kessler and McKenna [1978] 1985, 2).

In the Olympics, in cases of chromosomal ambiguity, women must undergo "a battery of gynecological and physical exams to see if she is 'female enough' to compete. Men are not tested" (Carlson 1991, 26). The purpose is not to categorize women and men accurately, but to make sure men don't enter women's competitions, where, it is felt, they will have the advantage of size and strength. This practice sounds fair only because it is assumed that all men are similar in size and strength and different from all women. Yet in Olympic boxing and wrestling matches, men are matched within weight classes. Some women might similarly successfully compete with some men in many sports. Women did not run in marathons until about twenty years ago. In twenty years of marathon competition, women have reduced their finish times by more than one-and-one-half hours; they are expected to run as fast as men in that race by 1998 and might catch up with means running times in races of other lengths within the next fifty years because they are increasing their fastest speeds more rapidly than are men (Fausto-Sterling 1985, 213–18).

WHAT SPORTS ILLUSTRATE

In professional and collegiate sports, physiological differences are invoked to justify women's secondary status, despite the clear evidence that gender status overrides physiological capabilities. Assumptions about women's physiology have influenced rules of competition; subsequent sports performances then validate how women and men are treated in sports competitions.

Gymnastic equipment is geared to slim, wiry, prepubescent girls and not to mature women; conversely, men's gymnastic equipment is tailored for muscular, mature men, not slim, wiry prepubescent boys. Boys could compete with girls, but are not allowed to; women gymnasts are left out entirely. Girl gymnasts are just that—little girls who will be disqualified as soon as they grow up (Vecsey 1990). Men gymnasts have men's status. In women's basketball, the size of the ball and rules for handling the ball change the style of play to "a slower, less intense, and less exciting modification of the 'regular' or men's game" (Watson 1987, 441). In the 1992 Winter Olympics, men figure skaters were required to complete three triple jumps in their required program; women figure skaters were forbidden to do more than one. These rules penalized artistic men skaters and athletic women skaters (Janofsky 1992). For the most part, Western sports are built on physically trained men's bodies. . . .

Organized sports are big businesses and, thus, who has access and at which level is a distributive or equity issue. The overall status of women and men athletes is an economic, political, and ideological issue that has less to do with individual physiological capabilities than with their cultural and social meaning and who defines and profits from them (Messner and Sabo 1990; Slatton and Birrell 1984). Twenty years after the passage of Title IX of the U.S. Civil Rights Act, which forbade gender inequality in any school receiving federal funds, the goal for collegiate sports in the next five years is 60 percent men, 40 percent women in sports participation, scholarships, and funding (Moran 1992).

Assumptions about men's and women's bodies and their capacities are crafted in ways that make unequal access and distribution of rewards acceptable (Hudson 1978; Messner 1988). Media images of modern men athletes glorify their strength and power, even their violence (Hargreaves 1986). Media images of modern women athletes tend to focus on feminine beauty and grace (so they are not really athletes) or on their thin, small, wiry androgynous bodies (so they are not really women). In coverage of the Olympics,

> loving and detailed attention is paid to pixie-like gymnasts; special and extended coverage is given to graceful and dazzling figure skaters; the camera painstakingly records the fluid movements of swimmers and divers. And then, in a blinding flash of fragmented images, viewers see a few minutes of volleyball, basketball, speed skating, track and field, and alpine skiing, as television gives its nod to the mere existence of these events. (Boutilier and SanGiovanni 1983, 190)

Extraordinary feats by women athletes who were presented as mature adults might force sports organizers and audiences to rethink their stereotypes of women's capabilities, the way elves, mermaids, and ice queens do not. Sports, therefore, construct men's bodies to be powerful; women's bodies to be sexual. As R. W. Connell says,

> The meanings in the bodily sense of masculinity concern, above all else, the superiority of men to women, and the exaltation of hegemonic masculinity over other groups of men which is essential for the domination of women. (1987, 85)

Given the association of sports with masculinity in the United States, women athletes have to manage a contradictory status. One study of women college basketball players found that although they "did athlete" on the court—"pushing, shoving, fouling, hard running, fast breaks, defense, obscenities and sweat" (Watson 1987, 441), they "did woman" off the court, using the locker room as their staging area: While it typically took fifteen minutes to prepare for the game, it took approximately fifteen minutes after the game to shower and remove the sweat of an athlete, *and* it took another thirty minutes to dress, apply make-up, and style hair. It did not seem to matter whether the players were going out into the public or getting on a van for a long ride home. Average dressing time and rituals did not change (Watson 1987, 443).

Such a redefinition of women's physicality affirms the ideological subtext of sports that physical strength is men's prerogative and justifies men's physical and sexual domination of women (Hargreaves 1986; Messner 1992, 164–72; Olson 1990; Theberge 1987; Willis 1982).

DIRTY LITTLE SECRETS

As sports construct gendered bodies, technology constructs gendered skills. Meta-analyses of studies of gender differences in spatial and mathematical ability have found that men have a large advantage in ability to mentally rotate an image, a moderate advantage in a visual perception of horizontality and verticality and in mathematical performance, and a small advantage in ability to pick a figure out of a field (Hyde 1990).

A woman mathematician and pioneer in data processing, Grace M. Hopper, was famous for her work on programming language (Perry and Greber 1990, 86). By the 1960s, programming was split into more and less skilled specialties, and the entry of women into the computer field in the 1970s and 1980s was confined to the lower-paid specialties. At each stage, employers invoked women's and men's purportedly natural capabilities for the jobs for which they were hired (Cockburn 1983, 1985; Donato 1990; Hartmann 1987; Hartmann, Kraut, and Tilly 1986; Kramer and Lehman 1990; Wright et al. 1987; Zimmerman 1983).

It is the taken-for-grantedness of such everyday gendered behavior that gives credence to the belief that the widespread differences in what women and men do must come from biology. To take one ordinarily unremarked scenario: In modern societies, if a man and woman who are a couple are in a car together, he is much more likely to take the wheel than she is, even if she is the more competent driver. . . . Men drive cars whether they are good drivers or not because men and machines are a "natural" combination (Scharff 1991). But the ability to drive gives one mobility; it is a form of social power.

I am not saying that physical differences between male and female bodies don't exist, but that these differences are socially meaningless until social practices transform them into social facts. West Point Military Academy's curriculum is designed to produce leaders, and physical competence is used as a significant measure of leadership ability (Yoder 1989). When women were accepted as West Point cadets, it became clear that the tests of physical competence, such as rapidly scaling an eight-foot wall, had been constructed for male physiques—pulling oneself up and over using upper-body strength. Rather than devise tests of physical competence for women, West Point provided boosters that mostly women used—but that lost them test points—in the case of the wall, a platform. Finally, the women themselves figured out how to use their bodies successfully. Janice Yoder describes this situation:

> I was observing this obstacle one day, when a woman approached the wall in the old prescribed way, got her fingertips grip, and did an unusual thing: she walked her dangling legs up the wall until she was in a position where both her hands and feet were atop the wall. She then simply pulled up her sagging bottom and went over. She solved the problem by capitalizing on one of women's physical assets: lower-body strength. (1989, 530)

In short, if West Point is going to measure leadership capability by physical strength, women's pelvises will do just as well as men's shoulders.

THE PARADOX OF HUMAN NATURE

Gendered people do not emerge from physiology or hormones but from the exigencies of the social order, mostly from the need for a reliable division of the work of food production and the social (not physical) reproduction of new members. The moral imperatives of religion and cultural representations reinforce the boundary lines among genders and ensure that what is demanded, what is permitted, and what is tabooed for the people in each gender is well known and followed by most. Political power, control of scarce resources, and, if necessary, violence uphold the gendered social order in the face of resistance and rebellion. Most people, however, voluntarily go along with their society's prescriptions for those of their gender status because the norms and expectations get built into their sense of worth and identity as a certain kind of human being and because they believe their society's way is the natural way. These beliefs emerge from the imagery that pervades the way we think, the way we see and hear and speak, the way we fantasize, and the way we feel. There is no core or bedrock human nature below these endlessly looping processes of the social production of sex and gender, self and other, identity and psyche, each of which is a "complex cultural construction" (Butler 1990, 36). The paradox of "human nature" is that it is *always* a manifestation of cultural meanings, social relationships, and power politics—"not biology, but culture, becomes destiny" (Butler 1990, 8).

When we rely only on the conventional categories of sex and gender, we end up finding what we looked for—we see what we believe, whether it is that "females" and "males" are essentially different or that "women" and "men" are essentially the same.

REFERENCES

Birrell, Susan J., and Sheryl L. Cole. 1990. Double fault: Renée Richards and the construction and naturalization of difference. *Sociology of Sport Journal* 7: 1–21.

Boutilier, Mary A., and Lucinda SanGiovanni. 1983. *The sporting woman.* Champaign, IL: Human Kinetics.

Butler, Judith. 1990. *Gender trouble: Feminism and the subversion of identity.* New York and London: Routledge & Kegan Paul.

Carlson, Alison. 1991. When is a woman not a woman? *Women's Sport and Fitness* March: 24–29.

Cockburn, Cynthia. 1983. *Brothers: Male dominance and technological change.* London: Pluto

———. 1985. *Machinery of dominance: Women, men and technical know-how.* London: Pluto.

Connell, R. W. 1987. *Gender and power.* Stanford, CA: Stanford University Press.

Donato, Katharine M. 1990. Programming for change? The growing demand for women systems analysts. In *Job queues, gender queues: Explaining women's inroads into male occupations*, written and edited by Barbara F. Reskin and Patricia A. Roos. Philadelphia: Temple University Press.

Fausto-Sterling, Anne. 1985. *Myths of gender: Biological theories about women and men.* New York: Basic Books.

Foucault, Michel. 1978. *The history of sexuality: An introduction.* Translated by Robert Hurley. New York: Pantheon.

Hargreaves, Jennifer A., ed. 1982. *Sport, culture, and ideology.* London: Routledge & Kegan Paul.

———. 1986. Where's the virtue? Where's the grace? A discussion of the social production of gender relations in and through sport. *Theory, Culture, and Society* 3: 109–21.

Hartmann, Heidi I., ed. 1987. *Computer chips and paper clips: Technology and women's employment.* Vol. 2. Washington, D.C.: National Academy Press.

Hartmann, Heidi I., Robert E. Kraut, and Louise A. Tilly, eds. 1986. *Computer chips and paper clips: Technology and women's employment.* Vol. 1. Washington, D.C.: National Academy Press.

Haskell, Molly. 1989. Hers: He drives me crazy. *New York Times Magazine*, 24 September, 26, 28.

Hudson, Jackie. 1978. Physical parameters used for female exclusion from law enforcement and athletics. In *Women and sport: From myth to reality*, edited by Carole A. Oglesby. Philadelphia: Lea and Febiger.

Hyde, Janet Shibley. 1990. Meta-analysis and the psychology of gender differences. *Signs: Journal of Women in Culture and Society* 16: 55–73.

Jaggar, Alison M. 1983. *Feminist politics and human nature*. Totowa, NJ: Rowman & Allanheld.

Janofsky, Michael. 1992. Yamaguchi has the delicate and golden touch. *New York Times*, 22 February.

Kessler, Suzanne J. 1990. The medical construction of gender: Case management of intersexed infants. *Signs: Journal of Women in Culture and Society* 16: 3–26.

Kessler, Suzanne J., and Wendy McKenna. [1978] 1985. *Gender: An ethnomethodological approach*. Chicago: University of Chicago Press.

Kolata, Gina. 1992. Track federation urges end to gene test for femaleness. *New York Times*, 12 February.

Kramer, Pamela E., and Sheila Lehman. 1990. Mismeasuring women: A critique of research on computer ability and avoidance. *Signs: Journal of Women in Culture and Society* 16: 158–72.

Laqueur, Thomas. 1990. *Making sex: Body and gender from the Greeks to Freud*. Cambridge, MA: Harvard University Press.

Levesque-Lopman, Louise. 1988. *Claiming reality: Phenomenology and women's experience*. Totowa, NJ: Rowman & Littlefield.

Messner, Michael A. 1988. Sports and male domination: The female athlete as contested ideological terrain. *Sociology of Sport Journal* 5: 197–211.

———. 1992. *Power at play: Sports and the problem of masculinity*. Boston: Beacon Press.

Messner, Michael A., Margaret Carlisle Duncan, and Kerry Jensen. 1993. Separating the men from the girls: The gendered language of televised sports. *Gender & Society* 7: 121–37.

Messner, Michael A., and Donald F. Sabo, eds. 1990. *Sport, men, and the gender order: Critical feminist perspectives*. Champaign, IL: Human Kinetics.

Money, John, and Anke A. Ehrhardt. 1972. *Man & woman, boy & girl*. Baltimore, MD: Johns Hopkins University Press.

Moran, Malcolm. 1992. Title IX: A 20-year search for equity. *New York Times*, Sports Section, 21–23 June.

Naftolin, F., and E. Butz, eds. 1981. Sexual dimorphism. *Science* 211: 1263–1324.

Olson, Wendy. 1990. Beyond Title IX: Toward an agenda for women and sports in the 1990s. *Yale Journal of Law and Feminism* 3: 105–51.

Perry, Ruth, and Lisa Greber. 1990. Women and computers: An introduction. *Signs: Journal of Women in Culture and Society* 16: 74–101.

Richards, Renée, with Jack Ames. 1983. *Second serve*. New York: Stein and Day.

Scharff, Virginia. 1991. *Taking the wheel: Women and the coming of the motor age*. New York: Free Press.

Slatton, Bonnie, and Susan Birrell. 1984. The politics of women's sport. *Arena Review 8*.

Theberge, Nancy. 1987. Sport and women's empowerment. *Women's Studies International Forum* 10: 387–93.

Vecsey, George. 1990. Cathy Rigby, unlike Peter, did grow up. *New York Times*, Sports Section, 19 December.

Watson, Tracey. 1987. Women athletes and athletic women: The dilemmas and contradictions of managing incongruent identities. *Sociological Inquiry* 57: 431–46.

Willis, Paul. 1982. Women in sport in ideology. In *Sport, culture, and ideology*, edited by Jennifer A. Hargreaves. London: Routledge & Kegan Paul.

Wright, Barbara Drygulski et al., eds. 1987. *Women, work, and technology: Transformations*. Ann Arbor: University of Michigan Press.

Yoder, Janice D. 1989. Women at West Point: Lessons for token women in male-dominated occupations. In *Women: A feminist perspective*, edited by Jo Freeman, 4th ed. Palo Alto, CA: Mayfield.

Zimmerman, Jan, ed. 1983. *The technological woman: Interfacing with tomorrow*. New York: Praeger.

EDITOR'S NOTE

Women's burgeoning physical prowess continues to encroach upon sacred male athletic domains that historically have been off limits to females. In the sport of running, for example, the first year that women were officially permitted to race in the Boston Marathon was 1972. That year, the winner in the women's category came in 410th overall. By 2003, the winner of the women's division finished 16th overall. In the world of marathons, since 1972, men's times have declined by less than four minutes while women's have declined by almost half an hour.[1] Selena Roberts, writing in *The New York Times*, notes that "Every year, American girls are developing more interest in sports, with about three million involved at the high school level."[2]

This year a teenage girl named Michelle Wie captivated all who watched her, poised and confident, compete against men, some of whom were twice her age in her quest to make it to the Masters. She came closer than any other female to advance to golf's men-only crème de le crème U.S. tournament, the Master's, historically off limits to women.

In yet another "male" sport, another close finish came for another young woman, twenty-three-year-old Danica Patrick finished a respectable fourth place in the 2005 Indianapolis 500. She was not the first female to race in the Indy 500, nor will she be the last, but she was the first to lead (in the 56th lap) for fourteen laps.

Are these women aberrations or are they the wave of the future? If it is the latter, what might it mean for women, for sports, and for female and male relationships?

NOTES

1. Allen St. John, "Marathon Women," *The Wall Street Journal*, 16 April 2004, p. W4.

2. Selena Roberts, "A Heady Apex for Women, but Is a Title IX Dead End Just Ahead?" *The New York Times*, 30 May 2005, p. D7.

18

Toward Safer Societies

Punishment, Masculinities, and Violence against Women

Laureen Snider

Economic "cushions" are under attack and income inequalities are increasing as nation-states reduce deficits by eliminating social services, health care, minimum wages, worker protection laws, and anything else that adds to the (corporate) cost of production. Removing social safety nets and public services is presented as necessary to allow developed countries (or the national and multinational corporations they shelter) to compete in cut-throat global markets. When capital, investment, and jobs can easily be shifted from Birmingham to Bangladesh, they will go wherever the potential for short-term profits is highest, or so we are told. Currency speculators have become key players in this game of capital roulette. George Soros, for example, ex-Hungarian financier, acts as a "global reality cop, pouncing on any government that overvalues or undervalues its currency" (Friedman 1995: A17). To appease investment-bankers and avert potentially disastrous runs on their currency nation-states have systematically begun campaigns to make their citizens less secure and more vulnerable, both psychologically and economically. Developed countries have entered a race to see who can create the most insecure, unhealthy, and violence prone population. The United States is ahead at the moment—but it had a head start, with fewer universal social programs to dismantle—and Canada, New Zealand, and the United Kingdom are catching up fast. . . . Public services are costly and inefficient; grants to poor people or provinces erode economic competitiveness and encourage dependence, according to right-wing think-tanks and politicians. But they also allow people to nourish their roots and remain in regions where they have traditions and histories, relatives and support networks. "Subsidies" are important in creating less desperate people.

Psychological "cushions," in the form of identification with values outside mass culture, are also under attack.[1] As many have pointed out, mass culture operates through consumerism, and consumerism works by creating and/or reinforcing personal and social insecurity. People with secure identities, independent of "lifestyle," are harder for advertisers to manipulate, cannot be trusted to buy on cue, may fail to grasp that they are inadequate, inferior, and socially irresponsible because they do not own the latest model cars, VCRs, and Nikes. Consumerism has to create hierarchies and reinforce individual identities because if I have the fastest car or most fashionable clothes, you obviously do not. This is not a capitalist conspiracy; it is a natural correspondence of interests between privately owned media and capital. Like most ideologies, that of consumerism has a core of truth—many products do save labor, increase comfort levels, and make life more pleasant. Add to this the socially created truths of consumerism, that not possessing certain "things" leads other social actors to cast aspersions on your trustworthiness, thrift, or credentials as a human being, and you have a very persuasive set of beliefs. But societies made up of people whose identities are solely dependent on purchased commodities are very vulnerable to capital's periodic cycles of contraction and expansion. Combining greater dependence with fewer social and economic supports leads inevitably to greater desperation, and some of this will emerge as increased interpersonal violence.

The content of mass culture is another factor linking desperation to violence. Without exploring the byzantine and endless debates over whether violent videos or television programs directly incite aggressive acts or produce desensitization, the omnipresence of these messages—the fact that a high percentage of people's leisure time, daily routines, and interactions with others revolve around violent events (be they fictional, news events, or sports)—indicates that the messages have, at minimum, the power to monopolize human attention. Of course actual effects of violent media will vary by individual, class, gender, values, and role in the community. The food we consume also has different effects depending on body type, mood, age, gender, weight, and level of nourishment. But if "you are what you eat," you are even more totally what you direct your attention to, what you think about, and value. And modern cultural diets promote insensitization, the quick thirty-minute fix, lists of winners and losers, the unambiguous black and white solution. Compromise means selling out, complexity is denied and violence, when used by "people like us," is a good thing, the only way to surmount omnipresent forces of evil and incompetence.

When all this is added up—polarized politics, an increased focus on individualism at the expense of community, greater heterogeneity, decreased equality, and the loss of older identities to mass consumerism—it appears to be a recipe for ever-greater violence, deprivation, desperation, and pain. It is hard to figure out modes of resistance, let alone transformation.

BUILDING LESS VIOLENT COMMUNITIES AND FAMILIES

While the difficulty of promoting micro- and middle-level patterns at odds with macro-level forces cannot be underestimated, it is essential to examine the context of subordination and understand the ways in which domination and violence are rooted inside the individual, in the patterns of daily life (Giddens 1981; Smart 1992; Foucault 1982). Thus, even while macro-level institutions are reinforcing one set of social relations, other social relations are undermining class and patriarchy, resisting and refusing hegemonic ways of thinking and acting. Macro-level transformation cannot be effective "if the agents upon whom [transformative politics] depends continue to be governed and defined by the very social contexts they are trying to transform" (Winter 1992; 812). The objective, then, is to examine how practices can be changed to foster subjectivities and identities that reject violent, dominator/dominated roles.

However, there is profound cultural resistance to wholesale and unqualified discouragement of individual aggression, particularly in the rearing of sons. Mothers as well as fathers, terrified of boys becoming "wimps," send contradictory messages about the acceptability of bullying and aggression. . . . To understand why some boys grow up embracing violent acts and identities, others eschew them, and the majority flounder in the middle, one must examine the relationship between micro-level patterns of control and systems of patriarchy. Literature on domestic assault tells us that many of the violent men who have been studied are frustrated individuals who see women as easy, weak, and available targets. They are often jealous and insecure, they believe in traditional sex roles and deny, to themselves and others, that their assaults have serious effects on the victimized. Frequently they witnessed or experienced physical or sexual abuse as children. Such men tend to see women as objects whose duty is to make their lives easier, a duty women frequently fail to fulfill being "by nature" unreliable, unfaithful, lazy, and so on. Violence for them is instrumental as well as expressive, a method of resolving conflict, establishing dominance, and claiming male entitlement (Tifft and Markham 1991; Dobash and Dobash 1992, 1975; Dekeseredy and Hinch 1991; Ptacek 1988*a*, *b*; Stets 1988; Buchwald et al. 1993).

Men construct masculinities in the same way that all identities are built, by choosing among the options they see as available and satisfying for "people like them," people who share their class, race, neighborhood, family, and society as well as gender. In heterogeneous Western societies a wide range of masculinities is available, offering much choice—and much confusion. However, the patriarchal man—silent, . . . emotionally constipated, and physically strong—is still the ideal, especially in mass culture. Hegemonic masculinities on this model are heavily promoted in dominant media and sport, and constitute the identities most visible, accessible, and appealing, particularly to boys lacking alternative male role models. Peer groups of adolescent males, alienated from mainstream authority, use sport, rap, and mass culture extensively to develop ideas of what it means to be a man in this class, race, region, culture, and time. Frequently this means borrowing the most violent and misogynous components of mainstream identities on offer. The price of questioning hegemonic masculinities can be high, producing feelings of uncertainty about one's own masculinity, rejection by peers, or even physical attacks.

Given dominant value-systems that glorify power as an end in itself, and the undeniable fact that force is useful in getting one's way (for it offers immediate gratification without the need to grovel, negotiate, or compromise and, in sexual matters, without vulnerability or risk of rejection), it can be hard for those who buy in to understand why anyone would reject the entitlement offered by hegemonic masculinities. When you can partake of an identity that allows you, by the simple fact of gender, to see yourself as stronger and smarter than half the world, entitled by birthright to deference and power if not wealth, why would you question such beliefs? Dissident males, who by their very existence show that these identities are cultural creations supporting privilege rather than biosocial necessities, threaten the entire structure.

Class and ethnic differences must be figured into this equation because they mediate the appeal of certain masculinities. Poor black or Hispanic men in marginalized under classes, for example, may find identities based on possession of turf or defense of honor appealing, or those that celebrate individualistic and collective force as badges of status, perhaps because a block of contested cityscape, a muscular body, and a gun are among the few resources they can claim in such environments (Polk 1994). For men in urban ghettos to claim identities where self-esteem or peer status depends on the successful attainment of professional credentials or higher degrees (as many reformers insist they should) would be psychological and cultural suicide. The economic and educational resources necessary to play this game are simply not available to the vast majority, however intelligent and industrious. The success of the handful who might make it would come at the psycho-social expense of the many who would not.

White working-class American men (and a small percentage of black men) have seen their relatively privileged positions, good wages, and strong unions, disappear in recent decades. Some of them have turned to militia-style movements celebrating turf and force (the equivalent of ghetto youth identities but more rural and collective), and/or to nationalistic identities based on citizenship, claiming entitlement as citizens of the richest, best, most powerful nation in the world. Working-class European men, typically less marginalized than urban under classes in the United States, and better protected from the vagaries of the global marketplace due to the psychological and economic cushions instituted in such states in the post-war period, have often used sport, particularly football (soccer to North Americans), to underpin and reinforce concepts of manhood that contain notions of fair play in addition to celebrating toughness, physicality, and the ability to take life's reverses stoically—"like a man" (Williams and Taylor 1994).

For middle-class North American white men, born into settings where masculinities can be centered in occupational success and higher education, dominant masculinities show wide generational splits. Adolescent middle-class masculinity is often premised on physical prowess, strength, and sport (all linked to sexual success as a source of status), but with maturity job performance becomes paramount. In the merciless, literally accurate language of the metaphor, occupational success "separates the men from the boys." Although phenomena such as the jobless recovery now threaten the economic prospects of the adult middle-class man, mainstream cultural goals of wealth, achievement, and success through upward mobility were realistic goals for many decades. There was therefore less need, *as a class*, to cling to older masculinities stressing physical toughness, patriarchal notions based on the power of the male body. Men in this class were not so much learning to labor as learning to rule. This does not mean that middle- or upper-class masculinities reject misogyny or violence on either the personal or professional level (Godenzi 1994); the difference is often one of packaging more than substance. M. Levi (1994) points out that the City (the financial center of London) is personalized by corporate executives and traders as a bitch goddess, a fickle female promising much but delivering little. Phrases such as "the City is a place for men, not for boys" (Levi 1994; 241) (and, therefore, not for women at all) suggest a subculture where exchange markets are exclusive boys' clubs, and trading and deals are dominance games, competitions for personal as well as occupational power. The self-images of urban currency traders reek of machismo—the cowboy mystique, the swaggering recklessness of the quintessential "twenty-five-year-olds in red suspenders," the "bad boy" heroes such as Nick Leeson, the twenty-eight-year-old bond trader who single-handedly brought down Barings Bank, the power of a George Soros, who "single-handedly broke the British pound" (Friedman 1995; A17). Such warrior power rivals that of earlier male heroes on the battlefields of Waterloo or the Plains of Abraham. Such identities celebrate dominance and patriarchy, but claims are based more on cerebral than physical power. This is hegemonic masculinity globalized.

It should, it *must* be possible to find ways of being manly that are not misogynous and do not require the repression of every human emotion except anger. It should not be necessary to denigrate male sexuality or insist that it be denied to address misogyny or assault, but it is essential to differentiate the sex drive from the need to dominate. To understand the limits as well as the potential for change it is useful to examine the decline and fall of traditional male spheres of action, male "imperatives" to impregnate, provision, and defend females and family groups (Gilmore 1990). These three have been central to male roles, male self-esteem, and male identities, historically and cross-culturally, for thousands of years. There is no reason to believe they are epiphenomena, mere social constructions that can be wiped out by laws or political tinkering. Indeed it is more plausible to see the blockage and denial of "maleness" symbolized by the denigration of these roles as fueling the male rage that animates the late twentieth century. Right-wing, racist, militia-style social movements and the reactionary, punishment-oriented political regimes which are their psychological equivalents (both of which, surveys tell us, are supported by men more than by women), are symptomatic.

In less than one generation male prerogatives to impregnate, provide, and defend have been radically altered. Take the responsibility to provide for one's family: as we have seen, technologies making many working-class jobs obsolete combined with right-wing policies to accommodate capital's quest for higher profit margins have destroyed union solidarity, wages, and benefits, and abolished thousands of jobs. Since few women occupied the well-paid unionized jobs in heavy industry or manufacturing that were the primary targets of this wave of downsizing, working-class men were the main losers. In the 1990s downsizing spread up the class ladder; this time men and women in middle management and public sectors took the hit. The ability to provide for oneself, let alone one's mates and children, was radically altered. Government programs, the economic cushions, softened the blow to an extent in some European countries, but these are temporary measures at best. To make matters worse, women sometimes found it easier to secure new jobs—they are typically better educated, more willing to accept low wage positions, and are sometimes viewed by employers as more reliable and less aggressive (positive traits in the job market of the 1990s for many McJobs). In the middle classes, the success of feminism in securing equal opportunity, independence, and promotion for women in formerly male domains, while relieving economic stress for men lucky enough to have partners with good jobs, added new stress to the pain of redundance and new fuel to the fires of backlash (Faludi 1991).[2] In North America, women's wages rose relative to men's as various equity programs made hiring women (and some minorities) beneficial, and their relative scarcity in many traditionally male professions such as science or engineering increased their market value. Thus in the 1990s, just when large numbers of middle-class white men began experiencing intense marginalization for the first time, middle-class women began making real, though often exaggerated, gains.

The imperative to impregnate has become less necessary as well. Advances in technology threaten to make males redundant, with frozen sperm, artificial insemination, and test-tube babies replacing humans. Patriarchy's historical monopoly over reproduction and hence over women has been challenged, and contraceptive pills, IUDs, and legalized abortion have allowed many women, in the developed world at least, to control when, how, and with whom they will reproduce. Backlash and resistance, as in laws requiring the consent of a partner or parent to procure an abortion, or "voluntary chastity" movements, have been largely unsuccessful. The arrival of AIDS has made heterosexual promiscuity, always the prerogative of men more than women, literally life-threatening. Meanwhile overpopulation has rendered patriarchal structures that value men for the number of (male) offspring they can sire increasingly unfashionable, particularly in first-world countries where each new person consumes seventeen times his or her share of the world's resources.

The need to defend oneself or one's mate against natural enemies (fire, flood, and wild animals) has largely disappeared as well, particularly in developed and urbanized countries. But the desire for enemies is obvious: invented villains permeate popular culture, and heroes are pressed into service to ward off everything from godless communists, aliens, and marauding rapists to killer hurricanes and runaway submarines. Unfortunately fulfilling the male imperative to defend in nonfictive realities runs up against state monopolies over the control of arms and the exercise of interpersonal violence. Thus we see the almost religious significance attached by militia movements to the "right" to bear arms, or the more recent but equally intense reaction to the banning of handguns larger than .22 caliber following the Dunblane massacre in Britain (*Guardian Weekly*, "Guns Go Abroad," 8 December 1996: 24). Public restrictions on private arsenals are essential, but they also benefit women as a group more than men as a group, since women are the more fearful and vulnerable sex. State social control deprives men of the right and obligation to display their (generally) superior physical strength and greater aggressive capacity, and another component of male identity disappears.

The heavy misogyny found in male identity formation is too widespread, culturally and historically, to be wholly accidental. Blatant rejection of femininity and an exaggeration of male-female differences is a primary component of virtually every known male subculture (including those among gay men) (Jefferson 1994). Whether this is biologically or psychologically necessary is not known, nor is it particularly relevant from a utilitarian perspective. What matters is that, to have any appeal to rebellious adolescent males with much clearer ideas of what they reject than what they accept, alternate male identities must be *different* from female identities. It may turn out that the biosocial psychology of male humans, not to mention eons of evolution, make it important for boys to exaggerate gender differences in order to reject the mother-figure and distance themselves from the dependence of childhood. But there is no reason to suppose that the need to create identities that are distinctively different from women's implies a need to hate, devalue, or dominate women. The latter are necessary components of patriarchy, not masculinity.

It also seems obvious that boys/men need roles, and therefore institutions and (sub) cultures, that allow them to be aggressive, risk-takers, and adventurers (which does not mean that women should be denied such roles). There are few cultural or social spaces in developed societies where boys can be constructively adventurous or aggressive. Fantasy roles abound, from cyberspace to video games, but many of these exploit racism or homophobia rather than satisfying needs. With the disappearance of wild animals, frontiers, and unexplored territory, the only adventurous legitimate *jobs* on offer are violent and destructive in nature (such as soldiers, police, and/or criminals), or they are restricted to a privileged elite (space explorers today require doctorates in astrophysics). No wonder male police and prison guards cling so desperately to machismo images and subcultures, fighting academic and political directives that would replace warrior roles with service orientations (Heidensohn 1992; Reiner 1992). No wonder, too, that virtually all businesses and political organizations are gendered in ways that relegate women to secondary roles responsible for emotional scutwork, while men claim the adventurous, aggressive roles and the prestige, power, and income such roles "deserve" (Hochschild 1983). It is not functionality, capitalism, or the dictates of efficiency that require such subcultures or organizational divisions of labor.

Heterosexual women do have important parts to play in struggles to recast male identities. Too often women as mothers reward violence and toughness in their sons (and weakness in their daughters), or devalue emotionality and vulnerability in men with negative labels. Women as lovers and mates, particularly young women, cannot continue to respond erotically to machismo and reject men exploring alternate masculinities or those who have refused emotional castration. Feminism as a movement is well placed to problematize and consciousness raise around women's roles in reinforcing violent masculinities.

Because knowledge is a form of power, there are important tasks in this struggle for those in the academy as well. New male identities need to be wideranging, they will vary with class, ethnicity, orientation, religious identification, occupation, and age (to name only a few factors), and they cannot be specified or prescribed in advance. They must be struggled for, forged by trial and error, and based in older masculinities and ways of being. But little is known about the structural and cultural forces forming masculinities and femininities, or about micro-level processes that mediate the process of identity formation among individual men and women (Foucault 1982). Violence has historically been connected with dominance, and both with eroticism, but the roots and consequences of these links are unclear. We know little about the various agendas and interests animating struggles around masculinities today, and we have not adequately explored the social or political consequences of the different visions of male-female natures and relationships now vying for power. Some groups attempting to recast male and female identities, for example, take the partial, political, and fragmented bits of biological knowledge we have about sex differences as facts, and argue for conservative policies on this basis (such as forcing women to stay home to bond with infants, or excluding them from higher education in mathematics because of alleged differences in left-right brain functions governing spatial abilities in men and women, for example). Naming the problems, specifying the implications, and identifying the interest groups at play is a necessary first step to securing transformative changes and, even more crucial right now, to averting reactionary ones.[3] This is all part of the process of creating alternative models, of envisaging different ways of seeing to counter the dead weight of hegemony, for acceptance of the status quo rests heavily on notions that it constitutes the necessary and inevitable ordering of the world.

Directing greater attention to an "ethics of care" might be a useful component of the process of constructing alternatives (Gilligan 1982; Smart 1989: 72–74; Kellough 1995). G. Kellough suggests that the intersecting values of capitalism and patriarchy have co-opted, through law, the common human urge to care for others and distorted it into a welfare/dependence frame. Women in particular are forced to choose between independence/autonomy and the obligation to care for others or nurture (Kellough 1995: 382–83). This is a false dichotomy because people must be nurtured (through socialization) in order to become autonomous, so caring and independence are intertwined not juxtaposed. Such a concept is useful insofar as it can be used as a counterbalance to voices advocating penalty and revenge, and a challenge to tyrannies of the binary. "Using the need of human beings for the caring attention of others" (Kellough 1995: 383) as a tool to evaluate macro-level processes (laws, structures, policies, and institutions) focuses attention on new concepts of human rights, concepts based in collectivist and dualistic rather than individualistic zero-sum terms. We know so little about the activities central to caring, or the institutions and implications of such an orientation, compared to those central to punishing.[4]

NOTES

1. Earlier collective identities based in craft guilds have largely disappeared. Religion, a primary source of alternative value systems in many parts of the world, has been marginalized in much of Europe and Canada, and "captured" by consumerism and capitalism in the United States (Bibby 1993). There has been talk about the potential of technology (the Net, for example) to re-create community and nourish alternate identities, but since it is still predominantly privileged classes, men, and increasingly commercial interests which are "on line," it is unduly optimistic to see anything "alternative" emerging here.

2. Jobs for married women are not new—all but the most privileged have worked outside the home since the dawn of the Industrial Revolution (except during the most intense periods of child-rearing), but their wages were kept low by a combination of sexism and glass ceilings, and their jobs were more likely to be seen, by women as well as men, as secondary.

3. The struggle for identity, the territory of internal or psychological change, is central to counter-hegemonic and ideological change. And it has not been claimed and politicized to the degree that structure-based change, now the apparently unchallengeable property of those who would make the world safe for profit maximization, has been. It may therefore be fertile soil politically, as well as essential knowledge.

4. Much caring labor, in the private sphere and in mainstream organizations ranging from airlines to government, is done by and expected from women rather than men (Hochschild 1983). However the consequences and implications this has for social policy, child-rearing, economic reform, and violence are unknown. Do male subcultures and identities lose the potential to express and develop caring identities because of the dominance of women in these spheres? Are women denied the chance to develop more instrumental abilities? With what consequences? The empirical and theoretical territory of caring needs to be explored as carefully as the terrain of penalty has been.

REFERENCES

Bibby, R. (1993), *Unknown Gods: The Ongoing Story of Religion in Canada*. Toronto: Soddart.

Buchwald, E., P. Fletcher, and M. Roth, eds. (1993), *Transforming a Rape Culture*. Minneapolis, MN: Milkweed Editions.

Dekeseredy, W. and R. Hinch (1991), *Woman Abuse: Sociological Perspectives*. Toronto: Thompson Educational Publishing.

Dobash, R. E. and R. Dobash (1975), *Violence Against Wives: A Case Against the Patriarchy*. New York: Free Press.

—— (1992), *Women, Violence and Social Change*. London: Routledge.

Faludi, S. (1991), *Backlash: The Undeclared War against American Women*. New York: Doubleday.

Foucault, M. (1982), "The Subject and Power," in H. Dreyfus and P. Rabinow, eds., *Michel Foucault: Beyond Structuralism and Hermeneuties*, 194–230. Chicago: University of Chicago Press.

Friedman, T. (1995), "Sorry, but this Group of Seven doesn't make the grade," *The Glove and Mail*, Tuesday, 30 May, A17 (reprinted from the *New York Times*).

Giddens, A. (1981), *The Class Structure of Advanced Societies*, 2nd ed. London: Hutchinson.

Gilligan, C. (1982), *In a Different Voice: Psychological Theory and Women's Development*. Cambridge: Harvard University Press.

Gilmore, T. (1990), *Manhood in the Making*. New Haven: Yale University Press.

Godenzi, A. (1994), "What's the Big Deal?" in T. Newburn and E. Stanko, eds., *Just Boys Doing Business?* 135–52. London: Routledge.

Heidensohn, F. (1992), *Women in Control*. Oxford: Oxford University Press.

Hochschild, A. R. (1983), *The Managed Heart: Commercialization of Human Feeling*. Berkeley: University of California Press.

Jefferson, T. (1994), "Theorizing Masculine Subjectivity," in T. Newburn and E. Stankol, eds., *Just Boys Doing Business?* 10–32. London: Routledge.

Kellough, G. (1995), *The Abortion Controversy: A Study of Law, Culture and Social Change*. Toronto: University of Toronto Press.

Levi, M. (1994). "Giving Creditors the Business: The Criminal Law in Inaction," *International Journal of the Sociology of Law*, 12: 321–33.

Polk, K. (1994). *When Men Kill—Scenarios of Masculine Violence*. New York: Cambridge University Press.

Ptacek, J. (1988a), "How Men Who Batter Rationalize their Behavior," in A. Horton and J. Williamson, eds., *Abuse and Religion*. Lexington, MA: Lexington Books.

—— (1988b), "Why Do Men Batter Their Wives?" in K. Yllo and M. Bograd, eds., *Feminist Perspectives on Wife Abuse*. Newbury Park, CA: Sage.

Reiner, R. (1992), "Police Research in the UK: A Critical Review," in M. Tonry and N. Morris, eds., *Modern Policing*. Chicago: University of Chicago Press.

Smart, C. (1989), *Feminism and the Power of Law*. London: Routledge.

—— (1992), "The Woman of Legal Discourse," *Social and Legal Studies*, 1: 29–44.

Stets, J. E. (1988), *Domestic Violence and Control*. New York: Springer-Verlag.

Tifft, L. and L. Markham, (1991), "Battering Women and Battering Central Americans," in H. E. Pepinsky and R. Quinney, eds., *Criminology as Peacemaking*, 114–53. Bloomington: Indiana University Press.

Williams, J. and Taylor, R. (1994), "Boys Keep Swinging: Masculinity and Football Culture in England," in T. Newburn and E. Stanko, eds., *Just Boys Doing Business? Men, Masculinities and Crime*, 214–34. London; Routledge.

Winter, S. (1992), "Don't Trust Anyone Not Over the Sixties," *Law and Society Review* 26/4: 789–818.

EDITOR'S NOTE

Laureen Snider argues that violence permeates our society in a variety of forms and that psychic violence is just as debilitating as the physical. It, too, leaves people feeling impotent, especially men who are working hard but failing at the role they have been primed for their entire youth—the "tough good provider." The problem is how to be a good provider in the United States where the economy is increasingly bifurcated—with a small minority at the top swimming in endless resources. *The Wall Street Journal* recently reported the salaries and bonuses of CEOs with earnings of upward of $1 million and with some earning between $17 to $32 million in 2004,[1] a worried middle class, and a petrified working class who are struggling to keep from scraping bottom.

Robert J. Samuelson describes the compensation for top corporate executives as "an artificial welfare system designed to ensure that even mediocre top executives do well."[2] According to Samuelson the median salary plus bonus of CEOs at 350 companies increased by 53 percent between 1993 and 2002.[3]

Still another report indicates that, between 1950 and 1970, for every dollar earned by the bottom 90 percent of workers, those in the top 1 percent earned $162 dollars; however, between 1990 and 2002, when those in the bottom 90 percent earned $1.00, those in the top 1 percent earned $18,000 dollars.[4] Compared with other industrial countries, the United States has the greatest concentration of wealth.[5] The 7.5 millionaire households in the United States controlled more than $11 trillion in assets.[6] Over one-third of the wealth in the United States is controlled by the top 1 percent and almost 60 percent is controlled by the top 5 percent.[7] Examined another way, 95 percent of the population has the remaining 40 percent to fight over. From that perspective, the desperation of workers can be understood.

In 2002, about 1 of every 436 high-income Americans paid no taxes and that figure is up from 1 in 1,010 in 2000. Among the high-income group, of those who did pay income taxes, 1 in 22 paid less than 10 cents for every dollar while the average American paid 13 cents for every dollar.[8]

On the other side of the bifurcated line are a worried middle class and a petrified working class who aren't in the top 5, 10, or even 40 percent. For these workers upward mobility seems elusive as they run in place, fear falling behind, and struggle to not lose ground. The Federal Reserve Bank reports that fewer families moved up in the 1980s than in the 1970s, and even fewer were upwardly mobile in the 1990s than in the 1980s.[9]

In the manufacturing sector, which has suffered the greatest loss of jobs, workers whose jobs have gone to Asia will eventually find work, but the average cut in pay will be about 14 percent. To give you an idea of why manufacturing jobs have gone off shore, the average wage of a Chinese worker is about 2.5 percent of a worker in the west![10] It is estimated that about 15 percent of jobs lost "have reappeared overseas."[11]

Even the middle-class worker has cause for worry. The recent high unemployment rate among tech workers—a sector that not too long ago was considered a growth industry—is due to off-shoring technology work in Asia. Sociologist Arne Kalleberg says: "We have a hollowing out of the job structure, and so these jobs that were once middle class are now low-skilled or disappear."[12] A least one thousand software engineering jobs were transferred to Asia by Intel while engineers in India repair Morgan Stanley's software problems in New York.[13] "Unemployment among tech workers . . . is now higher than the overall jobless rate for the first time in thirty years."[14] Companies that aren't moving operations overseas increasingly are using independent contractors; this means no job guarantees and no benefits, turning tech workers into migrant workers.[15]

Some economists argue that having workers stuck at the bottom doesn't necessarily hurt the economy. According to their perspective, the economy doesn't need minimum wages to keep the economy going. The rich will take care of consuming.[16] Do you suppose that's why the Senate failed so many times in the past to raise the minimum wage from $5.15 to $7.00 over a two-year period?[17] How does this bode for the psychological and physical well-being of working-class and middle-class families?

NOTES

1. "CEO Compensation Survey/2004," *The Wall Street Journal*, 11 April 2005, pp. R7–R11.
2. Robert J. Samuelson, "Welfare for Capitalists," *Newsweek*, 5 May 2003, p. 54.
3. Ibid.
4. Bob Herbert, "The Mobility Myth," *The New York Times*, 6 June 2005, p. A23.
5. Robert Frank, "U.S. Led a Resurgence Last Year Among Millionaires World-Wide," *The Wall Street Journal*, 12 June 2005, pp. A1, A8.
6. Robert Frank, "Millionaire Ranks Hit New High," *The Wall Street Journal*, 25 May 2005, pp. D1, D2.
7. Ibid.
8. David Cay Johnston, "More Wealthy People Paid No Tax," *The New York Times*, 3 July 2005, p. 13.
9. Janny Scott and David Leonhardt, "Class in America: The Shadowy Lines that Still Divide," *The New York Times*, 15 May 2003, pp. 1, 16–18.
10. Erika Kinetz, "Who Wins and Who Loses as Jobs Move Overseas," *The New York Times*, 7 December 2003, p. BU5
11. Louis Uchitelle, "A Missing Statistic: US Jobs That Have Moved Overseas, *The New York Times*, 5 October 2003, p. 21.
12. Greg Schneider, "Wandering for Work," *The Washington Post National Weekly Edition*, 15–21 November 2005, p. 18.
13. Uchitelle.
14. Schnider.
15. Ibid.
16. Eduardo Porter, "How Long Can Workers Tread Water?" *The New York Times*, 14 July 2005, p. C1.
17. Robert Pear, "Senate, Torn by Minimum Wage, Shelves Major Welfare Bill, *The New York Times*, 2 April 2004, p. A12.

19

Tomboys Yes, Janegirls Never

Barbara A. Arrighi

GENDER MESSAGES

The statements below comprise a collection of gendered directives assembled from various social and professional experiences, but primarily from classroom discussion when the topic was gender and masculinity. The name Billy is used here to demonstrate what a sustained barrage of gendered pointers would be like for one child to endure over time. Therefore, although Billy is fictitious, the comments are real. It is not out of the realm of possibilities that one child could hear most if not all of the following gender directives during childhood.

Immediate Family Members

Father to newborn Billy: "Little man, you take care of your mother while I'm gone."

Older brother to Billy: "Sissy, sissy, sissy. Billy is a sissy. Billy plays with dolls."

Older sister to Billy: "Billy is a sissy. Billy acts like a girl, looks like a girl, talks like a girl, walks like a girl."

Billy's father to no one in particular as Billy sits down to play the piano: "Oh, jeez, don't let him play the piano, the next thing he'll be walking around all limp-wristed."

Father to Billy: "Billy, give that doll back to your sister right now. I'm not raising no little fag."

Billy's father to Billy's mother: "How do you expect Billy to grow up and be a man when you're putting fingernail polish on him? I don't care if he is five years old. Before you know it, he'll be wearing your underwear."

Mother to Billy: "No, Billy, you can't play dress-up with your sister. Boys don't play dress-up, just girls do."

Mother to Billy: "No, Billy, you can't get an ironing board for Christmas. That's just for girls. Are you a girl?"

Father to Billy's female cousin: "Oh, Lord, don't let Billy play with that ironing board. Billy, get away from that ironing board. What's wrong with you?"

Extended Family Messages

Uncle to nephew Billy: "Stop crying, Billy, boys don't cry."

Uncle to nephew Billy: "Billy, what are you gonna do with that ironing board? Why don't you go play football or something, boy?"

Gender Messages from the Educational System

Billy's teacher (a female) punishing Billy and another male student in the school cafeteria: "The two of you will walk around the cafeteria five times holding hands, repeating: We're girls; we're girls."

Billy's coach: "Aw, come on, Billy, you throw like a girl."

Billy's coach to Billy and Billy's teammates: "You played like a bunch of girls today."

Peers and Gender Messages

A male friend chiding Billy (who is hugging him): "Get away from me, you faggot."

A male friend teasing Billy about the amount of time he spends with his girlfriend: "Man, she has you pussy-whipped."

Billy's girlfriend to Billy when Billy failed to do an allotted number of sit-ups: "You sissy, don't be such a wimp."

Media

Message on a boy's tee shirt advertised in the local Sunday paper: You Play Like a Bunch of Girls.

The Enduring Impact of Gender Messages

Taken individually, the statements presented above seem harmless, but collectively, the impact of messages that demean behavior viewed as feminine can be defining for both boys and girls. Admonishing male children for what has been labeled cross-gender behavior effectively brings boys back into line. Perhaps more important, by chastising boys for engaging in female-identified behaviors, both girls and boys become cognizant of the second-class status of females in society.

Acting out cultural scripts of masculinity accords status, power, and privilege; therefore, young girl children generally do not receive cautionary messages when they engage in culturally defined boy-typed play or act in a societally-defined boy-typed manner; nor do they suffer loss of status. Young tomboys are subjected to far fewer negative reactions (until adolescence) than are Janegirls. The same is not true for boys who engage in culturally-defined girl play (Macoby 1987). Because sanctions for behaviors perceived to be cross-gendered are more severe for boys, girls are more likely to imitate boys than vice versa (Bussey and Bandura 1992).

GENDERING IS AN INSIDIOUS PROCESS

What is remarkable about gendering is that males and females are more alike at birth than they are different, more alike than any other species. Within the first few moments of life, however, infants hear gendered words from mom, dad, doctor, and nurses. Newborn boys are busters or bouncing boys, while newborn girls are beautiful, delicate, petite. From infancy on, we experience gendered touches and gendered expectations. Acquiring gender is an insidious process, slow, subtle, unnoticed, until acquired behaviors appear natural, normal, appropriate. That said, by age five, compulsory masculinity has been established for the most part and God help the boy who is outside of the box (Nelson 1985).

A NETWORK OF SOCIALIZING AGENTS

Masculinity is not something that is simply transmitted from father to son. Everyone has a hand in the process, with family members at the top of the list. Laureen Snider notes in chapter 18 in this volume, "mothers as well as fathers, terrified of boys becoming 'wimps,' send contradictory messages about the acceptability of bullying and aggression."

The list doesn't stop with mom and dad; it includes siblings, extended kin, teachers, coaches, peers, and, of course, the media. What emerges is something akin to a network of gender police disallowing any semblance of societally defined feminine mannerisms or characteristics in boys and young men. It should come as no surprise, then, that frequently by adolescence males repress a range of emotions and actions lest they be associated with any and all things female and feminine (Bruch, Berko, and Haase 1998). In addition, by puberty, many young males have learned that the culturally correct, masculine way to relate with females is with the penis. Thus, one consequence of gendering that has implications for women and men is that some young boys learn to place a limited-use value on females.

No wonder young boys frequently refer to their female cohort with disdain—the "girls are yucky" syndrome. The need for self-protection causes boys to distance themselves from any activity that smacks of femininity. The fear of ostracism and alienation from those they revere (parents/teachers) and those they hold dear (peers) generally goes a long way toward constraining males from engaging in behavior that is seen as deviating from the norm of masculinity. After all, as social beings and conformists, what young boys would want to be considered odd men out? Individual gender transgressions, then, rather than dismantling gendered social structures, perhaps do more to strengthen gender-constructed boundaries. Boys will do whatever it takes to avoid being labeled a sissy. Analyzing, within that context, the gender statements given at the opening of this chapter offers insight into the overlapping systems of barrier-setting directives and actions that begin early in the lives of males and continue on into adulthood.

Looked at another way, children are socialized within a maze of linking, crosscutting, and/or interlocking social circles. If parents choose to raise their sons outside the bounds of our gender-typed culture—perhaps even androgynously—young boys will be exposed to many influences that are not consistent with their parents' way of thinking. For example, some parents might be slightly skittish but others might be outraged at the prospect of their young son coming home from a playmate's with painted nails and lips. The bottom line is that realistically, parents cannot control all messages their children receive.

SCHOOL DAZE AND PEERS

Beyond the family's sphere of influence lie other important contributors to the acquisition of gender. The educational system plays a major role. For at least twelve years, children spend the greater part of their daily lives within the regimented environments of schools; the only other systems to rival the regimen are the military, prison, and perhaps religious life. No bastions of liberalism, schools are staffed, for the most part, by bureaucrats—administrators and teachers who are steeped in middle-class gendered values. The expectation is that girls will be nice, neat, quiet, obedient, helpful, cooperative, and cheerful. Boys, however, will be boys: assertive/aggressive, competitive, boisterous, messy, athletic, and even unruly at times. Those who refuse to adjust are negatively sanctioned and even may be temporarily isolated from classmates until such time as their behavior conforms to the norm.

Teachers are not the only ones who play a crucial role in gendering children at school; students monitor each other for gender-appropriate behavior and sanction those children who transgress the norms, usually by ridicule or exclusion (who can forget cooties). School-related activities including recess, sports, and scouting separate students along gender lines that create, reinforce, and sustain gendered identities, gender boundaries, and a gendered system.

As children mature and become enmeshed in friendship groups at school and extracurricular activities, peer influence becomes paramount in providing gender guidelines, often overriding parental influence. Barbara Risman and Kristen Myers (1997) found that even in feminist households in which students espoused their parents' egalitarian views, the children did not adhere consistently to parental ideology. When family experiences conflicted with that of their friends, the influence of their friends prevailed.

CONFESSIONS OF A SMALL SAMPLE OF COLLEGE STUDENTS

How common are the admonishments listed at the beginning of this analysis? When students (a total of thirty-nine) in an introductory sociology class were asked anonymously if they had ever been referred to as a sissy, fag, or pussy, every male (twenty-one) answered yes. When asked if they had ever referred to a male using any of the three terms, all thirty-nine students indicated they had. While not a generalizable sample, the responses are indicative of a pattern that calls for further investigation.

What is particularly instructive and pertinent to the theme of this text is that all of the female students (eighteen) acknowledge that they too had used one or more of the terms to address males. The young women reported addressing younger brothers, older brothers, significant others, male friends, and classmates with these epithets. This is evidence of what Snider's argument suggests: that is, females as mothers (I would expand the circle to include friends, kin, wives, and lovers) contribute, perhaps unwittingly, to the perpetuation of machismo. More important, by chiding males who do not embody machismo or denigrating those males who act in a culturally defined feminine manner, women assist in the perpetuation of sexism. Simply put, by ridiculing behavior associated with that of their gender, women inadvertently and in subtle ways demean their own sex.

Even when used in a joking manner, the terms work to harness male behavior to narrow macho parameters. Thus, boys and men may feel compelled to separate themselves from all that is perceived in society as feminine and to embrace all that is defined in their culture as masculine. We have to ask ourselves: Is that what we want? Is that what society needs?

REFERENCES

Bruch, M. A., E. H. Berko, and R. F. Haase. 1998. Shyness, Masculine Ideology, Physical Attractiveness, and Emotional Inexpressiveness: Testing a Mediational Model of Men's Interpersonal Competence. *Journal of Counseling Psychology* 45: 84–97.

Bussey, K., and A. Bandura. 1992. Self-Regulatory Mechanisms Governing Gender Development. *Child Development* 63: 1236–50.

Macoby, E. E. 1987. The Varied Meanings of "Masculine" and "Feminine." In *Masculinity/Femininity: Basic Perspectives*, edited by J. M. Reinisch, L. A. Rosenblum, and S. A. Sanders, 227–39. New York: Oxford University Press.

Nelson, J. B. 1985. Male Sexuality and Masculine Spirituality. *Siecus Reports* 13: 1–4.

Risman, Barbara, and Kristen Myers. 1997. As the Twig Is Bent: Children Reared in Feminist Households. *Qualitative Sociology* 20: 229–52.

20

Hormonal Hurricanes

Menstruation and Female Behavior

Anne Fausto-Sterling

Is it possible that up to 100 percent of all menstruating women regularly experience emotional disturbance? Compared to whom? Are males the unstated standard of emotional stability? If there is but a single definition of what is normal and men fit that definition, then women with "female complaints" must by definition be either crazy or in need of medical attention. A double-bind indeed.

Some scientists explicitly articulate the idea of the naturally abnormal female. Professor Frank Beach, a pioneer in the field of animal psychology and its relationship to sexuality, suggests the following evolutionary account of menstruation. In primitive hunter-gatherer societies adult women were either pregnant or lactating, and since life spans were so short they died well before menopause; low-fat diets made it likely that they did not ovulate every month; they thus experienced no more than ten menstrual cycles. Given current life expectancies as well as the widespread use of birth control, modern women may experience a total of four hundred menstrual cycles. He concludes from this reasoning that "civilization has given women a *physiologically abnormal status* which may have important implications for the interpretation of psychological responses to periodic fluctuations in the secretion of ovarian hormones"— that is, to menstruation (emphasis added).[1] Thus the first problem we face in evaluating the literature on the premenstrual syndrome is figuring out how to deal with the underlying assumption that women have "a physiologically abnormal status."

Researchers who believe in PMS hold a wide variety of viewpoints (none of them supported by scientific data) about the basis of the problem. For example, Dr. Katharina Dalton, the most militant promoter of PMS, says that it results from a relative end-of-the-cycle deficiency in the hormone progesterone. Others cite deficiencies in vitamin B6, fluid retention, and low blood sugar as possible causes. Suggested treatments range from hormone injection to the use of lithium, diuretics, megadoses of vitamins, and control of sugar in the diet.[2] Although some of these treatments are harmless, others are not. Progesterone injection causes cancer in animals. What will it do to humans? And a recent issue of *The New England Journal of Medicine* contains a report that large doses of vitamin B6 damage the nerves, causing a loss of feeling in one's fingers and toes.[3] The wide variety of PMS "causes" and "cures" offered by the experts is confusing to put it mildly. Just what *is* this syndrome that causes such controversy? How can a woman know if she has it?

With a case of the measles it's really quite simple. A fever and then spots serve as diagnostic signs. A woman said to have PMS, however, may or may not have any of a very large number of symptoms. Furthermore, PMS indicators such as headaches, depression, dizziness, loss or gain of appetite show up in everyone from time to time. Their mere presence cannot (as would measle spots) help one to diagnose the syndrome. In addition, whether any of these signals connote disease depends upon their severity. A slight headache may reflect nothing more than a lack of sleep, but repeated, severe headaches could indicate high blood pressure. As one researcher, Dr. Judith Abplanalp, succinctly puts it: "There is no one set of symptoms which is considered to be the hallmark of or standard criterion for defining the premenstrual syndrome."[4] Dr. Katharina Dalton agrees but feels one can diagnose PMS quite simply by applying the term to "any symptoms or complaints which regularly come just before or during early menstruation but are absent at other times of the cycle.[5] Dalton contrasts this with men suffering from potential PMS "symptoms," because, she says, they experience them randomly during the month while women with the same physical indications acknowledge them only during the premenstruum.

PMS research usually bases itself on an ideal, regular, twenty-eight-day menstrual cycle. Researchers eliminate as subjects for study women with infrequent, shorter, or longer cycles. As a result, published investigations look at a skewed segment of the overall population. Even for those women with a regular cycle, however, a methodological problem remains because few researchers define the premenstrual period in the same way. Some studies look only at the day or two preceding the menstrual flow, others look at the week preceding, while workers such as Dalton cite cases that begin two weeks before menstruation and continue for one week after. Since so few investigations use exactly the same definition, research publications on PMS are difficult to compare with one another.[6] On this score, if no other, the literature offers little useful insight, extensive as it is.

Although rarely stated, the assumption is that there is but one PMS. Dalton defines the problem so broadly that she and others may well lump together several phenomena of very different origins, a possibility heightened by the fact that investigators rarely assess the severity of the symptoms. Two women, one suffering from a few low days and the other from suicidal depression, may both be diagnosed as having PMS. Yet their difficulties could easily have different origins and ought certainly to receive different treatments. When investigators try carefully to define PMS, the number of people qualifying for study decreases dramatically. In one case a group used ten criteria to define PMS only to find that no more than 20 percent of those who had volunteered for their research project met them.[7] In the absence of any clearly agreed upon definition(s) of PMS, examinations of the topic should a least state clearly the methodology used; this would enable comparison between publications, and allow us to begin to accumulate some knowledge about the issues at hand. At the moment the literature is filled with individual studies that permit either replication or comparison with one another—an appropriate state, perhaps, for an art gallery but not for a field with pretensions to the scientific.

Despite the problems of method and definition, the conviction remains that PMS constitutes a widespread disorder, a conviction that fortifies and is fortified by the idea that women's reproductive function, so different from that of "normal" men, places them in a naturally diseased state. For those who believe that 90 percent of all women suffer from a disease called PMS, it becomes a reasonable research strategy to look at the normally functioning menstrual cycle for clues about the cause and possible treatment. There are, in fact, many theories but no credible evidence about the origins of PMS. . . . Some of the theories are ingenious and require a sophisticated knowledge of human physiology to comprehend. Nevertheless, the authors of one recent review quietly offer the following summary: "To date no one hypothesis has adequately explained the constellation of symptoms composing PMS.[8] In short, PMS is a disease in search of a definition and cause.

If we continue to assume that menstruation is itself pathological, we cannot establish a baseline of health against which to define disease. If, instead, we accept in theory that a range of menstrual normality exists, we can then set about designing studies that define the healthy female reproductive cycle. Only when we have some feeling for *that* can we begin to help women who suffer from diseases of menstruation.

Many of those who reject the alarmist nature of the publicity surrounding PMS believe nevertheless that women undergo mood changes during the menstrual cycle. Indeed most Western women would agree. But do studies of large segments of our population support this generality? And if so, what causes these ups and downs? In trying to answer these questions we confront another piece of the medical model of human behavior, the belief that biology is primary, that hormonal changes cause behavioral ones, but not vice versa. Most researchers use such a linear, unicausal model without thinking about it. Their framework is so much a part of their belief system that they forget to question it. Nevertheless it is the model from which they work, and failure to recognize and work skeptically with it often results in poorly conceived research combined with implausible interpretations of data. Although the paradigm of biological causation has until very recently dominated menstrual cycle research, it now faces serious and intellectually stimulating challenge from feminist experts in the field.

LIFTING THE SHADOW TOWARD AN
UNDERSTANDING OF MENSTRUATION AND BEHAVIOR

During the forty-five years that have elapsed since Benedek and Rubenstein published the first "modern" experimental study of mood and menstrual cycle,[9] countless additional studies have appeared. Why, then, is it possible for a scientist in 1981 to write the following?

> The question is still being debated. Are women's moods a function of their rhythmic reproductive physiology or not? Unfortunately the literature does not agree on the answer to the more basic questions: Do women experience cyclic mood fluctuations?[10]

In looking for answers, we encounter a research field filled with poorly designed studies. Inadequate sample sizes and measures, inappropriate choice of subjects, tests designed to obtain a desired outcome, and poor or nonexistent use of statistical analysis are but some of the problems. That so many scientists have been able for so long to do such poor research attests to both the unconscious social agendas of many of the researchers and to the theoretical inadequacy of the research framework used in the field as a whole. Once again we encounter the failure of a simple linear model of biological causation, and must struggle instead with a more complex conceptualization in which mind, body, and culture depend so inextricably on one another that allegedly straightforward studies, ones claiming to find single causes for cyclic behavior, must be looked upon with deep suspicion.

Over the years specific critiques of menstrual-cycle studies have accumulated. As early as 1877 physician and medical researcher Mary Putnam Jacobi pioneered menstrual-cycle research with the publication of her book *The Question of Rest for Women During Menstruation*. In this critical literature review she pointed out the relative novelty of the idea that women are *more* rather than *less* vulnerable at menstruation. In a thorough analysis of her own careful interviews with 268 women about their menstrual experiences, she presented results that have a ring of feminist modernity, suggesting that by no means do all women suffer menstrual pain and that among those who do are many who are otherwise in poor health or under stress, or who have insufficient exercise and education.[11]

Psychologist Mary Brown Parlee deserves the credit for breaking ground more recently with her analyses of the menstrual cycle.[12] . . . Parlee categorizes studies on premenstrual emotionality into four types: correlational, retrospective questionnaires, daily self-reports, and thematic analysis of word lists describing various feelings and moods.

Correlational studies. Through correlational studies, scientists look to see if particular phases of the menstrual cycle coincide with reported or observed behaviors. Parlee points out that many studies don't even bother with independent confirmation of cycle phase. Properly done correlational studies also present problems. Early in their training, scientists learn that correlation gives no information about causation. As Parlee points out, most correlational studies seem to assume that when emotional changes correspond to changes in the menstrual cycle, hormones must be to blame. The model gives priority to biology by implication rather than by direct proof and leaves aside the idea that one's hormone biology might itself change under differing emotional conditions.

Retrospective questionnaires. Even today, one of the most widely used processes for studying premenstrual anxiety and depression is to ask women to fill out a form called the Menstrual Distress Questionnaire (abbreviated MDQ), on which they indicate which among a list of symptoms or moods they recall experiencing at different times of their menstrual cycle. . . . The questionnaire lists forty-seven "symptoms," only five of which—all found under the subheading "positive arousal"—have agreeable connotations. . . .[13] A rapid perusal alerts one to the fact that, starting out with the assumption of menstrual distress, one can design a test to prove one's point. Critics of this work recently designed a Menstrual Joy Questionnaire, which emphasizes positive feelings during the menstrual cycle.[14] The retrospective questionnaire holds additional problems, including the selective memory of the women completing it combined with their prior knowledge of the purpose of the study. Many women grow up with the expectation that they should feel bad just before their periods, and this belief can certainly predispose them to selectively remember feeling bad just before menstruation but not at other times of the month. As one researcher writes in a study on moods and menstruation in college students, "negative behavior exhibited premenstrually is perceived as evidence for the prevailing negative stereotype of female emotional behavior while positive behavior is ignored as something for which biology is irrelevant."[15]

The uncritical use of retrospective studies ignores the twin influences of negative cultural beliefs and outright ignorance about menstruation. A study of forty women at a Michigan clinic serving a poor, multiethnic clientele found patients to be "naive and misinformed about the true function of menstruation."[16] Most (63 percent) had no knowledge of menarche before they began to menstruate, while many thought that "cold" could enter the body during menstruation, "believing that a bath, a shampoo, a walk in the dew or rain might 'back up' menstrual flow and result in a stroke, insanity, or 'quick TB.'"[17]

A second type of investigation shows that middle-class children, presumably well educated about menstruation, still approach menarche with fixed ideas about what to expect. In one recent study most premenarcheal girls and boys of the same age believed menstruation to be a physically and emotionally disruptive event, while another found that 85 percent of the premenarcheal girls studied thought it inappropriate to discuss menstruation with boys.[18] Regardless of class or educational level, large numbers of women grow up with strong negative attitudes toward menstruation. . . . These firm beliefs might affect answers not only to retrospective questionnaires but also the physiology of menstruation itself.

Daily self-reports. Some researchers overcome the problem of selective memory on retrospective forms by using daily self-reports. With this method groups of women keep daily menstrual calendars on which they record their moods and the first day of menstruation. Until very recently, however, such studies have not been "blind"—the subject always knew that she was part of an attempt to correlate mood and menstrual phase.

Thematic analysis. In the fourth type of study reviewed by Parlee, researchers ask women to speak in unstructured fashion about daily life experiences. The interviewers then analyze the language content, scoring for indications of hostility and anxiety. By performing such analyses over the course of one or more menstrual cycles, investigators hope to correlate emotional changes with physiological ones. Although with this approach, the subject may be unaware of the study's purpose, the analyst isn't. In other words, this too is a "sighted" study with all the pitfalls of subjective analysis. The most reliable studies employ double blinds, in which neither the experimental subject nor the person gathering and categorizing the results knows the true purpose of the study. The few studies of premenstrual emotional changes done in this way fail to show cyclical mood alterations.[19]

Parlee's report merely scratches the surface, beneath which lies so huge a number of methodological problems that the thoughtful menstrual-cycle researcher risks paralysis in dealing with them, while they simply overwhelm the unwary layperson.

How is it that so many different and seemingly obvious things could be wrong with the bulk of menstrual-cycle research? The answer, hidden within the walls of the research structure, is usually plastered over with clever techniques and detailed measurements. Why, for instance, do researchers looking at women's hormone cycles and mood changes fail to mention the monthly cycle of testosterone?[20] The answer, I suggest, is that testosterone is seen as a male hormone, hence "normal," and thus not an obvious subject for inquiry when looking at the "abnormalities" of menstrual mood changes. How, too, can so many highly trained researchers fail even to discuss the problem of double-blind experimentation? The answer lies in their belief in biological primacy. One need worry about double blinds only if one remains conscious of the fact that thoughts, mind-sets, and emotions can affect one's physiology. Of course most women know this perfectly well, since overexcitement, exhaustion, travel, illness, and stress can alter the timing of one's period, change the number and intensity of premenstrual signals, and influence the presence or absence of the menstrual flow and its degree of discomfort; these are all variations in the physiological expression of the monthly cycle, influenced by one's emotional state.

Dr. Randi Koeske,[21] . . . paints in clear detail the consequences of reliance on a normative "disease-model" framework for the menstrual cycle, a framework that gives precedence to biological variables (which researchers view as representing the "real" underlying cause of behavior), while relegating social-cognitive variables to secondary positions.[22] It is a theoretical approach that emphasizes technical measurement even when it is devoid of meaning and focuses on "context-free factors inside the organism," as if the organism existed separately from its environment; at the same time the normative disease-model framework views "changeableness, emotionality, and rhythmicity" as either "inherently unhealthy" or as changes from norms (usually based on men) about how often and to what degree rhythmic variations are "appropriate." Such a viewpoint allows researchers to ignore the historical and cultural contexts of their work and, as Koeske so nicely puts it, reduces them to "capturing brief snapshots of time, rather than allowing processes to unfold in context."[23]

One can look forward to new illumination of this subject. A younger generation of scientists has begun to take fresh research initiatives, forging different theoretical approaches and using them to make their way toward better designed, more informative studies of the menstrual cycle. One of the most pleasurable aspects of reading the work of these scientists is that it stems from a full respect for women. A close second is the intellectual challenge encountered in considering complex, contextual research that precludes the reduction of human behavior to some simple biological variable. "The *real* alternative to biomedicine," Koeske writes, "is a system of health research . . . which finds a way to reintegrate the whole person from the jigsaw of parts created by modern scientific medicine. The strength of the feminist perspective is the recognition that the parts biomedicine currently recognizes cannot be reassembled into a whole."[24] The challenge presented to menstrual-cycle researchers is to find the missing pieces and light the way toward integration.

Koeske suggests several steps in that direction which, if followed inventively, will help deepen our understanding of the problem. These include:

1. Start with clearly stated and testable hypotheses, rather than creating a hypothesis after collecting the data.
2. Use more than one method to test the hypothesis, rather than relying solely on one highly modish approach.
3. Listen carefully to what women actually say about their bodies, lives, and perceptions, and treat their views as data, rather than restricting their choice of feelings in order to construct an "objective" measurement.
4. Beware (especially feminists) of replacing a biologically reductive theory with a socially reductive one.[25]

Like the merits of Mom and apple pie, Koeske's cautions may seem self-evident. When applied to actual research problems, however, they bring interesting results. Some examples follow.

1. Dr. Alice Rossi introduced "the social week" into her studies and found that both men and women experienced cyclical changes during this period. They tended to feel down on Tuesdays and happiest on weekends.[26]

2. Dr. Koeske bases some of her recent work on attribution theory, which tries to understand how people interpret their experiences. In one set of studies she asked students presented with made-up "case studies" that included menstrual-cycle information to interpret the behaviors of hypothetical "patients." Her findings bore out her hypothesis that only hostile or angry behaviors during the premenstruum were attributed to biology; the students believed that positive behaviors during the same period stemmed from individual personality traits or some external positive situation.[27]

3. Dr. Alice Dan, another member of the "new wave" of menstrual-cycle researchers, took up a point first made by Parlee—that we have yet to use two different measures to show the same menstrually related mood changes. In her study Dan compared self-reports of menstrual changes with analysis of open-ended conversations held at different times during the menstrual cycle. Her finding that the two independent assessments disagreed with one another raises some important questions, both about the validity of past studies and the interpretation of present ones. She considers reasonable the "suggestion that we stop measuring 'mood' changes over the menstrual cycle until we have developed a better understanding of what we are measuring."[28]

4. Dr. Sharon Golub found that premenstrually related increases in anxiety were far smaller than the heightened anxiety experienced by students subjected to the stress of an examination. In general she found premenstrually related mood changes to be of small magnitude, concluding that "the premenstrual hormonal changes appear to impose little psychological burden," and are often so slight that women "are sometimes not even aware of them."[29]

As Dr. Koeske puts it: "Who knows? With a little luck and a lot of hard work, the only thing that may turn out to be unusual or uninterpretable about female premenstrual emotionality is the fact that no one understood it before."[30] And understanding, I believe, will come from the type of research undertaken by the feminist biologists and social scientists of today.

NOTES

1. Frank A. Beach, preface to chapter 10, in *Human Sexuality in Four Perspectives* (Baltimore: Johns Hopkins University Press, 1977), 271.

2. M. B. Rosenthal, "Insights into the Premenstrual Syndromes," *Physician and Patient* (April 1983): 46–53.

3. Herbert Schaumberg et al., "Sensory Neuropathy from Pyridoxine Abuse," *New England Journal of Medicine* 309 (1983): 446–48.

4. Judith Abplanalp, "Premenstrual Syndrome: A Selective Review," *Women and Health* 8 (1983): 110.

5. Katharina Dalton, *Once a Month* (Claremont, CA: Hunter House, 1983), 12.

6. J. Abplanalp, R. F. Haskett, and R. M. Rose, "The Premenstrual Syndrome," *Advances in Psychoneuroendocrinology* 3 (1980): 327–47; and Judith Abplanalp, "Premenstrual Syndrome: A Selective Review," *Women and Health* 8 (1983).

7. Abplanalp, "Premenstrual Syndrome: A Selective Review."

8. Robert L. Reid and S. S. Yen, "Premenstrual Syndrome," *American Journal of Obstetrics and Gynecology* 139 (1981): 97.

9. T. Benedek and B. B. Rubenstein, "The Correlations between Ovarian Activity and Psychodynamic Processes: I. The Ovulative Phase," *Psychosomatic Medicine* 1 (1939): 245–70; and T. Benedek and B. B. Rubenstein, "The Correlations between Ovarian Activity and Psychodynamic Processes: II. The Menstrual Phase, *Psychosomatic Medicine* 1 (1939): 461–85.

10. Janet R. Swanby, "A Longitudinal Study of Daily Mood Self Reports and their Relationship to the Menstrual Cycle," in *The Menstrual Cycle*, vol. 2, eds. P. Komnenich et al. (New York: Springer, 1981), 94.

11. Mary Putnam Jacobi, *The Question of Rest for Women During Menstruation* (New York: G. P. Putnam's Sons, 1877).

12. Mary Brown Parlee, "The Premenstrual Syndrome," *Psychological Bulletin* 80 (1973): 454–65.

13. Rudolf Moos, "Typology of Menstrual Cycle Symptoms," *American Journal of Obstetrics and Gynecology* 103 (1969): 390–402.

14. J. Delaney, M. J. Lupton, and E. Doth, *The Curse. A Cultural History of Menstruation* (New York: Dutton, 1976).

15. Randi Koeske, "Premenstrual Emotionality: Is Biology Destiny?" *Women and Health* 1 (1976): 12.

16. Loudell Snow and Shirley M. Johnson, "Myths about Menstruation: Victims of Our Own Folklore," *International Journal of Women's Studies* 1 (1978): 70.

17. Ibid.

18. This study was reviewed by Sharon Golub, ed., "Lifting the Curse of Menstruation," *Women and Health* 8 (1983).

19. J. Brooks, D. N. Ruble, and A. E. Clark, "College Women's Attitudes and Expectations Concerning Menstrual-Related Changes," *Psychosomatic Medicine* 39 (1977): 288–98; and D. Ruble, "Premenstrual Symptoms: A Reinterpretation," *Science* 197 (1977): 291–92.

20. H. Persky, "Reproductive Hormones, Moods and the Menstrual Cycle," in *Sex Differences in Behavior*, ed. R. C. Friedman, R. M. Richart, and R. L. Vande Wiele (Huntington, N.Y.: Krieger, 1974), 455–66; W. P. Collins and J. R. Newton, "The Ovarian Cycle," in *Biochemistry of Women: Clinical Concepts*, eds. A. S. Curry and J. V. Hewitt (Boca Raton, FL: CRC Press, 1974).

21. Randi Koeske, "Premenstrual Emotionality: Is Biology Destiny?"; "Lifting the Curse of Menstruation: Toward a Feminist Perspective on the Menstrual Cycle," *Women and Healing* 8 (1983): 1–16; and "Theoretical Perspectives on Menstrual Cycle Research," in *The Menstrual Cycle*, vol. 1, eds. A. Dan, E. Graham, and C. P. Beecher (New York: Springer, 1980), 8–24.

22. Koeske, "Theoretical Perspectives on Menstrual Cycle Research."

23. Koeske, "Lifting the Curse of Menstruation," 6.

24. Ibid., 13.

25. Koeske, "Theoretical Perspectives on Menstrual Cycle Research."

26. Alice Rossi and P. Rossi, "Body Time and Social Time: Mood Patterns by Menstrual Cycle Phase and Day of the Week," *Social Science Research* 6 (1977): 273–308.

27. Koeske, "Theoretical Perspectives on Menstrual Cycle Research."

28. Alice Dan, "Free-Associative versus Self Report Measures of Emotional Change over the Menstrual Cycle," in *The Menstrual Cycle*, vol. 1, eds. Dan, Graham, and Beecher, 119.

29. Sharon Golub, "Premenstrual Changes in Mood, Personality and Cognitive Function," in *The Menstrual Cycle*, vol. 1, eds. Dan, Graham, and Beecher, 244.

30. Koeske, "Theoretical Perspectives on Menstrual Cycle Research," 24.

EDITOR'S NOTE

It has been established that some women have PMS, but might some men have testosterone syndrome? Testosterone has generally been held up as one of the most important and intractable aspects of the physical differences between females and males. The old science stated that men purportedly were more aggressive than women because men have high levels of testosterone. The new science now refers to women's testosterone, too. In fact, when a woman's libido is low, one of the recommended courses of treatments is a testosterone patch to bolster her natural testosterone level.

That's not all. A study at the University of Montreal dispels the long-held belief that aggression in boys is the result of higher levels of testosterone; a group of researchers led by Richard Tremblay, found that boys aged thirteen who exhibited the most aggressive behavior had below-average levels of testosterone, while boys who had higher levels of testosterone were the more socially dominate, more likely to be leaders.[1]

Now there is even research analyzing male menopause. It's only a matter of time, with all the baby boomers hitting age fifty, that male menopause will be at the epicenter of the medical radar screen. Clinical endocrinologists are beginning to examine the condition of male menopause called hypogonadism viropause and androgen decline in aging. Apparently, the symptoms of male menopause can include irritability, mood swings, depression, anxiety, palpitations, memory loss, decrease in libido, erectile dysfunction, and about 10 percent of men will experience hot flashes.[2]

As noted in the introduction of the text, women and men are more alike than different. Perhaps more knowledge and discussion of these issues where men and women share common ground can lead to greater empathy between the sexes.

NOTES

1. Stephen S. Hall., "The Bully in the Mirror," *The New York Times*, 22 August 1999, pp. 30–35, 58, 62, 64–65.

2. Richard A. Marini, "Men, too, have 'menopause' and signs very real," *The Cincinnati Enquirer*, 18 May 2001, p. F2.

VII

CORPORATE GATEKEEPING

Fitting In

21

Talking from 9 to 5

How Women's and Men's Conversational Styles Affect Who Gets Heard, Who Gets Credit, and What Gets Done at Work

Deborah Tannen

. . . There are many ways that women entering the world of work are entering "the men's house," to use the phrase coined by Captain Carol Barkalow as the title of her book about her military career. The very language spoken is often based on metaphors from sports or from the military, terms that are just idioms to many women, not references to worlds they have either inhabited or observed with much alacrity. Such expressions as "stick to your guns," "under the gun," "calling the shots," "an uphill battle," "a level playing field," "a judgment call," "start the ball rolling," "a curveball," "the ball's in their court," "batting a thousand," "struck out," "getting flak," "the whole nine yards," "in the ballpark," and "deep-six it" are part of our everyday vocabulary. . . .

Although there is evidence that women do adapt their styles to those of men when they find themselves in interaction with men, they rarely adopt mens' styles whole hog. And it is well that they don't, because men and women who model their behavior on someone of the other gender often get a very different reaction than their role models get. In a workplace situation, it is frequently a man who has been the model, while a woman who tries to behave like him is distressed to find that the reaction she gets is very different. . . .

THE GLASS CEILING AS A WALL OF WORDS

Here is a brief explanation of how conversational-style differences play a role in installing a glass ceiling. When decisions are made about promotion to management positions, the qualities sought are a high level of competence, decisiveness, and ability to lead. If it is men, or mostly men, who are making the decisions about promotions—as it usually is—they are likely to misinterpret women's ways of talking as showing indecisiveness, inability to assume authority, and even incompetence. . . . For example, a woman who feels it is crucial to preserve the appearance of consensus when making decisions because she feels anything else would appear bossy and arrogant begins by asking those around her for their opinions. This can be interpreted by her bosses as evidence that she doesn't know what she thinks should be done, that she is trying to get others to make decisions for her. . . .

Public speaking is frightening for almost everyone. But standing up in front of a large group of people, commanding attention, and talking authoritatively are extensions of the socialization most boys have been forced to endure, as boys in groups tend to vie for center stage, challenge the boys who get it, and deflect the challenges of others. Many of the ways women have learned to be likable and feminine are liabilities when it comes to public presentations. Most girls' groups penalize a girl who stands out or calls attention to herself in an obvious way.

A woman who works as a trainer for business people coming to the United States realized that a disproportionate amount of the criticism she and her colleagues delivered to the trainees was directed at women, especially in the nebulous category of "professional presence." They found themselves telling women, more often than men, that they did not speak loudly enough, did not project their voices, should stop cocking their heads to one side, should try to lower the pitch of their voices. A few women were told that their way of dressing was too sexy, their manner too flirtatious, if they wanted to be taken seriously in the American business environment. In a sense, they were appearing too "feminine." But there were also women who were told that they were too challenging and abrasive. They launched into questions without a lead-in or hedges; they asked too many insistent questions; they did not tilt their heads at all or seemed to be tilting them in challenging ways. Although the trainers did not think of it in these terms, you could say that these women were not "feminine" enough.

In at least one case, a particular trainee had to be told that she was coming across as both too flirtatious and too confrontational. In wondering why such a large percentage of women in her program (a small one to start with) had the basic skills down cold, yet seemed to be undermining their own effectiveness by their nonverbal behavior, the trainer concluded that they had a very fine line to walk: The range of behaviors considered acceptable for them was extremely narrow. And, perhaps most important, the American professional business culture in which they were learning to fit was not only American but also American male.

All of the factors mentioned by the trainer indicate that making presentations is a prime example of an activity in which behavior expected of women is at odds with what is expected of an effective professional. In fact, the very act of standing up in front of a group, talking about ideas is something that was unthinkable for women not so long ago.

Once a woman (or man) does make public presentations, she (or he) is open to challenge or even attack. . . .

THE DRAGON LADY

When I heard the same remark twice in one week about two different women, I knew there was something going on. "Before I came to work for Ann," a man who reports to her told me, "everybody warned me to watch out. They called her the dragon lady. But I don't know what they were talking about. I've always found her great to work with." A few days later, a woman at another company commented about the woman she works for, "I've heard people call Marie the dragon lady. But I've never seen anything to justify that. She's the best boss I've ever worked for." I wondered, Why the dragon lady? Not only was there nothing dragon-like about either Ann or Marie, but they were as different from one another as could be, in age, temperament, and personal style. The only thing they had in common was the "lady" part. Being women highly placed in their organizations seems to have caused people to look at them through conventional images of women in positions of authority. Our culture gives us a whole menagerie of stereotypical images of women: schoolmarm, head nurse, headmistress, doting mother, cruel stepmother, dragon lady, catwoman, witch, bitch.

An article about [former] President Clinton's health czar, Kristine M. Gebbie, began by saying she didn't look like a czar, then went on to say she had the air of a head nurse. Although there is nothing inherently negative about being head nurse, the image this term evokes in our culture is decidedly negative. In the tradition of Ken Kesey's Nurse Ratched, the villain in his novel *One Flew Over the Cuckoo's Nest*, it suggests a woman who is arbitrarily authoritarian, life-killingly humorless, and stiffly unfeminine. . . . The writer explains, "There is something at once no-nonsense and fussy about her—her erect posture, her precise and proper answers, her tendency to correct an interviewer's questions." Hmmm. Shouldn't a czar stand erect and have a no-nonsense manner? Shouldn't a czar give precise and proper answers? Correcting an interviewer's questions seems a good way to maintain control when being interviewed. But all these qualities took on a very different effect because they were found in a woman. . . .

. . . A newspaper announced in large type, summarizing an accompanying story, "A stuffy schoolmarm is a contender." I began reading the article and learned that an Illinois gubernatorial candidate named Dawn Clark Netsch had won the Democratic nomination after she managed "to alter her image to a down-to-earth contender from that of a stuffy schoolmarm." But further down, I was surprised to read that the "bookish" candidate, who had previously "talked too much" and sounded "like some kind of egghead," had been a law professor at Northwestern University for eighteen years. This seemed to explain why she might be "bookish," talk a lot, and be denigrated by some as an egghead. But none of these qualities is suggested by "schoolmarm," which has different connotations entirely: stuffy, yes, but a strict disciplinarian rather than bookish, and small-minded rather than an egghead. Forced to choose between a professional image, appropriate to the qualities the paper attributed to her as well as to her profession, and "schoolmarm," suggested by her gender, the newspaper went for the gender.

THE IMAGE OF AUTHORITY

Femaleness is associated with softeners, mitigation, and politeness, whereas maleness is associated with authority. This means that women who want to sound authoritative must risk sounding male. (It also means that men who want to sound polite must risk sounding female.) . . .

. . . When I asked people for their impressions of the men and women they worked with and for, I noticed a pattern: When they commented on women in managerial positions—but never when they commented on men—people often said, "She's abrasive," or, just as often, "She's not abrasive," "not aggressive," or "has a soft touch." It is one thing to describe how you think someone is—"abrasive," "aggressive," and so on. But why would people mention what someone is not? It makes sense only against the expectation that the person would be that way. So it seems that when a woman is in a high position, there is an expectation that she will be unfeminine, negative, or worse. When she isn't, it is perceived as worth mentioning. And these prevalent images ambush professional women as they seek to maintain their careers, a well as their personal lives—and their femininity. . . .

. . . Individuals in positions of authority are judged by how they enact that authority. This poses a particular challenge for women. The ways women are expected to talk—and many (not all) women do talk—are at odds with images of authority. Women are expected to hedge their beliefs as opinions, to seek opinions and advice from others, to be "polite" in their requests. If a woman talks this way, she is seen as lacking in authority. But if she talks with certainty, makes bold statements of fact rather than hedged statements of opinion, interrupts others, goes on at length, and speaks in a declamatory and aggressive manner, she will be disliked. Our language is rich in words to describe such unwomanly women—words that have been hurled at many prominent women in positions of authority such as Jeane Kirkpatrick, Geraldine Ferraro, and Margaret Thatcher, as well as innumerable women in offices, factories, and studios around the country. Looking closely at how women in positions of authority use language to do their jobs—and how others respond to them—sheds light on our images of women as well as our understanding of authority. . . .

When I talked to people about their work lives, I asked them, among other things, what they think management is all about, and what makes a good manager or a poor one. When I put this question to women in positions of authority, one of the most frequent statements they offered to explain what makes them good managers is that they do not act like an authority figure—insofar as an authority figure is thought to be authoritarian. They told me that they don't lord it over subordinates, don't act as though they are better than those who report to them. I began to wonder why women in authority are so concerned not to appear authoritarian—not to appear as if they think they are superior or are putting themselves in a one-up position, even though that is exactly the position they are in.

CREATING AUTHORITY AS A PROFESSOR

. . . Linguist Elisabeth Kuhn examined the way male and female university professors established their authority, and she came to conclusions comparable to Smith's for student preachers. Kuhn noticed that the American women professors she taped avoided giving their students direct orders at the beginning of the term. Instead, they spoke of "the requirements" of the course, as if these were handed down directly from the institution, and then told the students how they could fulfill the requirements. This is how three different women professors introduced their syllabi—written outlines of the courses:

"We are going to talk about the requirements."

"I also tell you what the course requirements are, since I'm sure you're interested in that. Um, there is going to be a midterm and a final. Okay?"

"Now, let me say a little bit about the requirements for the course. . . . There are two papers, the first paper, ah, let's see, is due it's back here [while looking at her sheet] at the beginning."

Kuhn contrasts this with the male professors in her study who also handed out lists of requirements in the form of syllabi but made it explicit that the syllabi set forth decisions they personally had made:

"I have two midterms and a final. And I added this first midterm rather early to get you going on reading, uh, discussions, so that you will not fall behind."

"I want you to read NN's XX. But I have not assigned a textbook for you to go out and buy because I assumed either you have a copy of XX which will include the NN, or you will be delighted to go out and provide yourself with it. . . . I'm gonna ask you to do one midterm, which will primarily be a reading check to make sure that you're with it."

. . . By using personal statements such as "I'm gonna ask you to do one midterm," the men professors called attention to their authority by going "on record" as the ones setting the requirements for the course.

In all these studies, women were found to downplay their authority while exercising it. It seems that creating their demeanor in a position of authority is yet another conversational ritual growing out of the goal of keeping everyone on an equal footing, at least insofar as appearances are concerned. This doesn't mean that women or men who speak this way really think everyone is equal; it means they have to do a certain amount of conversational work to make sure they maintain the proper demeanor—to fit their sense of what makes a good person, which entails not seeming to parade their higher status. If they have to tell others what to do, give information, and correct errors—all of which they will have to do on the job, especially if they are in a position of authority—they will expend effort to assure others that they are not pulling rank, not trying to capitalize on or rub in their one-up position. In contrast, since men's characteristic rituals have grown out of the assumption that all relationships are inherently hierarchical, it is not surprising that many of them either see less reason to downplay their authority or see more reason to call attention to it—to ward off inevitable challenges. . . .

I cannot emphasize enough that the appearance of equality I am referring to is ritual, not literal. I am not implying that individual women doubt their superior position in the hierarchy . . .

. . . Like many conversation rituals common among women, talking as if "we're all equals" but still expecting to receive the respect appropriate to the higher-status position depends on the participation of the other person to respect that position. The president of a women's college had a long and difficult meeting with a student who protested her choice of commencement speaker. Finally, the president said, "What it comes down to is that you don't accept my right to make this decision, after considering your point of view and everyone else's." The student thought about it and agreed. "When I see you on campus after hours dressed informally, I forget about your position," she said. . . .

When people told me about men who had "strictly business" or "no-nonsense" styles, they simply said, "He's a strictly business type," or they referred to his profession: "He's a typical accountant." But when they were commenting on the same style in a woman, I frequently heard, "She's got a pseudomasculine style." Because this style was expected of and associated with men, women who adopted it were seen not as trying to be efficient, competent, and businesslike, but as trying to be like men.

One man I interviewed mentioned the same characteristic—directness—in talking about three people in his company. But it was a complaint in the case of the two women and a compliment when applied to the man. About one woman he said:

> Well, her style was very direct. I think very direct and abrupt. Because that was one of the criticisms I had of her . . . was a, somewhat of a lack of tact. Because she could make statements which were right, but not tactfully made. And she tended to upset—or ruffle some feathers.

. . . And yet, in telling me why he particularly admired a man he worked with, he mentioned the same quality—directness:

And I had a great deal of admiration for him. I think he's direct, he's aggressive, he's very intelligent. . . . On the other hand, he does carry a big hammer! And if he needs to, he'll use it and you'll get squashed!

. . . But it is clear that the quality of directness made a different impression on him when it was used by the man and by the two women.

Another facet of this dynamic is that individuals within a culture may be punished by others if they do not conform to expectations for their sex. Anne Statham notes in her study of male and female managers that individuals of both sexes who departed from the norms for their own sex were viewed negatively by subordinates of the same sex. A male manager whose style approximated those of the women was seen as "fairly meek" and "weak" by men who worked for him, though he was highly praised by women subordinates. A woman manager whose style was more like those of the men in the study was criticized for neglect by a woman who reported to her (she "never shows any personal interest in me . . . she has only asked me to lunch once") and by her secretary for having "superior airs." The woman herself felt that women subordinates resisted accepting decisions she made independently.

Similar findings were uncovered by Susan Schick Case in a study of men and women managers talking together in groups of ten at a management school. Case concluded that two of the most influential members of the groups were a woman and a man whose styles combined ways of speaking expected of the two sexes. (She gauged influence by who talked more, how much, to whom, about what, and in what way.) The ways the particularly influential man spoke included hesitating, using rising intonation at the end of statements, mitigating statements with qualifiers, expressing feelings, and talking about himself. He also used "masculine traits" like swearing and joking. The particularly influential woman's style included using complex sentences, slang, resisting interruptions, and talking to the group as a whole. Her style also had many feminine aspects: She did not swear, did not talk "about competition, aggression, taking charge or one-upmanship," and her talk was often personal; Case found her to be the most supportive group member linguistically, but the only woman in the group who never said "mm-hmm." Case further describes her style in this way:

> She contributed 83 percent of all female usage of interruptions and all the incidents of disallowing interruption. That is not to say that she always disallowed interruptions. But the times she allowed interruptions accounted for only 18 percent of the female total. Although very assertive, her style was not confrontative, thus placing her in the bottom quartile in arguing, confronting, and attacking. She stated her own ideas, but also built on others' utterances and asked questions to elicit ideas, both female traits.

All in all, Case's description sounds quite appealing. So it comes as a surprise to learn that this woman was widely disliked and provoked openly hostile comments from others in the group whom Case describes as "male group members with prototypical male-style speech." Here are some of the things they said about her:

> "You're playing the role of a man in the group. There's an issue of competition."

> "Castrating bitch."

The men whose speech combined male and female traits, including the one Case singled out as being one of the most influential group members, did not, apparently, elicit the anger that this woman did, but neither were they pleased with the receptions they got. One man whose speech Case calls "balanced" measured in the middle in terms of influence, but he was the least influential of the men. . . .

. . . I have heard from many women in positions of authority who say the assertiveness required on the job causes problems at home. An attorney told me that she finds herself questioning her mother in a way that her mother protests, "You're not a lawyer now." Her husband too at times reminds her, "You're home now." One woman said that her husband told her, "Go out, come back in, and try saying that a different way. I'm not your secretary." Another woman told me that her husband became angry because instead of waiting on the sidewalk while he hailed a cab, she stepped into the street and raised her own arm, as she had come to do automatically when she needed to hail a cab in the course of her work. A third woman told of a similar experience: She and her husband arrived at an expensive restaurant for dinner. As usual, she had made the reservations. (This was no problem.) But as they approached the maître d', it was she who gave their name and helped the maître d' locate it on his list by pointing to it. By the time they were seated, her husband was livid. "Don't you ever do that again," he seethed. "You are the only woman in this whole restaurant who did that!"

In the case of the last example, I had to ask for clarification, to be sure I understood what exactly had angered the woman's husband. (It was that she took charge, dealing with the maître d' herself rather than hanging back and letting him do it.) But if women and men are to relate to each other as equals, shouldn't they be following the same norms in talking to each other? . . .

In considering these examples, I wondered why these women's husbands felt their wives were trying to dominate them, when the women did the very things that the men themselves wanted to do? . . .

WHAT'S A WOMAN TO DO?

. . . Our expectations for how a person in authority should behave are at odds with our expectations for how a woman should behave. If a woman talks in ways expected of women, she is more likely to be liked than respected. If she talks in ways expected of men, she is more likely to be respected than liked. It is particularly ironic that the risk of losing likability is greater for women in authority, since evidence indicates that so many women care so much about whether or not they are liked.

EDITOR'S NOTE

As Deborah Tannen's reading demonstrates, women in the corporate world have to achieve a balance between being too quiet and too boisterous; too passive and too aggressive; too girlish and too butch. Sometimes it seems that no matter what women do, they are welcome only as sex objects in the workplace. For example, at the National Institute for Health medical officer Betsy Smith and other women employees filed a class-action lawsuit alleging a culture of sexual harassment, including: a supervisor sending a red bra to a subordinate; female employees being hugged and kissed by their bosses; male employees e-mailing photos of bare-breasted women and even reserving one room at hotels to try to get female coworkers to sleep in the same room.[1]

Wall Street firms have had their share of lawsuits. Recently, E. Hydie Sumner won a $2.2 million lawsuit against Merill Lynch for sex discrimination. Sumner had an M.B.A and had experience in investment banking, earning six-figures, before she was hired with a base salary of $18,000 at Merrill Lynch. She agreed to the amount because she was told she would be given the opportunity to become a manager. Instead she was advised by her boss that her job was to be his "little ray of sunshine."[2] Sumner worked harder and harder, but instead of being rewarded, she was referred to as a "man hater" and "bitchy." It is instructive that Merrill Lynch is not alone in paying out millions to settle claims of sex discrimination filed by female employees. Other Wall Street firms include Morgan Stanley, that paid $54 million in settlement, and Smith Barney, that settled a class action lawsuit in the late 1990s.

Striking a balance or fitting in at the workplace doesn't end with the spoken word, but extends to the written word. Maureen Dowd, editorial columnist for *The New York Times*, argues that a man can write a column that criticizes those in power and will be seen as authoritative or just doing his job, but a woman would be called castrating or emasculating. After all, "Women are supposed to take it, not dish it out," says Dowd.[3]

Citing the snail's pace for appointing women to corporate boards, Judy Rosener reports that women "are frequently subjected to competency testing . . . women have to prove themselves over and over again by meeting a set of criteria which their male competitors need not meet."[4] Although Rosener's focus is the board level, her observations can be taken as indicators of women's acceptance within a corporation overall, because the corporate culture emanates from the board room.

It is instructive that women's delicate balancing act applies not only to women in the corporate boardroom but to women in the corporate man's bedroom. High-profile wives of high-profile men are expected to dress and behave in a way that does not detract in any way from their corporate man, even if he is on trial for stealing money from his company's coffers. Advice to wives attending the trial: Wives "should be present, but not ostentatious; attractive, but not excessively so . . . not look haughty and obscene.[5] Nancy Reagan was considered the perfect wife because she just sat there and knew when to "look like she cared; . . . when to nod, when to mist up . . . there is a talent to tearing up at the right moment . . . to looking hurt and concerned."[6] Of course, Nancy Reagan was an actress before she was a White House wife. All of this poses the question: What is the balance that the corporate man must strike?

NOTES

1. John Solomon, "Women at NIH claim harassment, lax safety," *The Cincinnati Enquirer*, 11 April 2005, p. A6.
2. Mimi Swartz, "Hydie Sumner Wants Her Job Back," *The New York Times Magazine*, 5 June 2005, pp. 70–74.
3. Maureen Dowd, "Dish It Out, Ladies," *The New York Times*, 13 March 2005, p. 11.
4. Judy B. Rosener, "Women on Corporate Boards Make Good Business Sense," *Directorship*, May 2003.
5. "The Wifely Art of Standing By," *The New York Times*, 19 October 2003, p. 7.
6. Ibid.

22

Women in the Power Elite

Richard L. Zweigenhaft and G. William Domhoff

In 1962, Felice Schwartz founded Catalyst, a nonprofit agency specializing in women's job issues. Over the years, Catalyst developed a dual mission: to assist women in business and the professions to achieve their maximum potential, and to help employers capitalize on the abilities of their female employees. In 1977, responding to requests from some major corporations, Catalyst began its Corporate Board Resource. This program was designed to draw on Catalyst's database of women of achievement "to help board chairmen carefully select and recruit female directors."[8] By the late 1970s, then, Catalyst was systematically monitoring the progress of women on boards and simultaneously working with boards to increase the presence of women.

Starting in 1993, Catalyst began to publish its annual Census of Female Board Directors based on the top one thousand companies, namely, the Fortune 500 and the Fortune Service 500, as a way of calling attention to how few women sit on corporate boards. As Sheila Wellington, president of Catalyst, wrote in Directorship Newsletter, "Hardly had the ink dried on the 1993 Census before more corporations were calling to alert us to the fact that they'd added a woman to their boards. For months, we fielded calls relaying names of female additions to boards. The day we began the 1994 count, the fax began a steady six-week hum, with company after company telling of their new women directors,"[9] Clearly, by 1994 "company after company" felt the need to demonstrate that they had included women on their boards.

There has been a steady increase in the number of corporate directorships held by women, from 9.5 percent in 1995 to 13.6 percent in 2003. In 2003, most all of the Fortune 500 companies had at least one woman director (446 of the 500, or 89.2 percent), and 47.6 percent had two or more, but only in 54 companies (10.8 percent) were 25 percent of the board seats filled by women. The larger Fortune companies tend to have more women on their

boards than the smaller ones. In a separate analysis of the directors on Fortune 100 companies as of September 30, 2004, a Catalyst-sponsored study
found that women held 16.9 percent of the total seats. Although the increases over the past decade have been steady, it is clear that it will take a
long time before women, who own 48 percent of all stock in the United
States, will achieve parity. Many women executives, not surprisingly, have
been disappointed by these data. [10]

Moreover, various Catalyst studies have shown that within the Fortune 500
corporations, even fewer women hold the most senior and highest-paying
positions. For example, in 2002, 5.2 percent of the top earners were women
(up from 2.4 percent in 1995), and 7.9 percent of those holding the most important positions in the corporation (what Catalyst calls the "clout titles" such
as chairman, chief executive, vice chairman, president, chief operating officer,
and executive vice president) were women (up from 6.2 percent in 1997, the
first year Catalyst assessed such data). [11]

Who are these women, and how did they come to be corporate directors?
Do they come from backgrounds similar to the white, Protestant, American-
board sons of the businessmen and professionals who constituted the corporate elite in 1956? What role do they play on the corporate boards: are they tokens, or have they assumed positions of importance equal to those of their
male counterparts on their boards?

Three studies help answer these questions. The first was performed in 1977
by Burson-Marsteller, a public relations and advertising firm, for a client. The
second was a 1986 doctoral dissertation by Beth Ghiloni. The third was done
by Catalyst in 1991. Although their methods and samples differ, together these
studies suggest some patterns and some changes over time in the characteristics of women on corporate boards.

All three studies found that the women directors were highly educated, better educated, in fact, than the male directors who sat on boards with them.
Moreover, using attendance at exclusive prep schools, listing in the Social Register, or membership in an exclusive club as evidence of membership in the social upper class, and using ownership of large amounts of stock in a Fortune-
level firm as evidence of membership in the economic upper class, Ghiloni
concluded that 33 percent of her sample were from either the economic or the
social upper class or both. This figure is similar to overall findings for samples
of predominantly male directors for 1963 by G. William Domhoff and for
1970 by Thomas Dye. [12]

Rosabeth Moss Kanter has suggested that the need to reduce uncertainty in
large and impersonal institutions leads to the strong emphases on conformity
in behavior and homogeneity in background: "It is the uncertainty quotient
that causes management to become so socially restricting; to develop tight inner circles excluding social strangers; to keep control in the hands of socially
homogenous peers; to stress conformity and insist upon a diffuse, unbounded

loyalty; and to prefer ease of communication and thus social certainty over the strains of dealing with people who are different." [13]

A few years after Kanter's book appeared, when we interviewed black and white Jewish and Gentile men and women who had MBAs from Harvard and were in (or had been in) the corporate world, this theme emerged again and again. Notably, the Jewish women we interviewed agreed that being a woman posed more of a hurdle than being Jewish. A number of them, however, explained that this did not mean that their Jewishness was completely without significance. As one put it, "It's not irrelevant. It's part of the total package. Ultimately, in the fishbowl-type environment you're in, they scrutinize you carefully. It's part of the question of whether you fit the mold. Are you like me or not? If too much doesn't fit, it impacts you negatively." Another explained, "I heard . . . how I would be perceived as a pushy Jewish broad who went and got an MBA. . . . I had to work against that stereotype from the first day."

As one manager explained, "What's important is comfort, chemistry, relationships, and collaborations. That's what makes a shop work. When we find minorities and women who think like we do, we snatch them up."

One Fortune 500 labor relations executive used the phrase "comfort zone" to make the same point about "chemistry" and reducing "uncertainty." "You need to build relationships," she said, "and you need to be pretty savvy. And for a woman or a person of color at this company, you have to put in more effort to get into this comfort zone." [14]

Much has been made of the fact that men have traditionally been socialized to play competitive team sports and women have not. . . . Just as football is often identified as the classic competitive and aggressive team sport that prepares men for the rough and tumble (and hierarchical) world of the corporation, an individual sport, golf, is the more convivial, but still competitive, game that allows boys to play together, shoot the breeze, and do business. As Marcia Chambers shows in *The Unplayable Lie*, the golf course, and especially the country club, can be as segregated by sex as the football field. Few clubs bar women, but some clubs do not allow women to vote, sit on their governing boards, or play golf on weekend mornings. [15]

When the editors of *Executive Female* magazine surveyed the top fifty women in line-management positions . . . one of the . . . most frequently identified problems, not unrelated to the comfort factor, was the exclusion from "the social networks—the clubs, the golf course—where the informal networking that is important to moving up the ladder often takes place." [16]

A few months before Bill Clinton was elected president, his future secretary of energy had some pertinent comments about the importance of fitting into corporate culture and the relevance of playing golf. "Without losing your own personality," said Hazel O'Leary, then an executive vice president at Northern States Power in Minnesota, "it's important to be part of the prevailing corporate culture. At this company, it's golf. I've resisted learning to play golf all my life, but I finally had to admit I was missing something that way." She took up golf. [17]

Whether or not playing golf is necessary to fit in, it is clear that women who make it into the corporate elite must assimilate sufficiently into the predominantly male culture to make it into the comfort zone. As Kathleen Jamieson points out, however, this can place them in a double bind. On the one hand, women in the corporate world are expected to be competitive and tough-minded, but not too competitive or tough-minded, or they risk being called ball busters. On the other hand women in the corporate world are expected to be feminine enough to be seen as attractive and caring, but not too feminine, lest their appearance and behavior be seen as inappropriate or as an indication that they are tender-minded. [18]

Aside from wanting their corporations to appear diverse (especially if they cater to a diverse clientele), does something more drive corporations to include women in higher management and on their boards? We think there is. It has to do with the use of women to create a "buffer zone."

As part of his analysis of the transition from a pure patriarchal system, in which all power is held by males, to modern capitalism Michael Mann proposes that "a kind of compromise between patriarchy and a more gendered stratification hierarchy has emerged," both in the households and in the marketplace. In this compromise, women now occupy buffer zones between the men of their own class and the men in the classes below. This phenomenon appears at every point in the class hierarchy. Women who are part-time and unskilled manual laborers in low-income jobs, for example, serve as a buffer between the mostly male unemployed below them and the mostly male skilled manual workers above them. Secretaries and other white-collar women interact with the blue-collar workers who do maintenance jobs and deliver packages for the male managers. Women are the nurses and paralegals for physicians and lawyers. And women in the higher reaches function as buffer between "capital and labor" by serving as volunteers, fund-raisers, and board members for a wide range of charitable and social service organizations. [19]

Drawing on this analysis, we conclude that men who run America's corporations have women in higher management and on their boards not only to present a corporate image of diversity but to provide a valuable buffer between the men who control the corporation and the corporation's labor force (and the general public). It is not surprising, therefore, that Catalyst has found that relatively few women officers who hold the titles of executive vice president, senior vice president, or vice president have positions with operational responsibility for profit and loss. Instead, many are channeled into positions specializing in such areas as labor relations and public relations. [20] It is in these jobs especially that women are used as effective buffers because these staff jobs seldom lead to positions in top management. Ghiloni concluded her study of the velvet ghetto of public affairs in a top-fifty corporation by noting that "women can play an increasingly important role in the corporation and still not gain power." [21]

Long before women joined corporate boards or were employed in personnel and public relations, women of the upper class interceded in the social system in ways that smoothed out the hard-edged, profit-oriented impact of a business-driven economy. In the Progressive Era, some upper-class women argued for protective labor legislation, maximum hours, and more respectful treatment of labor. They came to call themselves "volunteer" as they took a hand in running health, cultural, and social welfare agencies that added a human, socially concerned dimension to their lives of wealth and privilege. First in nonprofit institutions and now in corporations, we see the intersection of gender and class in a way that serves the power elite by providing a buffer zone between the wealthy few and the rest of society. [22]

NOTES

[8] "Women on Corporate Boards: The Challenge of Change," Catalyst, 1993, 4. See also, Enid Nemy, "Felice N. Schwartz, 71, Dies; Working Women's Champion," *New York Times*, February 10, 1996, 52.

[9] Sheila Wellington, "Women on Corporate Boards: The Challenge of Change," Directorship Newsletter, December 1994. Directorship describes itself as a "data-based firm specializing in corporate governance." In business since 1975, the company uses proxy statements to provide detailed information to its clients (mostly corporations, but also magazines and researchers) on more than 7,000 directors.

[10] 2003 Catalyst Census of Women Board Directors: A Call to Action in a New Era of Corporate Governance (New York: Catalyst, 2003); Kristin Downey, "Survey Finds Few Female Directors," *Washington Post*, June 18, 2004, E3; "Women and Minorities on Fortune 100 Boards, Alliance for Board Diversity," [AU: NEWSPAPER?] May 17, 2005. In contrast to these data for board memberships in the United States, in Norway, when it became apparent that businesses were slow to include women in executive positions, the government passed a law requiring that at least 40 percent of corporate board seats be filled by women; see Alan Cowell, "Oslo Journal: Brewmaster Breaks One Tradition, but Upholds Another," *New York Times*, December 24, 2005, A4.

[11] 2002 Catalyst Census of Women Corporate Officers and Top Earners in the Fortune 500 (New York: Catalyst, 2003), 8, 12.

[12] Beth Ghiloni, "New Women of Power: An Examination of the Ruling Class Model of Domination." (Ph.D. diss., University of California, Santa Cruz, 1986), 122–36; G. William Domhoff, *Who Rules America?* (Englewood Cliffs, NJ: Prentice Hall, 1967), 51, 57; Thomas R. Dye, *Who's Running America? The Carter Years*, 2nd ed. (Englewood Cliffs, NJ: Prentice Hall, 1979), 169–70.

[13] Rosabeth Moss Kanter, *Women and Men of the Corporation* (New York: Basic 1977), 49.

[14] Peter T. Kilborn, "A Leg Up on Ladder, but Still Far from Top," *New York Times*, June 16, 1995.

[15] Marcia Chambers, *The Unplayable Lie: The Untold Story of Women and Discrimination in American* Golf (New York: Golf Digest/Pocket, 1995). See also, Marcia Chambers, "For Women, the Country Club Is the Big Handicap," *New York Times*, April 4, 2001, C19. Some golf clubs continue to deny memberships to women. The best known is Augusta National Golf Club, the home of the Masters Golf Tournament.

[16] Basia Hellwic. "Executive Female's Breakthrough 50," *Executive Female* (September–October 1992), 46.

[17] Anne B. Fisher, "When Will Women Get to the Top?" *Fortune*, September 21, 1992, 44–56 (quotation appears on p. 56).

[18] Kathleen Hall Jamieson, *Beyond the Double Bind: Women and Leadership* (New York: Oxford University Press, 1995), 120–45.

[19] Michael Mann, "A Crisis in Stratification Theory? Persons, Households/Families/Lineages, Genders, Classes, and Nations," in *Gender and Stratification*, edited by Rosemary Crompton and Michael Mann (London: Polity, 1986) 40–56 (quoted material appears on p. 47).

[20] Catalyst Census of Women Corporate Officers and Top Earners, 8.

[21] Beth W. Ghiloni, "The Velvet Gheto: Women, Power and the Corporation," in *Power Elites and Organizations*, edited by G. William Domhoff and Thomas R. Dye (Beverly Hills: Sage, 1987), 21–36.

[22] G. William Domhoff, *The Higher Circles* (New York: Random House, 1970), 35; Susan Ostrander, *Women of the Upper Class* (Philadelphia: Temple University Press, 1984); and Diana Kendall, *The Power of Good Deeds: Privileged Women and the Social Reproduction of the Upper Class* (Lanham, MD: Rowman & Littlefield, 2002).

EDITOR'S NOTE

Richard L. Zweigenhaft and G. William Domhoff tell us that only about 14 percent of board seats are held by women in Fortune 500 corporations. That's up a whopping 5 percent in ten years!

Judy Rosener, who writes extensively about women as board members, asked CEOs of large firms why they had no women members on their boards. She reports that she was "given a list of qualities that many of their male board members didn't possess."[1] It is clear that women and other minorities are held to a different standard than are white men. Rosener found, too, that those making the recommendations or appointments to a board tend to look within their own professional network. Using that criteria means "there are few or no women on their radar screens."[2] When women finally break through the inner sanctum and achieve membership status, Rosener reports that the presence of women on the board not only ends "sexist language and jokes" but broadens the issues to be considered.[3] Should one infer from that that the reluctance to appoint more women to boards has to do with preserving sexist language and jokes?

Findings from Canadian research conclude that the addition of women to boards seems to make boards more accountable. For example, The Conference Board of Canada's May 2002 study reports that "72% of boards with two or more women conduct formal board performance evaluations, while only 49% of all-male boards do; [the study also found] that companies that provide boards of directors with formal, written limits to authority have a greater percentage of women directors than do organizations with no formal limits to authority."[4]

While Rosener's work indicates boards would do well to appoint more women, others, including author Barbara Ehrenreich, argue that one can't expect that appointing a few women who have assimilated—altered something about themselves to fit in with male board members—will change the culture of the board. What do you think?

NOTES

1. Judy B. Rosener, " Women on Corporate Boards Make Good Business Sense," *Directorship*, May 2003.

2. Ibid.

3. Ibid.

4. Ibid.

23

Women above the Glass Ceiling

Perceptions on Corporate Mobility and Strategies for Success

Sally Ann Davies-Netzley

The number of women who have attained elite positions in corporate offices and boardrooms in the United States remains considerably low. Women comprise roughly 4 percent of directors and 2 percent of corporate officers in Fortune 500 companies (Von Glinow and Krzyczkowska-Mercer 1988). More progress has been made in corporate boardrooms. In the mid-1970s, only 13 percent of the 1,350 major corporations in the United States had a female director on their board. By 1985, that figure rose to 41 percent (*The Wall Street Journal* 1986).

Some scholars interpret these gains as dismal progress for women and emphasize the lack of substantial numbers of women at the top. Others characterize women in elite corporate positions as token workers who are less integrated in the large, influential central circles of power (Kanter [1977] 1993; Moore 1988). While we can point to a limited number of studies discussing elite women as "outsiders on the inside," there is a lack of research focusing on women's experiences in elite corporate positions and their perspectives on corporate mobility and success.

This study builds on the existing literature on women in management in several ways. First, I question the extent to which men and women in elite corporate positions offer similar perspectives on corporate success and mobility. Second, I examine how women presidents and CEOs respond to a work situation that, ideologically, has been associated with masculinity and continues to be characterized by mostly men. What strategies do women use to succeed in their elite positions above the corporate glass ceiling?

METHODOLOGY

In the fall of 1995 and 1996, I interviewed men and women who occupy elite corporate positions in Southern California. I considered those in elite positions to be at the top of the corporate hierarchy. Consequently, I limited my sample to individuals who hold the title of president or chief officer. Participants were selected from a wide range of industries: a midsize law firm, a private university, a local bank, and one of the largest local hospitals. The financial and advertising companies have been reported among the top twenty-five of their industries in terms of employees and revenues, which ranged from $250,000 to $500,000. The bio- and high-technology firms had revenues exceeding $1 million annually, and some ranked in the top ten of their industries.

Most interviews were conducted face-to-face in the offices of the informants and lasted about one hour. Questions were open-ended and focused on the respondents' social origins, education, career path, business and social affiliations, characterization of social networks, and factors assisting them in their rise to the top and their ability to successfully function in their position. Respondents also were asked to characterize their views concerning social relationships between people in elite positions and the extent to which gender was a significant factor in influencing an individual's success.

Sixteen informants were interviewed. Nine were white women, and seven were white men. Considering the small size of my sample and that most corporate CEOs and presidents are white, it is not surprising that snowball sampling produced an all-white sample. An obvious drawback of this sample is that it does not allow for direct comparisons to men and women of color. The median age was fifty-two for men and fifty for women. In addition, all of the interviewees had earned bachelor's degrees. Six of the men and five of the women had degrees beyond the bachelor's level. The median years in current position was eight for men and seven for women. Six of the men and five of the women were presently married. All of the men and five of the women had children.[1]

IDEOLOGY AT WORK: ELITE MEN'S PERSPECTIVES

When discussing what it takes to make it to the top, the men primarily attribute their success and elite status to their own individual qualities.[2] These men uphold the dominant stratification ideology in the United States by emphasizing that success and economic reward come from individual talent and effort.

Overall, the men ranked hard work as the most important element for success. Douglas Strickland, president of a biotechnology corporation, comments, "Everyone in the game is smart enough. It takes hard work." In thinking about what is most important in achieving and maintaining a top position, Strickland notes, "Hard work is first, timing/luck, cold honest appraisal, and good, useful ideas."

Strickland mentions luck as the second factor in achieving success. Four other men also mention luck as one factor in success, but they always place luck after individual effort. For instance, Steven Putnam, a law firm partner, notes, "I think luck has something to do with it, but I don't think luck is a major factor." He continues, "It's a matter of some internal drive people develop." For Putnam, this inner drive, possessed by some but not all individuals, is important for a successful career. Similarly, Matthew Gilbert, president of a scientific institute, and John Holden, CEO of a private university, emphasize the importance of an individual's inner qualities, particularly leadership skills, in becoming successful.

The men highlight competitive qualities needed to succeed in business, and several drew parallels between being a corporate elite and an athlete. For instance, Holden makes the connection between sports and the business world:

> I don't think you'll find a successful CEO that doesn't thrive on competition. . . .
> To use a sports analogy, think of the person who wants the ball at the last of the
> game. A lot of people who don't want the ball say, "What if I miss?" I think com-
> petitors say, 'What if I make it?"

Likewise, Strickland uses a football analogy, comparing a president of a company to a quarterback: "The quarterback has got to do his job, even though he knows that within a split second of throwing the football, he's going to get creamed."

These men define their success in terms of performance and winning, dominant values of organized sports. The analogy they draw between business and organized sports is significant, because sports are an important organizing institution for the embodiment of masculinity and represent "a practice through which men's separation from and power over women is embodied and naturalized" (Messner 1989, 73).

When thinking about their own success and what it takes to make it to the top, all of the men downplay the importance of an "old boys' network" or peer similarities among men and underscore the significance of individual qualities. A good example of undermining the importance of all-male, elite networks is provided by Strickland. He initially denies the existence of an old boys' network but acknowledges that many boardrooms are occupied primarily by men: "Oftentimes I'll go to a meeting and it will be all white men in the room." Still, he undermines the assertion that gender plays an important role: "But I know these men and they don't give a damn. If there's a woman in there who can give them an edge, then get in there."

In addition to asking the men about success, I also asked for their thoughts on the paucity of women at the top. Assumptions inherent in patriarchal gender ideology were used by the men to explain why women are underrepresented in elite positions. Three men felt that women's lack of necessary skills and know-how had prevented them from attaining elite positions. James Olson, president of a financial institution, describes the recent addition of the first woman to the bank's board: "We talked about having a woman in the past but had been unable to settle on someone who we thought could make a major contribution."

Family conflict also was suggested by four of the men as the most significant reason why few women are at the top. These men equate women primarily with the homemaker role.

> No matter how much you want to fight it, there is this underlying thing for women that they always have to be the wife, the mother. The male, well, they're supposed to be the father and husband, but that doesn't mean quite the time commitment.

He states that married women do not perform as well because they can't commit the time that male counterparts can. Norton also argues that there is still conflict between work and home for women in senior positions that require twelve- to fourteen-hour workdays. These four men view single women without children as better suited to corporate elite positions than wives and mothers . . . they did not view their own family responsibilities as a hindrance for their work in elite positions.

Five men in the sample had wives who stayed at home for most of their children's school-age years. The two men with wives working in the paid workforce relied more heavily on paid child care. All of the men (all have children) state that they have sacrificed family time for work; however, they all underscore the benefits of an elite position for their families: private school attendance, a "nice home in a nice area," and recreational opportunities. Although it appears that men in the United States have shifted their attitudes toward the provider role in a more egalitarian direction (Wilkie 1993), the men in my sample typify primary breadwinning men who view their parental contribution in terms of income and financial support.

SUCCESS FROM THE STANDPOINT OF ELITE WOMEN

Unlike the men who describe moving up the ladder quickly or growing with the company, all of the women offered examples of experiencing gender discrimination in their corporate careers—whether it be in the form of comments from men colleagues questioning their ability to have a career and family or feeling left out of informal networking opportunities. To advance their careers, five of the women talked of fleeing larger corporations, working in smaller firms, networking in the local corporate community, and then moving into higher positions in more established corporations. The act of leaving large corporations and moving to "smaller, more hospitable organization(s)" is a common response among professional women experiencing workplace discrimination (Rosener 1995, 113). This is illustrated by Marie Johnson, president of a consulting company, who left a lucrative position in a large company because her advancement opportunities were blocked. She explains,

> I told my boss that I wanted to be more involved with customers. I wanted to take the next step. He said to me that he didn't think that women with children could do "marketing." I decided at that point to move on.

Likewise, advertising president Jennifer Anderson recalls gender discrimination in her previous place of business.

> I've been in meetings where men haven't listened to leadership from a woman. But women are needed and should be valued. You have to prove yourself more as a woman. There's a kind of silent hostility out there toward women in business. I think there's this, anger that men have to share "what belongs to them" with women.

An immediate difference emerges in the role played by hard work. In contrast to men, all of the women assert that hard work alone, or even intelligence or talent, is not enough to succeed, and that opportunities are often blocked to individuals who are not white males. All of the women assert that external barriers exist to hinder a hardworking woman from achieving upward corporate mobility. Tracy Newton, CEO of a biotechnology company, illustrates this point: "Some people feel it's just hard work, do a good job, and you'll get promoted. That might be true to a certain point and that point is wherever the glass ceiling is."

This is not to say that the women did not acknowledge individual qualities as factors for success. Overall, the women agreed that an individual's inner drive, high self-esteem, and communication skills are important for success. Ultimately, however, the women emphasize that corporate mobility to the top does not depend primarily on individual-level variables such as inner drive or work ethic. Their views on corporate mobility and success are different from the men's.

Male-Dominated Networks

Whereas the men legitimize their positions through the ideology of individualism, all the women I spoke with explain their success by referring to social-structural variables. They emphasize social networks as most significant for success at elite levels and argue that the existence of an old boys' network continues to make it more difficult for women to succeed. They assert that success depends largely on how entrenched male networks are and how willing elite men are to accept the women into the networks.

Most of the women talk of experiencing old boys' networks within more established corporations. . . . Newton describes the corporate atmosphere of a former workplace: "The only women they wanted at the top were the ones they placed there as tokens." Newton also adds that if women want to reach senior positions, they need to network with men in power positions. Newton argues, "The power is still in the males fifty-plus years old. If you want to reach the top, those are the people you have to network with."

Even after having reached an elite corporate position, all of the women still consider themselves outsiders to a system that accommodates men. "Fundraising is tougher for women in business because they don't have the network of 'good old boys' to put in money." Joan Miller, a former CEO who sits on several boards of directors, comments, "There is an old boys' network, and I have no doubt that there probably are opportunities (I've) missed, there probably are certain positions that I never could be in." Even though Miller and Wagner have obtained top corporate positions, they still feel excluded from business opportunities because of the existing old boys' network. This echoes the sentiments of Nancy Harrison, president of a high-technology corporation, who still does not consider herself "part of the group":

> The people at the top of this industry are still mostly men. I try not to let it bother me. I think they respect me as a professional, but I don't feel like I'm part of the group. I don't feel like I belong.

Likewise, Carrie Hughes, president of an investment corporation, describes feeling like an outsider after becoming a newly appointed board member:

> It doesn't occur to some men that a woman would be there to contribute to the board. There was this one incident when this board member thought I was part of the hotel staff and tried to pick me up. I introduced myself and he immediately backed off.

Such statements reinforce Moore's (1988) findings that even after reaching elite positions, women are still "outsiders on the inside" and often feel invisible or excluded from informal relationships and networks of all-men colleagues. . . . Wagner states, "The network will break down. Younger men are different. They respect your leadership more." Hughes adds, "The weight of the numbers in business are now such that they won't be able to use excuses for much longer."

Peer Similarities

These women also note that the rapport between elite men often hinders women's pathways to success. Feeling like outsiders, they recognize that the nature of the relationships developed between elite males is fundamentally different from that between men and women in elite positions. Katherine Frost, president of a scientific corporation, made this point:

> There is definitely a different rapport between men. It's subtle, but they can say to each other. "Hey, could you wait a minute, I'd like to talk over some ideas with you after the meeting." With me, I think there's the hesitation of, well, she might think I'm coming on to her.

WOMEN'S SURVIVAL STRATEGIES AT THE TOP

Earning advanced degrees and credentials (higher than those of most men) appears to be a way that women compete with men for elite positions. Three of the women purposefully returned to school to increase their credentials and make themselves more competitive for top positions. Hughes asserts, "I got an MBA in marketing ten years after my MA in communication because it was apparent that I wasn't going to go higher in the corporate world without it." Master's degrees in business and law degrees are most closely related to entry into elite positions (Ward, Orazem, and Schmidt 1992). A total of five women in my sample had graduate degrees but mentioned difficulties during their graduate programs with being taken seriously by male faculty. Miller talks of one dissertation committee member: "He thought they shouldn't waste graduate positions on women because they would just marry, have children, and not be as professional."

Rather than highlighting hard work, the women talk primarily of strategies they use for fitting in: altering appearance to fit the proper business attire and changing speech and behaviors to conform to situations with other elites. Frost notes, "There are certain ways of acting in these meetings, I mean for business investors or advisory meetings, I pull my hair back, wear a suit, don't act giggly . . . because you need to fit in." When meeting with other elites, Frost puts on a calculated performance. She modifies her appearance, . . . because she knows that this is the expected way to look and behave. Likewise, this conscious modification spills over into social situations with other corporate elites. Hughes discusses avoiding some country club activities with male peers. She jokes, "It's too tough to be taken seriously when you're wearing a tennis skirt!"

These modifications are predictably influenced by gendered expectations. For instance, one man I interviewed, Douglas Strickland, comments on appropriate behavior in board meetings: "If you're going to be a frilly little sweetheart and have people open your doors . . . that isn't what it's about. I mean it has its place." Encountering such kinds of attitudes, the women attempt to downplay their own feminine qualities to fit in. Newton makes this point: "I talk sports, politics, read the *Wall Street Journal*. I talk what the guys do. I have to. My belief is 'when in Rome, do as the Romans do.'" Newton consciously brings up topics she feels will be of interest to other male elites, topics she would not otherwise discuss outside these circles. Hughes also talks of "speaking 'their' language in board meetings." And Miller also notes, "There certainly is an old boys' network, but I've also found that you can enter it, I think, so long as you are sort of, not the word, asexual, but if you don't act like a female."

Finally, I questioned what strategies these women use to survive in such an elite position and reconcile their family lives. Two women made a conscious decision not to have children with such a demanding career. Hughes emphasizes that with her busy travel schedule and twelve-hour days, she could not devote the time necessary to raising children. "My career goals have definitely influenced my decision not to have children. I think for me, I just don't think it would be fair to have children and this kind of schedule."

Five of the women in my sample have children, two with school-age children, three with adult children. They all acknowledge that work and family have conflicted at some point in their careers.

While these women comment on work and family conflicts, they also are quick to suggest that they can juggle such responsibilities. As with all working parents, they talk of methods for reconciling work and family such as day care facilities and modifying schedules with partners to accommodate child care. They also are able to pay for live-in help, something most other American families cannot afford.

CONCLUSIONS

Most of the top executive positions and directorships in corporate America continue to be held by white men of upper- or upper middle-class origin. In recent years, however, there has been an increase of women, particularly white upper middle- to upper-class women, in top corporate positions. Most studies of women at the top have addressed their numbers in the leadership of the entire nation, using survey data to examine their gains within major national corporations and the U.S. government (Dye 1995; Moore 1988). This study provides a unique, detailed look at men and women who comprise part of a local community-based elite, how they think about corporate mobility, and women's strategies for success at the top.

My finding that men are less sensitive to external barriers facing women and minorities is supported by a recent survey of 325 men CEOs conducted by Catalyst (Townsend 1996). Eighty-two percent cited a lack of general management experience as the reason women are held back from corporate leadership (Townsend 1996). In contrast, among the 461 women in vice president or higher positions, male stereotyping of women was the number-one cited obstacle to women's advancement, with exclusion from informal ("old boy") networks the next most serious deterrent (Townsend 1996). This article also reveals strategies women use in maintaining their elite positions, such as displaying cultural capital in the form of advanced degrees or in modification of appearance and speech. . . .

Women's work experiences are not only affected by gender but also by race, ethnicity, nationality, and class. It is little surprise that women privileged within race and class hierarchies in the United States are moving up the corporate ladder. Understanding their perceptions of corporate mobility, and those of both women and men in ethnic minorities, continues to be crucial for revealing how outsiders climb the corporate ladder and break through the glass ceiling.

NOTES

1. All names of the interviewees and some biographical details have been changed.
2. Social psychologists also have found that American men in achievement situations tend to internalize and take credit for their successes, illustrated by male college students when passing an exam (Sweeney, Moreland, and Gruber 1982). For social psychologists, socialization is an important explanation for this internal attributional style among men. Contradictory evidence has been found with respect to women's attributions of success (Deaux 1976; Wiley, Crittenden, and Birg 1979). In response to the social psychology literature, I argue that it is important to keep in mind that attributional patterns are based on men's and women's social experiences and response to social context and cultural ideology.

REFERENCES

Deaux, Kay. Sex: A perspective on the attribution process. In *New Directions in Attributional Research*, vol. 1, ed. J. Harvey, W. Ickes, and R. Kidd. New York: Halsted.

Dye, Thomas, 1995. *Who's running America? The Clinton years*. Englewood Cliffs, NJ: Prentice Hall.

Kanter, Rosabeth Moss. (1977) 1993. *Men and women of the corporation*. New York: Basic Books.

Messner, Michael. 1989. Masculinities and athletic careers. *Gender & Society* 3: 71–88.

Moore, Gwen. 1988. Women in elite positions: Insiders or outsiders? *Sociological Forum* 3: 566–85.

Rosener, Judy B. 1995. *America's competitive secret: Utilizing women as a management strategy*. New York: Oxford University Press.

Sweeney, Paul, Richard Moreland, and Kathy Gruber. 1982. Gender differences in performance attributions: Students' explanations for personal success and failure. *Sex Roles* 8: 359–73.

Townsend, Bickley. 1996. Room at the top for women. *American Demographics* 18, 7 (July): 28–37.

Von Glinow, M. A., and A. Krzyczkowska-Mercer. 1988. Women in corporate America: A caste of thousands. *New Management* 6: 36–42.

The Wall Street Journal. 1986. The board game: More women are becoming directors but it's still a token situation, 24 March, section 4, 290.

Ward, Patricia A., Peter F. Orazem, and Steffen W. Schmitt. 1992. Women in elite pools and elite positions. *Social Science Quarterly* 73: 31–45.

Wiley, Mary Glenn, Kathleen Crittenden, and Laura Birg. 1979. Why a rejection? Causal attribution of a career achievement event. *Social Psychological Quarterly* 42: 214–22.

Wilkie, Jane Riblett. 1993. Changes in U.S. men's attitudes toward the family provider role, 1972–1989. *Gender & Society* 7: 261–79.

EDITOR'S NOTE

A study of 215 Fortune 500 companies by Adler found that those companies that had earnings above the median of other large companies had the highest proportion of executives who were women.[1] It simply makes good business sense for companies to reflect the population as well as their customers.[2]

The Conference Board of Canada noted similar findings about companies with female board members; that is, companies with women on their boards had higher revenue and profit than companies with all-male boards.[3]

The statistics are telling: Women are about half of the labor force, over half of college graduates, and about half of those receiving graduate training. With women's continued accumulation of human capital (education, training, experience, workplace commitment), all the qualities they were told for years they were lacking, it is doubtful that women will be content in staff positions—positions that traditionally do not lead to the top of organizations. Women are training for more![4]

NOTES

1. Judy B. Rosener, "Women on Corporate Boards Make Good Business Sense," *Directorship*, May 2003.

2. Ibid.

3. Ibid.

4. Ibid.

24

Invisible Women

Katha Pollitt

Women don't shout. Women don't like politics. Women shrink from intellectual debate. Women don't try. It's time for another round of "What's Wrong with Women?" Last month's category was science. This month it's punditry, sparked by a testy (well, nasty) letter from syndicated columnist and FOX-TV commentator Susan Estrich to Michael Kinsley, the courtly editorial and opinion editor of the *Los Angeles Times*, pointing out the lack of female talent on his op-ed pages: In nine weeks, only 20 percent of the pieces were written by women. Now everybody's jumping in: "Feminists Get Hysterical" (Heather MacDonald in *City Journal*) is a typical sentiment.

"There ought to be more women on op-ed pages in general. Over time, I intend to make that happen," said Fred Hiatt, editorial page editor of the *Washington Post*, which counts one woman, Anne Applebaum, among its nineteen pundits; in the first two months of 2005 one in ten op-ed pieces were by women. Take your time, Mr. Hiatt! As Applebaum warns, you don't want to hire untalented women who'll just write about "women's issues." *Her* friends got their bylines by "having clear views, knowing their subjects, writing well and learning to ignore the ad hominem attacks that go with the job." And you know how few women meet those lofty criteria! "The pool of available people doing opinion writing is still tilted toward men," said *New York Times* editorial page editor Gail Collins. "There are probably fewer women, in the great cosmic scheme of things, who feel comfortable writing very straight opinion stuff, and they're less comfortable hearing something on the news and batting something out." Come April, the *Times* will have seven male op-ed columnists, plus Maureen Dowd. Not to worry though, Dowd writes, there are "plenty of brilliant women. . . . We just need to find and nurture them."

Oh, nurture my eye. It may be true that more men than women like to bloviate and "bat things out"—socialization does count for something. So do social rewards: I have seen men advance professionally on levels of aggression, self-promotion, and hostility that would have a woman carted off to a loony bin—unless, of course, she happens to be Ann Coulter. But feminine psychology doesn't explain why all five of *USA Today*'s political columnists are male, or why *Time*'s eleven columnists are male—down to the four in Arts and Entertainment—or why at *Newsweek* it's one out of six in print and two out of thirteen on the Web. According to *Editor and Publisher*, the proportion of female syndicated columnists (one in four) hasn't budged since 1999. The tiny universe of political-opinion writers includes plenty of women who hold their own with men, who do not wilt at the prospect of an angry e-mail, who have written cover stories and bestsellers and won prizes—and whose phone numbers are likely already in the Rolodexes of the editors who wonder where the women are. How hard could it be to "find" Barbara Ehrenreich, who filled in for Thomas Friedman for one month last summer and wrote nine of the best columns the *Times* has seen in a decade? Or Dahlia Lithwick, legal correspondent for *Slate*, another Friedman fill-in, who actually possesses a deep grasp of the field she covers—which cannot always be said for John Tierney, who begins his *Times* column in April? What about Susan Faludi? The *Village Voice*'s Sharon Lerner? Debra Dickerson? Wendy Kaminer? *The Progressive*'s Ruth Conniff? Laura Flanders? Debbie Nathan? Ruth Rosen, veteran of the *LA Times* and the *San Francisco Chronicle*? Our own Patricia Williams and Naomi Klein? Natalie Angier, bestselling author and top *New York Times* science writer, would be a fabulous op-ed columnist. And, not to be one of those shrinking violets everyone's suddenly so down on, What about me? Am I a potted plant?

You'll note I've mostly named liberals and feminists—I'm sure there are good women writers on the right out there, too, and their job prospects are probably a lot rosier. A conservative woman who endlessly attacks feminists, like *The New Yorker*'s Caitlin Flanagan or the *Los Angeles Times*'s departed Norah Vincent or the *Boston Globe*'s Cathy Young—what could be hotter than that?

Besides being false and insulting, all this fuss about women not having the *cojones* for no-holds-barred debate overlooks the fact that, as Deborah Tannen pointed out in the *LA Times*, there are many ways to write political commentary. Not every male columnist is a fire-breather, an instant expert, a tub-thumper, an obnox. Think of the *Washington Post*'s E. J. Dionne Jr. or *USA Today*'s Walter Shapiro, both mannerly and sweet-natured to a fault. Some columnists use their perch to do crusading reporting—Bob Herbert's great strength to tell stories, to—analyze ideas and policies, to ask questions, to skewer received opinion with wit and humor. And then there are the ones who just drone boringly on. Surely there are women capable of that!

That opinion writing is a kind of testosterone-powered food fight is a popular idea in the blogosphere. Male bloggers are always wondering where the women are and why women can't/don't/won't throw bananas. After all, anyone can have a blog, right? In the wake of the Estrich-Kinsley contretemps, the *Washington Monthly* blogger Kevin Drum mused upon the absence of women bloggers and got a major earful from women bloggers, who are understandably sick of hearing that they don't exist. "I'm staring you right in the face, Kevin," wrote Avedon Carol, (http://sideshow.me.uk), "and even though you've said you read me every day you don't have me on your blogroll. It's things like this that make me tear out my hair when people wonder why women are underrepresented. . . ." There are actually lots of women political bloggers out there—spend half an hour reading them and you will never again say women aren't as argumentative as men! But what makes a blog visible is links, and male bloggers tend not to link to women (to his credit, Kevin Drum has added nineteen to his blogroll). Perhaps they sense it might interfere with the circle jerk in cyberspace—the endless mutual self-infatuation that is one of the less attractive aspects of the blogging phenom.

Or maybe, like so many op-ed editors, they just don't see women, even when the women are right in front of them.

EDITOR'S NOTE

Peter Jennings, the ABC anchor, has passed away, Tom Brokaw of NBC has retired, and Dan Rather of CBS was ousted. Tom Brokaw believed that when the three long-time anchors were gone that "would be the end of the white male anchor time."[1] However, he acknowledged, "I think we're still stuck in a society that looks at white males as authority figures."[2]

Roger Ailes of Fox News admitted that "network anchoring is still Mount Olympus."[3] In other words, don't look for change on the nightly network news any time soon. Brokaw, the father of three daughters, declared it unfair that biology (childbirth) causes "career interruptus" for so many women who "have to juggle all this stuff."[4] Perhaps if men, like Brokaw, did half of the juggling with their wives, more women could find fulfillment at home *and* in the marketplace.

It isn't just the electronic media and television networks. Susan Estrich expresses frustration when newspaper editors argue they can only hire one liberal female columnist. Can you imagine a newspaper editor saying we "can't take a Bob Novak because" we "have a George Will" or we "can't take Bill O'Reilly because" we "have Bill Safire?[5]

NOTES

1. Maureen Dowd, "There's No End to This Era for White Men," *New York Times*, 3 December 2004, p. B7.

2. Ibid.

3. Ibid.

4. Ibid.

5. Susan Estrich, "Kinsley's Days at the *LA Times* Are Numbered," Realpolitics.com, 18 February 2005.

VIII

WOMEN'S EQUALITY

Progress and Resistance

25

Women against Women

American Antisuffragism, 1880–1920

Jane Jerome Camhi

Although the origins of feminism in general and suffragism in particular can be traced back to the first decades of the nineteenth century, the antisuffrage movement did not surface until the last two decades of the century. Beginning in the 1880s and gathering momentum through the 1890s, the antisuffrage movement reached its peak of power and influence between 1895 and 1907. Nevertheless, it retained sufficient force in 1919 and 1920 to offer substantial opposition to suffrage efforts to ratify the federal woman suffrage amendment. At its height the movement encompassed more than twenty-five state associations, some having numerous city and local branches, and a national association.[1]

The movement was organized, led, and staffed by women who went to lengths inconsistent with their goals in order to prevent the extension of suffrage to women. Common to all antisuffragists was the belief that the entry of women into public life (which was considered the inevitable consequence of the ballot) would bring in its wake disaster not only for women themselves but for all of society. Despite this belief, the antisuffragists were so intent on resisting the coming of woman suffrage that they leaped midstream into the battle, adopting all of the techniques they were so eager for womankind to avoid, including campaigning and even lobbying.

The women who led this movement were usually members of the social aristocracy. They were, for the most part, urban, wealthy, native born, Republican, and Protestant—members of established families either by birth or marriage, or both. They claimed to be favorably disposed to the gradual improvements in the status of women that had taken place over the century and, in this sense, did not consider themselves unsympathetic to women's rights as such. Nevertheless, on one issue they remained unanimously and steadfastly opposed—the granting of suffrage to women.

The opponents of woman suffrage employed a wide variety of arguments in their efforts to influence the public to resist any extension of the elective franchise to women. The arguments, however, had two things in common. First, they were almost all predictive—intimating, if not explicitly detailing, the evil consequences that would ensue if woman suffrage were enacted. Second, they were usually imputative, that is, the arguments were presented in such a way that the suffrage question emerged as a mere symbol of what was assumed to be the real issue, the threat of the spread of feminist ideas. Most antisuffragists did not consciously intend to confuse the issue. If anything, their rhetoric belied the confusion in their own minds. However, whether conscious or not, it was one of the antisuffragists' most effective weapons.[2]

Obfuscating the issue by causing the advocates of suffrage to appear as feminists played upon contemporary uncertainties regarding the changing role of women. As a result, many who might not have taken issue with the justice or expedience of extending suffrage to women found themselves forced to take a stand either for or against what was made to appear to be two opposing value systems. The result was that the question of woman suffrage, which had over the years come to assume a symbolic significance for those in the suffrage movement, also began to assume a symbolic significance in the minds of the uncommitted and the unsure.

WOMAN'S SPECIAL ROLE

A primary assumption of the Antis was that the family was the basic nexus, the self-governing unit upon which the state was built. Therefore, as a microcosm of the state, every well-regulated family had to have one head. . . .[3] To be preserved as a unit the family must be represented in the state by the voting power of its head, the man of the family.[4] The notion that there should be one head of the family and that this head should be the man even influenced the Antis' position on child custody. The Antis were in accord with the laws giving custody of children to the father in cases of disagreement and argued against granting equal custody to each parent.

If woman's work in the home were always properly performed, declared the Antis, "there would be far fewer bosses, ringsters and grafters in the world at large." Even more extravagant was their contention that when woman fails to perform the work nature has assigned her she "leaves the world depleted by just so much of moral strength and all the best educators and scientists declare, lowers the entire race in its affectionate social and moral achievements."[5]

The distinctive genius of woman, it was argued, did not lie in her logical or executive abilities, but in her sensibilities, which made her irreplaceable in the home where her influence over the lives of those around her was much greater than any she could possibly wield as a voter, where she would count as only one man.[6]

PRIVILEGE AND POWER

The Antis argued that if women voted they would lose the power to mold the citizens of the future. Antisuffrage campaign material often included posters depicting the evil effects of woman suffrage on the domestic scene. In the antisuffrage litany, motherhood and participation in public life were always presented as mutually exclusive.

The business of state, on the other hand, was not only man's work but also his highest prerogative. To make and execute the laws of the country was equated with manhood. Therefore, men who favored the ballot for women "lowered their own dignity in the State and belittled their own importance as the true makers and enforcers of law."[7] From the lofty perspective of female Antis, governing was the one activity that "makes him a man, a being worthy to stand upon an equality with woman."[8]

Primaries, caucuses, conventions, courts, and legislatures were all involved in the simple casting of a ballot. These were man's work, however, and gave to man the inalienable quality that distinguished him from a mere brute. In other words, if politics were taken away, little would remain. Man's power to rule was what evened the balance between the sexes. Without it, man would be shorn of his manhood and the balance between the sexes destroyed. "What woman wants a man whose power of law-giving is no more than equal to her own?" She has her great gift from God to serve as mother of men, "the exemplar and expounder of all noble, moral and spiritual gifts." His birthright is equally inalienable. If he robs himself of it, "what would become of that mutual homage and respect which is the natural bond between the sexes? No, let him keep for himself something by which we may still reverence him, the horns of Moses, his manly power of law-giving!"[9]

On the one hand, taking their cues from the suffragists, who devoted most of their energies to foreseeing changes in the female role, the Antis, like the suffragists, did not really question the basic patriarchal norms that expected the male to be provider, authority, stoic, protector, or lawmaker. On the other hand, since in the Antis' view all of these roles depended primarily on the male's greater physical strength, and since they believed that governments operated by rule of force, the question of how man could harness this brute force and yet not lose his manhood was crucial. By employing it to enforce the dictates of a civilized state, man's brute strength was transmitted into a special social virtue. Man the animal became man the governor.

It undoubtedly worked to the advantage of the Antis, both in terms of morale and practical politics, to underscore the fact that the main opponents of woman suffrage were women and to urge that if women really wanted to vote, they would have it. For one thing, it enabled them to depict suffrage as the "only woman's movement which has been met by the organized opposition of women."[10] For another, it enabled them to claim that the weight of public opinion was on their side rather than just the self-interested forces that the suffragists consistently defined as the enemy:

> [C]hief opponents of woman suffrage are not the special interests nor those men who take a narrow and prejudiced view of woman's relation to the state, but those *women* who have grave doubts whether their duty lies in service to the state by the ballot, or by a fulfillment of present responsibilities which bear no relation to the ballot.[11]

It was inevitable that politicians and legislators reluctant to advance the cause of woman suffrage would find it to their advantage to stress the fact that women themselves were opposed to woman suffrage.

Although the Antis billed themselves as representing the "silent majority" of American women, they were certainly not representative. They came from families that had both money and power, and therefore they could not be construed as a cross section of society. As members of a native-born monied class, they shared all the prejudices of those who felt they had something to lose by the changes taking place in American society. They resented the immigrant and distrusted the poor and feared the swelling of the ranks of the electorate by what they regarded as an illiterate and ignorant vote. It was only natural that these class prejudices were reflected in their views concerning the types of women they felt ought *not* to vote and thus became part of their rationale for resisting the extension of suffrage.

Taking their cue perhaps from Catherine Beecher, who had classified women into five categories, the Antis were fond of visualizing womanhood as consisting of sex types. Although these varied somewhat as to particulars, for the most part they constituted three basic categories—the better class, the indifferent, and the degenerate. It was only natural that the Antis considered themselves, and were in fact, a representative segment of the first category.[12] This was the handful of women who carried on church, philanthropic, and reform work when they were not devoting themselves to their domestic tasks. The Antis felt that this kind of woman was capable of developing an interest in and an understanding of political questions but was usually too preoccupied with her primary tasks to take the time to cast her ballot.[13]

The indifferent women constituted the vast majority and included the following subgroups—women of the shopkeeper, clerk, artisan, and prosperous laborer class, wage-earning women, immigrant women, and black women. The first sort were assumed to be overburdened with domestic duties and uninterested in questions outside of their limited sphere.[14] The working women were thought to be exposed to political affairs, but deemed uninterested in questions outside of their own narrow interests.[15] The Antis could not place immigrant women as a group or black women as a race in the third category reserved for what was variously designated the evil, wrongminded, corrupt, and sordid women.[16] But they did cast them at the bottom of the heap of the indifferent. The Antis feared that the ignorance of immigrant women would make them subject to manipulation by their men, who would have no compunctions about selling not only their own votes, but those of their wives and daughters as well.[17] Sometimes, however, they were not too careful in distinguishing between the illiterate and the vicious:

> We must think of the tens of thousands of illiterate and vicious women in New York City, and just as carefully of the scores of thousands of ignorant negresses at the South. . . . Are we prepared to throw into political life all the women good and bad, intelligent and unintelligent, of the whole U.S., including the swarms which belong to Europe but have been adopted here? . . . Surely the well-trained, educated, intelligent boys of New York City, even though they be not more than ten years old, would make better voters than vicious tramps or stupid foreigners all but wholly ignorant of the English language.[18]

The third kind of woman—the degenerate—consisted of two general types, both considered beyond the pale of respectability and believed to far outnumber the first category of good women.[19] These were the prostitutes, manipulated by bosses, pimps, and saloon keepers, and who, it was feared, would vote because private (and sinister) interests would see to it that they did.[20] The following excerpt reflects this kind of thinking. Printed and reprinted by the Antis, this article appeared in the *San Francisco Examiner* the day after an election in which women voted:

> McDonough Brothers had several automobiles busy all day long hauling Barbary coast dance hall girls and the inmates of houses on Commercial street to the different booths, and always the women were supplied with a marked sample ballot.[21]

Arguing that the best women would remain at home, Senator Morgan of Alabama, in an 1887 Senate debate on woman suffrage, complained,

> The effect would be to drive the ladies of the land, as they are termed, the well-bred and well-educated women, the women of nice sensibilities, within their home circles, there to remain, while the ruder of that sex would thrust themselves out on the hustings and at the ballot-box, and fight their way to the polls through Negroes and others who are not the best of company even at the polls, to say nothing of the disgrace of association with them. You would paralyze one-third at least of the women of this land by the very vulgarity of the overture made to them that they should go struggling to the polls in order to vote in common with the herd of men.[22]

The degenerate women, argued the Antis, were powerless without the vote, but once enfranchised, the ballot would become a weapon they would use against reform measures because they would want to ensure that their way of life was not interfered with.[23] Whether they went to the polls on their own behalf or because they were forced to, a higher percent of this sort of woman than of respectable women would vote, they predicted:

> Apathetic, ignorant, sordid women—poor or rich—as things now stand, are at worst a negative evil. But such women, with votes, become potential reinforcements to the forces of vice, and those forces are always prompt in rallying their reenforcements.[24]

The other kind of degenerate or wrong-minded women were those who would devote their lives to public affairs, seeking conspicuous offices and "playing the role of bosses among the ignorant of their sex."[25] They would "employ the distinctive power of their sex in caucuses, in jury-boxes, and in legislative and congressional committees; thus adding another to the many deteriorating influences of public life." Thus the best of women would shun political life and the most unprincipled would have the field to themselves.[26]

Tallying up the score, the Antis felt that if women were enfranchised, the influence (and the interests) of the "better class of women" would be nullified. Woman suffrage would destroy the indirect power of the informed woman since the vote would give equal power to the uninformed.

Perhaps what most irritated the traditional type of woman was not that women were actually out there on platforms agitating for change but that they were willing to consider their own cause—that of women—as a priority. This went against the grain of womanly self-denial. What was admired in the male sex as initiative, independence, and self-esteem was looked upon in women as selfish and self-serving, bold and unwomanly. A short article in the January 1912 issue of *The Anti-Suffragist* singled out the dropping of the husbands' names on the visiting card or address of married women as the "most noticeable social innovation of the suffragists" and condemned it as "an assertion of separate and individual interests and bank account."

As if woman suffrage by itself were not sufficiently worthy of contempt, the Antis often embellished its horror by equating it with any one of the so-called radical -isms. If not actually equated with feminism, bolshevism, or socialism, then it was the necessary harbinger of these and similar horrors. In the charged atmosphere of the years surrounding World War I, the Antis consciously resorted to a campaign designed to discredit the suffragists by playing upon popular fears of bolshevism and social revolution.

In 1887 the Senate had witnessed a debate on woman suffrage in which various southern senators, reacting against a "wholesale and indiscriminate extension of the electorate," zeroed in especially on the black woman. According to Senator Beck of Kentucky, one mistake had already been made, when the ignorant "colored men of the South" had been enfranchised. It was going to take years not only to dispel their ignorance but also to turn them into intelligent voters. The colored woman, he argued, was even more ignorant, never having had the advantages of communication with the outside world:

> No one perhaps in a hundred of them can read or write. . . . Take them from their washtubs and their household work and they are absolutely ignorant of the new duties of voting citizens. . . . Why, sir, a rich corporation or a body of men of wealth could buy them up for fifty cents a piece, and they would vote, without knowing what they were doing, for the side that paid most.[27]

During the battle over ratification, the Antis would continue to exploit Southern prejudice by identifying women suffrage with racial equality. In a leaflet entitled "That Deadly Parallel," they quoted the Fifteenth Amendment and the proposed woman suffrage amendment in parallel columns in order to link woman suffrage with Negro suffrage. Another leaflet warned that woman suffrage meant reopening the Negro question, the loss of states' rights, and all the reconstruction horrors with "female carpet-baggers as bad as their male prototypes."[28]

Judge Joseph C. Higgins, president of the Tennessee Constitutional League, told the press that if the legislature ratified, the league "would be constrained to go into the courts and inhibit the Secretary of State from certifying."[29] On August 12, the Senate and House committees on constitutional amendments held a joint hearing. Both suffragists and Antis spoke. Charlotte Rowe of New York, a lawyer and inactive Anti, explained the attitude of the Antis:

> We feel that if you men are good enough to work for us, die for us, live for us, you are good enough to vote for us . . . to give woman the ballot is only to break up the home and the beginning of socialism.[30]

Viola Klein, although primarily a sociologist, has also been concerned with how women as members of an "out-group" have internalized society's attitudes toward them. By "out-group," Klein means that women are distinguished from the dominant (male) strata by virtue of their physical characteristics, historical tradition, and social role. Furthermore, as in the case of other groups in a similar position, women have been subjected to preconceived opinions and collective judgments instead of being treated on their own merits. The general effect of this stereotyping is to inhibit the development of individualism, resulting in an "incalculable amount of restrictions, discouragement, ill-feeling and frustration."[31]

Antisuffrage journalist Richard Barry, after interviewing Josephine Daskam Dodge Bacon, quoted her in "Why Women Oppose Woman's Suffrage":

> No, I do not believe in woman suffrage. Why? Because a woman can no more do a man's work that a man can do a woman's. There has never been a first-class

woman writer, statesman, general or executive. I write second-class stuff myself. All women writers are second-class the minute you compare their work with that of the best *workmen*. But while there have been no really great women writers . . . no really great generals . . . no really great painters . . . there *have* been a large number of good mothers.

And while women have repeatedly been great mothers I defy you to mention a man who has ever been a really first-class mother.

Therefore, I conclude it is possible for women to achieve greatness as mothers and in no other way, and I do not believe Nature intended us to enter a field of effort where the laws of our being declare us outsiders.[32]

Apparently some Antis believed that it was a fairly general phenomenon that women did not have faith in other women. Mrs. Augustine H. Parker, an antisuffrage essayist, contended that because most women "are unconvinced by the feminists' protestations, few women care to be represented by other women." This was only natural, she thought, since "women do not, as a rule, employ other women to take care of their business affairs." As evidence she pointed to the fact that one half of the stock of the Pennsylvania Railroad was owned by women who could have elected several women directors if they wished, and yet the board was composed entirely of men.[34]

What at first may seem a strictly fanciful model for understanding the Antis emerges from Albert Memmi's study of colonialism, *The Colonizer and the Colonized*. Racism serves the same function in colonialism as sexism does in a patriarchal system. That is, in the same way that "racism sums up and symbolizes the fundamental relation which unites colonialist and colonized," sexism functions to unite male and female. The analogy is even more striking if one looks at the three major ideological components that according to Memmi constitute colonial racism: a gulf between the culture of the colonialist and the colonized; exploitation of these differences for the benefit of the colonialist; and the use of these supposed differences as standards of fact.[35]

The colonialist stresses those things that keep him separate, just as does the male in a patriarchy. And once the behavioral feature that characterizes the colonialist (or male) and contrasts him with the colonized (or female) has been isolated, this gap must be kept from being filled:

> The colonialist removes the factor from history, time, and therefore possible evolution. What is actually a sociological point becomes labeled as being biological or, preferably metaphysical. It is attached to the colonized's basic nature.

If the colonizer (colonialist) wants to be the master, it is not enough for him to be so, in fact, "he must also believe in its legitimacy." Furthermore, in order for that legitimacy to be complete, it is not enough for the colonized to be a slave, "he must also accept his role."[36] In the history of the relationship between the sexes, women until quite recently also have accepted their role, thus helping to legitimize the condition of male supremacy.

One of the devices that maintain the subordination of women and prevent the formation of a shared community of interest between the sexes is the prevalence of stereotypes that conform to mankind's needs. So, too, in the cases of the colonizer and the colonized. Another similarity is that the traits ascribed to the weaker are in both cases often incompatible with one another. Both women and colonized are simultaneously regarded as inferior and wicked, lazy and backward, without desires (frigid) and gluttonous (insatiable):

> The humanity of the colonized, rejected by the colonizer, becomes opaque. It is useless, he asserts, to try to forecast the colonized's actions ("They are unpredictable!" "With them, you never know"). It seems to him that strange and disturbing impulsiveness controls the colonized. The colonized must indeed be very strange if he remains so mysterious after years of living with the colonizer.[37]

Another mark of the colonized's depersonalization is the "mark of the plural. . . ." The colonized does not exist as an individual. Neither women nor colonized are free to choose between being colonized or not being colonized.

One of the most compelling similarities between the plight of the colonized and that of all women is that they have been removed from history and from the community. As Memmi indicates, "Colonization usurps any free role in either war or peace." The colonizer "pushed the colonized out of the historical and social, cultural and technical current."[38] While Memmi feels that the colonizer did so in order to subdue and exploit, and it is certainly not clear that male domination involved such vindictive motives, nevertheless the dynamics in both situations were such that the success of the one depended on the failure of the other. If one looks at the culture, society, and technology of both women and colonized, one sees how seriously damaged they are. And the same holds true of women as of the colonized—one has no idea what they would have been without colonization (or subjection), but one can see what has happened to both as a result.

There are also remarkable similarities between the *experiences suffered* by the colonized and by women in general. For many women, as for the colonized, their first ambition was to assimilate, to "become equal to that splendid model and resemble him to the point of disappearing in him." Memmi points out that when the colonized rebelled, the rebels were laughed at because of their insistence on wearing khaki uniforms. They hoped to be considered soldiers, and by this tactic, "They laid claim to and wore the dress of history."[39] By the same token, women suffered ridicule when they first expressed belief in their autonomy by donning the female facsimile of male dress, namely bloomers.[40]

Considered incapable of governing, both women and colonized were kept away from power. And in both cases, long absence from autonomous government resulted in the loss of interest in and feeling for the control and skills that it requires.

As a result of colonization, says Memmi, the colonized almost never experiences nationality and citizenship, except privately. This social and historic mutilation (the absence of self-assurance or pride of citizenship) is perpetuated by the educational system where references to the community and nation are always in terms of the colonizing nation.[41] In what schools or textbooks could American women have derived any pride of citizenship in learning about the history of their country? Everything takes place outside of the experience of the oppressed. They are nonentities or exist only with reference to others. Neither women nor the colonized recognize that they had a past. They have no history, no leaders, no heroes.

In the historical experience of women, the Antis emerge as the young women who fall back on traditional values, with one important difference from the colonized. As domesticity engulfed them and removed them from the mainstream of civilization, they attempted to find comfort in the only way of life they ever knew by postulating that it was the highest kind of life for all women. Instinctively they rebelled against assimilation, against becoming "equal" to the male model and resembling man to the point of disappearing in him. This would have deprived them of what was uniquely their own. Psychologically wedded to the system, they sought to secure: their way of life by enveloping it in a self-perpetuating mystique.

Memmi argues that the colonial condition cannot be changed except by doing away with the colonial relationship. The relationship demands that there be both the colonizer and the colonized; therefore, if one or the other is eliminated the basic relationship is altered. Assimilation and colonization are contradictory, for if all the colonized were assimilated, the colonizers would have no one left to exploit. On the other hand, when assimilation does occur, the colonized is even further removed from being in touch with his culture.

Just as the colonized, excluded from the universality common to all men, begins to assert his differences, the Anti also had to assert hers. Both ran the same risks. By taking up the challenge of exclusion, the colonized and the Antis accepted being separate and different, *but* their individuality was that which was limited and defined by the colonizer. Thus both the colonized and the Antis drew pride from their differences, but they were differences that had been formulated by the dominant group. Therefore, rejection of the colonizer's values and system was based on the conviction that everything that belonged to the colonizer was *not* appropriate for the colonized. According to Memmi, this is just what the colonizer has always told the colonized. Therefore, the rebellious colonized takes the first step toward liberation by accepting and glorifying an image of himself that emphasizes the apparent differences between himself and the colonizer.

Both Antis and suffragists had benefited from advances in women's rights such as higher education, access to the professions, and control over their property; therefore, there was hardly any difference between them regarding the desirability of women's rights—in all areas, that is, except the vote. But, according to Kraditor, the significance of the latter for the feminists was that it represented *autonomy*, the desire to be recognized in economic, political, and social realms as individuals in their own right. It was this, rather than a redefinition of woman's proper sphere, that loomed as the feminist objective and served to differentiate feminists and suffragists from Antis.

But Antis and suffragists were "social feminists"—urban upper- and middle-class women whose social worlds often overlapped through their activities as clubwomen. Thus, in addition to the fact that these social justice activities became the principal justification for feminism, most of the organization Antis were also clubwomen.

Now one has to take into account the fact that often both Antis and suffragists shared a similar worldview and possibly even a similar experience. In many cases it was only their solutions that differed. Furthermore, this approach enables one to view both suffragism and antisuffragism simply as variations of a new and growing trend toward activism among women. Looked at this way, Antis and suffragists had more in common with each other than with the aggregate of women in general. In any event, it becomes necessary to delineate more flexible denominators in dealing with women's behavior in groups than simply saying that some were pro and some anti; this must be done so that the commonality of shared experience is not obscured by the differences that divided them:

> Women have been the only subordinated-group that has belonged to the same families as its rulers. The ambiguous status of well-to-do women, as both ruler and ruled, generated contradictions and ambiguities in both feminists' and antifeminists' attitudes toward women.[42]

NOTES

1. It is virtually impossible to arrive at an accurate number of state associations. In the last issue of *The Woman's Protest* (February 1918), the Antis claimed twenty-five state associations serving their purpose. Nevertheless, it is doubtful that all of these states had fully constituted statewide organizations such as those of Massachusetts or even New York. Many of them were probably no more than committees. Furthermore, the list omits the Tennessee chapter, which became one of the more active state groups. Until further work is done on each state association, one can only estimate the extent of the antisuffrage organization.

2. Some individuals deliberately exploited the relationship between suffragism and feminism, arguing that the ballot for women would lead inevitably to the latter. The Men's League Opposed to Women Suffrage, "Brief Argument against Woman Suffrage" (Philadelphia 1913) MHS.

3. James McGrigor Allan, *Woman Suffrage Wrong in Principle, and Practice* (London: Remington and Co., 1890), 23; Mrs. A. J. George, "Suffrage Fallacies," *Anti-Suffrage Essays by Massachusetts Women* (The Forum Publications of Boston, 1916), 29.

4. Mrs. Herbert Lyman, "The Anti-Suffrage Ideal," *Anti-Suffrage Essays by Massachusetts Women*, 118–22; Goldwin Smith, "Woman Suffrage," *Essays on Questions of the Day* (New York: Macmillan & Co., 1894), 183–218.

5. Illinois Association Opposed to Woman Suffrage, *Fifteenth Annual Report*, December 1911. Other statements reflecting these and similar sentiments include the following: "If men are doing poorly—it is due to the women who trained them. We need better voters, not more voters." Alice N. George, "Woman's Rights vs. Woman Suffrage" (New York: National Association Opposed to Woman Suffrage, 1913), 8.

> If women had conquered their own part of life perfectly, one might wish to see them thus leave it and go forth to set the world to rights. But on the contrary, never were domestic conditions so badly attended. Until woman settles the servant question, how can she ask to run the government? (Emily Bissell, "A Talk to Women on the Suffrage Question" [New York State Association Opposed to Woman Suffrage, 1909], 5.)

6. The Reverend Charles H. Parkhurst, "The Inadvisability of Women Suffrage," Supplement to the *Annals of the American Academy of Political and Social Science* 35 (May 1910), 36–37.

7. Elizabeth Jackson, "Suffrage and the School Teacher," *Anti-Suffrage Essays by Massachusetts Women*, 86.

8. Illinois Association Opposed to Woman Suffrage, *Fifth Annual Report*, 1901.

9. Letter to Editor, Chicago *Record-Herald*, May 17, 1911.

10. George, "Suffrage Fallacies," 28; Man-Suffrage Association, *The Case Against Woman Suffrage* (New York, 1915), 6.

11. George, "Woman's Rights vs. Woman Suffrage," 3 (my italics).

12. Margaret C. Robinson, "Woman Suffrage in Relation to Patroiotic Service" (Public Interest League of Massachusetts, Sophia Smith Collection, Smith College), 99, 102.

13. Ibid.; M. G. van Rensselaer, "Should We Ask for the Suffrage?" 47.

14. Rensselaer, "Should We Ask for the Suffrage?," Massachusetts Association Opposed to the Further Extension of Suffrage to Women (n.d.), 47.

15. Ibid., 49.

16. Robinson, "Woman Suffrage a Menace to Social Reform"; Catharine Esther Beecher, *Woman's Profession as Mother and Educator* (Philadelphia: G. Maclean, 1872), 11; Bissell, "A Talk to Women on the Suffrage Question"; Lilly Rice Foxcroft, "Why Are Women Opposing Woman Suffrage?" *Wellesley Alumnae Quarterly* (April 1917); Rensselaer, "Should We Ask for the Suffrage?," 52.

17. Rensselaer, "Should We Ask for the Suffrage?," 50.

18. Ibid., 9–10, 14.

19. The Antis feared that if women were given the vote, the larger number of degenerate or wrong-minded women would vote against the reform measure of "good" women, who would have only a few ballots to cast. Robinson, "Woman Suffrage a Menace to Social Reform," 106.

20. Rensselaer, "Should We Ask for the Suffrage?" 52.

21. The article from which this excerpt was taken was printed in the Cambridge *Chronicle* (October 16, 1915). It was republished by the Women's Anti-Suffrage Associ-

ation of Massachusetts and excerpted by Robinson in "Woman Suffrage a Menace to Social Reform," 107.

22. Quoted in Carrie Chapman Catt and Nettie Rogers Shuler, *Woman Suffrage and Politics* (New York: Charles Scribner's Sons, 1923), 233.

23. Robinson, "Woman Suffrage a Menace to Social Reform," 106.

24. Foxcroft, "Why Are Women Opposing Woman Suffrage?" 4.

25. Rensselaer, "Should We Ask for the Suffrage?" 52.

26. Beecher, *Woman's Profession*, 11. Beecher's choice of words is very revealing. If by "distinctive power of their sex" she means sexuality or even feminine wiles, why is this assumed to be such a deleterious influence on public life? She does not explain. Others certainly shared their feelings, yet none of the female Antis addressed herself to just how this evil influence would operate. Does this perhaps reflect the fear that women free to engage in public life might use their sexual attractiveness to allure other women's husbands? We have only the male reaction of historian and antisuffragist Francis Parkman, who felt that their sex would give women a political advantage. Women would be free to be aggressive and even attack the latter who, out of chivalry, would be unable to be forthright and fight back. Man-Suffrage Association, "Some of the Reasons Against Woman Suffrage," n.d., reprinted by MAOFESW, *Why Women Do Not Want the Ballot*, vol. 1, no. 7.

27. Burrill (no first name given), "Some Practical Aspects of the Question," *Anti-Suffrage Essays by Massachusetts Women* (n.d.), 43–52.

28. It is difficult to understand how the Antis failed to regard this situation as anything but obvious tokenism. Perhaps from the vantage point of that period, however, this did represent an advance for women.

29. A Tennessee constitutional league had been formed to oppose ratification as a violation of the state constitution, but it was not nearly as active as the Southern Women's Rejection League. A. Elizabeth Taylor, *The Woman Suffrage Movement in Tennessee* (New York: Bookman, 1957).

30. *Nashville Tennessean*, August 13, 1920, cited ibid.

31. Viola Klein, *The Feminine Character: History of an Idealogy* (London: K. Paul, Trench, Trubner, 1946), 4–5.

32. Richard Barry, "Why Women Oppose Woman's Suffrage," *Pearson's Magazine* (February/March 1910), 326–27.

33. Mrs. Richard Watson Gilder, "A Letter on Woman Suffrage," (Massachusetts Association Opposed to the Further Extension of Suffrage to Women, 1894), 11.

34. M. Augustin H. Parker, "Are Suffragists Sincere Reformers?," *Anti-Suffrage Essays by Massachusetts Women*, 83.

35. Albert Memmi, *The Colonizer and the Colonized* (New York: The Orion Press, 1965), 70–71.

36. Ibid., 71, 89.

37. Ibid., 85.

38. Ibid., 91, 114. Kate Millett points out: "In terms of industry and production, the situation of women is in many ways comparable both to colonial and to pre-industrial peoples. Although they achieved their first economic autonomy in the industrial revolution and now constitute a large and underpaid factory population, women do not participate directly in technology or in production." Even when they do participate in production of commodities, they do not "own or control or even comprehend the process in which they participate." Furthermore, women's distance from technology "is sufficiently

great that it is doubtful that (in the absence of males) they could replace or repair such machines on any significant scale. If knowledge is power, power is also knowledge, and a large factor in their subordinate position is the fairly systematic ignorance patriarchy imposes upon women." *Sexual Politics* (Garden City, NY: Doubleday & Company, Inc., 1970), 41–42.

39. Memmi, *Colonizer and Colonized*, 95, 116.

40. Mary Wollstonecraft, writing in 1792, was concerned about the fact that masculine virtues seemed excessively valuable to early feminists. Women resemble soldiers, she wrote, in that, "They both acquire manners before morals and a knowledge of life before they have, from reflection, any acquaintance with the grand ideal outline of human nature." *A Vindication of the Rights of Woman* (New York: W. W. Norton & Company, Inc., 1967), 40.

41. Memmi, *Colonizer and Colonized*, 96.

42. Eileen S. Kraditor, *Up from the Pedestal: Selected Writings in the History of American Feminism* (Chicago: Quadrangle Books, 1968), 10.

EDITOR'S NOTE

One hundred twenty Harvard professors signed a letter that stated, in part, that "an institutional culture at Harvard erects numerous barriers to improving the representation of women on the faculty."[1] The letter was in response to Larry Summers, president of Harvard, who ruffled more than a few feathers when he proposed that innate differences between males and females explain why fewer women succeed in math and science. Regarding Summers' notion of biology over social learning, Ann Hulbert, writing in *The New York Times*, analyzes the data differently. Hulbert and others argue that boys' overall better math scores on standardized tests are the result of high scores for a small number of boys, not all boys, and that there are many, many low-scoring boys in the pool.[2]

Pointing to statistics that suggest something other than genetics might be going on at Harvard, Hulbert reports that since Summers became president, the percentage of tenure offers to women in the arts and sciences at Harvard have declined from 37 percent to 11 percent.[3]

It's possible, then, to believe that President Summers recently stated that it wasn't "too much [of an exaggeration] to say that" universities like Harvard "were designed by men for men."[4]

Finally, there is evidence that biology has something to do with women's predicament in academic, but not what Summers had in mind. Research by Ehrenberg, found that "men who had children within five years of receiving Ph.D.s were 38 percent more likely to have received tenure than their female counterparts who had children within five years of receiving their Ph.D.s."[5] It shouldn't take a rocket scientist to understand what can be inferred from Ehrenberg's finding, should it?

NOTES

1. Rebecca Winters, "Harvard's Crimson Face," *Time*, January 24, 2005, 52.

2. Ann Hulbert, "Boy Problems," *The New York Times*, April 3, 2005, 13.

3. Ibid.

4. Phillip Kennicott, "Summers Storm," *The Washington Post National Weekly Edition*, May 2–8, 2005, 8–9.

5. Review News & Notes, *TIAA-CREF*, Summer 2005, 7.

26

Where the Girls Are

Growing Up Female with the Mass Media

Susan J. Douglas

I was not yet in college in the spring and summer of 1968; I wasn't a member of any of the various oppositional political groups that organized against and did battle with government authorities. I was, like the vast majority of young people, still only a spectator. Yet spectatorship in 1968—even in the confines of your own home—was a politicizing activity.

Just think about what we saw in this one year. In January, Dr. Spock, who had helped our mothers raise us, was indicted for "aiding and abetting" draft evasion. In February, we watched the Tet Offensive on TV, which suggested that maybe Vietnam wasn't going to be the Sunday football game rout the president and the Pentagon had assured us it would. On March 12, Eugene McCarthy won the New Hampshire primary, and four days later, Bobby Kennedy declared his candidacy for president. Just two weeks after this, in what I thought would be yet another lie-filled address to the nation, Lyndon Johnson stunned us all by announcing that he was stepping down from the presidency when his term expired. The elation I felt over this blockbuster development lasted exactly four days until, at 6:00 P.M. on April 4—just in time for the nightly news—Martin Luther King Jr. was assassinated.

Less than three weeks after this disaster, on April 23, somewhere between 800 and 1,000 students at Columbia barricaded themselves inside campus buildings to protest the university's ties to the Pentagon and its ongoing appropriation of poor, residential neighborhoods in upper Manhattan. The takeover ended the next week when 1,000 cops stormed the buildings, arresting 700 college kids and injuring at least 150 of them. And it was only five weeks later that we watched those sickening images of Bobby Kennedy lying on the floor of the Ambassador Hotel in Los Angeles, his wife cradling his bloody head in her lap.

The public activism of young people was one of the biggest ongoing stories 1968. After all, between January and June of that year alone, there were 221 major demonstrations at 101 colleges and universities involving some 39,000 students.[1] Public demonstrations were automatically newsworthy because they provided news organizations with provocative pictures, they represented conflict, and they sometimes produced arrests and violence, two of the news media's yardsticks for determining whether an event merited coverage. But precisely because of such criteria, and the news media's ingrained preference for covering events rather than explaining underlying causes or processes, their desire to identify leaders and spokesmen even in groups that refuse to have them, and their insistence that there are two sides—no more, no less—to every news story, such coverage was a mixed blessing for the young people of the New Left. It would prove to be a mixed blessing for feminism as well.

When feminists staged their own demonstrations, they encountered not just deeply entrenched journalistic conventions but also the most recently established routines and biases shaping the coverage of social movements and demonstrations. By the time of the Miss America demonstration, certain precedents in the press coverage of dissent were well established. The news media cast the protests of young people as simultaneously dangerous and ineffectual, deeply subversive yet of little consequence. Solemn references to "Communist elements" and constant reliance on two incendiary images—burning draft cards with Vietcong flags—were intermixed with dismissive comments like this wrap-up from CBS's Bruce Morton: "Most people have doubts that U.S. foreign policy can be changed on the streets."[2] *The New York Times* and CBS, by turns, emphasized the extremism of antiwar demonstrators yet ridiculed their beards and blue jeans as signs that they were nothing more than naïve, style-over-substance poseurs. The "other side" the media gave time to were often ultra right-wing types, as if there was some equivalence between their politics and those of kids trying to stop the war.[3]

The important precedent was that the news media routinely divided the antiwar movement into what Todd Gitlin termed "legitimate main acts and illegitimate sideshows," meaning the moderate, conciliatory positions worth listening to and all the rest that the news media indicated were not.[4]

The treatment of the Miss America protest made it clear that the media coverage of the women's movement would be strikingly similar to that of the antiwar movement. But where women were involved, there were some extra, important touches. How feminists used, or failed to use, their faces and their bodies, and the extent to which their faces and bodies conformed to those in a Max Factor ad, were central features of the coverage. If these girls were out on the streets and swinging bras around, why, they must be closet exhibitionists, narcissists, or simply hysterical, and language that suggested witchcraft or secret cults resonated darkly with the magical powers of sitcom characters. The media also paid inordinate attention to the way feminists violated physical and social boundaries, and suggested that, by doing so, they were making spectacles of themselves, just as Beatles fans had done a few years earlier. Feminists were cast as unfeminine, unappealing women who were denouncing the importance of the male gaze, yet who secretly coveted that gaze for themselves by protesting in public. These poor girls, it was suggested, sought to get through political flamboyance what they were unable to get through physical attractiveness.

It was not just what was said to or about women in the media that was important; news stories and TV shows were structured so that feminism was positioned as deviant. The standards by which something was judged newsworthy were, in fact, deeply masculine. The emphases on conflict in the public sphere, on crime, on dramatic public events rather than behind-the-scenes processes, on the individual rather than the group, and on competition rather than cooperation all biased the news toward masculine public enterprise. The public sphere was defined, visually and rhetorically, as the place where men make history. The news also exploited the highly emotional as spectacle while denigrating overly emotional commentary about events as not objective and therefore invalid. Because of these journalistic conventions, the only places any female had in the news were as victim, hysteric, sex object, or wife of a prominent man. . . . The overwhelming dismissive coverage of the women's movement that followed was in many ways inevitable.

These biases, of course, were reinforced by the structures of the news organizations themselves, which were rigidly hierarchical and male-dominated. In the late 1960s, women journalists were confined to writing about spring hats and thirty-one new ways to cook squash, or they were researchers for male reporters, and they were rarely seen on television except as weather girls. Women trying to break out of these confines faced enormous pressures to conform to how the boys did things, and they also faced editors and publishers deeply hostile to the women's movement.

Perhaps one reason that the Miss America demonstration is not remembered as frequently as it should be is that it happened amidst the swirl of so many shocking events in 1968. Yet retrospectives today on the late 1960s seem all too eager to show young girls smoking pot and dancing partially clad at love-ins while they completely ignore Atlantic City in September. But anyone who cares about the sick proliferations of the anorexic body as the ideal for all women, or who is tired of the constant equation between crow's-feet and female worthlessness, should keep the memory of this protest alive and well, for us and for future generations. Robin Morgan and her organization, the New York Radical Women, took direct aim at what they called "the degrading mindless-boob-girlie symbol" so prevalent in the media and decried the "ludicrous 'beauty' standards we ourselves are conditioned to take seriously." They also attacked "the unbeatable madonna-whore combination" and the mixed messages women had been socialized to internalize. "To win approval, we must be both sexy and wholesome, delicate but able to cope, demure yet titillatingly bitchy. . . . Miss America and *Playboy*'s centerfolds are sisters over the skin."[5]

The New York Times's coverage of the protest in Atlantic City indicated how the women's movement would be framed by the news media over the next five years, and some female journalists were just as dismissive as their male counterparts. *Times* reporter Charlotte Curtis, emphasizing what she saw as these women's desperate need for attention, observed, "Television and news photographers were allowed and even encouraged to photograph the pickets, and the women . . . escalated their activities when the cameramen arrived."

Throughout the article, the demonstrators were made to appear ridiculous, frivolous, and hypocritical. All the women's charges about sexism in the United States were placed in quotation marks, suggesting that these were merely the deluded hallucinations of a few ugly, angry women rather than a fact of life. The demonstrators' rhetoric was cast as highly inflated and thus absurd, and their complaints about female oppression seen as representing a wacky, self-seeking, publicity-hungry fringe of distinctly unrepresentative women. So the women who were protesting the public exhibition of women's bodies were themselves cast as nothing more than needy exhibitionists. The contrast was stark: Miss America contestants, beautiful, docile, and compliant, who eagerly sought out and competed for the male gaze, deserved their day in the public spotlight; the demonstrators, unruly, rebellious, excessive, who attacked the institutionalization of male voyeurism, did not.

One year later, *Newsweek* would describe the Miss America demonstration as one in which 150 women "gathered in front of Convention Hall and burned their brassieres," even though no bra burning had occurred in Atlantic City.[6] But bra burning had become the news peg for media coverage of the women's movement, a metaphor that trivialized feminists and titillated the audience at the same time. For the press, burning bras was a natural segue from burning draft cards. It fit into the dominant media frame about women's liberation and equated the women's movement with exhibitionism and narcissism, as if women who unstrapped their breasts were unleashing their sexuality in a way that was unseemly, laughable, and politically inconsequential, yet dangerous. Women who threw their bras away may have said they were challenging sexism, but the media, with a wink, hinted that these women's motives were not at all political but rather personal: to be trendy, and to attract men.

Even for those of us who didn't recognize it at the time, 1968 was a turning point. All the prefeminist glimmerings in girl group music, Beatlemania, perky teens, and women with magical powers, the exhortations to make something of ourselves and change the world, and the image of the political woman we first saw in Joan Baez and Mary Travers—these shards started coming together and magnified one another during 1968. The acceptance by millions of us of some version of feminist ideology was a fitful process, during which we began questioning, rethinking, and revising our sense of what it meant—or ought to mean—to be an American woman.

So where are we now, in the era of "I'm not a feminist, but . . .?" We are an overlay of imprints, bearing, in some way or another, the fossilized remains of *Queen for a Day, Sputnik,* the Sexual Revolution, the Chiffons, Beatlemania, perkiness, the women's movement, the catfights, *Charlie's Angels,* and buns of steel. We have learned to be masochistic and narcissistic, feisty and compliant, eager to please and eager to irritate and shock, independent and dependent, assertive and conciliatory. We have learned to wear a hundred masks, and to live with the fact that our inner selves are fragmented, some of the pieces validated by the mass media, others eternally ignored. All our lives, we have watched women from Beatles fans to Anita Hill and Hillary Rodham Clinton breaching barricades and crossing boundaries they weren't supposed to: we have seen how stepping out of line has been punished and how effective—and utterly futile—such punishments have been. Certain women are demonized, but they, and others emboldened by their actions, come back for more. We have grown up with these ever discrepant representations of women, and related to them all our lives, and while we have shaped them, they have had more power to shape us. We have grown up and continue to live with media images not of our making, so, on some level, we will always feel like outsiders looking in at a culture that regards us unknowable, mysterious, laughable, other.

We are fed up with ads that tell us we're too old, too fat, and too marked up in some way but we feel, nonetheless, too old, too fat, and too marked up. We are tired of blockbuster movies that glorify beefy, rippled men who speak monosyllabically and carry extremely well-endowed sticks, but we go to them anyway, nursing our fury and enjoying our catharsis. We get the bends as we escape into the schizophrenic landscape of *Glamour* or *Vogue,* in which editorials, advice columns, and articles urge us to be assertive, strong, no-nonsense feminists while the fashion and beauty layouts insist that we be passive, anorexic spectacles whose only function is to attract men and who should spend our leisure time mastering the art of the pedicure. We throw half-eaten bagels at Saturday morning kids' shows and commercials that train our daughters to be giggling, air-headed Valley Girls, but we go ahead and buy them Glitter Ken and the Fisher-Price toy kitchen on the theory that we played with Barbie and we came out OK—well, sort of. We think that news programs must be getting less sexist because there are now famous women newscasters like Connie Chung, Diane Sawyer, and Nina Totenberg, but we also see how so-called women's issues are either sensationalized (have one more drink and you'll die of breast cancer) or trivialized (so what if a woman has to drive three hundred miles to get an abortion, or a sixteen-year-old has to get permission to do so from a father she never sees?), while women's voices about major areas of national policy are ignored.

This is what it has come to. On the one hand, few women want to take on the baggage of the feminist stereotype. On the other hand, they embrace much of what feminism has made possible for them—which they also learned about, initially, from the media—and are uninterested in returning to the days of woman as doormat. Since the 1960s, legitimation of feminism in the mass media and backlash against it have smacked against each other with the force and chaos of billiard balls colliding. Individual women, too often isolated by the pressures of juggling work, relationships, kids, and trying to see a movie once a year, are left on their own to arrange the balls neatly in some psychic rack that makes sense for them, if only momentarily.

What the mass media don't convey, and can't convey, is that feminism is an on-going project, a process, undertaken on a daily basis by millions of women of all ages, classes, ethnic and racial backgrounds, and sexual preferences. Feminism is constantly being reinvented, and reinvented through determination and compromise, so that women try, as best they can, to have love and support as well as power and autonomy. As they do so, they have certainly taken note, with Susan Faludi's help, of a backlash filled with wishful thinking pronouncements about the "death" of feminism and the heralding of a new "postfeminist" age.[7]

The news media, for their part, are today a schizophrenic mess about feminism, and there is a powerful reverberation between their schizophrenia and our own. They continue to cover feminism and describe feminists as if the movement is monolithic and feminists are all alike. At the same time, in their stories and their hiring practices, we see that in the news media (as elsewhere) feminism is many things to many women; that there is not one feminism but many; and that there are beautiful, amiable women who claim feminism and shrill, mean-spirited ones who condemn it.

Women's voices are rarely heard on the news. Feminism is still kept in ideological purdah. Female "experts" are interviewed for the nightly news when the topic is abortion, child care, or affirmative action; but when the topic is war, foreign policy, the environment, or national purpose, female voices, and feminist voices in particular, are ignored. A recent study revealed that in 1988 only 10.3 percent of the guests on *Nightline* were female, and of the twenty most frequent guests, none were women. Another study from 1990 found that the ten individuals who appeared most frequently as analysts on the CBS, ABC, and NBC nightly news were all men, and some of them appeared as many as fifty-eight times in a single year.[8] Betty Friedan's Women, Men and Media Project found that the percentage of female correspondents was only 15 percent in 1989, and that there were some nights when you could watch the news and see no women reporters at all. Of the one hundred most frequently seen correspondents on TV, only eight were women.

Thanks to the women's movement, my consciousness as a woman and as a mother was very different from my mother's. I was aware of our country's pathological schizophrenia about mothers and children: revere them in imagery, revile them in public policy. But this wasn't my own lonely observation; unlike my mother, I could read, hear, and see other women, in a variety of places, articulating these same criticisms. I also had the language, as well as the sense of obligation, to dissect the media's role in sustaining this hypocrisy.

Nowhere is the gap between image and reality wider than the one separating the smiling, serene, financially comfortable, and perfectly coiffed media mom from her frazzled, exhausted, sputum-covered, real-life counterpart. Everywhere I turned, as I read child-care books, watched TV, or went shopping for baby paraphernalia, I found myself navigating the powerful crosscurrents of middle-class motherhood. Like all the other messages surrounding us—about sex, about assertiveness, about women in politics, and about independence—the messages about motherhood and babies crash into each other like tidal waves. Shooting these ideological rapids on a daily basis, while also taking care of a baby, can produce a certain astringency in the new mom's worldview. And I found myself getting more astringent as I took inventory of the completely unrealistic images of motherhood we imbibed. Here was my love-hate relationship with the mass media writ large.

In the early months of my daughter's life, I watched more TV than usual, but with a more jaundiced eye. Yet even my old standbys let me down. On *L.A. Law*, Ann Kelsey and Stuart Markowitz, who had been trying unsuccessfully to have a baby, adopted an infant girl.

Motherhood had virtually no impact on this woman's life or work, while those of us sitting at home in our sputum-covered bathrobes and ratty slippers were wondering how we were going to survive the next day at work on no sleep. This baby, like most media babies, was a trouble-free, ecstasy-producing, attractive little acquisition; if you "get" one, it will make you feel real good, look great in a rocking chair, and make you fall in love with your spouse all over again. Now, while babies are, at times, an indescribable joy, caring for them makes you feel like you've been tortured in an especially sadistic sleep-deprivation experiment. The feel-good images are a complete lie, and you know it. But they burrow into you, forcing you to castigate yourself for not being serene enough, organized enough, or spontaneous enough as a mother.

Talk about getting the bends! On the one hand, we had the TV supermoms, size six women with perfectly applied makeup who could do anything and apparently didn't need any sleep. On the other hand, we got a recognition that motherhood might be just a tad demanding, but acknowledged only in the age-old blame-the-victim solution of the mommy track. Between these two extremes were millions of us, the real mothers of America, with no place to stand. We were either supposed to act as if children don't hamper our ability to be overachieving workaholics and we can do everything we did before plus raise a baby or two or acquiesce to second-class citizenship, acknowledging that being a mother is so debilitating that we're only capable of having dead-end, place-holding jobs while men, including fathers, and women without kids step on our backs to get the next promotion. Either way, the real-life mother is humiliated, especially if she has a job, as opposed to a "career," in which the whole notion of advancement or a "track" is patently absurd.

These contradictions surrounding motherhood and children differ from what our mothers confronted, but they have their roots firmly and deeply in the 1950s. For even now, no matter what you do, you can't ever be good enough as a mother. If you don't work, you're a bad mom, and if you do work, you're a bad mom. Then there's all the advice that comes at us from *Working Mother, Parents, Newsweek,* the nightly news, *20/20,* and *Oprah.* Let your baby cry herself to sleep; never let your baby cry. Don't be too rigid, but don't be too permissive. Don't ever spank your child; an occasional swat on the butt is good for a kid. Encourage your child to learn, but don't push her to learn. Be her friend; never be her friend. Rein her in; cut her some slack. The tightrope walks are endless. Once again we find ourselves under surveillance, not only as sex objects, or as workers, but as mothers. And on all sides of us are voices with megaphones, yelling completely opposite things to us as we figure out whether we have time to do a wash or will simply have to turn the kid's underwear inside out tomorrow.

And here, again, we feel the pull between sisterhood and competitive individualism. At 4:00 A.M., when it seemed like everyone in the world except my daughter and I was asleep, I felt myself part of that transhistorical and transcultural group called mothers, the ones who get up, no matter what, listening to the soft snorings of others, while tending to the needs of a child. Now this may sound overly romantic and sentimental, but I didn't expect to feel such a powerful bond with other space and time.

This is why Roseanne Barr, now Arnold, became the top female sitcom star in America in the early 1990s. Despite the incredibly hostile treatment she has gotten in the press—because she's four things TV women are not supposed to be, working-class, loudmouthed, overweight, and a feminist—Roseanne became a success because her mission was simple and welcome: to take the schmaltz and hypocrisy out of media images of motherhood. Her famous line from her stand-up routine—"If the kids are alive at five, hey, I've done my job"—spoke to millions of women who love their children more than anything in the world but who also find mothering boring and, at times, infuriating. Most moms are not corporate attorneys, Roseanne insisted, nor do they fit a size six, carry a briefcase, or smile most of the time. They are waitresses, or work in factories, or in tiny office cubicles, or in other dead-end jobs, and they don't have $700 suits or nannies.

Both the news and entertainment media have had enormous power to set the agenda about how people consider, react to, and accept women's changing roles and aspirations. Frequently, and without obvious collusion, the various media have managed to settle on what becomes the prevailing common sense about women's place in the world. Having that common sense repeated and reenacted in sitcoms, movies, and newscasts has a powerful effect on women's self-perceptions and on men's perceptions of them. To point out that these dominant images are perforated with rifts and contradictions that have sometimes emboldened women does not undercut their basic power.[9] The media have helped instigate change for women while using a host of metaphors—women with magical powers, the catfight, the choked-off female voice—to contain and blunt that change.

So, for us, the question about whether the mass media lead social change or lag behind it sets up a false dichotomy, for we have seen and felt them do both at the same time. Yet sometimes the mass media lag much more than they lead, and today we live in an especially conservative media environment, in which ownership of media outlets is increasingly concentrated in the hands of fewer megacorporations and the voices of those not smack dab in the moderate political center are vilified or silenced. Images of scores of women in satin teddies and garter belts hopping in and out of bed with whomever is handy suggest, to some, an overly "liberal" media when such images are, in fact, deeply reactionary.

The only advice I have for women today is to purchase two things: extra slippers, for throwing at the TV set, and extra stationary, for writing letters to soda companies telling them we'll never buy their swill again and will organize boycotts if they keep pitting Cindy Crawford against older women and keep pitting us against one another.

NOTES

1. Rita Lang Kleinfelder, *When We Were Young: A Baby-Boomer Yearbook* (New York: Prentice Hall, 1993), 472.

2. Todd Gitlin, *The Whole World Is Watching* (Berkeley: University of California Press, 1980), 121.

3. See ibid., 47–52 and 90–94.

4. Ibid., 6.

5. "No more Miss America!" in Robin Morgan, ed., *Sisterhood is Powerful* (New York: Vintage, 1970), 521–24.

6. "The Big Letdown," *Newsweek*, September 1, 1969, 49–50.

7. S. Susan Faludi, *Backlash: The Undeclared War Against American Women* (New York: 1991), 76–77.

8. Susan Douglas, "The Representation of Women in the News Media," EXTRA!, March–April 1991, 2.

9. Justin Lewis, *The Ideological Octopus* (New York: Routledge, 1991), 203–5.

EDITOR'S NOTE

Maureen Dowd, editorial columnist for *The New York Times*, could be responding to Susan Douglas's reading when she says: "Every culture has its own way of tamping down female power, be it sexual, political, or financial. Americans like to see women who wear the pants be beaten up and humiliated . . . women being degraded has an entertainment value far greater than men being degraded."[1]

Dowd fears there's no one to turn to for help because in her view feminism was merely a "flash," while the backlash has been around for years.[2]

She thinks "People liked Hillary [Rodham Clinton] and Martha [Stewart] a lot more once they were "broken. . . ."[3] Dowd argues that some men, especially alpha men, find successful women unnerving and feel somewhat comforted when "alphettes" are pushed down a bit.[4]

The questions: 1.Why are women unnerved by successful women? 2. Is feminism or the women's movement gone?

NOTES

1. Maureen Dowd, "Taming of the Shrews," *The New York Times*, March 6, 2005, 13.
2. Maureen Dowd, "There's No End to This Era for White Men," *The New York Times*, December 3, 2004, B7.
3. Dowd, "Taming."
4. Dowd, "Taming."

27

Mating, Marriage, and the Marketplace

A Survey of College Student's Attitudes and Expectations

Barbara A. Arrighi

Those of you reading this text have experienced the economic recession, corporate mergers, and massive layoffs of the late twentieth century. In your lifetime you have undoubtedly acquired some familiarity with terms like merger mania, corporate downsizing, corporate rightsizing, bull markets, bear markets, day trading, e-commerce, and the NASDAQ. Politically, you have lived through the country's shift from democratic liberalism to an embracing of Reagonomics, a turn toward Clinton's democratic conservatism, with compassionate conservatism ushering in the twenty-first century.

You have come of age in the midst of the continuing fallout of the liberalized sexual mores of the 1960s. The culture has bequeathed to you spiraling divorce rates, increased remarriage rates, destigmatization of and an increasing occurrence of cohabitation, legalization of abortion, premarital sex as normative, higher rates of out-of-wedlock births (even as birth control has become more accessible and more reliable), and an increasing proportion of wives and mothers as full-time, year-round workers. In general, though many young women have not embraced feminism as a social or political ideology, they have practiced its tenets: higher levels of education for women, delayed first marriage, fewer children, and a sustained commitment to the workplace.

You have been subjected to televised discussions, debates, and even U.S. Senate hearings about formerly taboo subjects like domestic violence, sexual harassment, the health risks of unprotected sex, and the unforgettable, tortured definition of sex by a sitting president. All of this has played out, synchronized to the beat of successive political and religious calls for a return to family values.

Within an environment of changing sexual mores and lifestyle patterns, what can be gleaned about the future from this generation's attitudes and expectations concerning mating, marriage, and the marketplace? This study provides a descriptive analysis of a sample of members of the cohort born in the late 1970s and early 1980s and their views on these issues, all within the context of a culture in flux.

SEX-ROLE ATTITUDES AND EGALITARIANISM

Research indicates that attitudes and education are linked, and that values change with increased education (Ross 1987). For example, there is evidence that those with higher levels of education are more accepting of equality between the sexes. In marital relationships, husbands' level of education is a predictor of their willingness to share household tasks (Farkas 1976). Furthermore, there is evidence that husbands with twelve or more years of education do more housework than those with fewer years of education (Presser 1994).

Societal definitions of what women and men should be emerge within the process of doing gender (West and Zimmerman 1987); that is, designations of appropriately masculine or feminine behavior are constructed within institutional contexts. Thus, they are socially constructed as well as structured in family systems and educational systems, to name just two. Gendered role performances reinforce and legitimate existing gender-patterned behaviors that are interwoven into our institutions and thus our social relationships.

As an institution, the family provides the initial and perhaps most enduring inculcation of gender. For example, at birth males and females are more alike than different; however, because of the institutionalized gender expectations of significant others, the gender division—a mere seam at birth—becomes a chasm by young adulthood. The structure of gendering means the similarities between females and males are denied (Rubin 1975). The patterns of gender behavior and power relations in one's family of origin influences the gender development of a child as well as the gender organization of family life when two people marry. In analyzing the data in this study, I am interested in determining to what extent college students in the sample give gendered responses concerning mating, marriage, and the marketplace.

METHODS

A convenience sample of 354 students completed surveys in four sections of introductory sociology courses during the fall semester of 1997. One hundred thirty-three respondents were males and 221 were females. The majority of students were freshmen between seventeen and twenty-one years of age. What we learn about these students cannot be generalized to other college-age women and men, but the findings can provide a sense of the direction future research should take.

RESULTS

The attitudes and expectations of the young women and men in the sample converged on many issues, especially those relating to marriage and family. The most notable gender differences emerged on workplace issues.

GENDER AND MATING

Traditionally, women were to remain virginal until marriage (no matter how late they wed); men, however, were expected, even encouraged, to become experienced sexual partners. Indeed, the prevailing thinking until the 1960s was that women were void of any "carnal motivation" (Collins and Coltrane 1991; Cott 1978). Even today the messages about appropriate sexual behavior for women are ambiguous at best. In light of this, it is instructive that almost half of the college males (46 percent) expressed a centuries-old preference to marry a virgin, and that about a third of young women in the sample responded that they, like the young men in the sample, would prefer to marry a virgin.

The student responses could reflect the religious influence of the larger community in which the university is situated. Located along the northern edge of the Bible Belt, the university is also in an area that is heavily Catholic. Virgin Mary sightings, attracting hundreds of faithful, have been reported in the last few years at a Catholic church located not far from the university.

However, something other than religious dogma could be motivating the responses. For example, fear of deadly sexually transmitted diseases could be informing their responses. Then again, women's responses might be nothing more than a desire for equity concerning the sexual behavior of their partner. Simply put, if men prefer virgins, women can too.

While a substantial proportion of college men surveyed expressed a traditional preference for a virgin, the expectations of many appeared grounded in contemporary sexual mores. Almost half of the men (44 percent) and more than half of the women (51 percent) stated that they do not expect to marry a virgin. However, if national data are accurate, a substantial proportion of students in the sample are going to be disappointed, because virgins appear to be an endangered species. At the turn of twentieth century, less than 25 percent of women reportedly had engaged in premarital sex, but by the late 1980s the proportion had increased to 66 percent (Family Planning Perspectives 1985). The shift for men went from 66 percent in the 1920s who reported having engaged in premarital sexual activity to about 95 percent in the 1980s (Collins and Coltrane 1991). Clearly, the expectations of students surveyed do not reflect the national shift toward premarital sexual activity.

STUDENTS AND A DOUBLE STANDARD

Both male and female students in the sample thought a double standard exists concerning sexual behavior. For example, a majority of the men (68 percent) and women (85 percent) disagreed with the statement: "Today a woman can be as sexually active as a man and it will not reflect negatively on her." The finding suggests that the students in this sample would think the 66 percent of young women in the national sample (noted above) who reportedly engage in premarital sex do so at risk to their reputation. While both groups of students in this sample agree that being sexually active is problematic for women, the young men appear to welcome the idea of women taking the lead in a relationship. More than half of the college men surveyed disagreed with the statement: "In relationships, it is best for the man to pursue the woman." However, less than half (45 percent) of women in the sample were willing to forgo tradition and take on the role of the pursuer. No doubt their hesitancy was related to their awareness of the resiliency of the double standard.

GENDER, MARRIAGE, AND HOUSEWORK

The issue of who should be the pursuer may be debatable, but most survey respondents seemed prepared to follow the traditional path of marriage and family. The overwhelming majority of students expect to marry (87 percent of men and 93 percent of women) and raise a family (86 percent of males and 89 percent of females).

How couples set up their households has been central to research examining equally within the family. Prevailing cultural norms define men by their ability to provide for their families (Bernard 1981). Within that context many, if not most, men view paid work as the arena in which their success will be measured and the family as a separate institution that provides a "haven in a heartless world" (Lasch 1977). Being a provider is steeped in gender and confirms men's masculine identity (Bernard 1981).

Because being a homemaker, like being a provider, is steeped in gender too, men who engage in housework do not fit the cultural definition of masculinity (Bernard 1981). Men might resist sharing household tasks because "real" men wouldn't do them (Fowlkes 1980). Even at that, the work and family literature has reported that men and women support the notion of men contributing to household labor, especially when wives are employed outside the home (Pleck 1993; Thompson and Walker 1989).

Though there is consensus that men should share housework with their significant others, the research consistently has found that men typically do no more than a third of household labor. Yet in a departure from tradition, the expectation of the majority of this sample of college students is that they will share household tasks equally (men 77 percent, women 88 percent). It should be noted that in the face of this seemingly egalitarian view, almost half of the male respondents indicated that some household tasks were better suited to women! That 40 percent of women agreed with the men sheds some light on why the proportion of housework completed by men has not changed dramatically. Could it be that some women resist giving up tasks that they think display being a woman? Should future research shift the focus from why men do not do more to why women will not do less? Are men reluctant to take on work that they feel best displays being a woman? Is it that men are reluctant to take on more than a third of household work, or is it more that too many women resist giving up the home as their primary responsibility, possibly even acting as gatekeepers for men sharing housework?

Indeed, two-thirds of the sample agreed with the statement: "There are natural differences between men and women and we shouldn't try to change things." The responses to the survey statements are at the core of the gender perspective's argument about gender displays. Although being a man or woman socially is not the inevitable outgrowth of biological features, it is made invisible through gendering and thus comes to be viewed as natural (Ferree 1990; Gerson and Peiss 1985). The college sample's responses align with a 1993 Gallup Poll (Newport 1993) in which 56 percent of men and 73 percent of women agreed that "not including purely physical differences, men and women are basically different." If the dominant thinking of both sexes is that women and men are innately different, appeals by a minority of women and men for equality between the sexes will be resisted by the majority.

STUDENTS' VIEWS ABOUT CHILD CARE

Although the men surveyed believed there are some tasks for which women are better suited, there was ambivalence concerning child care. Half of the male respondents (and 69 percent of women) believed that women are not automatically better caretakers of children than men. The students' responses concerning child care correspond with prior research that suggests that, of all the household duties, men are more likely to assist with child care than with other tasks. As we forge a new century, some foresee the increasing expectation for fathers to become equal coparents (Doherty, Kouneski, and Erickson 1998; Pleck and Pleck 1997). Men can even find child care rewarding (Gerson 1993).

STUDENT ATTITUDES ABOUT WORK AND FAMILY

Should wives stay home? Not according to a majority of the students surveyed. Overall, two-thirds disagreed with the statement, "It is better for the family if the wife stays home and the husband goes to work." Nationally, well over half of women with school-aged children are in the workplace, and student responses are consistent with that data. It is possible that for many of the students their own childhood experiences included having a working mom. Unfortunately, that information about students in the sample is unavailable in these data.

Despite reports indicating that 48 percent of employed married women provide half or more of family income (Families and Work Institute 1995), they tend to be thought of as supplemental rather than co-providers (Ferree 1990). Research has suggested that even in the face of harsh economic reality, many couples think the provision of family income should be the husband's sole responsibility (Vannoy-Hiller Philliber 1989). And cross-cultural research supports the notion that the breadwinner status is attached to the man, not the woman. What does our sample think?

Not only do the men surveyed not object to the prospect of working wives, they report not being threatened by the prospect of their mates earning more than they do. Seventy percent of the men and 65 percent of the women do not think that it is better for the family if the husband earns more than the wife.

GENDER AND THE WORKPLACE

The young college men have thus far presented somewhat egalitarian attitudes and expectations concerning mating and family matters; they appear to draw the line, however, when it comes to the workplace. Seventy-three percent of the men think that "there are some jobs in the workplace that are better suited for men than for women." If, as Bernard and others suggest, men view paid work as the arena in which their success is measured and their manhood is defined, within that context their response makes sense. Their thinking here provides further evidence that the students subscribe to the natural difference argument. More than half (57 percent) of the young women in the sample agreed with the men, which is alarming and indicates the complexity of the issue of resistance to full integration of women in the workplace. Is the glass ceiling being held in place with the help of some women?

Although these data are not generalizable, the students' responses are consistent with the results of a 1993 Gallup Poll cited above (Newport 1993), in which the majority of both sexes concurred with the notion that men and women are basically different. Taken together, it is a conundrum for women. Can equality between the sexes be achieved if difference is the paradigm?

STUDENTS AND AFFIRMATIVE ACTION

It is instructive that although the women surveyed did not seem to consider "his and her jobs" problematic, at least 41 percent of women did not agree with this statement: "Affirmative Action is no longer needed to help women get ahead." While not a majority, it is nearly double the 24 percent of college men who disagreed. The findings correspond with a 1995 Gallup Poll that found only 43 percent of women and 38 percent of men approved of Affirmative Action for women. Thompson's (1991) argument that women and men typically compare their situations with others of the same sex rather than with those of the opposite sex may be appropriate here in explaining men's lack of support for Affirmative Action and women's lukewarm support.

Thirty-nine percent of women and 35 percent of men responded "don't know" to the above statement about Affirmative Action. Their response could reflect their inexperience with and/or lack of knowledge of Affirmative Action issues in the workplace. It is worth noting that, though support for the Affirmative Action statement above was minimal, 72 percent of the college women and 50 percent of the young men disagreed with this statement: "if women and men have the same qualifications and do the same job, they are paid the same wage." Interestingly, students surveyed are cognizant that inequality exists in the workplace, but their lack of endorsement for Affirmative Action indicates they do not support a policy to change it. As noted above, if male identity and financial well-being are attached to the marketplace, men's self-interested stance on Affirmative Action is logical.

But what can be said of women's lack of support for Affirmative Action? It could be that inequality that has the potential to lead to conflict is suppressed or denied by those who are victimized by it. It could be that women are a colonized group and do not fully grasp their subordination. It could be too, as Ferree (1990) argues, that rather than look at the structure of inequality we try to resolve it "by invoking supposed differences in the characters of men and women" (876). It is less disruptive, less messy, less risky to blame the individual rather than to take on the daunting task of structurally addressing issues of inequality. It allows the status quo to remain intact.

CONCLUSION

If education liberalizes attitudes, some of the responses from this sample of college students point to an egalitarian perspective, especially about issues concerning home life and children. It appears that for the most part the students expect to share household tasks and child care as some have predicted will happen in the twenty-first century.

If this group of college students has its way, however, the workplace will remain divided into his and hers. A gender perspective is at work here. The men clearly do not favor Affirmative Action to ameliorate job segregation, and women are not much more enthusiastic. Furthermore, while endorsing equality in the home, a sizable proportion of the college women seem to accept a segregated status for women and men at work. If this sample is in any way representative of the next generation of workers, equality in the workplace will continue to elude us.

The study has provided a snapshot of college students' attitudes concerning work and family issues. While it provides some insights, the findings are not generalizable. Longitudinal research is needed so that we can understand the process by which students form their attitudes and the extent to which students' attitudes about family predict their behaviors.

The direction of future research should be threefold. One should focus on explaining men's role in the household division of labor as well as men's gatekeeping function in the workplace. A second should focus on women as gatekeepers in the home—that is, to what extent are women resistant to men's encroachment on their turf? Finally, the third focus of the analysis should examine women's role in perpetuating workplace job segregation.

REFERENCES

Bernard, Jessie. 1981. The Good Provider Role: Its Rise and Fall. *American Psychologist* 36: 1–12.

Collins, Randall, and Scott Coltrane. 1991. *Sociology of Marriage and the Family: Gender, Love, and Property.* Chicago: Nelson Hall.

Cott, Nancy F. 1978. Passionlessness: An Interpretation of Victorian Sexual Ideology 1790–1850. *Signs* 4: 219–36.

Doherty, William J., Edward F. Kouneski, and Martha F. Erickson. 1998. Responsible Fathering: An Overview and Conceptual Framework. *Journal of Marriage and the Family* 60, 277–92.

Families and Work Institute. 1995. *Women: The New Providers.* Benton Harbor, MI: Whirlpool Foundation.

Family Planning Perspectives. 1985. Recently Wed Women More Likely to Have Had Premarital Sex. 17 (September/October): 142.

Farkas, George. 1976. Education, Wage Rates, and the Division of Labor between Husband and Wife. *Journal of Marriage and the Family* 38: 473–83.

Ferree, Myra Marx. 1990. Beyond Separate Spheres: Feminism and Family Research. *Journal of Marriage and the Family* 38: 473–83.

Fowlkes, Martha. 1980. *Behind Every Successful Man.* New York: Columbia University Press.

Gerson, Kathleen. 1993. *No Man's Land.* New York: Basic Books.

Gerson, Judith, and Kathy Peiss. 1985. Boundaries, Negotiations, Consciousness: Reconceptualizing Gender Relations. *Social Problems* 32: 317–31.

Lasch, Christopher. 1977. *Haven in a Heartless World.* New York: Basic Books.

Moore, David W. 1995. Americans Today Are Dubious about Affirmative Action. *The Gallup Monthly Poll* (March): 36–38.

Newport, Frank. 1993. Americans Now More Likely to Say: Women Have It Harder than Men. *The Gallup Monthly Poll* (October): 11–13.

Pleck, Joseph. 1993. Are 'Family-Supportive' Employer Policies Relevant to Men? In *Men, Work and Family,* edited by Jane C. Hood, 217–37. Newbury Park, CA: Sage.

Pleck, E. H., and J. H. Pleck. 1997. Fatherhood Ideals in the United States: Historical Dimensions. In *The Role of the Father in Child Development,* 3rd ed., edited by M. E. Lamb. New York: Wiley.

Presser, Harriet. 1994. Employment Schedules among Dual-Earner Spouses and the Division of Household Labor by Gender. *American Sociological Review* 59: 348–64.

Ross, Catherine E. 1987. The Division of Labor at Home. *Social Forces* 65: 816–33.

Rubin, Gayle. 1975. The Traffic in Women: Notes on the "Political Economy" of Sex. In *Toward an Anthropology of Women,* edited by R. Reiter. New York: Monthly Review Press.

Thompson, Linda. 1991. Family Work: Women's Sense of Fairness. *Journal of Family Issues* 12: 181–96.

Thompson, Linda, and Alexis J. Walker. 1989. Gender in Families: Women and Men in Marriage, Work and Parenthood. *Journal of Marriage and the Family* 51:41–57.

Vannoy-Hiller, Dana, and William W. Philliber. 1989. *Equal Partners: Successful Women in Marriage.* Newbury Park, CA: Sage.

West, Candace, and Don H. Zimmerman. 1987. Doing Gender. *Gender and Society* 1: 125–51.

IX

THE PRICE OF DEVIANCE

28

The Unruly Woman

Gender and the Genres of Laughter

Kathleen Rowe

Since Sigmund Freud, few people question laughter's entanglements with aggression. Both spring from the unconscious and both are, to varying degrees, taboo for women. The notion of "angry young women" films like the "angry young men" films popular in the 1950s and 1960s has itself been laughable, at least until *Thelma and Louise*. Ridley Scott's 1991 take on the buddy movie/road movie, shocked, moved, and polarized audiences on the issue of women's violence against men. Women's anger more often remains unspoken, as Julia Lesage writes, repressed beneath "all of women's depression—all our compulsive smiling, ego-tending, and sacrifice; all our psychosomatic illness, and all our passivity" ("Women's Rage" 421). Because women lack acceptable aesthetic or social structures through which to express or even "think" anger, it rarely erupts into the violence or transgressive laughter of *A Question of Silence* or *Thelma and Louise*. In melodrama and film noir, for example, women's anger appears as insanity or perversity, including grotesque images of lesbianism. Even art has rarely contained direct expressions of women's rage. What's needed are "self-conscious, collectively supported, and politically clear articulations of our anger and rage," in Lesage's words—articulations that cannot be made in the model of "nice girls" ("Women's Rage" 420, 427). That is, women must be willing to offend and to be offensive, to look beyond the doomed suffering women of melodrama and the evil ones of film noir.

I would like to suggest that those structures for expressing women's anger do enlist—in the genres of laughter, and, at least in rudimentary form, in the structure of narrative itself.

All narrative forms contain the potential to represent transformation and change, but it is the genres of laughter that most fully employ the motifs of liminality. From romance to satire to the grotesque, these genres are built on transgression and inversion, disguise and masquerade, sexual reversals, the deflation of ideals, and the leveling of hierarchies. It is to these motifs, which are also the motif of the carnivalesque, that B. Rudy Rich refers when she advocates the feminist potential of the "Medusan film," a type of film about sexuality and humor.[1] She argues that comedy should not be overlooked as a weapon of great political power, which women should cultivate for "its revolutionary potential as a deflator of the patriarchal order and an extraordinary leveler and reinventor of dramatic structure" (353).[2]

The name "Medusan" is borrowed from Hélène Cixous's "The Laugh of the Medusa," an essay that might well have inspired *A Question of Silence*. Medusa, of course, is a mythological woman whose story bears important implications for theories of sexuality, spectacle, and cinema. When Medusa boasted of her beauty to Athena, Athena became jealous and changed Medusa and her sisters into monsters with fangs for teeth, snakes for hair, and staring eyes that could transform people into stone. Perseus killed her by looking at her reflection in his mirrorlike shield and then beheading her. The blood from her left side was fatally poisonous, and that from her right could restore life to the dead. Medusa remains an evocative symbol in contemporary culture, appearing, for instance, as an evil woman who threatens an androgynous male hero and the furry creatures who follow him in *Captain EO*, a Michael Jackson video shown in the early 1990s in Disneyland.[3] One could say that among the many things Medusa embodies is extreme ambivalence toward women—toward their bodies, their beauty, their celebration of self, and their blood.

Whereas for Freud, Medusa incarnates male fears of castration, Cixous uses her to mock those theories built on such notions of female lack. In the most widely quoted passage from the essay, she writes that what Perseus averted his eyes from was not a deadly monster but a woman without the deformities "male" theories attempt to inflict on her: "You have only to look at the Medusa straight on to see her. And she is not deadly. She's beautiful and she's laughing" (255). While underscoring yet another failure, like that of Bakhtin, to "hear" women's laughter, this rewriting of Medusa's story exemplifies the kind of creative destruction Bakhtin associates with the grotesque.

Feminist film theory has yet to pursue fully the implications of Medusa's power both to draw Perseus's gaze as spectacle and to fix her own gaze, her "staring eyes," on him.[4] By using her power to draw his gaze, she can halt his quest for his Oedipal patrimony, robbing him, in fact, of his own eyes. From Cixous's perspective, that power becomes deadly only because of Perseus's refusal to meet her gaze. A more courageous meeting of her gaze would allow Perseus to apprehend not petrifying monstrosity but beauty: "You have only to look at the Medusa straight on." As long as men avert their eyes from her, fearing the sight of her *and* her gaze, "woman" can be only a phantasm of castration for them, deadly and grotesque. And more important, as long as women do not look at *each other* straight on, they can see only distorted reflections of themselves.

Medusa, like Bakhtin's grinning pregnant hags, contains some of the earliest outlines of the unruly woman, an ambivalent figure of female outrageousness and transgression with roots in the narrative forms of comedy and the social practices of carnival. The unruly woman represents a special kind of excess differing from that of the femme fatale (the daughters of Eve and Helen) or the madonna (the daughters of Mary), whose laughter, if it ever occurred, no longer rings in the myths still circulating around them. Like Medusa, the unruly woman laughs. Like Roseanne Arnold, she is not a "nice girl." She *is* willing to offend and be offensive. As with the heroines of the romantic film comedy, from Ellie in *It Happened One Night* (1934) to Loretta in *Moonstruck* (1987), her sexuality is neither evil and uncontrollable like that of the femme fatale, nor sanctified and denied like that of the virgin/madonna. Associated with both beauty and monstrosity, the unruly woman dwells close to the grotesque.

The figure of the unruly woman contains much potential for feminist appropriation, for rethinking how women are constructed as gendered subjects in the language of spectacle and the visual. The parodic excesses of the unruly woman and the comedic conventions surrounding her provide a space to "act out" the "dilemmas of femininity," in Mary Russo's words (225), to make not only "fantastic" and "incredible" but also laughable those tropes of femininity valorized by melodrama. Russo asks in what sense women can produce and make spectacles of themselves *for* themselves. The unruly woman points to new ways of thinking about visibility as power. Masquerade concerns itself not only with a woman's ability to look, after all, but also with her ability to affect the terms on which she is seen.

Such a sense of spectacle differs from the one that shaped early feminist film theory. Granting that visual pleasure and power are inextricably bound, this position would see that relation as more historically determined, its terms as more mutable. It would argue that visual power flows in multiple directions and that the position of spectacle isn't necessarily one of weakness. Because public power is predicated largely on visibility, men have long understood the need to secure their power not only by looking but by being seen, or rather, by fashioning—as subject, as author, as artist—a spectacle of themselves.

The topos of the unruly woman . . . reverberates whenever women disrupt the norms of femininity and the social hierarchy of male over female through excess and outrageousness. Historian Natalie Davis does not provide an inventory of qualities associated with female unruliness but instead a wide-ranging collection of examples of "women on top" and a powerful theoretical framework for understanding them.[5]

1. The unruly woman creates disorder by dominating, or trying to dominate, men. She is unable or unwilling to confine herself to her proper place.

2. Her body is excessive or fat, suggesting her unwillingness or inability to control her physical appetites.
3. Her speech is excessive, in quantity, content, or tone.
4. She makes jokes, or laughs herself.
5. She may be androgynous or hermaphroditic, drawing attention to the social construction of gender.
6. She may be old or a masculinized crone, for old women who refuse to become invisible in our culture are often considered grotesque.
7. Her behavior is associated with looseness and occasionally whorishness, but her sexuality is less narrowly and negatively defined than is that of the femme fatale. She may be pregnant.
8. She is associated with dirt, liminality (thresholds, borders, or margins), and taboo, rendering her above all a figure of ambivalence.

These are some of the tropes or signifiers of female unruliness. Ideology holds that the "well-adjusted" woman has what Hélène Cixous has described as "divine composure" (246). She is silent, static, invisible—"composed" and "divinely" apart from the hurly-burly of life, process, and social power. Such is not the case with the unruly woman. Through her body, her speech, and her laughter, especially in the public sphere, she creates a disruptive spectacle of herself. The tropes of unruliness are often coded with misogyny. However, they are also a source of potential power, especially when they are recoded or reframed to expose what that composure conceals. Ultimately, the unruly woman can be seen as prototype of woman as subject—transgressive above all when she lays claim to her own desire.

In July 1990, Roseanne Barr Arnold, star of the top-rated ABC sitcom *Roseanne*, was invited to sing the national anthem at a double-header between the Cincinnati Reds and the San Diego Padres. Tom Werner, coproducer of the TV show and owner of the Padres, thought that the fat and noisy comedian would give a boost to his losing team. It was Working Women's Night at the San Diego stadium, and Arnold was nationally known for her depiction of working-class family life in her character Roseanne. With thirty thousand fans in the stands, Arnold screeched out the song, grabbed her crotch, spit on the ground, and made an obscene gesture to the booing crowd. Werner had been right; the team won its next two games. But the performance, intended as a parody of baseball rituals, unleased a firestorm in the press. CNN broadcast the story with interviews of outraged "people on the street." In one segment, baseball fans drove a steamroller over a boom box containing a tape of her voice. Angry calls flooded the switchboards at ABC. On national television, President George Bush called her performance "disgraceful." Arnold received threats on her life.

The incident boosted media coverage of the already controversial Arnold from the tabloids to the establishment press and from the gossip columns to page one. Headlines joked about "the fat lady singing" or the "Barr-mangled banner," while the tabloid *Star* more graphically exclaimed "Barrf!" and then listed "Her 10 most gross moments." From sports writers to political commentators, all felt compelled to say something about the incident. William C. Rhoden wrote in the *New York Times*: "Barr is merely the symptom of the excess of greed in American sports."

Obviously Arnold had struck a nerve. Other singers have been criticized for their highly stylized renditions of "The Star Spangled Banner"—among them José Feliciano, Bobby McFerrin, Marvin Gaye, and Willie Nelson. And one could argue that Arnold, as a comedian, was doing nothing more than they had, shaping the performance according to her own comedic artistry. But none provoked a reaction like this one. Arnold jested about it—"I must be the greatest singer. My voice can stop a fucking nation."

If it is dangerous "to be a woman, period," it is especially so to be an *unruly* woman, and Arnold's performance in San Diego that summer confirmed her status as such.

Women rarely have the opportunity to claim the kind of public space that Arnold did that day, and her experience offers abundant lessons about the relation between social power and public visibility. Invisibility helps constrain women's social power; as long as women are not seen in the public sphere, they do not exist. Arnold heightened her visibility by forcing herself from one—less visible—category of popular discourse into another usually unavailable to women—from "soft news" to "hard news." Soft news includes gossip, the tabloids, *People* magazine, lifestyle and entertainment sections of the newspaper; hard news covers events clearly in the public sphere and appears on the front pages and op-ed pages of newspapers and at the beginning of newscasts. If sports is not exactly hard news, it's not soft either, because of its particular status in masculine culture. When Arnold walked into that stadium, she made herself the subject of hard news, subject to those voices that had never touched her when she was safely contained in a place marked "sitcom" or "HBO Comedy Special," or in the feminized discourse of gossip columns and tabloids.

Implicit in the unruly woman's heightened visibility is her potential to bring about a process Erving Goffman describes as "breaking frame." Goffman suggests that social life is an "endless negotiation" about which cultural frame should surround, and thereby give meaning to, various events and bits of behavior. He argues that the meaning of a social situation can be radically altered by changing the frame in which it is perceived and that frames are most vulnerable at their margins. Because she is dangerously situated in the margins of social life, the unruly woman enjoys heightened "frame-busting" power.

Arnold entered a space that day already defined as liminal or sacred in patriarchal culture. Baseball is not merely a game, something that is played, but a collective, public, and masculine ritual, a quasi-religious reaffirmation of patriarchy, patriotism, and the myth of our nation's Edenic history. . . . Free of the narrative constraints of her television series, Arnold staged a joke that reframed that ritual event and turned it into something else—a carnivalized moment of leveling, mockery, and inversion. By exceeding the limits of play tolerated on that diamond, parodying the gestures of the Boys of Summer, and singing the national anthem less than reverentially—in effect, by being who she was, a comedian, joke-maker, and unruly woman—she violated the space of that ritual and, indeed, the national airwaves that had been given over to its celebration. What might have been a harmless spoof of the tropes of masculinity and patriotism became a threat to the sanctity of all American institutions, invoking that "perilous realm of possibility," in Victor Turner's words where "anything *may* go" (41).

According to Turner, at times of dramatic social change, sacred symbols—such as baseball, the national anthem, and the flag—burst into the public arena to mobilize people to defend their cultures. In the summer of 1990, the U.S. government was laying the groundwork for its showdown with Saddam Hussein and preparing to deploy sixty thousand troops in Kuwait. Flag burning had become a controversial issue, with proposals in Congress for a constitutional ban against it. Arnold's performance made her vulnerable to the official voices of masculine authority, the voices of news and government from George Will to George Bush, which projected onto her all perceived threats to the dominant culture. Indeed, Will's near loss of control over his own rhetoric exposed his column's subtext—the range of repressed fears this disorderly fat woman released about racial threats to the nation's "alabaster" cities, about mass culture with its "slob" values encroaching on the tidy domain of those who know Walt Whitman's poetry well enough to paraphrase it.[6]

Not only in this incident but throughout her career Arnold has used the semiotics of unruliness to break frame, to disrupt, to expose the gap between, on the one hand, the New Left and the women's movement of the late 1960s and early 1970s, and on the other hand, the realities of working-class family life two decades later. On one level, of course, Arnold's joke backfired. On another and more important one, however, it succeeded as a powerful demonstration of the disruptive power of the unruly woman. Even as fans were booing her in the stadium, others were cheering.[7] As Arnold's career has unfolded, her fat, unruly body—and her noisy, angry, funny persona—have shape-shifted into forms that might appear less transgressive than the ones that first defined her.

The cover of the December 1990 issue of *Vanity Fair*—headlined "Roseanne on Top"—shows Arnold holding the wrists of her husband Tom Arnold to pin him beneath her. Her mouth is open in what appears to be a laugh. She is wearing a low-cut red dress, a strawberry-blonde wig, diamonds, and a white fox fur, a look that parodically recalls the blonde bombshells and gold diggers of early classical Hollywood film. The photograph, a medium shot, centers on Arnold's massive cleavage. Tom Arnold's face, looking at the camera and registering little emotion, is upside down.

The words and images of the cover suggest that Arnold wields power in multiple dimensions—power over men, financial power, celebrity power, sexual power. These words and images also acknowledge that she has achieved that power by cultivating a particular persona defined by gender inversion.

Arnold's success has not generated universal enthusiasm, as the national anthem incident made clear. Nor was that incident an isolated event, but merely the most provocative in a series of episodes that included dropping her pants at other public events, cracking jokes about menstruation on national television, and generally, "making a spectacle of herself." Many people find Arnold's persona deeply offensive and controversy has followed her up almost every rung of the ladder to success. She and her series have been trashed by the tabloids, snubbed by the Emmies, and condescended to by media critics.[8] At the same time, her fans have been loyal and numerous enough to propel her to, and sustain, her success.

While this ambivalence cuts across media and class lines, the supermarket tabloids have perhaps played the largest role in creating and popularizing Arnold's unruly persona. The tabloids are the carnivalesque of the popular print media, giving heightened representations of the kinds of "weirdness or disjunction" their readers experience in everyday life (Fiske 114). They are popular with the same demographic group targeted by Arnold's show, women aged eighteen to thirty-four, or, as comedian Alan King more colorfully describes them, "the hopeless underclass of the female sex. The polyester-clad, overweight occupants of the slow track. Fast-food waitresses, factory workers, housewives—members of the invisible pink-collar army. The despised, the jilted, the underpaid." "In other words," as Arnold replies, "the coolest people" (both quoted in O'Connor B27). Arnold shares with the tabloids a taste for the self-consciously excessive, vulgar, and sensational. Both Arnold and the tabloids carnivalize, invert, and mock the norms of bourgeois taste.

One explanation for the contradictions that have characterized Arnold's reception in U.S. culture lies in the phenomenon of stardom itself. . . . In Arnold's case, her copious body could be seen as a site which makes visible, and reconciles, the conflicts women experience in a culture that says consume (food) but look as if you don't. Or it makes visible the conflict any member of the working class might experience in a culture than says consume (goods—conspicuously and lavishly) but don't expect a job that provides you with the means to do so. This explanation is apt, but it doesn't fully explain the extreme ambivalence that has marked Arnold's career from its outset.

Such an explanation, I believe, would locate Arnold in the historical and theoretical context of female unruliness. In an article on the op-ed page of the *New York Times* ("What Am I, a Zoo?"), Arnold describes her own awareness of the carnivalesque heterogeneity of her image by enumerating the groups she has been associated with—the regular housewife, the mother, the postfeminist, the "Little Guy," fat people, the "Queen of Tabloid America," the "body politic," sex, "angry womankind herself," "the notorious and sensationalistic La Luna madness of an ovulating Abzugian woman run wild"—and so on.

Arnold's unruliness is more dearly paradigmatic than syntagmatic, less visible in the stories her series dramatizes than in the image cultivated around her body. Roseanne Arnold-the-person who tattooed her buttocks and mooned her fans, Roseanne Connor-the-character for whom farting and nose picking are as much a reality as dirty dishes and obnoxious boy bosses. It is Arnold's *fatness*, however, and the *looseness* or lack of personal restraint her fatness implies, that most powerfully define her and convey her opposition to middle-class and feminine standards of decorum and beauty. Indeed, the very appearance of a 200-plus-pound woman on a weekly primetime sitcom is significant. More than anything, I believe, her fatness is the source of the hostility directed against her. Even if a fat woman says or does nothing, her very appearance, especially in public space, can give offense. Fatness has carried more positive implications for women in other historical periods and among other ethnic and racial groups, but in white, late-twentieth-century America, it signifies a disturbing unresponsiveness to social control.

As Michel Foucault has shown, social groups exercise control over their members by inscribing standards of beauty and perfection, of social and sexual "normalcy," on their bodies. At the same time, the body serves as a vehicle for communication from subject to social world—a nonverbal communication that is often hidden by the social privileging of speech (Douglas 87). Body language conveys the individual's relation to the social group along a continuum of control, from strong to weak, from total relaxation to total self-control. Among the socially powerful, relaxation signifies "ease." Among those deemed in need of social control, it signifies "looseness" or "sloppiness." The body that "refuses to be aestheticized," that does not control its "grotesque, offensive, dirty aspects," can thus communicate resistance to social discipline (Fiske 97). George Will could find no better way to express his reaction to Arnold's rebelliousness than by describing her as a "slob."

Arnold's body epitomizes the grotesque body Bakhtin described, an affinity that is clear from the first paragraph of *Roseanne: My Life as a Woman* (Barr), where her description of her "gargantuan appetites" even as a newborn baby brings to mind Bakhtin's study of Rabelais. Arnold compounds her fatness with a looseness of body language and speech. She sprawls, slouches, and flops on furniture: her speech—even apart from its content—is loose, its enunciation and grammar "sloppy," and its tone and volume "excessive."

In twentieth-century U.S. culture, these qualities have long lost the positive charges they might have carried in the cultures Bakhtin described. Our culture stigmatizes all fat people by psychologizing or moralizing their obesity.[9] For *women*, body size and bearing are governed by especially far-reaching standards of normalization and asetheticization, which forbid both looseness and fatness. Women of ill-repute, whether fat or thin, are described as "loose," their bodies, especially their sexuality, are seen as out of control. Similarly, fat women are seen as having "let themselves go." To protect themselves against the threat of rape, violence, come-ons, and offensive male vulgarity, poor women, especially women of color, may assume a bearing that is "stiff" and "ladylike." Anita Hill displayed extreme dignity and reserve during the 1991 Senate hearings on the appointment of Supreme Court Justice Clarence Thomas, although that bearing did not protect her from sexual innuendoes by men or charges of "aloofness" by women.

The cult of thinness is among the most insidious means of disciplining the female body in contemporary U.S. culture. Because a woman's social well-being is largely dependent on her appearance, heavy women suffer more than heavy men from the culture's tendency to stigmatize fat people. Comedians make fat jokes about Arnold but they usually spare John Goodman, the equally fat actor who plays her husband on her sitcom. While other cultures have considered round and fleshy women as sensuous and feminine, our culture considers them unfeminine, rebellious, and sexually deviant, either undersexed or oversexed. In her studies of women's relation to food (*Fat is a Feminist Issue* and *Hunger Strike*), Susie Orbach has described anorexia as the "metaphor of our times," an expression of the extreme contradictions women experience when they are socialized to tend to the needs of others but deny their own. Femininity is gauged by how little space women take up; women who are too fat or move too loosely appropriate too much space, obtruding upon proper boundaries (Henley 38). It is no coincidence, Orbach writes, that since the 1960s, when women accelerated their demands for more space in the public world, the female body ideal has become smaller and ever more unattainable. At the same time, the incidence of anorexia has sharply increased. The anorectic takes the imperative to deny her desire and "aestheticize" her body beyond healthful limits, her emaciated form becoming a grotesque exposure of the norms that seek to control women's appetites in all areas of their lives.

The transgressive, round female body is also the maternal body, and maternity ties women to the process of generation and aging. As a result, the figure of the grotesque old woman often bears a masculinist culture's projected fears of aging and death. While Arnold is hardly an old woman and the media do not attempt to portray her as such, fatness and age are closely related because both foreground the materiality of the body.

Women are expected to keep not only their bodies but their utterances unobtrusive. As Henley notes, voices in any culture that are not meant to be heard are perceived as loud, when they do speak, regardless of their decibel level. The description of feminists as "shrill"—with voices that are too loud and too high-pitched—quickly became a cliché in accounts of the women's movement. Dominant cultures characterize minorities among them as loud—Americans in Europe, Japanese in the United States. In white U.S. culture, the voices of blacks are characterized as not only "loud" but "unclear," "slurred," and "lazy"—in other words, loose. Farting, belching, and nose picking convey a similar failure—or refusal—to restrain the body. While boys and men can make controlled use of such "uncontrollable" bodily functions to rebel against authority, such an avenue of revolt is generally not available to women. But, as Henley suggests, "if it should ever come into women's repertoire, it will carry great power, since it directly undermines the sacredness of women's bodies" (91).

Arnold describes how Matt Williams, the producer she eventually fired from her show, tried to get *her* fired: "He compiled a list of every offensive thing I did. And I do offensive things. . . . That's who I am. That's my act. So Matt was in his office making a list of how gross I was, how many times I farted and belched—taking it to the network to show I was out of control" (quoted in Jerome 85–86). Of course she was out of control—*his* control.

By being fat, loud, and ever willing to "do offensive things," the star persona "Roseanne Arnold" displays, above all, a supreme ease with her body—an ease which triggers much of the unease surrounding her because it diminishes the power of others to control her. Pierre Bourdieu describes such a manner as an "indifference to the objectifying gaze of others which neutralizes its power . . . [and] appropriates its appropriation" (208). It marks her rebellion against not only the codes of gender but those of class, for a culture's norms of beauty or the "legitimate" body—fit and trim—are accepted across class boundaries while the ability to achieve them is not. Ease with one's body is the prerogative of the upper classes. For the working classes, the body is more likely to be a source of embarrassment, timidity, and alienation.

She learned about madness and institutionalization at the age of sixteen when she spent eight months in a mental hospital because of nightmares and other symptoms of psychological trauma she experienced after being hit by a car. Like other labels of deviancy, madness is often attached to the unruly woman, and it is a leitmotif in Arnold's autobiography and the tabloid talk about her.

What finally convinced her to cast her lot with comedy was "the thought of woman, any woman, standing up and saying NO . . . a huge, cosmic NO." She explains, "The first time I went on stage, I felt *myself* say it, and I felt chilled and free and redeemed" (Barr, *Roseanne* 152). This "no" draws on laughter's power to negate. It refuses the affirmation men often like to attribute to women, as in Molly Bloom's famous, unconditional, rhapsodic "yes" at the end of James Joyce's *Ulysses*.

Arnold discovered her stance (or attitude, if you will) when she realized that she could take up the issue of female oppression by adopting its very language. . . . So she built her act and her success by exposing those "tropes of femininity" stylized and valorized, as Mary Ann Doane explains in *The Desire to Desire*, in the women's melodrama. Arnold attacked the ideology of "true womanhood"—how to be the perfect wife and mother—by cultivating the opposite, an image of the unruly woman. Appropriating Andelin's words but to very different ends, she called this figure the "Domestic Goddess."

It is no accident that a tradition of funny, angry women is hard to find, for the closeness between laughter and anger produces deep constraints on how women may express or participate in both. These constraints are illuminated by Freud's theory of wit (*Jokes and Their Relation to the Unconscious*), which points to the importance of gender in much comedy and laughter. For Freud, joke work arises from the unconscious much as dream work does. It has three related forms—the joke itself, the comic, and the humorous—which all release energy otherwise spent in repression.

In Freud's account, the joke in its basic form requires three parties—two men and a woman. The first man initiates the joke to release an aggressive impulse, originally sexual, toward the woman. He forces her to participate in the joke through her embarrassment, her acknowledgement that she understands its content. (Such was the case when Anita Hill was made to repeat Clarence Thomas's remarks to her about pubic hair on a Coke bottle.) Through its cleverness, the joke veils and makes socially acceptable its underlying aggression. The joke does not exist until the laughter of the second man confirms it; the woman, as the joke's passive butt, thus enables the formation of a bond between the two men. According to Freud, the replacement of an actual woman by a symbolic substitute marks the advance of civilization, as does the joke's evolution from smut to content that is less overtly sexual.[10]

Freud's account of the joke suggests why so much laughter is directed *at* women and why so much comedy is misogynistic. It also explains why women so often feel alienated from many traditions of comedy, whether the slapstick of early silent film or the routines of standup comedians from Andrew Dice Clay to Eddie Murphy. For this reason, standup comedy—highly dependent on the dynamics of joke making—has, until the 1960s, been an unfriendly place for female performers. Until then, women rarely appeared in a comic act without a male partner. Even after the 1960s, women who succeeded as standup comedians tended, in a sense, to occupy the "male" position by directing their jokes at themselves in self-deprecating barbs, or at other women. Much of the humor of Phyllis Diller and Joan Rivers falls into this category.

Freud's analysis explains how precariously the unruly woman is poised between serving as a target of hostile laughter herself and hurling that laughter back at its sources. It also gives yet another explanation for the furor Arnold provoked in San Diego. Not only did she violate the space of baseball, but she also encroached on another sacred masculine territory—that of the jokemaker. Arnold "made" a joke, and a tendentious one, containing a thinly veiled message of aggression. Refusing to play the passive victim herself, she forced men into that role. As in her standup routine, she used the social pressure mobilized by the joke to force men to assume a perspective, even if only briefly, they ordinarily would not—to laugh at their symbols of masculine pride. In order to laugh, men had to adopt the double perspective that characterizes women's lives, experiencing the joke as both subject and object, as butt and complicitous second party. For many, obviously, that was impossible.

NOTES

1. See "In the Name of Feminist Film Criticism." An example of such a film is Jacques Rivette's *Celine and Julie Go Boating* (1974), which was almost universally denounced by male critics for its "silliness" but has become a favorite of feminists. Pitting a new kind of comedy against the genre of melodrama, the film suggests a seemingly unending capacity for prolonging the middle section of narrative with its invention, liminality, and play. See also Lesage's *"Celine and Julie Go Boating*: Subversive Fantasy."

2. Rich warns against an overemphasis on form or "signifying practices" in judging a film's feminist potential. Her call for "a bit of phenomenology" about the existence and experience of the female spectator remains as cogent today as when she made it in 1978. Comedy's potential for feminism has long been recognized as well by Patricia Mellencamp, whose persuasive and witty work on the subject began with articles on the Marx Brothers ("Jokes and Their Relation to the Marx Brothers"), Lucille Ball, and Gracie Allen and has continued through her recent books on the avant-garde, television, and the discourses of scandal.

3. Medusa retains even greater currency in the avant-garde. Her story is rewritten, feminized, and conflated with that of Eve in Monique Wittig's *Les Guérillères* (see Suleiman 132). Her face appears on the cover of a recent book about female performance artists (Juno and Vale, *Angry Women*). Suleiman describes the laughing Medusa as a "trope for women's autonomous subjectivity and for the necessary irreverence of women's writing—and rewriting" (168).

4. De Lauretis makes a provocative move in this direction when, in the context of a "politics of the unconscious," she rewrites the Medusa story so that Medusa is not sleeping but is awake when Perseus slays her (*Alice Doesn't* 134–136). By doing so, she points to the fact that our culture demands that women be "asleep" whenever it asks us to identify with the images of dead women it parades before us and when it privileges "aesthetic" standards at the expense of any other kind of identification. I take a similar position in relation to high cultural modes of criticism in "Romanticism, Sexuality, and the Canon."

5. That framework is based on the notion of sexual inversion, which I will discuss in more detail later in this chapter. I substitute *gender inversion* for *sexual inversion*, to avoid any ambiguity that might arise from the latter's associations with homosexuality in psychoanalytic discourse. While the list that follows is my own, it is largely indebted to Davis, as is this entire study. Like Mary Russo's, her work has made immeasurable contributions to my own.

6. As Arnold herself noted, the reaction to her performance, not the performance itself, carried the more alarming message. As for Bush, she says, he "should have been paying attention to Kuwait" (quoted in Hirschberg 224).

7. Later that year, the incident appeared in an episode of the courtroom drama series, *L.A. Law*, where it was rewritten as a conflict between a sympathetically portrayed, heavy black male blues singer and a team owner, whose stuffiness was shown to be un-American.

8. In July 1991, she beat four male competitors—Dan Quayle, Saddam Hussein, U.S. Senator Jesse Helms, and developer Donald Trump—to win the first annual "Sitting Duck" award given by the National Society of Newspaper Columnists ("People" 2A).

9. Marcia Millman writes that fat people arouse "horror, loathing, speculation, repugnance, and avoidance" (71). In the working class, fatness becomes a sign of a failure to achieve upward mobility. She also notes that some men hold a secret attraction to fat women.

10. Other studies confirm this scenario. As Mary Douglas suggests, people tend to direct jokes "downward," toward groups that are lower in social power (*Implicit Meanings* 95). Or, as lesbian comedian Kate Clinton writes, "Male penile humor—the ultimate in stand-up comedy—is based on the hierarchical power structure of the put-down" (quoted in Pershing 224). Studies of the socialization of women (McGhee) show that in mixed company, women look to men for permission to laugh. Girls learn early in their lives that their role is not to "make" jokes themselves, to be comic artists, but to smile or laugh at the jokes men make, often at women's expense. Joke making is considered unfeminine.

REFERENCES

Andelin, Helen. *Fascinating Womanhood*. Santa Barbara, CA: Pacific Press, 1965.

Arnold, Roseanne. Interview with Kathleen Rowe. 20 June 1991.

——. See also Barr, Roseanne.

Bakhtin, Mikhail. *The Dialogic Imagination*. Edited by Michael Holquist. Translated by Caryl Emerson and Michael Holquist. Austin: University of Texas Press, 1981.

——. *Rabelais and His World*. Translated by Helene Iswolsky. Bloomington: Indiana University Press, 1984.

Barr, Roseanne. *Roseanne: My Life as a Woman*. New York: Harper and Row, 1989.

——. "What Am I, a Zoo?" *New York Times* (national ed.), 31 July 1989, I15.

——. See also Arnold, Roseanne.

Bourdieu, Pierre, *Distinction: A Social Critique of the Judgement of Taste*. Translated by Richard Nice. Cambridge, MA: Harvard University Press, 1984.

Cixous, Hélène. "The Laugh of the Medusa." Translated by Keith Cohen and Paula Cohen. In *New French Feminisms*, edited by Elaine Marks and Isabelle de Courtivron, pp. 245–64. Brighton: Harvester, 1980. Originally published as "Le Rire de la Méduse." *L'Am* 61 (1975): 39–54.

Davis, Natalie Zemon. *Society and Culture in Early Modern France*. Stanford, CA: Stanford University Press, 1975.

de Lauretis, Teresa. *Alice Doesn't: Feminism, Semiotics, Cinema*. Bloomington: Indiana University Press, 1984.

Doane, Mary Ann. *The Desire to Desire: The Woman's Film of the 1940s*. Bloomington: Indiana University Press, 1987.

Douglas, Mary. *Implicit Meanings: Essays in Anthropology*. Boston: Routledge & Kegan Paul, 1975.

Dyer, Richard. *Heavenly Bodies: Film Stars and Society*. New York: St. Martin's Press, 1986.

Fiske, John. *Understanding Popular Culture*. Boston: Unwin Hyman, 1989.

Foucault, Michel. *Discipline and Punish: The Birth of the Prison*. Translated by Alan Sheridan. New York: Random House, 1979.

Freud, Sigmund. *Jokes and Their Relation to the Unconscious*. Translated by James Strachey. New York: W. W. Norton, 1960.

Georgatos, Dennis. "When the Fat Lady Sings. . . . Some San Diego Padre Fans Are Glad When It's Over." *Eugene* [Oregon] *Register-Guard*, 27 July 1991, A1, A4.

Goffman, Erving. *Frame Analysis: An Essay on the Organization of Experience*. Boston: Northeastern University Press, 1986.

Henley, Nancy M. *Body Politics: Power, Sex and Non-Verbal Communication*. Englewood Cliffs, NJ: Prentice-Hall, 1977.

Hirschberg, Lynn. "Don't Hate Me Because I'm Beautiful." *Vanity Fair* (December 1990): 182–86+.

Jerome, Jim. "Roseanne Unchained." *People* (9 October 1989): 84–98.

Juno, Andrea, and V. Vale, eds. *Angry Women*. San Francisco: Re/search Publications, 1991.

Lesage, Julia. "*Celine and Julie Go Boating*: Subversive Fantasy." *Jump Cut* 24–25 (19): 37–43.

———. "Women's Rage." In *Marxism and the Interpretation of Culture*, edited by Carol Nelson and Lawrence Grossberg. Chicago: University of Illinois Press, 1988, 419–28.

Maynard, Joyce. "Domestic Affairs." *The Oregonian*, 11 February 1989: C1.

McGhee, Paul E. "The Role of Laughter and Humor in Growing Up Female." In *Becoming Female: Perspectives on Development*, edited by Clair B. Kopp. New York: Plenum Press, 1979, 183–206.

Mellencamp, Patricia. *High Anxiety: Catastrophe, Scandal, Age & Comedy*. Bloomington: Indiana University Press, 1992.

———. *Indiscretion: Avant-Garde Film, Video, & Feminism*. Bloomington: Indiana University Press, 1990.

———. "Jokes and Their Relation to the Marx Brothers." In *Cinema and Language*, edited by Stephen Heath and Patricia Mellencamp. Frederick, MD: University Publications of America, 1983, 63–78.

———. "Situation Comedy, Feminism and Freud: Discourses of Gracie and Lucy." In *Studies in Entertainment*, edited by Tania Modleski. Bloomington: Indiana University Press, 1986, 80–95.

Millman, Marcia. *Such a Pretty Face: Being Fat in America*. New York: W. W. Norton, 1980.

Mitchell, Elvis. "Smug Trafficking." *The Village Voice*, 25 April 1989, 47–48.

O'Connor, John J. "By Any Name, Roseanne is Roseanne is Roseanne." *New York Times*, 18 August 1991, B1, B27.

Orbach, Susie. *Fat is a Feminist Issue II*. London: Arrow, 1982.

———. *Hunger Strike: The Anorectic's Struggle as a Metaphor for Our Age*. New York: W. W. Norton, 1986.

"People." *Eugene* [Oregon] *Register-Guard*, 1 July 1991, A2.

Pershing, Linda. "There's a Joker in the Menstrual Hut: A Performance Analysis of Comedian Kate Clinton." In *Women's Comic Visions*, edited by June Sochen. Detroit, MI: Wayne State University Press, 1991, 193–236.

Rhoden, William C. "Sports of the Times: In the Land of the Free." *New York Times* (national ed.), 31 July 1990, B9.

Rich, B. Ruby. "In the Name of Feminist Film Criticism." In *Movies and Methods II*, edited by Bill Nichols. Berkeley: University of California Press, 1985, 340–58. (Originally published in *Jump Cut* 19 [1978].)

Rowe, Kathleen K. "Romanticism, Sexuality, and the Canon." *Journal of Film and Video* 42 (1990): 49–65.

Russo, Mary. "Female Grotesques: Carnival and Theory." In *Feminist Studies, Critical Studies*, edited by Teresa de Lauretis. Bloomington: University of Indiana Press, 1986, 213–29.

Suleiman, Susan Rubin. *Subversive Intent: Gender, Politics, and the Avante-Garde*. Cambridge, MA: Harvard University Press, 1990.

Turner, Victor. "Frame, Flow and Reflection: Ritual and Drama as Public Liminality." In *Performance in Postmodern Culture*, edited by Michel Benamou and Charles Caramello. Milwaukee: University of Wisconsin–Milwaukee Press, 1977, 33–55.

Waters, Harry F., with Steven Waldman, Daniel Glick, and Kim Fararo. "Rhymes With Rich: A Queen on Trial." *Newsweek*, 21 August 1989, 46–51.

Will, George. "Cities Gleam with Gunfire." Syndicated column in *Eugene* [Oregon] *Register Guard*, 1 August 1990, A15.

EDITOR'S NOTE

Kathleen Rowe paints a picture of Roseanne Arnold as a strong woman. Karen Heller, columnist for the *Philadelphia Inquirer*, asks "Why are so many people afraid of strong women . . . ?" Heller was referencing the latest book to trash Hillary Clinton because the book implies that because Hillary is intelligent, ambitious, and likes to hang out with other intelligent, ambitious women she must be a lesbian.[1]

Heller asks, too, why Jane Fonda has endured decades of vitriolic media coverage for her anti-Vietnam activities and for having "opinions contrary to those very men who ogled her as Barbarella [a film Fonda starred in when she was very young]."[2] Why does the public (including Vietnam veterans) persist in castigating Fonda, while anger with the likes of Lyndon Johnson, Richard Nixon, or Henry Kissinger—those whose failed policies bear responsibility for the conflict in which almost 60,000 American soldiers died—dissipated with the end of the 1970s?[3]

It isn't just liberal-leaning women who are publicly pummeled. The attacks on strong women know no partisanship. Consider that conservative political commentator Ann Coulter, no shrinking violet, gets more scathing comments—much of it focusing on her appearance or delivery style—than do her male counterparts: Bill O'Reilly or Rush Limbaugh.[4]

Perhaps a strong woman has to be a clone of Condoleeza Rice in order to avoid the personal flak. Clearly, Rice could not have risen to secretary of state without a savvy mixture of intelligence, ambition, and political astuteness, so why no fodder in her direction? Heller refers to Rice as a "policy nun" who seems "to have forsaken a private life in . . . her absolute devotion to country and leader."[5] Maureen Dowd, writing in *The New York Times* observes this about Rice: "[S]he does not need to play the victim to make people feel better about her power because she was never seen as a termagant. . . . She always seemed subservient to President Bush . . . a willing handmaiden"[6] Does a woman have to be strong, smart, ambitious, *and* subservient to "make it"? Are some folks more fearful of women than of bombs as Heller suggests?[7]

NOTES

1. Karen Heller, "Attacks on Strong Women Arise from Fear," *The Cincinnati Enquirer*, 14 July 2005, C13.

2. Ibid.

3. Ibid.

4. Ibid.

5. Ibid.

6. Maureen Dowd, "Taming of the Shrews," *The New York Times*, 6 March 2005, p. 13.

7. Heller.

29

Black Man with a Nose Job

How We Defend Ethnic Beauty in America

Lawrence Otis Graham

For my entire life, until yesterday, I had displayed my father's same nostrils, bridge, and profile. Tomorrow I wouldn't. Tomorrow I'd took like someone else. Staring up at the back of my father's head, I realized that the success of my operation would be measured in direct proportion to how much differently my nose looked from his. It was a shameful contrast to make with someone I loved so much, but when looking at my sketches, it was an accurate one nevertheless.

Having torn more than fifty or sixty shots of sharp-nosed, square-jawed, model-handsome, near-black-looking or practically black-looking men from some of the best store catalogs and hippest fashion magazines in New York, I felt I'd done more than my share of the legwork. I was now ready to pay whatever it cost and submit myself to whatever tests, X-rays, computer imaging, or painful surgical procedures were necessary.

"Mr. Graham," the sensitive doctor began as he reached for my chin and turned my head to either side. "There is only a certain amount of alteration that is possible, or even desirable, for any one nose."

He looked down at the brownest of all my men. "Mr. Graham, that nose would never be in harmony with your lips and chin. They would never work together."

"My lips and chin?" I asked. I had to pause a few seconds and consider the significance of his remark. "Then change them," I finally howled. "Change them, I'll pay whatever it costs. Change them. Just change them!"

Sometimes, it takes very little to send some of us down the slippery slope toward black self-hatred. . . . Eventually I entered a hospital on Manhattan's Upper West Side to undergo that common surgical procedure we all call rhinoplasty. While this procedure is performed nearly a hundred thousand times each year, I had the feeling that my case was different. It was shortly after

277

being wheeled into the large, brightly lit recovery room that I became certain that I had just launched an assault on my identity and my people. But now it was too late to go back. I was, forever, a black man who had gotten a nose job.

Although I'd grown up in a white neighborhood where male and female adolescents got their noses narrowed, chins and cheeks enhanced, and skin chemically peeled as a coming-of-age ritual during junior high and high school vacations, I had never seriously considered plastic surgery for myself. Yes, I wanted to be thought of as more handsome, but no one in my family had ever undergone cosmetic surgery. For these white friends and classmates who had undergone surgical changes, their explanations focused simply on cosmetics. They wanted to look "better." Not surprisingly, no one ever seemed to impute any other motive or to psychoanalyze the real meaning of "better." For me and my family, physical appearance and its alteration were issues of ethnicity and heritage. Black people had wide nostrils, thick lips, protruding mouths, and dark skin—and any desire to change those features was, by definition, a negative commentary on our people and our own racial identity.

For the most part, I never even compared my looks to those of the white kids or white adults around me. During my adolescence, I did, however, draw contrasts with the young blacks in my own world of black professionals and their families who socialized in our black social clubs and vacation places. There were numerous occasions as a child, and later as an adult, when hosting summer cookouts in Sag Harbor, Long Island, or Oak Bluffs, Martha's Vineyard; attending our Jack & Jill family gatherings; or partying at the Sisters of Ethos all-black dances at Wellesley College, when I'd run into dozens of well-to-do, light-skinned, straight-haired, thin-featured black childhood friends. After returning to the security of my own bedroom mirror, I would critique my features against those other blacks in my life who had "sharper," "nicer," "finer" (all words that meant more attractive and less Negroid) physical characteristics.

My color ambivalence manifested itself in many different ways during my adolescence. I'm reminded of the Hasbro G.I. Joe army and astronaut set I used to play with. One afternoon I put brown shoe polish all over my 1967 G.I. Joe astronaut's entire pink body and later melted his tiny nose away with the heat from my Mattel "Creepy Crawlers" cooking iron. I don't know if I can ascribe my actions to black pride or a desire to punish Joe, but I never took him out in public after that.

Finally, after considering hundreds of magazine and catalog layouts and doctor's sketches, after writing a check for $4,000 to a black surgeon, and after having the operation, I still sometimes feel like I've upset the standard of blackness that I'd been raised to accept and appreciate. When I told a black former classmate about my operation, she accused me of trying to pass out of the black race. It was hardly the sympathetic response I had expected from an intelligent woman who had been one of my first friends in law school. In fact, her contempt was so great and questions so numerous, I really began to wonder if she was right about my motives.

Did I have this operation in order to become less black—to have features that were more white? Had I bought into the white definition of beauty—the sharp nose, the thin lips, the straight hair? Did I think that my less Negroid-looking black friends were more attractive than me?

My wife says my decision is personal and that I shouldn't feel compelled to defend it or explain it to anyone else. I'd like to think she is right. Maybe she's right about not needing to justify my acts to white coworkers or white neighbors. But what about my black relatives, my black friends, my black coworkers, my black secretary? Don't I owe them an explanation? Don't I have to let them know I wasn't saying that I wanted to be white when I pared down my wider, rounder Negroid nose?

Of course, I could take the easy way out and tell onlookers that one's racial identity is not embodied in one's nose. It certainly should be obvious in my case. After all, my dark brown skin and curly black hair are still intact. A different nose won't make me look white. But that's really not the point I need to address, is it?

For two years prior to my operation, I agonized over the ethnic ramifications of cosmetic surgery. According to the American Society of Plastic and Reconstructive Surgeons, 640,000 cosmetic procedures were performed in the United States in 1994. Since the preponderance of those patients were white, I am fairly certain that many of them felt no obligation to justify their surgery to members of their ethnic group.

All of this leads me to conclude that my defenses are a wasted effort. While my white friends have guiltlessly selected profiles and implants with their surgeons, I was making a futile attempt to validate my ethnic loyalty by developing arguments to prove that a nose job would not make me less black.

I shouldn't have to defend my surgery any more than those 640,000 patients who pass under the scalpel each year—or for any person who makes any type of cosmetic changes in his or her natural appearance. After all, an Italian person rarely feels guilty for turning his brown hair blond. Few Jewish people apologize for having their noses shaved down. Not many Asian people have to justify putting waves into their straight hair. Many people, in fact, are surprised to learn that in both Japan and Korea, as well as in the United States, it is quite common for male and female Japanese and Korean people of all ages to have their eyes done (for less than $1,500, a surgeon creates a more westernized eye by creating a fold in the eyelid that makes it appear rounder) and their noses enhanced (for about $2,500, a surgeon creates a more Caucasian nose by raising the bridge and tip by inserting a plastic or cartilage implant). With so many other groups undergoing the same procedures, it is ludicrous for black cosmetic surgery to be taken as a form of heresy against the race.

I am discovering that many whites as well as blacks perceive a black person's cosmetic surgery as a sign of self-hatred or the desire to be less black—an accusation often aimed at singer Michael Jackson, who in spite of his claims about rare skin diseases and naturally changing bone structure, pinched his nose, bleached his skin, tattooed his eyes, enhanced his chin, and straightened his hair. Even black talk-show host Montel Williams felt compelled to explain his nose job to his viewers. His claim: He'd done it because he'd had difficulty breathing. Whether we believe his explanation or not, none of us have the right to challenge such a decision.

An equally presumptuous attitude prevailed a while back with regard to colored contact lenses. No one objected when white actors, models, and consumers wore the cosmetic lenses, but when black talk-show host Oprah Winfrey wore them on TV, there was an immediate avalanche of attacks from both whites and blacks who could not understand why a black person would wear green contacts. White people seemed to be threatened by the notion that black people could actually avail themselves of cosmetic advances and appropriate beauty characteristics that white people had theretofore defined as exclusively their own. Black audiences, too, looked at rich, powerful, and famous Oprah and feared that she was somehow about to "buy" herself out of the black race and leave us bereft of one more black heroine and role model. In the end, when the host held her ground on her black identity, black and white viewers wised up and realized that the ever dedicated and down-to-earth Winfrey wasn't going anywhere she didn't belong. Colored contacts weren't going to change her.

Black plastic-surgery patients or lens-wearers should not have to address the isse of ethnicity any more than white people who go to a tanning salon or get a collagen shot to thicken their lips—as so many white actors, models, and fashion-conscious citizens are doing today. Black people who get their hair straightened each month should be able to do so just because they want to sample a noncurly style.

Because I've narrowed my nose, some of my black friends say I have sought to deny my ethnicity, and oddly enough, some of my white friends—even those who have had nose jobs themselves—say I'm representative of the young black professional who wants to assimilate into the white culture. Perhaps it is true that the media images and the white kids who surrounded me as a child sometimes caused me to judge my own attractiveness on some other group's standard of beauty, but I dismiss the suggestion that any black who seeks to alter his natural physical characteristics has turned on his people and attempted to "pass" as a member of some other race.

Once the bandages were finally taken off (a few years ago), friends discovered that I am no less black than I was before the operation. I still had the same black friendships, still supported the same black causes, and still maintained the same black consciousness. As my father, the stoic black southerner, was able to do, my friends continue to allow me to take pleasure in my new appearance. For them to view this as anything more than a cosmetic procedure would be to suggest that the culture, feelings, and history of black people are awfully superficial.

30

Hitting Bottom

Homelessness, Poverty, and Masculinity

Timothy Nonn

In the dangerous and impoverished Tenderloin district of San Francisco live the men we consider failures. Urban deterioration and public neglect has created a "dumping-ground for unwanted individuals" (North of Market Planning Coalition 1992: 4). Low rents attract immigrants, welfare recipients, and low-income workers. The population is about 40 percent white, one-third Asian American, and one-tenth black and Latino, respectively. There are severe problems with homelessness, AIDS, violence, substance abuse, and unemployment.

In studies of men, poor men are rarely the object of research.[1] This article examines the coping mechanisms poor men develop to resolve their status as "failed men."

Using a snowball sample, twenty men were interviewed during a six-month period, including twelve whites, six blacks, and two Latinos; twelve were heterosexual, and eight were homosexual. Their ages ranged from twenty-nine to fifty-four; the majority had a high-school education. Many had been homeless, but most were now living in single-room occupancy hotels. Twelve were single, seven were divorced or separated, and one was married. Several had left children behind. Their interactions with women at the time of the interview were very limited. Few had contact with families or had long-term relationships with women.

FAILED MEN

A discussion of failure among men must begin with hegemonic masculinity. R. W. Connell writes:

> Hegemonic masculinity is constructed in relation to women and to subordinated masculinities. These other masculinities need not be as clearly defined—indeed,

281

achieving hegemony may consist precisely in preventing alternatives gaining cultural definition and recognition as alternatives, confining them to ghettos, to privacy, to unconsciousness. (1987: 186)

Connell defines hegemonic masculinity as men's dominance over women. While individuals may change, men's collective power remains embedded in social and cultural institutions. Michael Messner interprets change among white, middle-class men as a matter of personal lifestyle rather than a restructuring of power and politics (1993).

Hegemonic masculinity is the standard by which Tenderloin men are judged. The media refers to them as "thugs and bums."[2] Forced to live amidst poverty, drugs, and violence, they are stripped of or denied access to a masculine identity constructed around the role of "the good provider" (see Bernard 1995). As white heterosexuals, they are stripped of an identity associated with privilege and power. As gays or men of color, they are denied access to a masculine ideal associated with heterosexual whites.

Tenderloin men sometimes refer to each other as "invisible." George describes a homeless man's life:

I call it the "invisible-man syndrome." That's what you become. Most homeless, but not all, self-medicate. It's that thing that you can turn to when you're suffering. You feel disenfranchised from society. You feel less than human. It tells him— in between those periods where he has some lucidity, in between drug or alcohol bouts—that he is a total failure.[3]

Tenderloin men face a lonely end. Before death—having been stripped of everything that qualifies a man for full participation in society—there is the shame of surviving as less than a man. Tenderloin men belong to a "shamed group" (Goffman 1963: 23).

Tenderloin men feel trapped in the role of failure.[4] Many hang out day and night on streets "drinking and drugging," talking and begging. The ubiquitous drug trade, routine violence, and crushing poverty combine to form an atmosphere of continual dread and hopelessness within the neighborhood. The men wait in line for hours at churches to receive food, clothing, and lodging. Because it is equally painful to be seen as to be invisible, they are silent and avoid eye contact. They spend a lot of time waiting. The wait transforms them. They dress in a similar ragged way. They walk and talk in a dispirited way. Their faces have the same blank stare or menacing hardness. Some turn into predators in search of victims.[5] Others turn into victims in search of sympathy. George says:

Your antenna is up for people feeling sorry for you. Part of you becomes a predator. The predator part wants to take advantage. So you can get resources to continue your downward spiral to total destruction. The other part of you feels ashamed because you have violated every man-code that you were ever taught. So you're stuck on stupid. You get to a point where you don't know what to do.

The invisibility of Tenderloin men is part of "a pervasive two-role social process" in which failure and success are interrelated (Goffman 1963: 138). They are stigmatized merely by living in an area decimated by poverty, sex, and drug markets, and high levels of crime and violence. William Julius Wilson calls them "the permanent underclass" (Wilson 1987: 7).

Trapped at the bottom of society and stigmatized as failures, Tenderloin men have limited opportunities to claim an identity that fosters self-worth. Charles, a fifty-year-old white gay man, says: "Once you go in there, it's like being an untouchable. You're stigmatized as being this type of sleazy person that does dope and needles, and the whole thing."[7]

Virtually all heterosexual white men interpret their present hardship as the result of personal failure. Richard Sennett and Jonathan Cobb argue that the "code of respect" in American society demands that "a man should feel responsibility for his own social position—even if, in a class society, he believes men in general are deprived of the freedom to control their lives." Failure is defined according to cultural values in which a man is expected to have the desire and opportunity to work (Sennett and Cobb 1972: 36).

Heterosexual white men experience a high level of cultural shock in moving to the Tenderloin.[8] A walk to the store is a challenge to their self-esteem. They confront black and Latino men who threaten their sense of racial superiority and gays who threaten their sexual identity.

Heterosexual whites are confused and angry because others appear to violate social norms. Most retreat into isolation. A few imitate other men's behavior. Brad, a twenty-nine-year-old single, heterosexual white man, admires the "sense of family" among Latinos.[9] Many appreciate the nurturing qualities of gays. But other men criticize whites for not knowing themselves. Miguel, a divorced fifty-year-old heterosexual Latino man, says:

> The white man tries too hard to make friends. . . . If you're going to come in here and start trying to be black, they see that already. You're not! But here's a guy and he's trying to talk like us and be cool. It's a front.[10]

Wanting to belong, and forced to confront their prejudices, heterosexual whites discover that genuineness is vital. But it is difficult for them to adapt. Quinn, a fifty-four-year-old gay white man, says whites are aloof because: "White is right. White isn't going to be criticized. White isn't going to be stopped by police."[11]

HETEROSEXUAL BLACK AND LATINO MEN: COOL POSE

Heterosexual blacks and Latinos dominate street life and display what Richard Majors and Janet Mancini Billson (1992) call "cool pose." Cool pose is a counter-masculinity that structures identity around the value of respect. Power is interpreted as group solidarity in a racist society. Blacks and Latinos establish social position by displaying aggressiveness or showing deference (Almaguer 1991: 80). . . . [Miguel] says:

> One of the techniques you use—and this is a prison technique—is getting big. You work out hard. You carry yourself in an intimidating manner. Your body language says, "I'll kill you if you even think about approaching my space."

The mask of hypermasculinity establishes a man's position in his group.[12] Miguel describes putting on his mask:

> Whenever I walk, I look mean. I make my face look like I got an attitude. Like I just got ripped off. I don't look at the person. I look through them. I'm cutting him. And this guy's thinking, "Hmmm. Let me move out of the way." You could get busted. "Oh, you ain't that tough." But out there you gotta act that way.

"Getting busted" means that someone is able to see through a man's mask. Whites have difficulty distinguishing between actual threats and posturing by blacks and Latinos, and often feel threatened. But Jack, a heterosexual black man, explains that cool pose conceals a sense of failure among men of color living in a white-dominated society:

> The one thing I hear from white guys is, "You guys act like you're so proud." They don't realize why we're doing it. It's to survive amongst our own peers. We feel just as bad as he does. The white guy resents that; "How in the hell can he act like that and I'm white? I come from the superior race and I can't act like that. I feel dead." They come from two different worlds.[13]

Ned interprets cool pose in relation to a definition of masculinity that excludes black men in American society:

> A black man has to be tough out there on the street. The reason they have to be that way is that they don't have any other outlet for their manhood. They can't show their manhood by being a success economically because society simply will not give them a chance, I mean a black man is even lucky to have a full-time—or even a part-time-job. So he has to show his manhood by acting physically tough. Because mentally tough won't get him anywhere.

Cool pose is depicted as "a creative strategy devised by African-American males to counter the negative forces in their lives" (Majors and Billson 1992: 105). Yet, the counter-masculinity of cool pose does not allow heterosexual black and Latino men to escape from failure by structuring identity around the value of respect. While the coping mechanism of cool pose weakens the stigma of failure, it undermines identity by organizing social relations around poles of dominance and submission. What heterosexual men of color view as respect, others view as hostility. By adopting an identity based upon fear and violence, men of color in the Tenderloin in part contribute to their own alienation from other groups and society at large. They are further marginalized in an environment where different social groups demand to live in equality with one another.

HOMOSEXUAL BLACK AND WHITE MEN: PERFECT COPY

Gays in the Tenderloin blur gender and sexual boundaries by constructing identity around performance of a series of roles. "Perfect copy" of hypermasculinity redefines and subverts masculinity (Butler 1990: 31). Klaus, a thirty-four-year-old gay white man, interprets his experience with heterosexual men in the Tenderloin:

> They feel like their manhood or sexuality has been threatened because I'm more butch than they are. I am more of a man than a straight man can be around here. They're threatened. Not only to me but to themselves.[14]

Gays structure identity around the value of acceptance. Power is interpreted as inclusion of persons who challenge gender and sexual categories. Because identity is in flux, and gender and sexual identity are rendered uncertain, "homosexuality undermines masculinity" (Edwards 1990: 114). Larry, a thirty-three-year-old gay white man, says heterosexuals are simultaneously confused and intrigued by gays:

> I think [they] are very jealous of gay men because we're so open and free with our feelings. We speak what we have to say. We don't hide our feelings. We cry at sad movies. Heterosexual men think that men don't cry.

Another gay man believes single heterosexuals are in a predicament because they normally rely on women to provide them with gender identity. Charles says:

> Most men depend on women to define that role for them. So a man is what a woman defines him to be. So if you don't have a woman in your life to define you as a man, then you have to depend on all these macho apparatuses. Then you have to prove to other men that you are a man.

VERSATILE MASCULINITY

Versatile masculinity is a unique masculine identity that emerges from everyday encounters of Tenderloin men as they collectively resolve the contradictions of counter-masculinities. Versatile masculinity allows men to identify with a transcendent set of values without destroying their group identity or value systems. This new set of values—while not distinctively masculine—is the basis of a masculine identity that binds Tenderloin men together in genuine community.

Versatile masculinity is not a fixed identity but a growing capacity for relating to difference.[15] As a fluid construction that sorts and combines practices, values, and attitudes in a strategic movement, it enables men to flourish in a diverse and dynamic environment. Most important, it is not a way of being but a way of becoming in relationships.

H. Richard Niebuhr writes that ultimate value is not identifiable with a particular mode of being but "is present whenever being confronts being, wherever there is becoming in the midst of plural, interdependent, and interacting existences. It is not a function of being as such but of being in relation to being" (1970: 106–7).

As marginalized persons, Tenderloin men are innovative survivors who manifest "creative strategies for survival that then open up new possibilities for everyone" (Duberman 1993: 24).

NOTES

1. There are several noteworthy works that examine the lives of poor and working-class men. See Eugene V. Debs, *Walls and Bars* (Chicago: Charles H. Kerr and Company, 1973); George Orwell, *Down and Out in Paris and London* (New York: Berkeley Medallion, 1959); James Agee and Walker Evans, *Let Us Now Praise Famous Men* (Boston: Houghton Mifflin Company, 1939); Studs Terkel, *Hard Times: An Oral History of the Great Depression* (New York: Washington Square Press, 1970); Elliot Liebow, *Tally's Corner* (Boston: Little, Brown and Company, 1967); William Julius Wilson, *The Truly Disadvantaged: The Inner City, the Underclass, and Public Policy* (Chicago: University of Chicago Press, 1987); Lillian Rubin, *Worlds of Pain: Life in the Working-Class Family* (New York: Basic Books, 1976); Richard Sennet and Jonathan Cobb, *The Hidden Injuries of Class* (New York: Vintage Books, 1972).

2. Local newspapers regularly describe Tenderloin residents in derogatory terms. See "Cheap wine ban sought in Tenderloin," *San Francisco Chronicle*, 5 April 1989; "Group wants Tenderloin as family neighborhood," *San Francisco Chronicle*, 21 July 1992; "Community policing," *San Francisco Chronicle*, 20 November 1992.

3. Interview with George on 30 April 1993. All names are fictitious.

4. Interview with Peter, a recently married, forty-eight-year-old heterosexual white man, on 27 July 1993.

5. The term "predator" is commonly used to refer to persons (often drug users) who prey on the more vulnerable sectors of the Tenderloin neighborhood, such as the elderly, children, and tourists.

6. Interview with Samuel on 26 August 1993.

7. Interview with Charles on 28 July 1993.

8. Bruno Bettelheim (1960: 120) reports that of Jews sent to Nazi concentration camps, middle-class German men experienced the greatest level of initial shock and were the least adaptable prisoners.

9. Interview with Brad on 28 July 1993.

10. Interview with Miguel on 23 July 1993.

11. Interview with Quinn on 29 July 1993.

12. Pleck (1987: 31) defines "hypermasculinity" as exaggerated, extreme masculine behavior.

13. Interview with Jack on 23 April 1993.

14. Interview with Klaus on 13 March 1993.

15. Versatility is defined as "the faculty or character of turning or being able to turn readily to a new subject or occupation," or "many-sidedness." In *The Compact Edition of the Oxford English Dictionary* 1971, Oxford University Press.

REFERENCES

Almaguer, Tomas. 1991. "Chicano Men: A Cartography of Homosexual Identity and Behavior." *Differences* 3 (2).

Bernard, Jessie. 1995. "The Good-Provider Role." In Michael S. Kimmel and Michael A. Messner, eds., *Men's Lives*. New York: Macmillan.

Bettelheim, Bruno. 1960. *The Informed Heart: Autonomy in a Mass Age*. New York: The Free Press.

Butler, Judith. 1990. *Gender Trouble: Feminism and the Subversion of Identity*. New York: Routledge & Kegan Paul.

Connell, R. W. 1987. *Gender and Power*. Palo Alto, CA: Stanford University Press.

Duberman, Martin. 1993. "A Matter of Difference." *Nation*, 5 July.

Edwards, Tim. 1990. "Beyond Sex and Gender: Masculinity, Homosexuality and Social Theory." In Jeff Hearn and David Morgan, eds., *Men, Masculinities, and Social Theory*. London: Unwin Hyman.

Gershick, Thomas J., and Adam S. Miller. 1994. "Coming to Terms: Masculinity and Physical Disability. " In M. Kimmel and M. Messner, eds., *Men's Lives*, 3rd ed. Boston: Allyn and Bacon.

Goffman, Erving. 1963. *Stigma: Notes on the Management of Spoiled Identity*. New York: Touchstone.

hooks, bell. 1990. "Feminism: A Transformational Politic." In Deborah L. Rhode, ed., *Theoretical Perspectives on Sexual Difference*. New Haven: Yale University Press.

Koenig, Karen. 1993. "Transgenders Unite to Fight for Justice and Recognition." *Tenderloin Times*, August.

Maitland, Zane. 1993. "Tenderloin Hotel Has a Rooftop Garden." *San Francisco Chronicle*, 23 July.

Majors, Richard, and Janet Mancini Billson. 1992. *Cool Pose: The Dilemmas of Black Manhood in America*. New York: Lexington Books.

Messner, Michael A. 1993. "'Changing Men' and Feminist Politics in the United States." *Theory and Society*, August/September.

Niebuhr, H. Richard. 1970. *Radical Monotheism and Western Culture*. New York: Harper Torchbooks.

North of Market Planning Coalition (NOPC). 1992. *Final Report: Tenderloin 2000 Survey and Plan*. San Francisco: NOPC.

Pleck, Joseph H. 1987. "The Theory of Male Sex-Role Identity: Its Rise and Fall, 1936 to the Present." In Harry Brod, ed., *The Making of Masculinities: The New Men's Studies*. New York: Routledge & Kegan Paul.

Sennett, Richard, and Jonathan Cobb. 1972. *The Hidden Injuries of Class*. New York: Vintage Books.

Tong, Ben. 1971. "The Ghetto of the Mind: Notes on the Historical Psychology of Chinese America." *Amerasia Journal*, 1 (3) November.

Wilson, William Julius. 1987. *The Truly Disadvantaged: The Inner City, the Underclass, and Public Policy*. Chicago: University of Chicago Press.

31

Older Men as Invisible Men in Contemporary Society

Edward H. Thompson

There are already nearly 13 million men age sixty-five and older. The minority among elders, and especially the minority among the very elderly, 13 million older men is still a sizable population. It is greater than the number of all undergraduates enrolled full-time in four-year colleges in 1992 (U.S. Department of Education, 1992), greater than the number of children living in single-parent families in 1980 (Thompson and Gongla, 1983; U.S. Bureau of the Census, 1992), nearly twenty times greater than the number of physicians practicing medicine in 1993 (Roback, Randolph, and Seidman, 1993) and ten times the number of people incarcerated in correctional institutions in 1990 (U.S. Bureau of the Census, 1993). Mainstream journals and opinion makers have made us much more familiar with these folks, however smaller their population size.

REASONS FOR VISIBILITY

Older men have remained invisible for reasons besides their smaller number. For one, gerontologists have not encouraged the distinction between the concepts of "sex" and "gender." *Gender* is often accepted as if synonymous with sex, serving fundamentally as a categorical construct for grouping the aged. Consequently, the literature introduces us to older biological males by virtue of describing a sex difference in aging. However, what surely distinguishes older biological males, as a group, is their cohort-specific, gendered social lives. As much as research has treated all men as if they were genderless (Kimmel and Messner, 1992), fewer researchers have paid attention to the masculinities that older men encounter or those they disclose.

Another reason for older invisibility is that aging and ageism do not affect men and women equally. From a political economy perspective, it is true that older men have a more comfortable, privileged life compared to older women of the same generation. Consequently, when gender is taken into consideration, elderly women have a much higher profile in gerontological research because the view of aging places women in double jeopardy relative to older men (Sontag, 1972) and because sociological research on "advantaged" groups has traditionally attracted less sustained attention than studies of the disadvantaged (Berger, 1963). In this frame, the pernicious concept of "the aged" is synonymous with a disadvantaged group and thus more synonymous with the providence of older women than older men.

Similarly, the organizations, interest groups, industries, professional societies, and political bodies that make up "the aging enterprise" and serve the elderly in one capacity or another (Estes, 1979, 1993) also furnish ideas about aging and images of elder men. These are elaborately constructed images pressed into public consciousness, and the images that aging enterprise has fabricated are just that—"constructed." To illustrate, for two decades the medical-industrial complex has profited handsomely by medicalizing elderly men's lives more than meeting elderly men's and women's needs. Cardiac catheterization laboratories, fourth- and fifth-generation ventricular pacemakers, arthroscopic surgical technology, and cardiac bypass surgery all derive great profit by "servicing" the elderly male population's health problems and yield much greater profit for the enterprise than would programming to raise the standard of living and health status of all elders. The socially constructed image of elderly men— former breadwinners and national leaders—as "old" and by definition in poor health fuels compassion and, of course, greater profit than the image of most elderly men (and women) as having poor access to health and medical care services. This "compassionate ageism" (Binstock, 1983) is also sexist. It has medicalized elderly men's lives and their perceived well-being, perhaps more than elderly women's. One unintended consequence, for example, of the "compassion" and profiteering is that older men's nonmedical needs become frivolous. The everyday needs of healthy, elder males, as well as elder men's need for services other than medical interventions become remote concerns when compared to the life-and-death emphasis.

In much the same way that gerontologists have inadvertently homogenized elders to make older men genderless, scholars working in the field of gender studies have not paid much notice to men in late life. Older men's masculinities are couched as an invisible part of the dynamics of hegemony or, more simply, ignored. Whether in the research traditions or contemporary theorizing "about men," age is truncated. To illustrate, Daniel Levinson and his colleagues (1978) discuss men's late adulthood in their landmark *The Seasons of a Man's Life* in just seven pages (33–39) and characterize this age in "discontinuous" imagery, as if aging is a negation of masculinity: "A primary developments task of late adulthood is to find a new balance of involvement with society and with the self. A man in this era is experiencing more fully the process of dying and he should have the possibility of choosing more freely his mode of living" (p. 36). The widely praised second edition of *Men's Lives* that Kimmel and Messner organized for gender scholars has not one article among the fifty-six that directly probes older men's masculinities. At this point in the development of gender studies, the masculinities of older men have been subordinated to the concerted effort to understand middle-aged and younger men's lives, who are, as Ortega y Gasset (1958) suggests, "the dominant" group. Even when a life course perspective is recognized (e.g., Connell, 1992; Segal, 1990), the theoretical discourse on masculinities has concentrated on social practices of young to middle-aged men and, by default, marginalized the masculinities of elderly men. But, meta-theoretically, has the marginalization of older men in the scholarship on gender contributed to the preservation of conventional discourses on masculinity? Failing to acknowledge elderly men as a distinct group of men may have homogenized not only adulthood but also theory on masculinity.

One can see, with retrospective clarity, how these four initiatives have helped conceal older men's lives. My interest is to examine them collectively in greater detail. The task is to advance the conceptual and theoretical underpinnings for a more long-term discussion of older men as men and as elders.

SOCIALLY CONSTRUCTED IMAGES OF AGED MEN

Visualize the image. The men hold themselves upright and proud—these middle-aged men whose time of life is shifting from "early' to "middle adulthood" and who are perhaps at a peak in their impact on the world outside the home. They are the "dominant" generation, as Ortega y Gasset defined the ages forty-five to sixty. They make their ideas and aims the pivotal ones in every sector of society: business, politics, religion, science. But soon they . . . embrace the season of life that Levinson and his colleagues (1978) call "late adulthood" and, for some, "late, late adulthood."

In the popular culture, men in late adulthood no longer occupy center stage. Their generation is no longer the dominant one: it has been displaced by a younger, "Pepsi" generation. Men in late life are classed as "senior" or "old." They become "socially opaque" (Green, 1993). They are presumed to have completed the major part—perhaps all—of their life work. The older man sees himself living in his shadow or death's (Levinson et al., 1978). Writing in *Esquire*, novelist Thomas Morgan (1987, p. 162) describes a memory of his father's sixtieth birthday: "I do not remember his exact words, only that he seemed to be telling me he was conceding at sixty, perhaps welcoming at sixty that he need not be a part of the future. . . . As it happened, he worked ten more years, but lived, I'm sorry to say, as though it were all an anti-climax."

Television commercials, newspaper presentations, and magazine advertisements fully impart this image, too. No longer in control, wealthy, and urbane, old men are pictured as living neither in the city nor the suburbs but in a small rural town, or in the country, near the pasture. Homes are smaller, plainer, without gadgets and machines. Bodies are not virile, rather pleasantly plump. Checked flannel shirts have replaced the dark blue suit. As part of the "grandparent" generation, advertisements will show that the older man's soft lap cat has replaced the younger man's spirited black Labrador retriever. Lemonade is now the drink of choice (Bucholz and Bynum, 1982; Ferraro, 1992; Kaiser and Chandler, 1988; Powell and Williamson, 1985; Swayne and Greco, 1987).

It seems that the constructed images of older men leave these elders with two strikes against them. First is the prejudice within public (and professional attitudes regarding "old age" in general (Butler, 1969; Walsh and Connor, 1979). Elders—in particular, elderly men—are thought to suffer significant losses: Their occupational role, their livelihood and community of coworkers, their health and independence, and their masculinity are commonly thought to be displaced by aging. The traditional discourses of masculinity and aging separate adult men into two categories: old and all others. The older man is depicted in a yo-yo fashion, with both positive and negative content (Hummert, 1990). He is portrayed as interactively and psychologically involved in more expressive and caring roles within the family. He is also, by default, contrasted with an image of the younger, justly preoccupied father and husband whose primary concern is with productive labor and power management. The underlying core values in the discourse extol youth, independence, and economic productiveness and an aversion to aging and anything feminine (Cole, 1986; Fischer, 1978; Green, 1993, p. 53).

The second strike is older men's perceived genderlessness. Ask people to complete the sentence "An old man . . ." and then listen to ungendered ageism and his feminization. Older men are depicted as sedentary, resting on a park bench, passing time, asexual. Images of older men basically portray diminished masculinity (Kite, Deaux, and Miele, 1991; Puglisi and Jackson, 1980–81; Silverman, 1977). To many people, aging is a negation of masculinity, and thus older men become effeminate over time. Given this cultural assumption, older men are used, however, unwittingly. The degendered imagery of the older man keeps afloat a masculinity and a discourse that sustains younger men. The conventional discourse describes gender in simply binary terms, wherein aging diminishes men's masculinity and, by default, heightens their femininity over time. Framed this way, images of age-specific and cohort-specific masculinities never rise to a threshold of public consciousness. Rather, the social construction maintains that "old men" are not men at all.

DISCOURSES IN THE ACADEMY

As the size of elderly female population increased between 1930 and 1990, the importance of gender and aging commanded greater and greater attention among academics and policy makers (Haug, Ford, and Sheafor, 1985; Herzog, Holden, and Seltzer, 1989; Lesnoff-Caravaglia, 1984; Markson, 1985; Matthews, 1979; also see Coyle, 1989). Ironically, as older women's lives and their profound needs gained visibility, older men became more marginal and invisible. In fact, being elderly appears in some quarters to have become synonymous with being female. For example, in *Gender and Later Life*, Arber and Ginn (1991, p. vii) state, "Later life is primarily an experience of women." Their first chapter is powerfully titled "The Feminization of Later Life," because the demographics of aging show that elderly women outnumber elderly men in later life, especially as age advances. The message that is constructed, however, goes beyond making note of a sex differential in longevity. Rather, as women's experience in later life is brought to the foreground, older men's fade from attention. Arber and Ginn's otherwise very fine work makes "later life" as synonymous with women as "gender" has become.

Homogenizing elders—as reflected by mid-century discourses on "the aged" or the new academic discourse on feminization—was once said to be akin to "tabloid thinking" (Binstock 1983, p. 140). Homogenizing sets the stage to ignore individual differences and to think about "the elderly" only at the collective level as disadvantaged individuals beset by common problems.

Although the core value behind older men's invisibility is academics' "compassionate ageism" for older women (Binstock, 1983), knowledge production in gerontological studies currently makes for blind spots and a lack of understanding of older men. As Cook (1992, p. 293) warned in an editorial in *The Gerontologist*, "If we want the public and the media to abandon the oversimplifying generalities they often make about age and aging and look instead at the diversity among older people, then gerontologists must stop asking attitudinal and factual questions about 'the elderly' as if they were a homogeneous group."

In the sociologies of the life course and family life, elderly men were not often studied as men but served as the referent point to better understand late-life families, elderly women's lives as caregivers, or younger men. Small wonder than that as much as "wives' sociology" once informed us about family life (Safilios-Rochschild, 1969), there is a "midlife sociology" that has tried to theorize about older men's lives. To illustrate, role-theory sociologies directed attention to the rolelessness of late life. Retired men were envisioned outside the "normal" work spaces, and, by default, they were invading their wives' space—the family home (see literature review in Brubaker, 1990). This early sociological discourse of older men defined their lives as a period of indispensable disengagement from former, power-brokering statuses. Older men were portrayed as obsolete currency in a culture that cherishes power; in disengagement terms, the spotlight was on younger men's welfare. Later discourses of activity theory similarly emphasized the core values of a masculinity that best fits younger employed men's lives. Neither did these theoretical accounts reveal much about men as a group or about subgroup and individual differences.

Logically, the diversity among young and middle-aged men does not disappear at age sixty-five, seventy, or seventy-five, when older men leave the workplace to take up more assiduously their semipublic and private social worlds. Their gendered lives continue. Their relationships with institutions, women, other men, and children press on. Dannefer (1988) pointed out that as men grow older, their accumulated decisions about life course options produce increased differentiation among them. But in what ways? Do age and gender interact to affect older men's thoughts, feelings, behaviors, and relations with others? Do the two interact to affect men as a group?

REFERENCES

Arber, S., and J. Ginn. (1991). *Gender and later life: A sociological analysis of resources and constraints*. London: Sage.

Berger, P. L. (1963). *Invitation to sociology: A humanistic perspective*. New York: Anchor.

Binstock, R. H. (1983). The aged as scapegoat. *The Gerontologist* 23, 136–43.

Brubaker, T. H. (1990). Families in later life: A burgeoning research area. *Journal of Marriage and the Family* 52, 959–81.

Buchholz, M., and J. E. Bynum. (1982). Newspaper presentations of America's aged: A content analysis of image and role. *The Gerontologist* 22, 83–88.

Butler, R. N. (1969). Age-ism: Another form of bigotry. *The Gerontologist* 9, 243–246.

Cole, T. R. (1986). "Putting off the old": Middle class morality, antebellum Protestantism, and the origins of ageism. Pp. 49–65 in D. van Tassel and P. N. Stearns (eds.), *Old age in a bureaucratic society*. Westport, CT: Greenwood Press.

Connell, R. W. (1992). A very straight gay: Masculinity, homosexual experience, and the dynamics of gender. *American Sociological Review* 57, 735–51.

Cook, F. L. (1992). Ageism: Rhetoric and reality. *The Gerontologist* 32, 292–93.

Coyle, J. M. (1989). *Women and aging: A selected, annotated bibliography*. Westport, CT: Greenwood Press.

Dannefer, D. (1988). Differential gerontology and the stratified life course: Conceptual and methodological issues. Pp. 3–36 in G. L. Maddox and M. P. Lawton (eds.), *Annual review of gerontology and geriatrics*, vol. 8. New York: Springer.

Estes, C. L. (1979). *The aging enterprise*. San Francisco: Jossey-Bass.

———. (1993). The aging enterprise revisited. *The Gerontologist* 33, 292–98.

Feraro, K. F. (1992). Cohort changes in images of older adults, 1974–1981. *The Gerontologist* 32, 296–304.

Fischer, D. H. (1978). *Growing old in America* (expanded ed.) New York: Oxford University Press.

Green, B. S. (1993). *Gerontology and the construction of older age: A study in discourse analysis*. Hawthorne, NY: Aldine.

Haug, M., A. B. Ford, and M. Sheafor. (1985). *The physical and mental health of aged women*. New York: Springer.

Herzog, A. R., K. C. Holden, and M. M. Seltzer. (1989). *Health and economic status of older women*. Amityville, NY: Baywood.

Hummert, M. L. (1990). Multiple stereotypes of elderly and young, adults: A comparison of structure and evaluation. *Psychology and Aging* 5, 182–93.

Kaiser, S. B., and J. L. Chandler. (1988). Audience responses to appearance codes: Old-age imagery in the media. *The Gerontologist* 28, 692–99.

Kalish, R. A. (1979). The new ageism and the failure models: A polemic. *The Gerontologist* 19, 398–402.

Kimmel, M. S., and M. A. Messner. (1992). *Men's lives* (2nd ed.). New York: Macmillan.

Kite, M. E., K. Deaux, and M. Miele. (1991). Stereotypes of young and old: Does age outweigh gender? *Psychology and Aging* 6, 19–27.

Lesnoff-Caravaglia, G. (1984). *The world of the older woman: Conflicts and resolutions.* New York: Human Sciences Press.

Levinson, D. J., C. N. Darrow, E. B. Klein, M. H. Levinson, and B. McKee. (1978). *The seasons of a man's life*. New York: Knopf.

Markson, E. W. (1985). *Older women: Issues and Prospects*. Lexington, NIA: Lexington Books.

Matthews, S. H. (1979). *The social world of old women: Management of self-identity*. Beverly Hills, CA: Sage.

Morgan, T. B. (1987, May). What does a sixty-year-old man see when he looks in the mirror? *Esquire*, 161–67.

Ortega y Gasset, J. (1958). *Man and crisis*. New York: Norton.

Powell, L., and J. B. Williamson. (1985). The mass media and the aged. *Social Policy* 16, 38–49.

Puglisi, J. T., and D. W. Jackson. (1980–1981). Sex role identity and self esteem in adulthood. *International Journal of Aging and Human Development* 12, 129–38.

Roback, G., L. Randolph, and B. Seidman. (1993). *Physician characteristics and distribution in the United States*. Chicago: American Medical Association.

Safilios-Rochschild, C. (1969). Family sociology or wives' family sociology? A cross-cultural examination of decision-making. *Journal of Marriage and the Family* 31, 290–301.

Segal, L. (1990). *Slow motion: Changing masculinities, changing men*. New Brunswick, NJ: Rutgers University Press.

Silverman, M. (1977). The old man as woman: Detecting stereotypes of aged men with scale. *Perceptual and Motor Skills* 44, 336–38.

Sontag, S. (1972). The double standard of aging. *Saturday Review* 55, no. 39, 29–38.

Swayne, L. E., and A. J. Greco. (1987). The portrayal of older Americans in television commercials. *Journal of Advertising* 16, no. 1, 47–54.

Thompson, E. H., and P. A. Gongla. (1983). Single parent families: In the mainstream of American society. In E. D. Macklin and R. H. Rubin (eds.), *Contemporary families and alternative lifestyles: Handbook on research and theory*. Beverly Hills, CA: Sage.

U.S. Bureau of the Census. (1992). *Marital status and living arrangements*. Washington, D.C.: Government Printing Office.

U.S. Bureau of the Census. (1993). *Statistical abstracts of the United States, 1992*. Washington, D.C.: Government Printing Office.

U.S. Department of Education. (1992). *Projections of education statistics to 2003*. Washington, D.C.: Government Printing Office.

Walsh, R. P., and C. L. Connor. (1979). Old men and young women: How objectively are their skills assessed? *Journal of Gerontology* 34, 561–68.

X

PATRIARCHY AND ITS CONSEQUENCES

32

The Subjection of Women

John Stuart Mill

The object of this Essay is to explain as clearly as I am able, the grounds of an opinion which I have held from the very earliest period when I had formed any opinions at all on social or political matters, and which, instead of being weakened or modified, has been constantly growing stronger by the progress of reflection and the experience of life: That the principle which regulates the existing social relations between the two sexes—the legal subordination of one sex to the other—is wrong in itself, and now one of the chief hindrances to human improvement; and that it ought to be replaced by a principle of perfect equality, admitting no power or privilege on the one side, nor disability on the other.

The difficulty is that which exists in all cases in which there is a mass of feeling to be contended against. So long as an opinion is strongly rooted in the feelings, it gains rather than loses in stability by having a preponderating weight of argument against it. For if it were accepted as a result of argument, the refutation of the argument might shake the solidity of the conviction; but when it rests solely on feeling, the worse it flares in argumentative contest, the more persuaded its adherents are that their feeling must have some deeper ground, which the arguments do not reach; and while the feeling remains, it is always throwing up fresh entrenchments of argument to repair any breach made in the old. And there are so many causes tending to make the feelings connected with this subject the most intense, and most deeply rooted of all those which gather round and protect old institutions and customs, that we need not wonder to find them as yet less undermined and loosened than any of the rest by the progress of the great modern spiritual and social transition; nor suppose that the barbarisms to which men cling longest must be less barbarisms than those which they earlier shake off.

In the first place, the opinion in favour of the present system, which entirely subordinates the weaker sex to the stronger, rests upon theory only; for there never has been trial made of any other; so that experience, in the sense in which it is vulgarly opposed to theory, cannot be pretended to have pronounced any verdict. And in the second place, the adoption of this system of inequality never was the result of deliberation, or forethought, or any social ideas, or any notion whatever of what conducted to the benefit of humanity or the good order of society. It arose simply from the fact that from the very earliest twilight of human society, every woman (owing to the value attached to her by men, combined with her inferiority in muscular strength) was found in a state of bondage to some man. Laws and systems of polity always begin in by recognising the relations they find already existing between individuals. They convert what was a mere physical fact into a legal right, give it the sanction of society, and principally aim at the substitution of public and organized means of asserting and protecting these rights, instead of the irregular and lawless conflict of physical strength. Those who had already been compelled to obedience became in this manner legally bound to it. Slavery, from being a mere affair of force between the master and the slave, became regularized and a matter of compact among the masters, who, binding themselves to one another for common protection, guaranteed by their collective strength the private possessions of each, including his slaves. In early times, the great majority of the male sex were slaves, as well as the whole of the female. And many ages elapsed, some of them ages of high cultivation, before any thinker was bold enough to question the rightfulness and the absolute social necessity, either of the one slavery or of the other.

Less than forty years ago, Englishmen might still by law hold human beings in bondage as saleable property; within the present century they might kidnap them and carry them off, and work them literally to death. This absolutely extreme case of the law of force, condemned by those who can tolerate almost every other form of arbitrary power, and which, of all others, presents features the most revolting to the feelings of all who look at it from an impartial position, was the law of civilized and Christian England within the memory of persons now living: and in one half of Anglo-Saxon America three or four years ago, not only did slavery exist, but the slave trade, and the breeding of slaves expressly for it, was a general practice between slave states. . . . The yoke is naturally and necessarily humiliating to all persons, except the one who is on the throne, together with, at most, the one who expects to succeed to it. How different are these cases from that of the power of men over women! I am not now prejudging the question of its justificableness. I am showing how vastly more permanent it could not but be, even if not justifiable, than these other dominations which have nevertheless lasted down to our own time. Whatever gratification of pride there is in the possession of power, and whatever personal interest in its exercise, is in this case not confined to a limited class, but common to the whole male sex. Instead of being, to most of its supporters, a thing desirable chiefly in the abstract, or, like the political ends usually contended for by factions, of little private importance to any but the leaders; it comes home to the person and hearth of every male head of a family, and of every one who looks forward to being so. The clodhopper exercises, or is to exercise, his share of the power equally with the highest nobleman. And the case is that in which the desire of power is the strongest: for every one who desires power, desires it most over those who are nearest to him, with whom his life is passed, with whom he has most concerns in common, and in whom any independence of his authority is oftenest likely to interfere with his individual preferences. If, in the other cases specified, powers manifestly grounded only on force, and having so much less to support them, are so slowly and with so much difficulty got rid of, much more must it be so with this, even if it rests on no better foundation than those. We must consider, too, that the possessors of the power have facilities in this case, greater than in any other, to prevent any uprising against it. Every one of the subjects lives under the very eye, and almost, it may be said, in the hands, of one of the masters—in closer intimacy with him than with any of her fellow-subjects; with no means of combining against him, no power of even locally overmastering him, and, on the other hand, with the strongest motives for seeking his favour and avoiding to give him offence. In struggles for political emancipation, everybody knows how often its champions are bought off by bribes, or daunted by terrors. In. the case of women, each individual of the subject-class is in a chronic state of bribery and intimidation combined. In setting up the standard of resistance, a large number of the leaders, and still more of the followers, must make an almost complete sacrifice of the pleasures or the alleviations of their own individual lot. If ever any system of privilege and enforced subjection had its yoke tightly riveted on the necks of those who are kept down by it, this has.

All causes, social and natural, combine to make it unlikely that women should be collectively rebellious to the power of men. They are so far in a position different from all other subject classes, that their masters require something more from them than actual service. Men do not want solely the obedience of women, they want their sentiments. All men, except the most brutish, desire to have, in the woman most nearly connected with them, not a forced slave but a willing one; not a slave merely, but a favorite. They have therefore put everything in practice to enslave their minds. The masters of all other slaves rely, for maintaining obedience, on fear; either fear of themselves, or religious fears. The masters of women wanted more than simple obedience, and they turned the whole force of education to effect their purpose. All women are brought up from the very earliest years in the belief that their ideal of character is the very opposite to that of men; not self-will, and government by self-control, but submission, and yielding to the control of others. All the moralities tell them that it is the duty of women, and all the current sentimentalities that it is their nature, to live for others; to make complete abnegation of themselves, and to have no life but in their affections. And by their affections are meant the only ones they are allowed to have—those to the men with whom they are connected, or to the children who constitute an additional and indefeasible tie between them and a man. When we put together three things—first, the natural attraction between opposite sexes; secondly, the wife's entire dependence on the husband, every privilege or pleasure she has being either his gift, or depending entirely on his will; and lastly, that the principal object of human pursuit, consideration, and all objects of social ambition, can in general be sought or obtained by her only through him, it would be a miracle if the object of being attractive to men had not become the polar star of feminine education and formation of character. And, this great means of influence over the minds of women having been acquired, an instinct of selfishness made men avail themselves of it to the utmost as a means of holding women in subjections, by representing to them meekness, submissiveness, and resignation of all individual will into the hands of a man, as an essential part of sexual attractiveness. Can it be doubted that any of the other yokes which mankind have succeeded in breaking, would have subsisted till now if the same means had existed, and had been as sedulously used, to bow down their minds to it? If it had been made the object of the life of every young plebeian to find personal favour in the eyes of some patrician, of every young serf with some seigneur; if domestication with him, and a share of his personal affections, had been held out as the prize which they all should look out for, the most gifted and aspiring being able to reckon on the most desirable prizes; and if, when this prize had been obtained, they had been shut out by a wall of brass from all interests not centering in him, all feelings and desires but those which he shared or inculcated; would not serfs and seigneurs, plebeians and patricians, have been as broadly distinguished at this day as men and women are? and would not all but a thinker here and there, have believed the distinction to be a fundamental and unalterable fact in human nature?

But I may go farther, and maintain that the course of history, and the tendencies of progressive human society, afford not only no presumption in favour of this system of inequality of rights, but a strong one against it; and that, so far as the whole course of human improvement up to this time, the whole stream of modern tendencies, warrants any inference on the subject, it is, that this relic of the past is discordant with the future, and must necessarily disappear.

For, what is the peculiar character of the modern world—the difference which chiefly distinguishes modern institutions, modern social ideas, modern life itself, from those of times long past? It is, that human beings are no longer born to their place in life, and chained down by an inexorable bond to the place they are born to, but are free to employ their faculties, and such favourable chances as offer, to achieve the lot which may appear to them most desirable. Human society of old was constituted on a very different principle. All were born to a fixed social position, and were mostly kept in it by law, or interdicted from any means by which they could emerge from it. As some men are born white and others black, so some were born slaves and others freemen and citizens; some were born patricians, others plebeians; some were born feudal nobles, others commoners and *roturiers*. A slave or serf could never make himself free, nor, except by the will of his master, become so. . . . In modern Europe, and most in those parts of it that have participated most largely in all other modern improvements, diametrically opposite doctrines now prevail. Law and government do not undertake to prescribe by whom any social or industrial operation shall or shall not be conducted, or what modes of conducting them shall be lawful. These things are left to the unfettered choice of individuals. . . . The modern conviction, the fruit of a thousand years of experience is, that things in which the individual is the person directly interested, never go right but as they are left to his own discretion; and that any regulation of them by authority, except to protect the rights of others, is sure to be mischievous. This conclusion, slowly arrived at, and not adopted until almost every possible application of the contrary theory had been made with disastrous result, now (in the industrial department) prevails universally in the most advanced countries, almost universally in all that have pretensions to any sort of advancement. It is not that all processes are supposed to be equally good, or all persons to be equally qualified for everything; but that freedom of individual choice is now known to be the only thing which procures the adoption of the best processes, and throws each operation into the hands of those who are best qualified for it. Nobody thinks it necessary to make a law that only a strong-armed man shall be a blacksmith. Freedom and competition suffice to make blacksmiths strong-armed men, because the weak-armed can earn more by engaging in occupations for which they are more fit. In consonance with this doctrine, it is felt to be an overstepping of the proper bounds of authority to fix beforehand, on some general presumption, that certain persons are not fit to do certain things. It is now thoroughly known and admitted that if some such presumptions exist, no such presumption is infallible. Even if it be well grounded in a majority of cases, which it is very likely not to be, there will be a minority of exceptional cases in which it does not hold; and in those it is both an injustice to the individuals, and a detriment to society, to place barriers in the way of their using their faculties for their own benefit and for that of others.

If this general principle of social and economical science is not true; if individuals, with such help as they can derive from the opinion of those who know them, are not better judges than the law and the government, of their own capacities and vocation; the world cannot too soon abandon this principle, and return to the old system of regulations and disabilities. But if the principle is true, we ought to act as if we believed it, and not to ordain that to be born a girl instead of a boy, any more than to be born black instead of white, or a commoner instead of a nobleman, shall decide the person's position through all life—shall interdict people from all the more elevated social positions, and from all, except a few, respectable occupations. Even were we to admit the utmost that is ever pretended as to the superior fitness of men for all the functions now reserved to them, the same argument applies which forbids a legal qualification for members of Parliament. If only once in a dozen years the conditions of eligibility exclude a fit person, there is a real loss, while the exclusion of thousands of unfit persons is no gain for if the constitution of the electoral body disposes them to choose unfit persons, there are always plenty of such persons to choose from. In all things of any difficulty and importance, those who can do them well are fewer than the need even with the most unrestricted latitude of choice; and any limitation of the field of selection deprives society of some chances of being served by the competent, without ever saving it from the incompetent.

At present, in the more improved countries, the disabilities of women are the only case, save one, in which laws and institutions take persons at their birth, and ordain that they shall never in all their lives be allowed to compete for certain things.

The social subordination of women thus stands out an isolated fact in modern social institutions; a solitary breach of what has become their fundamental law; a single relic of an old world of thought and practice exploded in everything else, but retained in the one thing of most universal interest. . . .

If it be said that the doctrine of the equality of the sexes rests only on theory, it must be remembered that the contrary doctrine also has only theory to rest upon. All that is proved in its favour by direct experience, is that mankind have been able to exist under it, and to attain the degree of improvement and prosperity which we now see; but whether that prosperity has been attained sooner, or is now greater, than it would have been under the other system, experience does not say. On the other hand, experience does say, that every step in improvement has been so invariably accompanied by a step made in raising the social position of women, that historians and philosophers have been led to adopt their elevation or debasement as on the whole the surest test and most correct measure of the civilization of a people or an age. Through all the progressive period of human history, the condition of women has been approaching nearer to equality with men. This does not of itself prove that the assimilation must go on to complete equality; but it assuredly affords some presumption that such is the case.

Neither does it avail anything to say that the nature of the two sexes adapts them to their present functions and position, and renders these appropriate to them. Standing on the ground of common sense and the constitution of the human mind, I deny that any one knows, or can know, the nature of the two sexes, as long as they have only been seen in their present relation to one another. If men had ever been found in society without women, or women without men, or if there had been a society of men and women in which the women were not under the control of the men, something might have been positively known about the mental and moral differences which may be inherent in the nature of each. What is now called the nature of women is an eminently artificial thing—the result of forced repression in some directions, unnatural stimulation in others. It may be asserted without scruple, that no other class of dependents have had their character so entirely distorted from its natural proportions by their relation with their masters; for, if conquered and slave faces have been, in some respects, more forcibly repressed, whatever in them has not been crushed down by an iron heel has generally been let alone, and if left with any liberty of development, it has developed itself according to its own laws; but in the case of women, a hot-house and stove cultivation has always been carried on of some of the capabilities of their nature, for the benefit and pleasure of their masters.

Hence, in regard to that most difficult question, what are the natural differences between the two sexes—a subject on which it is impossible in the present state of society to obtain complete and correct knowledge—while almost everybody dogmatizes upon it, almost all neglect and make light of the only means by which any partial insight can be obtained into it. This is, an analytic study of the most important department of psychology, the laws of the influence of circumstances on character. For, however great and apparently ineradicable the moral and intellectual differences between men and women might be, the evidence of their being natural differences could only be negative. Those only could be inferred to be natural which could not possibly be artificial—the residuum, after deducting every characteristic of either sex which can admit of being explained from education or external circumstances. The profoundest knowledge of the laws of the formation of character is indispensable to entitle any one to affirm even that there is any difference, much more what the difference is, between the two sexes considered as moral and rational beings; and since no one, as yet, has that knowledge, (for there is hardly any subject which, in proportion to its importance, has been so little studied), no one is thus far entitled to any positive opinion on the subject. Conjectures are all that can at present be made; conjectures more or less probable, according as more or less authorized by such knowledge as we yet have of the laws of psychology, as applied to the formation of character.

Even the preliminary knowledge, what the differences between the sexes now are, apart from all questions as to how they are made what they are, is still in the crudest and most incomplete state.

One thing we may be certain of—that what is contrary to women's nature to do, they never will be made to do by simply giving their nature free play. The anxiety of mankind to interfere in behalf of nature, for fear lest nature should not succeed in effecting its purpose, is an altogether unnecessary solicitude. What women by nature cannot do, it is quite superfluous to forbid them from doing. What they can do, but not so well as the men who are their competitors, competition suffices to exclude them from; since nobody asks for protective duties and bounties in favour of women; it is only asked that the present bounties and protective duties in favour of men should be recalled. If women have a greater natural inclination for some things than for others, there is no need of laws or social inculcation to make the majority of them do the former in preference to the latter. Whatever women's services are most wanted for, the free play of competition will hold out the strongest inducements to them to undertake. And, as the words imply, they are most wanted for the things for which they are most fit; by the apportionment of which to them, the collective faculties of the two sexes can be applied on the whole with the greatest sum of valuable result.

The general opinion of men is supposed to be, that the natural vocation of a woman is that of a wife and mother. I say, is supposed to be, because, judging from acts—from the whole of the present constitution of society—one might infer that their opinion was the direct contrary. They might be supposed to think that the alleged natural vocation of women was of all things the most repugnant to their nature; insomuch that if they are free to do anything else— if any other means of living, or occupation of their time and faculties, is open, which has any chance of appearing desirable to them—there will not be enough of them who will be willing to accept the condition said to be natural to them. If this is the real opinion of men in general, it would be well that it should be spoken out. I should like to hear somebody openly enunciating the doctrine (it is already implied in much that is written on the subject)—"It is necessary to society that women should marry and produce children. They will not do so unless they are compelled. Therefore it is necessary to compel them." The merits of the case would then be clearly defined. It would be exactly that of the slaveholders of South Carolina and Louisiana. "It is necessary that cotton and sugar should be grown. White men cannot produce them. Negroes will not, for any wages which we choose to give. *Ergo* they must be compelled." An illustration still closer to the point is that of impressment. Sailors must absolutely be had to defend the country. It often happens that they will not voluntarily enlist. Therefore there must be the power of forcing them. How often has this logic been used! and, but for one flaw in it, without doubt it would have been successful up to this day. But it is open to the retort—First pay the saviors the honest value of their labour. When you have made it as well worth their while to serve you, as to work for other employers, you will have no more difficulty than others have in obtaining their services. To this there is no logical answer except "I will not": and as people are now not only ashamed, but are not desirous, to rob the labourer of his hire, impressment is no longer advocated. Those who attempt to force women into marriage by closing all other doors against them, lay themselves open to a similar retort. If they mean what they say, their opinion must evidently be, that men do not render the married condition so desirable to women, as to induce them to accept it for its own recommendations. It is not a sign of one's thinking the boon one offers very attractive, when one allows only Hobson's choice, "that or none." And here, I believe, is the clue to the feelings of those men, who have a real antipathy to the equal freedom of women. I believe they are afraid, not lest women should be unwilling to marry, for I do not think that any one in reality has that apprehension; but lest they should insist that marriage should be on equal conditions; lest all women of spirit and capacity should prefer doing almost anything else, not in their own eyes degrading, rather than marry, when marrying is giving themselves a master, and a master too of all their earthly possessions. And truly, if this consequence were necessarily incident to marriage, I think, that the apprehension would be very well founded. I agree in thinking it probable that few women, capable of anything else, would, unless under an irresistible *entrainement*, rendering them for the time insensible to anything but itself, choose such a lot, when any other means were open to them of filling a conventionally honourable place in life: and if men are determined that the law of marriage shall be a law of despotism, they are quite right, in point of mere policy, in leaving to women only Hobson's choice. But, in that case, all that has been done in the modern world to relax the chain on the minds of women, has been a mistake. They never should have been allowed to receive a literary education. Women who read, much more women who write, are, in the existing constitution of things, a contradiction and a disturbing element: and it was wrong to bring women up with any acquirements but those of an odalisque, or of a domestic servant.

33

Real Rape

Susan Estrich

MY STORY

In May 1974 a man held an ice pick to my throat and said: "Push over, shut up, or I'll kill you." I did what he said but I couldn't stop crying. When he was finished, I jumped out of my car as he drove away.

I ended up in the back seat of a Boston police car. I told the two officers I had been raped by a man who came up to the car door as I was getting out in my own parking lot (and trying to balance two bags of groceries and kick the car door open). He took the car, too.

They asked me if he was a crow. That was their first question. A crow, I learned that day, meant to them someone who is black. That was the year the public schools in Boston were integrated.

They asked me if I knew him. That was their second question. They believed me when I said I didn't. Because, as one of them put it, how would a nice (white) girl like me know a crow?

Now they were really listening. They asked me if he took any money. He did; but though I remember virtually every detail of that day and night, I can't remember how much. It doesn't matter. I remember their answer. He did take money; that made it an armed robbery. Much better than a rape. They got right on the radio with that.

We went to the police station first, not the hospital, so I could repeat my story (and then what did he do?) to four more policemen. When we got there, I borrowed a dime to call my father. They all liked that.

In many respects I am a very lucky rape victim, if there can be such a thing. Not because the police never found him: looking for him myself every time I crossed the street, as I did for a long time, may be even harder than confronting him in a courtroom. No, I am lucky because everyone agrees that I was "really" raped. When I tell my story, no one doubts my status as a victim. No one suggests that I was "asking for it." No one wonders, at least out loud, if it was really my fault. No one seems to identify with the rapist. His being black, I fear, probably makes my account more believable to some people, as it certainly did with the police. But the most important thing is that he was a stranger; that he approached me not only armed but uninvited; that he was after my money and car, which I surely don't give away lightly, as well as my body. As one person put it: "You really didn't do anything wrong."

But most rape cases are not as clear-cut as mine, and many that are, like mine, are simply never solved. It is always easier to find the man when the woman knows who he is. But those are the men who are least likely to be arrested, prosecuted, and convicted. Those are the cases least likely to be considered real rapes.

Many women continue to believe that men can force you to have sex against your will and that it isn't rape so long as they know you and don't beat you nearly to death in the process. Many men continue to act as if they have that right. In a very real sense, they do. That is not what the law says: the law says that it is rape to force a woman "not your wife" to engage in intercourse against her will and without her consent. But while husbands have always enjoyed the greatest protection, the protection of being excluded from rape prohibitions, even friends and neighbors have been assured sexual access.[1] What the law seems to say and what it has been in practice are two different things. In fact, the law's abhorrence of the rapist in stranger cases like mine has been matched only by its distrust of the victim who claims to have been raped by a friend or neighbor or acquaintance.

The latter cases are cases of "simple rape." The distinction between the aggravated and simple case is one commonly drawn in assault. It was applied in rape in the mid-1960s by Professors Harry Kalven and Hans Zeisel of the University of Chicago in their landmark study of American juries.[2] Kalven and Zeisel defined an aggravated rape as one with extrinsic violence (guns, knives, or beatings) or multiple assailants or no prior relationship between the victim and the defendant. A simple rape was a case in which none of these aggravating circumstances was present: a case of a single defendant who knew his victim and neither beat her nor threatened her with a weapon. They found that juries were four times as willing to convict in the aggravated rape as in the simple one. And where there was "contributory behavior" on the part of the woman—where she was hitchhiking, or dating the man, or met him at a party—juries were willing to go to extremes in their leniency toward the defendant, even in cases where judges considered the evidence sufficient to support a conviction for rape.[3]

Juries have never been alone in refusing to blame the man who commits a "simple rape." Three centuries ago the English Lord Chief Justice Matthew Hale warned that rape is a charge "easily to be made and hard to be proved, and harder to be defended by the party accused, tho' never so innocent."[4] If it is so difficult for the man to establish his innocence, far better to demand that a woman victim prove hers; under Hale's approach, the one who so "easily" charges rape must first prove her own lack of guilt. That has been the approach of the law. The usual procedural guarantees and the constitutional mandate that the government prove the man's guilt beyond a reasonable doubt have not been considered enough to protect the man accused of rape. The crime has been defined so as to require proof of actual physical resistance by the victim, as well as substantial force by the man. Evidentiary rules have been defined to require corroboration of the victim's account, to penalize women who do not complain promptly, and to ensure the relevance of a woman's prior history of unchastity.

Although rape has emerged as a topic of increasing research and attention among feminists in recent years,[5] the law of rape, particularly of the "simple rape," has not been widely addressed.[6] When I began law school, a few months after being raped, I expected to learn the law of rape. I was wrong. Rape was, I discovered, just not taught. When I started teaching, seven years later, rape was still not being taught. When I asked why, I was told that it was not interesting enough, or complicated enough, or important enough to merit a chapter in a criminal law casebook or a week in a course. That attitude is, at long last, beginning to change. But it is not enough that lawyers begin to understand the law of rape as a serious subject. Rape law is too important, too much a part of all of our lives, and too much in need of change, to leave to the lawyers.

IS IT RAPE?

The man telling me this particular story is an assistant district attorney in a large Western city. He is in his thirties, an Ivy League law school graduate, a liberal, married to a feminist. He's about as good as you're going to get making decisions like this. This is a case he did not prosecute. He considers it rape—but only "technically." This is why.

The victim came to his office for the meeting dressed in a pair of tight blue jeans. Very tight. With a see-through blouse on top. Very revealing. That's how she was dressed. It was, he tells me, really something. Something else. Did it matter? Are you kidding!

The man involved was her ex-boyfriend. And lover; well, ex-lover. They ran into each other on the street. He asked her to come up and see *Splash* on his new VCR. She did. It was not the Disney version—of *Splash*, that is. It was porno. They sat in the living room watching. Like they used to. He said, let's go in the bedroom where we'll be more comfortable. He moved the VCR. They watched from the bed. Like they used to. He began rubbing her foot. Like he used to. Then he kissed her. She said no, she didn't want this, and got up to leave. He pulled her back on the bed and forced himself on her. He did not beat her. She had no bruises. Afterward, she ran out. The first thing she did was flag a police car. That, the prosecutor tells was the first smart thing she did.

The prosecutor pointed out to her that she was not hurt, that she had no bruises, that she did not fight. She pointed out to the prosecutor that her ex-boyfriend was a weightlifter. He told her it would be nearly impossible to get a conviction. She could accept that, she said: even if he didn't get convicted, at least he should be forced to go through the time and the expense of defending himself. That clinched it, said the D.A. She was just trying to use the system to harass her ex-boyfriend. He had no criminal record. He was not a "bad guy." No charges were filed.

Someone walked over and asked what we were talking about. About rape, I replied; no, actually about cases that aren't really rape. The D.A. looked puzzled. That was rape, he said. Technically. She was forced to have sex without consent. It just wasn't a case you prosecute.

This case is unusual in only one respect: that the victim perceived herself to be a victim of rape and was determined to prosecute. That is unusual. The prosecutor's response was not.

A recent study in Seattle found that prior relationship was the single most important factor in the underreporting of rape to the police.[7] The author found a positive correlation between prior relationship and other variables (force, injury, circumstances of initial contact) that were positively related to reporting. But notably, even those women raped by friends or relatives, who did experience serious threats, force, or injury, were less likely to report. Similarly, a study of women who contacted rape crisis centers in Massachusetts found that nearly two-thirds knew their attackers and that the majority did not report the victimization to the police. The closer the relationship between victim and assailant, the less likely the woman was to report.[8]

What is most noteworthy about such studies is not the reporting rates themselves but the extent to which, contrary to the picture of the official victimization surveys, nonstranger rapes outnumber assaults by strangers. In both Massachusetts and Seattle the overwhelming majority of women who contacted rape centers had been attacked by men they knew. And women who contact these centers are women who at least perceive themselves to be "rape" victims, even if they do not report to the police. It appears that most women forced to have sex by men they know see themselves as victims, but not as legitimate crime victims.

The reasons given in these studies for the failure to perceive forced sex as rape, let alone report it as such, reflect an understanding of rape that discounts the "simple" case. Some women do not report because they were "successful" in resisting the actual penetration, suggesting an erroneous belief that sexual aggression is a crime only when it ends in unwanted intercourse.[9] Other women do not report because they ended up "giving in" to the sexual pressure without a "fight," suggesting the equation of nonconsent with utmost or at least reasonable physical resistance.[10] And many young women believe that sexual pressure, including physical pressure, is simply not aberrant or illegal behavior if it takes place in a dating situation. Thus, one study concluded that most adolescent victims do not perceive their experience of victimization "as legitimate," meaning that "they do not involve strangers or substantial violence." Forced sex does not amount to criminal victimization "unless it occurs outside a dating situation or becomes especially violent."[11]

These findings confirm what has been learned through tests posing hypothetical examples. In those tests almost no one has any difficulty recognizing the classic, traditional rape—the stranger with a gun at the throat of his victim forcing intercourse on pain of death—as just that. When the man in the hypothetical (even a stranger) "warns her to do as he said" and "tells her to lie down" instead of "slashing her with a knife" or at least "waving" it in the air and shoving her down, those who are certain that a "rape" has taken place decrease significantly in every category except women who generally held "pro-feminist" views.[12] In situations where a woman is presented as being forced to engage in sex after a "date with a respected bachelor" or with a man she met in a bar who takes her to a deserted road (instead of home) or with her boss after working late, less than half of the female respondents in another survey were certain that a "rape" had occurred. Notably, where the two were strangers and the circumstances of the initial contact were involuntary—accosted in parking lots, house break-ins—nearly everyone was certain that a rape had occurred.[13] Adolescents in one survey were least likely to label clearly forced sex as "rape" when the couple was presented as dating. According to that study, "teenagers of both genders are quite accepting of forced sex between acquaintances and often don't view it as rape."[14]

Why would fully half of the women who not only perceived themselves to be the victims of nonstranger rape but also went so far as to report it to the police remain silent when asked about criminal victimization by a survey interviewers? One possibility is that they were simply tired of talking about it and considered it too private or too painful to discuss with a stranger who wanted the information for a survey. But that possibility would seem to apply equally to all rape victims, not only to those raped by nonstrangers; it does not explain why the stranger victims were so willing to disclose and the nonstranger victims so unwilling. A second possibility does: that the victims who did not disclose were those who had in effect been told that they were not legitimate victims by the police and the criminal justice system.

The woman raped by her ex-boyfriend the weightlifter, in the "technical" rape my acquaintance so easily dismissed, clearly thought she had been raped. She flagged down a police car; she went to meet with the prosecutor; she was willing to persist, regardless of the odds. The response from the system was negative. I wonder what she would say if a survey interviewer came to her house one day and asked if she had been victimized in the last year. I would not be surprised if she said nothing at all.

Distrust by Definition

Nonconsent has traditionally been a required element in the definition of a number of crimes, including theft, assault, battery, and trespass.[15] Rape may be the most serious crime to allow a consent defense, but it is certainly not the only one.[16] Rape is unique, however, in the definition that has been given to nonconsent—one that has required victims of rape, unlike victims of any other crime, to demonstrate their "wishes" through physical resistance. And the law of rape is striking in the extent to which nonconsent defined as resistance has become the rubric under which all of the issues in a close case are addressed and resolved.

Brown v. State, a 1906 Wisconsin decision,[17] is a classic statement of the definition of nonconsent in rape as "utmost resistance."[18] It is also a classic simple rape.

The victim in *Brown*, a sixteen-year-old (and a virgin), was a neighbor of the accused. She testified at the trial that on a walk across the fields to her grandmother's house, she greeted the accused. He at once seized her, tripped her to the ground, and forced himself upon her. "I tried as hard as I could to get away. I was trying all the time to get away just as hard as I could. I was trying to get up; I pulled at the grass; I screamed as hard as I could, and he told me to shut up, and I didn't, and then he held his hand on my mouth until I was almost strangled." Whenever he removed his hand from her mouth she repeated her screams. The jury found the defendant guilty of rape.

On appeal, the Supreme Court of Wisconsin did not reverse Brown's conviction on the ground that the force used was insufficient to constitute rape. Nor did they conclude that he lacked the necessary *mens rea* or criminal intent for rape. Rather, they reversed his conviction on the grounds that *the victim* had not adequately demonstrated her nonconsent: "Not only must there be entire absence of mental consent or assent, but there must be the most vehement exercise of every physical means or faculty within the woman's power to resist the penetration of her person, and this must be shown to persist until the offense is consummated."[19]

Here the victim failed to meet that standard: she only once said "let me go"; her screams were considered "inarticulate"; and her failure actually to "resist"— to use her "hands and limbs and pelvic muscles," obstacles which the court noted that "medical writers insist . . . are practically insuperable"—justified reversal of the conviction.[20] In fact, the court rioted that "when one pauses to reflect upon the terrific resistance which the determined woman should make," her absence of bruises and torn clothing was "well-nigh incredible."[21]

Still, such courts' equation of nonconsent with resistance was questionable even on their own terms. A system of law that truly celebrated female chastity, which is the system that these judges purported to uphold, should have erred on the side of less sex and presumed nonconsent in the absence of affirmative evidence to the contrary. The resistance test accomplished exactly the opposite.

Chastity may have been celebrated, but consent was presumed. A system of law which at that time treated women, in matters ranging from ownership of property to the pursuit of the professions to participation in society, as passive and powerless, nonetheless demanded that in matters of sex they be strong and aggressive and powerful.[22]

That is only the half of it. It was bad enough to say—and the cases do—that seizing and tripping a woman, and telling her to shut up and covering her mouth with your hands (the *Brown* case) is the sort of romantic foreplay that neighborhood teenagers must endure; or that sex with the master comes with the job, at least where there is no gun or beating (the *Dohring* case).

What is worse is that the resistance requirement accomplished this not by judging the man and finding his behavior legitimate, but by judging the woman and finding her conduct substandard. She failed to behave as judges thought a chaste woman would; therefore she consented; she wanted it; she was unchaste. It was her behavior that was scrutinized, and her conduct that was found wanting. By choosing to resolve these cases of simple rape under the resistance standard, rather than standards of force or intent, the common law courts chose the course most punitive toward the woman victim.

The virtue of the woman and the force used by the man obviously are factors to be taken into account, but they are not the only ones; the "appropriateness" of the relationship may be equally important. Strangers need not be resisted, even if unarmed; dates must be.[23] A stepdaughter is not required to resist her stepfather, but she is required to resist the boy or man next door.[24] Adult women are required to resist when the man is an adult neighbor, but not when he is a drunken youth.[25] White women are not required to resist black men, but black women are.[26]

Thus, the broadened sexual access permitted by the resistance requirement generally applied only in "appropriate" relationships. The genius of these common law judges, if it can be called that, was in framing and applying the requirement so as to ensure just such access, no more and no less, while at the same time protecting men like themselves from the dreaded lies of the appropriate women they spurned.

By the 1950s and 1960s, the "utmost resistance" standard had been generally replaced by a reasonable resistance standard.[27] Chastity was still valuable, but judges no longer suggested that it was more valuable than life itself. . . .

In the literature of the 1950s and 1960s special scrutiny of women complaining of simple rape was required because men understood women to be confused and ambivalent in these potentially appropriate relationships. According to an article published in the *Stanford Law Review* in 1966:

> Although a woman may desire sexual intercourse, it is customary for her to say, "no, no, no" (although meaning "yes, yes, yes") and to expect the male to be the aggressor. . . . It is always difficult in rape cases to determine whether the female really meant "no."[28]

In order to remedy these problems, the *Stanford Law Review* concludes that the resistance standard, at least as applied in simple rape cases involving a single unarmed defendant, must be "high enough to assure that the resistance is unfeigned and to indicate with some degree of certainty that the woman's attitude was not one of ambivalence or unconscious compliance and that her complaints do not result from moralistic afterthoughts." At the same time, the standard must be "low enough to make death or serious bodily injury an *unlikely outcome* of the event."[29] That death or serious bodily injury remains a *possible* outcome of ignoring a woman's words is, apparently, not too great a price to pay.

Perhaps the most influential of all such commentary is the often-cited *Yale Law Journal* article on what women want.[30] Relying on Sigmund Freud, the author points out that it is not simply that women lie, although there is an "unusual inducement to malicious or psychopathic accusation inherent in the sexual nature of the crime."[31] Even the "normal girl" is a confused and ambivalent character when it comes to sex with men she knows. Her behavior is not always an accurate guide to her true desires, for it may suggest resistance when in fact the woman is enjoying the physical struggle:

> When her behavior looks like resistance although her attitude is one of consent, injustice may be done the man by the woman's subsequent accusation. Many women, for example, require as a part of preliminary "love play" aggressive overtures by the man. Often their erotic pleasure may be enhanced by, or even depend upon, an accompanying physical struggle.[32]

And if a woman is ambivalent about sex, it follows that it would be unfair to punish the man who was not acting *entirely* against her wishes:

> [A] woman's need for sexual satisfaction may lead to the unconscious desire for forceful penetration, the coercion serving neatly to avoid the guilt feeling which might arise after willing participation. . . . Where such an attitude of ambivalence exists, the woman may, nonetheless, exhibit behavior which would lead the fact finder to conclude that she opposed the act. To illustrate . . . the anxiety resulting from this conflict of needs may cause her to flee from the situation of discomfort, either physically by running away, or symbolically by retreating to such infantile behavior as crying.[33]

The problem accordingly is not only Hale's fear that some women simply lie, but that many women do not know what they want, or mean what they say—at least when they say no to a man they know. And the presence of force hardly proves rape since many women enjoy, and even depend for their "pleasure" on "an accompanying physical struggle."

Resistance therefore emerges not only as a test that ensures mate access, but as an imperative to ensure adequate notice. A man is free to ignore a woman's words (for his own pleasure, as well as the woman's), but resistance signifies that, no, in this case, means no. Resistance thus serves to give notice that sex is unwelcome, that force is just that, and that the man has crossed the line.

The requirement that the victim of a simple rape do more than say no was virtually without precedent in the criminal law. Many other crimes encompass a consent defense; none other has defined it so as to mandate actual physical resistance. In trespass, the posting of a sign or the offering of verbal warnings generally suffices to meet the victim's burden of nonconsent; indeed, under the Model Penal Code, drafted by the elite American Law Institute and followed by many states, the offense of trespass is aggravated where a defendant is verbally warned to desist and fails to do so.[34] A defendant's claim that the signs and the warnings were not meant to exclude *him* generally serves to indicate his intent or *mens rea* in committing the act, not the existence of consent.[35]

In robbery, claims that the victim cooperated with the taking of the money or eased the way, and thus consented, have been generally unsuccessful.[36] Only where the owner of the property actively participates in planning and committing the theft will consent be found; mere "passive submission"[37] or "passive assent"[38] does not amount to consent[39]—except in the law of rape.

In spite of the law's supposed celebration of female chastity, a woman's body was effectively presumed to be offered at least to any appropriate man she knows, lives near, accepts a drink from, or works for. The resistance requirement imposed on her the burden to prove otherwise and afforded courts a convenient vehicle to reverse convictions of simple rape where the woman had, in the words of the *Yale Law Journal*, done no more than "retreat" to "such infantile behavior as crying." But as important as the resistance requirement was to the accomplishment of these goals, it was not the only tool available to the common law courts. If the definition of the crime did not exclude the simple rape, the rules of proof would.

Evidentiary Distrust

The requirement that the victim's testimony be corroborated in order to support a conviction was, in its heyday, formally applied in a significant minority of American jurisdictions. In practice, it continues to be a critical factor in determining the disposition of rape charges even today.[40] The justification for the formal rule was, quite explicitly, that women lie. As the *Columbia Law Review* explained in the late 1960s: "Surely the simplest, and perhaps the most important, reason not to permit conviction for rape on the uncorroborated word of the prosecutrix is that that word is very often false. . . . Since stories of rape are frequently lies or fantasies, it is reasonable to provide that such a story, in itself, should not be enough to convict a man of a crime."[41] The writer felt no need to cite a single authority for the long-held, if never-tested, proposition that women frequently lie, voluntarily exposing themselves to the potential humiliation of a rape prosecution.

Rhetorically, a number of courts agreed. Without the corroboration rule, "every man is in danger of being prosecuted and convicted on the testimony of a base woman, in whose testimony there is no truth."[42] The corroboration rule is required because of the "psychic complexes" of "errant young girls and women coming before the court," which take the form "of contriving false charges of sexual offences by men."[43] If proof of opportunity to commit the crime were alone sufficient to sustain a conviction, no man would be safe."[44] Corroboration is required because sexual cases are particularly subject to the danger of deliberately false charges, resulting from sexual neurosis, phantasy, jealousy, spite, or simply a girl's refusal to admit that she consented to an act of which she is now ashamed."[45]

The key question is not simply whose intent should govern, but what we should expect and demand of men in the "appropriate" and "ambiguous" situations where rape has been most narrowly defined. It is not unfair, *Morgan* notwithstanding, to demand that men behave "reasonably" and to impose criminal penalties when they do not. Even more important, the reasonable man in the 1980s should be one who understands that a woman's word is deserving of respect, whether she is a perfect stranger or his own wife. . . .

In holding a man to a higher standard of reasonableness, the law would signify that it considers a woman's consent to sex significant enough to merit a man's reasoned attention and respect. It would recognize that being sexually penetrated without consent is a grave harm; and that being treated like an object whose words are not even worthy of consideration adds insult to injury. In effect, the law would impose a duty on men to open their eyes and use their heads before engaging in sex—not to read a woman's mind, but to give her credit for knowing it herself when she speaks it, regardless of their relationship. . . .

Many feminists would argue that so long as women are powerless relative to men, viewing a "yes" as a sign of true consent is misguided. For myself, I am quite certain that many women who say yes to men they know, whether on dates or on the job, would say no if they could. I have no doubt that women's silence sometimes is the product not of passion and desire but of pressure and fear. Yet if yes may often mean no, at least from a woman's perspective, it does not seem so much to ask men, and the law, to respect the courage of the woman who does say no and to take her at her word.

In the nineteenth century and on into the twentieth, courts celebrating female chastity in the abstract were so suspicious of the women who actually complained of simple rape that they adopted rules that effectively presumed consent. I have heard the same response justified in the 1980s by those who would seize on women's liberation as a basis to celebrate female unchastity. I could not disagree more. If in the 1980s more women do feel free to say yes, that provides more reason—not less—to credit the word of those who say no. The issue is not chastity or unchastity, but freedom and respect. What the law owes us is a celebration of our autonomy, and an end at long last to the distrust and suspicion of women victims of simple rape that has been the most dominant and continuing theme in the cases and commentary.

In sentencing a man who pled guilty to the aggravated rape of his fourteen-year-old stepdaughter in exchange for the dismissal of charges of sexual assault on his twelve-year-old stepson, a Michigan trial judge in 1984 commented:

> On your behalf, there are many things that you are not. You are not a violent rapist who drags women and girls off the street and into the bushes or into your car from a parking lot, and I have had a lot of these in my courtroom. . . . You are not a child chaser, one whose obsession with sex causes him to seek neighborhood children or children in parks or in playgrounds, and we see these people in court. You are a man who has warm personal feelings for your stepchildren, but you let them get out of hand, and we see a number of people like you in our courts.[46]

The judge is absolutely wrong. What makes both the "violent rapist" and the stepfather whose feelings "get out of hand" different and more serious offenders than those who commit assault or robbery is the injury to personal integrity involved in forced sex. That injury is the reason that forced sex should be considered a serious crime even where there is no weapon or beating. Whether one adheres to the "rape as sex" school or the "rape as violence" school, the fact remains that what makes rape, whether "simple" or "aggravated," different from other crimes is that rape is a sexual violation—violation of the most personal, most intimate, and most offensive kind.

Conduct is labeled criminal "to announce to society that these actions are not to be done and to secure that fewer of them are done."[47] It is time—long past time—to announce to society our condemnation of simple rape, and to enforce that condemnation "to secure that fewer of them are done." The message of the law to men, and to women, should be made clear. Simple rape is real rape.

NOTES

1. Even today, husbands remain completely immune from rape prosecutions in at least nine states; only ten states allow prosecution under all circumstances. In the rest, husbands can be prosecuted only in limited circumstances, as where they are living separately under court order or where one spouse has filed for divorce. See generally Note, "To Have and To Hold: The Marital Rape Exemption and the Fourteenth Amendment," *Harvard Law Review* 99 (1986): 1258–60; *People v. Liberta*, 65 N.Y.2d 152, 474 N.E.2d 567 (1984), *cert. denied*, 105 S.Ct. 2029 (1985).

2. Harry Kalven and Hans Zeisel, *The American Jury* (Boston: Little, Brown, 1966).

3. Ibid., 252–55.

4. Sir Matthew Hale, *The History of the Please of the Crown*, I (London: Professional Books, 1971), LVIII: *635. This statement is the usual basis, if not the exact wording, of the "cautionary" instruction given to juries in rape cases.

5. See, for example, Susan Brownmiller, *Against Our Will. Men, Women and Rape* (New York: Simon & Schuster, 1975); Diana E. H. Russell, *The Politics of Rape* (New York: Stein & Day, 1975); Nancy Gager and Cathleen Schurr, *Sexual Assault: Confronting Rape in America* (New York: Grosser & Dunlap, 1976); Andra Medea and Kathleen Thompson, *Against Rape* (New York: Farrar, Straus and Giroux, 1974); Susan Griffin, "Rape: The All-American Crime," *Ramparts* (September 1971): 26–36; Catharine MacKinnon, "Feminism, Marxism, Method, and the State," *Signs* 8 (1983): 635.

6. There are "major" articles in the late nineteenth and early twentieth centuries on the problems of consent in the law of rape. But what fascinated Professors Beale and Puttkammer, the leading authors, was not the consent of competent, adult women, but rather the problem of "consent" when a snake-oil salesman convinces a woman that he is really her husband and that sex is really a physical examination of her wooden leg. I am exaggerating, but only a very little. See Joseph Beale, "Consent in the Criminal Law," *Harvard Law Review* 8 (1895): 317, Ernst Wilfred Puttkammer, "Consent in Rape," *Illinois Law Review* 19 (1925): 410. With few exceptions—as, for example, Vivian Berger, "Man's Trial, Woman's Tribulation: Rape Cases in the Courtroom," *Columbia Law Review* 77 (1977): 1—the best of the more modern writing in the legal literature is found in "notes" prepared by students. See, for example, Note, "The Rape Corroboration Requirement: Repeal not Reform," *Yale Law Journal* 81 (1972): 1365; Note, "Recent Statutory Developments in the Law of Rape," *Virginia Law Review* 61 (1975): 1500; Comment, "Towards a Consent Standard in the Law of Rape," *University of Chicago Law Review* 43 (1976): 613.

7. Linda S. Williams, "The Classic Rape: When Do Victims Report?" *Social Problems* 31 (April 1984): 464. See also Menachem Amir, *Patterns in Forcible Rape* (Chicago: University of Chicago Press, 1971); Diana E. H. Russell, *Sexual Exploitation* (Beverly Hills, CA: Sage, 1984), 96–97; Richard L. Dukes and Christine L. Mattley, "Predicting Rape Victim Reportage," *Sociology and Social Research* 62 (October 1977): 63; K. Weiss and S. S. Borges, "Victimology and Rape: The Case of the Legitimate Victim," *Issues in Criminology* 8 (1973): 71.

8. Candace Waldron and Elizabeth Dodson-Cole, "An Analysis of Sexual Assaults Reported to Rape Crisis Centers in Massachusetts" (Boston: Massachusetts Department of Public Health, 1986). See also Judy Foreman, "Most Rape Victims Know Assailant, Don't Report to Police, Report Says," *Boston Globe*, 16 April 1986, 27.

9. See, for example, Ageton, *Sexual Assault among Adolescents*, 129–130.

10. See, for example, David Knox and Kenneth Wilson, "Dating Problems of University Students," *College Student Journal* 17 (1983): 226.

11. Ageton, *Sexual Assault among Adolescents*, 48.

12. Judith E. Krulewitz and Elaine Johnson Payne, "Attributions about Rape: Effects of Rapist Force, Observer Sex and Sex Role Attitudes," *Journal of Applied Social Psychology* 8 (1978): 291.

13. Susan H. Klemmack and David L. Klemrnack, "The Social Definition of Rape," in Marcia J. Walker and Stanley L. Brodsky, eds., *Sexual Assault: The Victim and the Rapist* (Lexington, MA: Lexington Books, 1976), 135–46.

14. Gail L. Zellman and Jacqueline D. Goodchilds, "Becoming Sexual in Adolescence," in Elizabeth Rice Allgeier and Naomi B. McCormick, eds., *Changing Boundaries:*

Gender Roles and Sexual Behavior, 1st ed. (Palo Alto, CA: Mayfield, 1983), 60–61. See also Kathellen L'Armand and Albert Pepitone, "Judgments of Rape: A Study of Victim-Rapist Relationship and Victim Sexual History," *Personality and Social Psychology Bulletin* 8 (March 1982): 134.

15. See Graham Hughes, "Consent in Sexual Offences," *Modern Law Review* 25 (November 1962): 673–76; Glanville Williams "Consent and Public Policy," *Criminal Law Review* (February–March 1962): 74, 154; Ernst Wilfed Puttkammer, "Consent in Criminal Assault," *Illinois Law Review* 19 (1925): 617.

By contrast, sexual offenses are deservedly criticized examples of "morals" offenses for which consent is no defense. See Sanford H. Kadish, "The Crisis of Overcriminalization," *The Annals of the American Academy of Political and Social Science* 374 (November 1967): 157. "Deviant" sex punishable by law has included homosexual sex, sex with children, oral sex, sex for money, let alone, under older laws, sex outside of marriage, or at least adultery. But in the long list of prohibited sexual relations, a separate category of "consensual" violent heterosexual sex is conspicuously absent; to the extent such sex has been prohibited, it is because it is sex (as fornication or adultery), not because it is violent, and both man and woman are considered equally guilty.

16. Virtually the only exception to the rule requiring nonconsent in cases of rape or sexual assault is one oft-cited (and criticized) English case. In *The King v. Donovan* [1934] 2 K.B. 498, the accused was charged with caning a girl of seventeen "in circumstances of indecency" for purposes of sexual gratification. His defense was consent, and he appealed his conviction on the ground that the trial judge had failed to instruct the jury that the burden was on the prosecution to establish lack of consent as an element of the offense of indecent assault. The court quashed his conviction on the grounds of misdirection of the jury, but in doing so it held that where the blows were likely or intended to do bodily harm, consent was no defense. It treated as an exception those cases of "cudgels, foils, or wrestling" which are "manly diversions, they intend to give strength, skill and activity, and many fit people for defence," as well as cases of "rough and undisciplined sport or play, where there is no anger and no intention to cause bodily harm." According to the court, "nothing could be more absurd or more repellent to the ordinary intelligence than to regard his conduct as comparable with that of a participant in one of those 'manly diversions.' . . . Nor is his act to be compared with . . . rough but innocent horse-play." For criticism of *Donovan's* "breadth," see, for example, Williams, "Consent and Public Policy," 154–55.

17. 127 Wis. 193, 106 N.W. 536 (1906).

18. See also *Reynolds v. State*, 27 Neb. 90, 91, 42 N.W. 903, 904 (1889); *Moss v. State*, 208 Miss. 531, 536, 45, So.2d 125, 126 (1950), "resistance [must] be unto the uttermost"; *People v. Dohring*, 59 N.Y.374, 386 (1874), "until exhausted or overpowered"; *King V. State*, 210 Tenn. 150, 158, 357 S.W.2d 42, 45 (1962), "in every way possible and continued such resistance until she was overcome by force, was insensible through fright, or ceased resistance from exhaustion, fear of death, or great bodily harm." In effect, the "utmost resistance" rule required that the woman resist to the "utmost" of her capacity and that such resistance not have abated during the struggle. See Note, "Recent Statutory Developments in the Definition of Forcible Rape," *Virginia Law Review* 61 (November 1975): 1506.

19. 127 Wis. at 199,106 N.W. at 538.

20. 127 Wis. at 199–200, 106 N.W. at 538. According to the court, a woman "is equipped to interpose most effective obstacles by means of hands and limbs and pelvic

muscles. Indeed, medical writers insist that these obstacles are practically insuperable in absence of more than the usual relative disproportion of age and strength between man and woman, though no such impossibility is recognized as a rule of law." The latter qualification is, by the court's own opinion and holding, open to question. The view that an unwilling woman could not physically be raped was not limited to Wisconsin or to the nineteenth century; and it provided support for insisting that the least women should do was resist to the utmost. See W. Norwood East, "Sexual Offenders— A British View," *Yale Law Journal* 55 (1946): 543.

21. 127 Wis. at 201, 106 N.W. at 539.

22. See, for example, *Muller v. Oregon*, 208 U.S. 412 (1908), upholding an Oregon law restricting hours of work for women by invoking scientific and sociological materials linking female biology and female dependency; *Goesart v. Cleary*, 335 U.S. 464 (1948), upholding legislative judgment that women who were not the wives or daughters of tavern owners should not be permitted to work as bartenders. It was not until 1971 that the United States Supreme Court for the first time struck down a state law as sex discrimination: *Reed v. Reed*, 404 U.S. 71 (1971).

23. See, for example, *People v. Kinne*, 76 P.2d 714 (Cal. App. 1938), conviction in a stranger case upheld, notwithstanding the absence of resistance; *State v. Dizon*, 390 P.2d 759 (Hawaii 1964), the same as the preceding; *People v. Blankenship*, 225 P.2d 835 (Cal. App. 1951), a repeat rapist convicted on four counts, notwithstanding the absence of resistance; *State v. Hunt*, 135 N.W.2d 475 (Neb. 1965), the requirement of "utmost resistance" was not applied where a woman was attacked by three men. For a particularly strict application of the resistance requirement to reverse a conviction in the context of a date, see *State v. Hoffman*, 280 N.W. 357 (Wis. 1938). See also *Territory v. Nishi*, 24 Hawaii 677 (1919), reversing for lack of resistance because the defendant and the victim were "friends and companions" and she voluntarily accompanied him to the park.

24. See Bailey, 82 Va. at 111; *Lewis v. State*, 154 Tex. Crim. 329, 226 S.W.2d 861 (1950).

25. Compare *Prokop v. State*, 148 Neb. 582, 28 N.W.2d 200 (1947), a drunken youth who broke in, with *People v. Serrielle*, 354 111. 182, 188 N.E. 375 (1933), an adult neighbor allegedly invited in.

26. See, for example, *State v. Hinton*, 333 P.2d 822 (Cal. App. 1959). See also *Perez v. State*, 94 S.W. 1036, 1038 (Tex. Crim. App. 1906), conviction reversed in a case involving Mexicans on the ground that "something more was required of the prosecutrix. . . . A virtuous woman and her companions would naturally be expected to exercise more force in opposition to the alleged outrage than is manifested by the testimony in this record."

27. See, for example, *Satterwhite v. Commonwealth*, 201 Va. 478, 1 11 S.E.2d 820 (1960), "woman is not required to resist to the utmost of her physical strength, if she reasonably believes resistance would be useless and result in serious bodily injury"; *People v. Tollack*, 233 P.2d 121 (Cal. App. 195 1), utmost resistance not required; *State v. Herfel* 49 Wis.2d 513, 518–19, 182 N.W.2d 232, 235 (1971), good-faith resistance measured by total circumstances; Note, "Towards a Consent Standard in the Law of Rape," *University of Chicago Law Review* 43 (1976): 613, 620.

28. Note, "The Resistance Standard in Rape Legislation," *Stanford Law Review* 18 (February 1966): 682; citing Gray and Mohr, "Follow-Up of Male Sexual Offenders," in Ralph Slovenko, ed., *Sexual Behavior and the Law* (Springfield, IL: Charles C. Thomas, 1965), 742, 746; Ralph Slovenko, "A Panoramic Overview: Sexual Behavior and the Law," in ibid., 5, 51.

29. Note, "The Resistance Standard in Rape Legislation," 685; emphasis added.

30. Note, "Forcible and Statutory Rape: An Exploration of the Operation and Objectives of the Consent Standard," *Yale Law Journal* 62 (December 1952): 55. This note is cited, and its influence apparent, not only in the Model Penal Code provisions adopted in the 1950s but in the comments to them edited in the 1970s and published in 1980. See American Law Institute, *Model Penal Code and Commentaries*, part II (Philadelphia: American Law Institute, 1980), vol. 1, sec. 213.1, pp. 301–3. The Code cites the Yale article for the proposition that overemphasis on nonconsent would compress into a single statute conduct ranging from "brutal attacks . . . to half won arguments . . . in parked cars." The Code, echoing the earlier commentary, goes on to note that: "often the woman's attitude may be deeply ambivalent. She may not want intercourse, may fear it, or may desire it but feel compelled to say 'no.' Her confusion at the time may later resolve into nonconsent. . . . The deceptively simple notion of consent may obscure a tangled mesh of psychological complexity, ambiguous communication, and unconscious restructuring of the event by the participants."

31. Note, "Forcible and Statutory Rape," p. 61. This and subsequent citations to the article reprinted by permission of The Yale Law Journal Company and Fred B. Rothman & Company from *The Yale Law Journal* 62.

32. Ibid., 66.

33. Ibid., 67–68.

34. See Model Penal Code, sec. 221.2(2) (1980), defiant trespasser.

35. The Model Penal Code requires that the person enter the place, "knowing that he is not licensed or privileged to do so." It also provides an affirmative defense that the "actor reasonably believed that the owner of the premises, or other person empowered to license access thereto, would have licensed him to enter or remain." Model Penal Code, sec. 221.2(3) (C)

36. In *Smith v. United States*, 291 F.2d 220 (9th Cir. 1961), for example, a bank teller pretended to agree, but told the manager, who instructed him to hand the defendant a bag when he was "held up." On appeal, the defendant argued that the bank had consented to giving him the money, thus there was no robbery. The court of appeals rejected the argument and affirmed the conviction, concluding that the bank had not consented but merely smoothed the way for the crime's commission.

37. *State v. Neely*, 90 Mont. 199, 300 P. 561 (1931).

38. *State v. Natalie*, 172 La. 709, 135 So. 34 (1931).

39. See also *Alford v. Commonwealth*, 240 Ky. 513, 42 S.W.2d 711 (193 1); *People v. Teicher*, 52 N.Y.2d 638, 422 N.E.2d 506, 439 N.Y.S.2d 846 (1981); *Carens v. State*, 134 Tex. Crim. 8, 113 S.W.2d 542 (1938). Nor is contributory behavior afforded exculpatory significance in property crimes. Leaving keys in the ignition does not exculpate from motor vehicle larceny, nor does leaving a front door unlocked excuse the trespass. See *State v. Plaspohl*, 239 Ind. 324, 157 N.E.2d 579 (1959); *State v. Moore*, 129 Iowa 514, 106 N.W. 16 (1906); Wayne LaFave and Austin Scott, *Handbook on Criminal Law* (St. Paul, MN: West, 1972).

40. See Chapter 2; corroboration is a key factor in virtually every study in determining the disposition of rape complaints.

41. Note, "Corroborating Charges of Rape," *Columbia Law Review* 67 (1967): 1137–38.

42. *Davis v. State*, 120 Ga. 433, 48 S.E. 180, 181 (1904).

43. *State v. Wulff*, 194 Minn. 271, 260 N.W. 515, 516 (1935).

44. *Power v. State*, 43 Ariz. 329, 332, 30 P.2d 1059, 1060 (1934).

45. *State v. Anderson*, 272 Minn. 384, 137 N.W.2d 781, 783, n. 2 (1965), quoting Glanville Williams, "Corroboration-Sexual Cases," *Criminal Law Review* 1962 (October 1962): 662–71.

46. The defendant was sentenced to probation, conditional on his receiving experimental drug treatment with Depo-Provera. Both the defendant and the state appealed, and the 134 Mich. App. 737, 352 N.W.2d 3 10, sentence was reversed on appeal. *People v. Gauntlett*, 313 (Mich. Ct. App. 1984).

47. Hart, *Punishment and Responsibility*, p. 6.

EDITOR'S NOTE

Did the late Senator Strom Thurmond of South Carolina rape his family's African American maid, Carrie Butler, in 1925? Senator Thurmond's private behavior and public stance are important to analyze not only because it fits well with Susan Estrich's reading, but also because it fits well within the context of patriarchy and the entitlement of elite men.

Senator Thurmond's early public life is well documented as being anti-African American. As a senator in the 1960s Thurmond bolted from the Democratic Party because of its support of civil rights for African Americans and he worked hard to block civil rights legislation.[1] Even before that Thurmond, as a judge in 1942, sentenced a black man to death for allegedly raping a white woman.[2]

While taking an extreme public stance against African Americans, in 1925, Thurmond, the man who preached black inferiority fathered a child with his family's maid, Carrie Butler. It is unclear whether he committed statutory rape because Ms. Butler's exact age at the time of impregnation is not known; however, the baby was born when Ms. Butler was sixteen.[3]

Even if Ms. Butler were aged sixteen at the time, as a Negro maid in the South in 1925, Butler was legally powerless to refuse the advances of a white man, especially the young scion of an influential white family like Thurmond's. Though Thurmond argued later in his life that he was a changed man, he never publicly acknowledged his daughter and she apparently felt compelled to collude with his misdeeds until after his death. She did not share in his inheritance with his other children. Clearly, Thurmond's behavior fits well with the colonial masters of the plantation era—treating African Americans as chattel—like property—that then allowed for inhumane treatment.

Although the rape laws in the United States are far from ideal but certainly better now than in 1925, there are places where women have no legal rights over their person and/or property. Nicholas Kristof, in *The New York Times*, recounts a horrific crime against a young woman in a village in Pakistan.[4] A village tribal council wanted to punish her family so they forced the family's daughter to be gang raped by her neighbors after which she was forced to walk home naked. The amazing thing is she did not do what the council had anticipated which was to commit suicide. Instead, she acted outside the box and demanded that her attackers be prosecuted. Amazingly, she won the first round.[5] Then a Pakistani court overturned the convictions of her attackers and they were released. Under Muslim law four men must be witnesses to a rape in order for it to have happened. A woman without witnesses can be charged with a crime, be publicly beaten, and sent to prison.[6]

Two different cultures, two different eras; two women without rights.

NOTES

1. Anna Quindlen, "Do As I Say, Not As I Do," *Newsweek*, 29 December 2003/5 January 2004, 131.
2. "Was Strom a Rapist?" *The Nation*, 1 March 2004, 5.
3. Ibid.
4. Nicholas Kristof, "When Rapists Walk Free," *The New York Times*, 5 March 2005, A27.
5. Ibid.
6. Ibid.

34

Clarence Thomas, Patriarchal Discourse, and Public/Private Spheres

Mary F. Rogers

Generically, patriarchy is a system of domination whereby men dominate women, with high-status men dominating other men as well. In contemporary Western societies, high-status men are white, heterosexual, able-bodied, and upper class or, at least, upper middle-class professionals commanding enviable salaries and benefits.

My interest lies in exploring the empirical shape of "patriarchal discourse," that is, any network of meanings that both justifies male dominance, whether in general or in specific institutions, and is widely used as an interpretive resource among members of a given society or community. In societies where men control all the major institutions—government, religion, economy, education, family, and so forth—patriarchal discourse would seem commonplace. Indeed, it is. As the Hill-Thomas hearings illustrate, however, this widespread discourse is plied with a benign cast that paints patriarchy as a fair and humane way of organizing social life.

To some extent all men share in masculine privilege and the institutionalized subordination of women. Yet masculine privilege varies with class, age, race, able-bodiedness, and sexual orientation. Put differently, gender cannot be experienced apart from these and other circumstances of our lives. Thomas thus came to the extended hearings patriarchally disadvantaged. Minimally, his race and class of origin mark him as less than elite. He could not assume that the fourteen white men on the Senate Judiciary Committee would consider him fully entitled to masculine privilege. Not surprisingly, Thomas invoked imagery whereby he could claim a masculinity, albeit racialized, commensurate with theirs for all practical and political purposes.

With testimony framed in narrowly patriarchal terms, Thomas established grounds whereon his fellow males could seem reasonable in sympathizing with him while also appearing appropriately concerned about Hill. Significantly, the patriarchal imagery he and most of the other participants put into play left Hill no clear-cut place to stand. Nowhere does her gender resound with its full subordinate force; nowhere does her race scream out for attention the way Thomas's did. Hill was "constructed . . . as a generic or universal woman with no race or class (or with race or class being unimportant to her experience)" (Brown 1995, p. 105).

METHOD

In 1994, the transcripts of the Thomas/Hill hearings became available in softcover (Miller 1994). They include only the testimony, affidavits, and other evidence gathered in response to Hill's allegations that Thomas sexually harassed her, first at the Department of Education and then at the Equal Employment Opportunity Commission (EEOC). That part of the confirmation process—its "extended" or "reopened" hearings—occurred 11, 12, and 13 October 1991.

I treat the transcripts broadly as an expression of what Dorothy E. Smith (1990, p. 6) calls the "relations of ruling," which include "the complex of discourses . . . that intersect, interpenetrate, and coordinate the multiple sites of ruling." I was curious about what types of discourse predominated in the words of Hill, Thomas, committee members, and various witnesses. So I sought narrative patterns in this mass of words about the workplace, professionalism, careers, and government service, about Hill's and Thomas's "backgrounds," careers, and "propensities," about power, privilege, and the politics of upward mobility. I approached the transcripts, then, as a knot of narratives reflective of how the relations of ruling are structured not only around gender but also around race and heterosexuality (among other axes).

I found that the masculinity of Thomas and his interlocutors emerged early and strongly, while the femininity of Hill and other female witnesses was less easily pinpointed. The transcripts show that masculinity means being a "protector" and "provider," especially in connection with literal and figurative families. In large measure, then, this article focuses on narrative data about heterosexual men's claims about their protection, provisioning, and power in connection with their real or rhetorical families. Following Adrienne Rich (1977, p. xvi), I treat "family" in terms "defined and restricted under patriarchy," that is, as an institution built up around heterosexual pairing where the man typically dominates the woman in socially accepted, culturally prescribed ways.

As I have implied, one learns little by looking at only one axis of patriarchal domination. In other terms, the "matrix of domination" demands attention alongside the relations of ruling. As Patricia Hill Collins (1991) defines it, that matrix comprises overlapping but distinct axes, such as gender and race, whereby some members gain advantages and others incur disadvantages.

Collins's conceptualization implies that most of us are both privileged and disprivileged to some degree. It also implies that

> [t]he way in which race, gender, and class categories are constructed in political discourse reinforces inequalities, obscures common interests, and denies the experiences of many women (and men). When both the dominant and the oppositional discourse tend to construct *women*, *Blacks*, and *labor* as separate and distinct categories or constituencies, the underlying interconnections are distorted. (Deitch 1993, p. 201)

Thomas had a vested interest in distorting those interconnections; he could scarcely come across as privileged and oppressive. Alleged to have harassed his colleague/supervisee with claims about his sexual prowess and details from pornographic films, Thomas needed to make a presentation of self (Goffman 1959) as an oppressed individual less interested in his own advancement than in the welfare of "subordinates" such as Hill. What better way than to present himself as a loving father? And what better way to seal that image than by extending it into the workplace? As protector, provider, and power wielder, Thomas spoke a language widely accepted in American life. His was the language of "family values" associated with backlash and traditionalism, as well as patriarchy.

PROTECTOR

From beginning to end, Thomas presents himself as a "family man." First, in his opening statement, he insists, "this apparently calculated public disclosure has caused me, my family, and my friends enormous pain and great harm." He goes on, "My family and I have been done a grave and irreparable injustice" (Miller 1994, p. 16). Soon Thomas mentions his mother, jarred enough by the turn of events to be "confined to her bed, unable to work and unable to stop crying." He asks, "Let me and my family regain our lives." Later, Thomas reiterates how his "family has been harmed, [his] friends have been harmed" (p. 18).

Thomas illustrates how men in patriarchal society can speak as victims while claiming their masculinity. By focusing on how events victimize those for whom he is responsible, the male victim deflects attention from his vulnerability while bolstering his status as patriarchal protector. Not surprisingly, then, Thomas recurrently refers to his family's pain and suffering: "This has devastated me and it has devastated my family"; "I can't tell you what my wife has lived through or my family. I can't tell you what my son has lived through; "My family has been harmed"; "I don't think that my family and I should have been put through this kind of ordeal"; "This has caused me great pain—and my family great pain"; "My family has suffered enough" (pp. 140, 155, 160,

161, 190, 195). Indeed, Thomas says the instigators of the, extended hearings "should at some point have to confront [his] family" (p. 183).

In the end, Thomas sits before the Judiciary Committee narratively and visually constructed not primarily as a careerist eager to reach the pinnacle of the American judicial system but as a family man: "I am here for my name, my family, my life and my integrity" (p. 117).

Second, Thomas presents himself as a "family man" in the workplace. As Homi K. Bhabba (1992, p. 236) puts it, Thomas translates the workplace into "familial space." Repeatedly, he offers variations of the following:

> I tend to be the proud father type who sees his special assistants go on and become successful and feels pretty good about it. (Miller 1994, p. 137)

> I view my special assistants as charges of mine. They are students, they are kids of mine and I have an obligation to them. It is the same way I feel toward interns and individual co-ops or stay-in-school students. (p. 142)

> I have had some [interns] who were nineteen or twenty years old who I would treat more like my son or daughter. (p. 172)

Among his workplace "charges" was Hill, whom Thomas says he treated "the same" as his *other special assistants who were successful or who performed well*" (p. 217, emphasis added). Note how Thomas implies that patriarchal protection presupposes compliance with the patriarch's expectations. In any case, Thomas reports that because a mutual friend recommended Hill, he felt a "special responsibility" for her. He "felt very strongly that [he] could discharge" it, in part by "be[ing] careful about her career." Thus did Hill join Thomas's special assistants: "They are family. My clerks are my family. They are my friends" (p. 151). Thomas claims he "looked out for" his workplace kin (p. 169). In the process, he "paint[s] a picture of a fatherly relationship" with Hill (Muir and Young 1996, p. 62).

By themselves, Thomas's invocations of family, country, and protective responsibilities might seem woefully contrived. The senators interrogating him, however, articulated parallel stances that lent credibility to Thomas's claims. They did this, first, by expressing sympathy for him and his family, thereby bolstering his protective stance.

The chair of the judiciary committee, Joseph Biden (D-DE,), said no one could fully appreciate how Thomas was feeling (Miller 1994, p. 223). Orrin Hatch (R-UT) noted that the president himself had asked Thomas whether he and his "family could take what would follow in the process" (p. 203).

Fully half ($N = 7$) of the committee explicitly expressed sympathy for Thomas, and four included his family in their expression. Whatever their motives, these senators gave Thomas what he rhetorically needed, namely, acknowledgment of his family-man characteristics. Thomas the protector thus gained rhetorical life partly from the teamwork (Goffman 1959) of senators broadly playing that same family-man role.

Yet patriarchy generally disallows the public destruction of a woman, even a woman of color in white-supremacist society who commands professional credentials and exhibits a feminine (neither assertive nor self-centered) demeanor. Since Hill never did "lose her poise, become angry, or break into tears" (Phelps and Winternitz 1992, p. 328), she came across as a properly feminine professional woman. Thus, the senators needed to appear to "protect" her in order to maintain their patriarchal standing. They did so by speaking to, about, and for Anita Hill in seemingly protective ways. In the process, they strengthened Thomas's rhetorical hand.

When they speak *to* Hill, the senators inject two topics traditionally linked with women: feelings and family. [Herbert] Kohl [(D-WI)] tells Hill, "I am sure this has been very painful for you" (p. 217). Paul Simon (D-IL) reports, "I sensed you were really agonizing on this whole thing" (p. 108). Howard Metznbaum (D-OH) tells Hill he is "sure" that "areas so sensitive . . . are so difficult for you to talk about" (p. 99). Arlen Specter's [(R-PA)] protective stance is similar: "I can understand that it is uncomfortable and I won't want to add to that. If any of it—if there is something you want to pause about, please do" (p. 39). Other senators ask Hill about her feelings. Biden wants to know how she "felt at the time" of the alleged harassment. "Were you uncomfortable, were you embarrassed, *did it not concern you?*" (p. 34, emphasis added) [Patrick] Leahy [D-VT] is interested in her current feelings: "Now, that was years ago. . . . How do you feel today? (p. 95) [Dennis] DeConcini's (D-AZ) query is diagnostic: "Do you feel put upon? Do you feel exposed?" (p. 101).

Besides concerning themselves with her feelings, committee members sometimes cast Hill in the role of daughter or sister in sharp contrast to Thomas as *head* of a family. After Hill's opening statement, Biden turns attention to her family before questioning her: "Professor Hill, . . . would you be kind enough to introduce your primary family members to us?" (p. 26). After Hill introduces her parents, four sisters, and a brother, she faces Biden's first question: "You are the youngest in the family, is that correct?" Like Biden, Simon acknowledges Hill's family before asking her anything: "First, Professor Hill, let me say to your parents, you have a daughter you ought to be very, very proud of" (p. 107).

Another way the senators constituted a supportive chorus for Thomas's patriarchal rhetoric was by directing protective remarks to other female witnesses. DeConcini says to J. C. Alvarez, a Thomas witness, "Nobody would call you arrogant. You are such a very nice lady" (p. 347). Generally, Biden excels along this dimension. He thanks [Susan] Hoerchner "for coming all the way across the country" from California but gives [John] Doggett no thanks for traveling from Arizona. At another gendered juncture, Biden says, "I am going to ask the women on the panel whether they need a break. They have been sitting there a long time" (p. 345).

PROVIDER AND POWER WIELDER

With the role of protector recurrently invoked on both sides of the table, Thomas was narratively positioned to invoke its correlates: provider and power wielder. His rhetoric illustrates that one can presume to protect only if one appears to have more power than the protected. Moreover, one can protect with the greatest legitimacy if one dispenses desirable resources. All the while, patriarchs' protection goes hand in hand with subordinates' compliance. As his former colleague Alvarez said of Thomas,

> With his immediate staff, he was very warm and friendly, sort of like a friend or a father. You could talk with him about your problems, go to him for advice, but, like a father, he *commanded* and he *demanded* respect. He *demanded* professionalism and performance, and he was *very strict* about that. (p. 296, emphasis added)

With reference to Hill, Thomas claims the role of provider but abjures the role of power wielder. He describes her as someone he "helped at every turn in the road," someone who "sought [his] advice and counsel" (p. 16).

Missing from this picture of collegiality and mentoring is power. That Thomas was the boss and that, by his own report, his "staffs were almost invariably predominantly women" (p. 174) are circumstances that his rhetoric obscures. Thomas the power wielder surfaces in the hearings but not in connection with Hill. For example, he claims to have taken "swift and decisive action when sex [sic] harassment raised or reared its ugly head" (p. 16). When he "was in a position to do something about it," he "did something about it" (p. 149). Thomas's assertions speak not to procedures but abrupt decisions, not to fair hearing but quick outcomes. His are the words of power, not leadership or fair play as such.

Nowhere do his words have that cast more than when he says, "I terminated [Angela Wright] very aggressively a number of years ago. And very summarily" (p. 196). Wright worked with Thomas as director of public affairs at the EEOC. Having made allegations strikingly similar to Hill's, she was only interviewed over the telephone by staff from six committee members' offices.

Wright describes coming to work one day and finding "a letter in [her] chair" saying "your services here are no longer needed" (p. 388). Consistent with the implications of Thomas's recollection, Wright reports no prior discussion—indeed, no discussion at all except the one she immediately demanded. Asked about dismissing her, Thomas said, "That is the way I am with conduct like that, whether it is sex [sic] harassment or slurs [alleged in Wright's case] or anything else, I don't play games" (p. 209).

Not only on but also off the job Thomas openly wielded power. For instance, Wright says he once came to her apartment uninvited and unannounced (pp. 384, 396). [Rose] Jourdain recalls that Wright had seen Thomas's visit as "rather presumptuous" (p. 423). Such presumptuousness also punctuated the hearings, as when Thomas advised the senators: "If you really want an idea of how I treated women, then ask the majority of the women who worked for me" (p. 125). Why only the "majority"? The power wielder is not asked.

That Thomas is not asked such hard questions implies how much narrative momentum he built up during the hearings. Judith K. Bowker (1996, p. 160) notes. "Using race as the vehicle, he established a relationship of power where he had authorization to indict his prosecutors." Particularly in collaboration with Orrin Hatch, as we will see, Thomas made "race trump sex" (Roper, Chanslor, and Bystrom 1996, p. 52; cf. Jordan 1995, p. 38). To some extent, then, "gender-based (Hill) and race-based (Thomas) frames vied" with each other during the hearings (Robinson and Powell 1996, p. 297). Yet Thomas's was a gendered as well as a racialized rhetoric. As David Frye (1996, p. 11) emphasizes, "maleness is not marked in the national politician"; it is presumed. Thus, a man in Clarence Thomas's position "faces the peculiar problem of keeping his gender invisible by keeping it sufficiently 'male'" (Frye 1996, p. 11).

PATRIARCHY, RACE, AND CLEAN HETEROSEXUALITY

Thomas describes the alleged harassment as "grotesque conduct" and thrice refers to its "grotesque language" (pp. 149, 155, 156). He describes the allegations about it as "impossible to wash off" (p. 156). Thomas refers to "this whole affair" as "garbage" (p. 161).

A brief exchange ensues, with Hatch querying Thomas about whether various of Hill's allegations invoke stereotypes of black men. As that exchange nears its end, Thomas says,

> I feel as though I have been abused in this process. . . . I feel as though something has been lodged against me and painted on me and it will leave an indelible mark on me. This is something that . . . plays into the worst stereotypes about black men in this society. And I have no way of changing it and no way of refuting the charges. (Miller 1994, p. 158)

Thomas's use of the "discourse of dirt and defilement" (Thomas 1992, p. 383) put the finishing rhetorical touch on his and Hatch's teamwork. Drawing from Joel Kovel (1984), Kendall Thomas (1992, pp. 384–85) emphasizes the cultural association of black bodies with dirt, filth, bodily wastes, and contamination. . . . Rhetorically, he dares his interlocutors to make judgments of him consistent with stereotypes of black men. In effect, Thomas claims his masculinity by judiciously racializing it and then challenging the stereotypes making nonwhite masculinity profoundly problematic. All the while Thomas lays grounds for claiming, in tandem with the senators, a clean heterosexuality.

Most of the senators fall into rhetorical line with Thomas. They sensational-
ize the allegations enough to support a perception of monstrosity and, therefore, the need for a perceptible monster. In Thomas the family man—protector
and provider on and off the job—they find no monster. The senators cannot,
then, see a peddler of sleaze, dirt, and trash any more than they can see a sick,
perverted, or emotionally disturbed person sitting across from them.

PATRIARCHY DISCOURSE AND THE PUBLIC/PRIVATE DIVIDE

Throughout the hearings, Thomas insists on his right to a private life. He refuses to discuss conversations "about my personal life or my sex life with any
person outside the workplace" (pp. 149–150). He says, "I didn't want my personal life and allegations about my sexual habits or anything else broadcast in
every living room in the United States" (p. 211).

Lurking beneath most such comments are assumptions about a reliable, if
not clear-cut, boundary between people's private and public lives. Thomas
claims, for instance, "I do not and did not co-mingle my personal life with my
work life nor did I co-mingle [staff members'] personal life with the work life"
(p. 176). Yet Thomas brought his son to the office; he listened to colleagues'
"personal" problems; he regarded them as "family" and "friends." Even
Thomas's insistence that "my relationship with my staff, although I care about
them, is in the workplace" fails to hold up. By his own admission he visited
Hill's apartment several times; Wright says he once dropped by her apartment.

Only Metzenbaum latches onto the inconsistencies in Thomas's public/
private rhetoric. He comments to [Phyllis] Berry-Myers that Thomas "says
that he kept his personal life extremely private. You seem to indicate that it
was sort of public" (p. 333). In fact, Berry-Myers reports that she "got to
know [Thomas's] private life, his private travails and things." She says that
was the case, though, because her job entailed "preparing him for processes
like this one" (p. 333). Further, Alvarez admits that she and Thomas "had
been friends for many, many years" but says, "at the office [they] were colleagues" (p. 351). Her stance reflects a discourse about friendship that runs
through the transcripts.

In these and other ways, "a discussion of sexual harassment . . . takes us back
to private/public distinctions" (Brown 1995, p. 119). One reason is that privacy is "connected to a politics of *domination*." As hooks (1994, p. 224) sees it,
we cannot undercut the matrix of domination until we "challenge the notions
of *public* and *private*." Like many other feminist theorists, hooks points to how
much nastiness in our lives is anchored in the so-called private sphere—child
abuse, wife battering, elder abuse, temper tantrums, emotional neglect, cheat-
ing, betrayal, violation. When such wrongs occur in one's "home" or behind
"closed doors" in the workplace, they become much harder to talk about, let
alone "prove." To say in public—to mere acquaintances and even strangers—

that intimates and close acquaintances have done wrong is to tell a most painful story under circumstances likely to feel traumatic.

As the sine qua non of respectable "public" personae, privacy gives the powerful grounds for acting offended or even victimized when called to give an accounting. That the very notion of a private sphere serves patriarchal interests seems straightforward enough, though in need of continual reworking under shifting material and social conditions. That that idea also falsifies people's experiences is less clear and more in need of theoretical clarification and empirical grounding.

Feminists aim to extend into the "private" sphere those standards of conduct mandated by law and custom in the "public" sphere. Their theorizing suggests the fruitfulness of conceptualizing the private sphere as that arena where the law falters and civility becomes unreliable.

"As an aspect of liberal theory" privacy certainly entails "a right to exclude others" (Young 1990, p. 108), but its *focus* cannot be exclusion for the sake of greater control or firmer domination. In principle, the private sphere is socially permeable (and often congenially so). It is not radically discontinuous with the public sphere, as Thomas and some of his interlocutors portrayed it. Indeed, when it is—when a household's members rarely interact with neighbors and rarely invite guests into their home—we suspect abuse of some sort or, more generally, a "dysfunction" household. Thus, feminists commonly contest the dualism that stamps the public sphere as "formalized, calculating, and hierarchical" while romanticizing the private sphere as its polar opposite (Kalberg 1987, p. 160).

Yet the private sphere broadly revolves around needs and desires that by definition (and often by law) cannot be satisfied in public. The private sphere thus concerns those social regions where we slough off our formal roles as best we can and are "ourselves"—"off" in Goffman's (1959) terms—without fearing censure of any palpable sort. Thus conceptualized, privacy is dramatically curtailed when one moves from home to the workplace, school, or mall where opportunities for intimacy plummet along with opportunities to be "known" as a biographical unique person. In this conceptual light, sexual harassment is a violation of privacy, an attempt within a predominantly impersonal sphere to introduce personal matters conventionally associated with intimacy or the prospect thereof. Thus, sexual harassment mangles privacy.

Alternatively, sexual harassment comprises efforts by one person to impose his—occasionally, her—privacy on some part of another person's public life. From this vantage point sexual harassment is deformed privacy, a holdover from a prefeminist age when male privilege equally left its stamp beyond and within the home. It is exclusionary for the sake of augmenting control and ensuring deniability, not for the sake of promoting intimacy. Sexual harassment denies women the privacy routinely granted men in the workplace. It is the workplace equivalent of the whistles, catcalls, and worse that women often face on the street.

Thus, during the reopened hearings on Thomas's nomination "the law's definition of public and private spheres . . . was at stake and under scrutiny." Ironically, "in the course of the hearings, the public import of sexual harassment was consistently privatized, in Hill's case," while "Thomas's attempt to protect his privacy was consistently respected." All the while, much in line with the separate spheres ideology consigning women to the "private" sphere, Hill was portrayed "as an essentially private individual, with private motives" (Ross 1992, pp. 56–57). The extended hearings thus illustrate that "in the public imagination the feminine world has the same flavor as a fictional world. It is present but not entirely real" (Griffin 1993, p. 2).

In this light, Thomas's insistence on his privacy entails a great deal more than restricting access to the details of his "personal" life. Above all, such insistence allows him to present a radically privatized self-centered on protecting, providing, and power wielding on behalf of his literal and figurative families. In that same discursive space, Thomas could publicize a heavily gendered family-man persona alongside a racially problematic clean-heterosexual persona. His construction of those personae heavily involved the rhetorical cooperation (Hatch, Specter, Biden) or relative silence (Kennedy, Grassley, Brown) of the senators across the room. . . .

I conclude that the private/public dichotomy is as central to patriarchal discourse as notions about protection, provision, and power. Indeed, that dichotomy allows men ultimately to privatize their public responsibilities and thus dodge accountability. Until the public/private dichotomy is fully interrogated and reworked in our culture, men such as Clarence Thomas will continue to have the upper hand whenever "private" violations of trust and abuses of power precipitate "public" occasions for separating victims from victimizers. To that extent, the relations of ruling remain undisturbed, and the matrix of domination is reinforced.

REFERENCES

Bhabba, Homi. 1992. "A Good Judge of Character: Men, Metaphors, and the Common Culture." Pp. 232–50 in *Race-ing Justice, En-Gendering Power*, edited by Toni Morrison. New York: Pantheon Books.

Bowker, Judith K. 1996. "Believeability: Narratives and Relational Messages in the Strategies of Anita Hill and Clarence Thomas." Pp. 149–67 in *The Lynching of Language*, edited by Sandra L. Ragan et al. Urbana: University of Illinois Press.

Brown, Elsa Barkley. 1995. "Imaging Lynching: African American Women, Communities of Struggle, and Collective Memory." Pp. 100–24 in *African American Women Speak Out*, edited by Geneva Smitherman. Detroit, MI: Wayne State University Press.

Collins, Patricia Hill. 1991. *Black Feminist Thought: Knowledge, Consciousness, and the Politics of Empowerment*. New York: Routledge.

Deitch, Cynthia. 1993. "Gender, Race, and Class Politics and the Inclusion of Women in Title VII of the Civil Rights Act." *Gender & Society* 7: 183–203.

Epstein, Cynthia Fuchs. 1988. *Deceptive Distinctions: Sex, Gender, and the Social Order*. New Haven, CT, and New York: Yale University Press and the Russell Sage Foundation.

Frye, David. 1996. "The Gendered Senate: National Politics and Gendered Imagery after the Thomas Hearings." Pp. 3–15 in *Outsiders Looking In*, edited by Paul Siegel. Cresskill, NJ: Hampton Press.

Fuss, Diana. 1991. "Inside/Out." Pp. 1–10 in *Inside/Out*, edited by Diana Fuss. New York: Routledge.

Goffman, Erving. 1959. *The Presentation of Self in Everyday Life*. New York: Anchor Books.

Griffin, Susan. 1993. "Red Shoes." Pp. 1–11 in *The Politics of the Essay: Feminist Perspectives*, edited by Ruth-Ellen B. Joeres and Elizabeth Mittman. Bloomington: Indiana University Press.

hooks, bell. 1994. *Outlaw Culture: Resisting Representations*. New York: Routledge.

Jordan, Emma Coleman. 1995. "The Power of False Racial Memory and the Metaphor of Lynching." Pp. 37–55 in *Race, Gender, and Power in America*, edited by Anita Faye Hill and Emma Coleman Jordan. New York: Oxford University Press.

Kalberg, Stephen. 1987. "The Origin and Expansion of *Kulturpessimismus*: The Relationships Between Public and Private Spheres in Early Twentieth Century Germany." *Sociological Theory* 5: 150–65.

Kovel, Joel. 1984. *White Racism: A Psychohistory*. New York: Columbia University Press.

Lubiano, Wahneema. 1992. "Black Ladies, Welfare Queens, and State Minstrels: Ideological War by Narrative Means." Pp. 323–363 in *Race-ing Justice, En-gendering Power*, edited by Toni Morrison. New York: Pantheon Books.

Miller, Anita, ed. 1994. *The Complete Transcripts of the Clarence Thomas Anita Hill Hearings: October, 11, 12, 13, 1991*. Chicago: Academy Chicago Publishers.

Muir, Janette Kenner, and Marilyn J. Young. 1996. "Evidence, Credibility, and Narrative Structures: The Case of Anita Hill." Pp. 57–77 in *Outsiders Looking In*, edited by Paul Siegel. Cresskill, NJ: Hampton Press.

Phelps, Timothy M., and Helen Winternitz. 1992. *Capitol Games: Clarence Thomas, Anita Hill, and the Story of a Supreme Court Nomination*. New York: Hyperion.

Rich, Adrienne. 1977. *Of Woman Born: Motherhood as Experience and Institution*. New York: Bantam.

Robinson, Cherylon, and Lawrence Alfred Powell. 1996. "The Postmodern Politics of Context Definition: Competing Reality Frames in the Hill-Thomas Spectacle." *The Sociological Quarterly* 37: 279–305.

Roper, Cynthia S., Mike Chanslor, and Diane G. Bystrom. 1996. "Sex, Race, and Politics: An Intercultural Communication Approach to the Hill/Thomas Hearings." Pp. 44–60 in *The Lynching of Language*, edited by Sandra L. Ragan et al. Urbana: University of Illinois Press.

Ross, Andrew. 1992. "The Private Parts of Justice." Pp. 40–60 in *Race-ing Justice, En-gendering Power*, edited by Toni Morrison. New York: Pantheon Books.

Smith, Dorothy. 1990. *Texts, Facts, and Femininity: Exploring the Relations of Ruling*. New York: Routledge.

——. 1992. "Sociology from Women's Experience: A Reaffirmation." *Sociological Theory* 10: 88–98.

Thomas, Kendall. 1992. "Strange Fruit." Pp. 364–89 in *Race-ing Justice, En-gendering Power*, edited by Toni Morrison. New York: Pantheon Books.

Young, Iris Marion. 1990. *Throwing Like a Girl and Other Essays in Feminist Philosophy and Social Theory*. Bloomington: Indiana University Press.

XI

EQUALITY AND THE MILLENNIUM

The Crisis in Education Has Consequences for the *-Isms*

35

How Harvard Helped Curb Title IX's Role in Admitting Women

Karen Blumenthal

More than thirty years before Harvard University President Lawrence H. Summers suggested that innate differences may keep women out of science and engineering, Harvard took a stand on women's affinity for science—and helped limit the scope of a key civil-rights law.

In a 1971 letter to a congressman, a spokesman for new Harvard President Derek C. Bok argued that accepting more female undergraduates at Harvard University "might underutilize our science facilities and require expensive additions to our faculty and staff in already crowded departments in the humanities and social sciences."

The university was trying to head off some little-noticed legislation making its way through Congress. Then known as Title X, and later formally known as Title IX of the Education Amendments of 1972, this short section would have required all schools receiving federal funds to end discrimination on the basis of sex. In other words, schools would no longer be able to set quotas, or ceilings, on how many women they would accept.

But Harvard and many other private universities, including Yale and Princeton, feared the new law would actually impose quotas on them, requiring them to admit just as many women as men. That simply wasn't a good idea, wrote a special adviser for Yale, which had just begun admitting women.

Harvard's approach was more novel. Radcliffe graduates donate less to the university than Harvard alumni do, it argued, so it would suffer financially from accepting more women. And then there was the issue of those empty science buildings.

In fact, the student newspaper reported, in the classes entering in 1971, 46 percent of Radcliffe freshmen intended to major in science, compared with just 40 percent at Harvard. (In an e-mail this week, Mr. Bok noted that many potential science majors later change their minds.)

Citing letters from prominent universities, Rep. John N. Erlenborn, offered an amendment. Title IX could outlaw sex bias in hiring at schools and universities, and in admission to graduate schools. But it wouldn't apply to undergraduate admissions.

"I do not oppose the right of women to attend college," Mr. Ertenborn said, according to the Congressional Record. But if Congress took away "from colleges the right to determine the composition of their own student bodies, it will plant the seed of destruction for our system of higher education as we know it."

Edith Green, who sponsored the original bill, argued that she wasn't trying to impose quotas but to end quotas that routinely placed a ceiling on female admission.

Patsy Mink recalled that her daughter had been rejected from Stanford, "even though the university acknowledged that she was abundantly qualified," because Stanford limited women to 40 percent of the student body. "Millions of women pay taxes into the federal treasury," she argued, supporting schools "to which we are denied equal access."

When the final House vote was taken, the Erlenborn amendment passed by five votes, but the Senate version of the education bill included undergraduate admissions. The conference committee compromised: State-supported public universities couldn't discriminate against women in undergraduate admissions. But private colleges could.

Since it was enacted, Title IX has become almost notorious for its impact on college athletics, but its original intent was simply to expand women's access to higher education, a move that, in turn, was expected to aid the pursuit of a broader range of careers, including those in science.

Indeed, once those doors were cracked open, women stormed through. In 1972, women earned about 44 percent of the nation's bachelor's degrees. In 1982, they surpassed men. Today, more than 57 percent of all undergraduate degrees are earned by women. What's more, in 2001–2002, according to Education Department figures, women earned more undergraduate degrees than men in agricultural sciences, biological sciences, and health sciences. They also earned 47 percent of the mathematics degrees and 42 percent of the physical science degrees. In some ways, Harvard has lagged behind: Last year was the first time it admitted more women than men to its freshman class.

Meanwhile, the common application for admission, accepted by Harvard and dozens of other colleges, states in a footnote, that "the admission process at private undergraduate institutions is exempt" from Title IX.

EDITOR'S NOTE

One hundred twenty Harvard professors signed a letter that stated, in part, that "an institutional culture at Harvard erects numerous barriers to improving the representation of women on the faculty."[1] The letter was in response to Larry

Summers, then president of Harvard, who ruffled more than a few feathers when he proposed that innate differences between males and females explain why fewer women succeed in math and science. Regarding Summers's notion of biology over social learning, Ann Hulbert, writing in *The New York Times*, analyzes the data differently. Hulbert and others argue that boys' overall better math scores on standardized tests are the result of high scores for a small number of boys, not all boys, and that there are many, many low-scoring boys in the pool.[2]

Pointing to statistics that suggest something other than genetics might be going on at Harvard, Hulbert reports that since Summers became president, the percentage of tenure offers to women in the arts and sciences at Harvard have declined from 37 percent to 11 percent.[3]

It's possible, then, to believe that Summers recently stated that it wasn't "too much [of an exaggeration] to say that" universities like Harvard "were designed by men for men."[4]

NOTES

1. Rebecca Winters, "Harvard's Crimson Face," *Time*, 24 January 2005, p. 52.

2. Ann Hulbert, "Boy Problems," *The New York Times*, 3 April 2005, p. 13.

3. Ibid.

4. Phillip Kennicott, "Summers Storm," *The Washington Post National Weekly Edition*, 2–8 May 2005, pp. 8–9.

36

Downsizing Higher Education

Confronting the New Realities of the High-Tech Information Age Global Economy

Walda Katz-Fishman

EDUCATION AS GATEKEEPER OR LIBERATOR? KNOWLEDGE AND FACULTY JOBS FOR WHOM?

The mythology of American democracy has rested squarely on the assertion that education—and especially higher education—is the key to achieving the American dream, that education is the great equalizer. The American dream has turned into the American nightmare for the working class and the poor and has begun to turn bad even for the more privileged middle class. As we take a sober look at what is going on, we find that while higher education was never what it was alleged to be, that it, too, is under siege. Colleges and universities are being restructured and downsized. Staff are fired with no notice. Intense efforts are underway to cut full-time faculty and eliminate faculty tenure and, with this, academic freedom and faculty governance. Faculty are overworked—they teach more and larger classes with less support staff under deteriorating conditions. The flow of government research funds is slowing, sometimes to a trickle and sometimes to an end. Teaching hospitals, mired in the economic crisis of health care, are being downsized, closed, or spun off from universities. Graduate student teaching assistants are being forced to do basically full time faculty teaching, at one fraction the compensation. Tuition is soaring, student aid is failing behind, and enrollments are beginning to drop off. If and when students graduate, they are drowning in debt. Censorship is on the rise in subtle and not so subtle ways. Why?

In reality, education perpetuates rather than transforms the social order and its inequalities of class, race, ethnicity, nationality, and gender. In turn, the economic revolution and crisis of the larger society are expressed within the institutions of higher education and in the day-to-day operations of colleges and universities. Thus, to better understand the attack on higher education—which is really an attack on faculty, students, and staff, and the communities from which we come—we must examine the economic and political realities of this historic moment.

The global integration of the market economy (driven by the necessity for maximum profits) and the high technology revolution are at the very heart of the transformation and crises in our society—including that within higher education. America's 128 million workers today compete in a global labor market with more than 3 billion workers worldwide, including over 900 million un/underemployed. The once high-paid American workers have seen their real wages steadily decline over the last twenty years as they compete with low-waged labor in the developing world. Computers and automation are eliminating millions of jobs, leading to reengineering (downsizing) in manufacturing, the service sector, government, and even the knowledge sector. This creates a further surplus of workers who further drive down wages as they compete for fewer and fewer good jobs—full-time secure jobs at a living wage with benefits.

The political attack spearheaded by today's politicians—both Democrats and Republicans—is a reflection of this new economic reality. The reform agenda of the New Deal and civil rights eras—including government support for health, education, and welfare—is being shredded. White supremacy is intensifying. The prison industrial complex is mushrooming. Censorship and cultural repression are at a new high. The right wing is in elected office. And the danger of a police state is upon us. . . .

EDUCATION, SOCIETY, AND THE ECONOMY— SOME ENDURING RELATIONSHIPS

Education, including higher education, is a key institution in the reproduction of the existing social order and the maintenance of the *status quo*. This occurs in two critical spheres: (1) in the material sphere of work, the labor force, and the struggle for survival (the social relations of production)—with their inequalities of class dynamically and historically related to race, ethnicity, nationality, and gender; and (2) in the ideological sphere of knowledge, ideas, theories, and values that legitimate or challenge the existing social order—and give direction to political motion in society.

Education, at its various levels of varying quality, prepares the current and future generations to do the work that needs to be done in society. Unskilled workers rarely, if ever, go to college and many do not even complete high school. In contrast, the most skilled technical and professional workers in our society often go to graduate and professional school and earn advanced degrees. As industry expanded from the 1940s through the 1970s, and the service and knowledge sectors of the economy grew—the development of this mass work required a corresponding development of mass education and higher education. This period saw the expansion of public education and of higher education—of land grant colleges and universities and historically black colleges and universities, which had historically served "special" groups in the society, as well as of public two- and four-year colleges and private colleges and universities. The new expanding work force needed a new kind of education for the post–World War II industrial and service economy that was taking off.

All that has changed in the 1990s. Today's postindustrial high-tech global information society has witnessed the end of "mass labor" and, with it, the end of "mass education." Yesterday's public education, organized in the image of the factory and largely preparing youth for factory jobs, is in deep crisis. Higher education and those aspiring to teach and learn there are also in deep crisis. The shrinking labor markets for all kinds of workers—not just manufacturing workers, but also service, and knowledge workers—means a downsizing of higher education that was, in reality, never available to the masses, but was accessible to the growing middle class and some sections of the working class of all racial ethnic groups.

In the 1990s, soaring tuition and student aid that does not keep pace call that accessibility—however limited it may have been—into question. More and more students work one or even two jobs while trying to complete their degrees in a reasonable amount of time. With fewer jobs available for college graduates, there is less and less reason for those in power to ensure easy and affordable access to higher education for today's youth.

Faculty who entered or have maintained their position in the middle class as knowledge workers to do the research needed by government and the corporate sector and to teach the next generation in our colleges and universities are less and less needed as the number of students going to college begins to decline. Full-time faculty are being increasingly replaced by part-time, contingent academic workers—mirroring the dynamics occurring in the larger labor force. A multi-tiered academic work force for faculty brings home to the academy the harsher realities of work in the larger society. The top tier consists of privileged full-time tenured faculty, the second tier of full-time tenure track faculty in the race for tenure, and the bottom tier of part-time and contract faculty often working multiple jobs at subsistence wages with no benefits. For those doing research, some funds are still available. But they are most available for researchers willing to do the bidding of the corporate class and its drive for maximum profits and maximum social control—however much these purposes may be disguised or denied—often at unimaginable expense to the quality of life on the planet and to the dignity and freedom of the world's peoples.

Whenever there have been changes in the economic foundation of society—how we produce and distribute the goods and services necessary for social life—there have been corresponding changes in the institutions of education and in the production and application of knowledge. If we examine higher education in the United States historically and today, we find a definite relationship between the social and economic order and changes within it and the quantity and quality of higher education.

The Types and Number of Institutions of Higher Education

In 1970 there were 891 two-year colleges and 1,665 four-year+ colleges and universities, for a total of 2,556. Between 1970 and 1992 the biggest jump in the number of institutions was in 1980. The number of two-year colleges increased by almost 50 percent to 1,274 and of four-year+ institutions to 1,957, for a total of 3,231. By 1992 there was some additional increase to 1,469 two-year colleges and 2,169 four-year+ colleges and universities, for a total of 3,638 institutions (U.S. Bureau of the Census 1994, p. 180, table no. 274). This greater increase in two-year colleges suggests that even though the overall number of higher education institutions increased dramatically, the greatest increase was at the low end of two-year colleges—hardly preparation for the high-tech information-age jobs of the future.

Who's in College? Who Graduates When?

In 1972 total student enrollment in all higher education institutions was 9.1 million, including 8.2 million whites, 727,000 blacks, and 242,000 Latina/os (U.S. Bureau of the Census 1994, p. 179, table no. 272). By 1982 these figures had increased to 12.4 million total students: 10 million whites, 1.1 million blacks, 519,00.0 Latina/os, 351,000 Asian Americans, and 88,000 American Indians. In 1992 they further increased to 14.5 million total students: 10.9 million whites, 1.39 million blacks, 955,000 Latina/os, 697,000 Asian Americans, and 119,000 American Indians. . . . The patterns for 1994 are similar to those for 1993. Overall enrollment declined 0.2 percent to 14.28 million, with white enrollment declining 1.7 percent to 47 million, black enrollment increasing 4.9 percent to 3.42 million, Latina enrollment increasing 6.9 percent to 1.06 million, Asian American enrollment increasing 6.8 percent to 774,000 and American Indian enrollment increasing 5 percent to 52,400 (Carter and Wilson 1996, p. 60; table 3).

We do not yet know the patterns of college enrollment in the new high-tech global economy. College education in this period is much like a high school education was in the earlier expanding industrial era—it is essential for obtaining the skills needed for employment. The problem, however, is that high technology is eliminating more and more jobs so "that even if every youth 18–24 years old got a college degree, many would still be unemployed and underemployed." In addition, it seems that the increases in enrollment that characterized the earlier years have slowed significantly and that those students who make it to college accumulate much greater debt that those who graduated prior to the 1990s. And, despite their increasing enrollment, students of color remain a long way from parity with white students. In addition, many of us may have thought that going to college was far more widespread than it actually is and has been. At its best, roughly one-third of all eighteen- to twenty-four-year-olds are in college, or 42 percent of high school graduates. This still excludes two-thirds of the youth in this age group and well over half of those who graduate from high school.

Class position and family income are critical in terms of who will graduate from college by age twenty-four. The lowest income youth (whose family income is less than $21,300) have a 6 percent or one in sixteen chance of graduating by age twenty-four. This figure has been constant since 1970. Youth whose family income is between $21,300 and $38,700 have between an 8 percent and 12 percent chance—fluctuating over the period from 1970 to 1993. Youth whose family income is between $38,700 and $63,800 have seen their chances of earning a college degree by age twenty-four increase from 14 percent in 1980 to 23 percent in 1993. *Those most likely to earn a college degree by age twenty-four are, of course, the youth whose families have the highest income—above $63,800. Their chances went from 29 percent in 1980 to 81 percent in 1993* (Common Agenda Coalition and National Priorities Project [CAC & NPP] 1995, pp. 20–21).

Given the disproportionate number of blacks at the low end of the class structure, we find that half as many—or fewer—blacks as whites had completed four or more years of college among those twenty-five years and older from the late 1950s through 1990. In 1957 these percentages were 2.9 percent for blacks and 8 percent for whites. By 1964 these percentages increased slightly to 3.9 percent for blacks and 9.6 percent for whites. They increased more dramatically to 6.4 percent of blacks and 14.5 percent of whites by 1975. These figures almost doubled by 1989 to 11.8 percent of blacks and 21.8 percent of whites. For blacks this number decreased to 11.3 percent in 1990 (the latest year for which these data are available), though it continued to increase for whites to 22 percent (Kominski and Adams 1992, p. 96).

The bleakest picture is for African American working-class youth, especially men. It has been much noted in recent years that more young black men are in the criminal injustice system (in prison or jail, on probation or parole) than are in college. More precisely, in 1989 19.6 percent of black men eighteen to twenty-four years old were in college while 23 percent were under criminal "justice" supervision. While the proportion of young black men in college increased to 22.8 percent by 1993 (the latest year for which data are available), the proportion of young black men twenty- to twenty-nine years old under criminal "justice" supervision soared to 30.2 percent in 1994 and to 32.2 percent in 1995 (Carter and Wilson 1995, pp. 66, Table 2; Mauer and Huling 1995, p. 4).

How Much Does It Cost? Who Pays?

The Sentencing Project estimates the cost of criminal "justice" control for the 827,440 young black men in the system in 1995 to be $6 billion a year

(Mauer and Huling 1995, p. 1). Consider how much cheaper it would be to send a young man to college (average cost of tuition and fees, and room and board at a public four-year college was about $5,400 in 1993) compared to the cost of prison at about $35,000 (U.S. Bureau of the Census 1994, p. 184, table no. 280; Joint Center for Political and Economic Studies [JCPES] 1995, p. 2). From 1980 to 1995 the federal government has decreased the education budget by $59 billion and increased the "corrections" budget in the criminal "justice" system by the same $59 billion (CAC & NPP 1995, p. 7). Is this a coincidence? Probably not! In the last decade alone the government spent $34.6 billion of our tax dollars to build one thousand new prisons and jails to hold the soaring inmate population—now over 1.5 million (*Washington Post* 1995, p. A25).

These numbers suggest that it is surely much cheaper and more cost effective to educate a young black man than to put him in jail. Yet those in power who insist on jail rather than college know the danger of educating those for whom there is no good job and no future! A study for the Justice Policy Institute, *From Classrooms to Cell Blocks* (1997), found that states have dramatically cut their funding for higher education. In the 1980s state expenditures for higher education decreased 6 percent while expenditures for corrections increased 95 percent. From 1987 to 1995 higher education state spending decreased 18.2 percent, while corrections gained 30 percent (Ambrosio and Schiraldi 1997, p. 6). In the 1994–1995 period, state bond fund expenditures for higher education declined in the amount of $954 million, and expenditures for corrections increased $926 million—almost an identical amount (Ambrosio and Schiraldi 1997, p. 10). The ruling class, despite its rhetoric about education, is pouring millions and billions into the prison-industrial complex at the expense of higher education for the youth of this country.

In addition, the cost of a college education, while affordable relative to the cost of prison, has soared in recent years. Between 1980 and 1993 the average cost of a college education increased roughly 300 percent. Average tuition and fees for all public institutions (two- and four-year colleges and other four-year schools) more than tripled from $583 in 1980 to $1,787 in 1993.[1] If room and board are included, these figures go from $2,165 in 1980 to $5,394 in 1993.[2] Average tuition and fees for all private institutions also tripled from $3,130 in 1980 to $10,031 in 1993. When room and board are included, the average cost goes from $4,912 in 1980 to $14,741 in 1993 (U.S. Bureau of the Census 1994, p. 184, table no. 280).

While college costs were tripling, the average Pell Grant—the largest federal program for grants to college students, did not *triple*. In 1980 the average Pell Grant was $882, which represented 41 percent of average college costs (tuition, fees, room and board at a public institution). By 1993 the average Pell Grant had increased to $1,418, but college costs had tripled; thus Pell Grants covered only 26 percent of average college costs (U.S. Bureau of the Census 1994, p. 183, table no. 278).

The remainder of student aid in the 1990s comes from student loans, work study, or just plain work. In 1980 the federal government spent $2.4 billion on Pell Grants and a total of $10.3 billion on all student financial assistance programs. In 1993 it spent $6.1 billion on Pell Grants and a total of $24.7 billion on all assistance (U.S. Bureau of the Census 1994, p. 183, table no. 278). Clearly, with only a quarter of college costs for only 30 percent of college students covered by Pell Grants, most students are drowning in debt if and when they graduate. This is a strange way to show the next generation how important a college education is to their success and well-being and to that of society as well. Or, are they lying to us?

How Many Faculty (Full-Time/Part-Time)? What's the Pay?

Much is made by college administrators and some corporate elites of the drain placed on the resources of our society by the full-time tenured faculty of the country. When we actually look at the numbers, we find that this charge is much exaggerated. Not only are there *not* that many tenured faculty, but faculty salary and benefits are modest compared to that of many corporate CEOs and even that of college administrators and professional workers in the corporate sector.

The total number of college faculty went from 474,000 in 1970 to 686,000 in 1980, to 840,000 in 1990 (the latest year for which these data are available). In *toto* this is less than 1 million faculty. But wait—of these, in 1970, 78 percent were full-time and 22 percent part-time. In 1980, 66 percent were full-time and 34 percent part-time, and in 1990 only 61 percent were full-time and 39 percent part-time (U.S. Bureau of the Census 1994, p. 180, table no. 274). Thus, in 1990, 512,400 faculty (slightly over one-half million) were full-time while 327,600 were part-time. If this trend continues—as is happening—by the early years of the twenty-first century more college faculty will be part-time contingent workers than full-time. This hardly speaks to a societal (or governmental) priority on the importance of a quality college education for all our youth.

DISMANTLING HIGHER EDUCATION AS WE KNOW IT: HIGHER EDUCATION CONFRONTS THE CORPORATE MODEL OF MAXIMUM PROFITS AND "LEAN AND MEAN"

The high-technology revolution in the productive process that has been eliminating jobs in the manufacturing and service sectors by the millions has finally hit the knowledge industry and higher education itself, including the Ivy League. In the larger economy, 25 million jobs were lost from the 1960s to the 1990s, some of these quality jobs in "blue chip" companies (Mills 1996; Rifkin 1995). By early in the next century another 35 million jobs are slated for elimination. In general, the new jobs created—when they are created—tend to be part-time and contingent jobs with low wages, no security, and no benefits. This shrinking of economic opportunity means a shrinking need for educational preparation.

The corporate model of lean and mean that has swept the corporate and government sectors—that will do whatever is necessary to maximize profits even if it means destroying the social fabric of our communities and creating chaos—is being implemented in higher education. The corporate class and those who represent its interests in government are setting the agenda locally, regionally, nationally, and internationally. If there are no good jobs for middle-class and working-class youth, the government and corporate sectors will not support their education. This is the reality rather than other way round—as it is presented by the ruling class with their individualistic and "blame the victim" ideology and propaganda.

It is essential that we understand how these processes of change operate in society, that we expose the lies constantly put forth by the power elite and its scholar "experts." They assert that poor and working-class youth and young adults cannot get jobs because they lack the necessary education. The truth is that the number of youth in college and with college degrees has nothing to do with the number of jobs in the economy locally, nationally, or globally. The massive elimination of jobs in recent years has proceeded despite roughly the same proportion of youth in college and an increase in their actual numbers. And many of those thrown out of good jobs as a result of downsizing have college degrees and often advanced degrees.

The truth is that *because* there are fewer and fewer good jobs for today's college graduates, those in power are making higher education less and less accessible for the majority of our youth—with working-class youth and youth of color especially hard hit. Thus, the elimination of good jobs and the shrinking job market for college graduates is what is at the root of the attack on higher education and the thorough restructuring and downsizing being imposed under the guise of fiscal accountability and "rightsizing."

For faculty this means fewer and fewer good jobs—part-time and contract work replacing full-time tenured positions, more and larger classes, deteriorating laboratory and teaching conditions, and graduate teaching assistants replacing faculty. Increasingly, too, research funds come only to those who ask the "right" questions—from the point of view of profits, domination, and control. Censorship is intensifying. This includes both self-censorship for fearful faculty looking over their shoulder trying to hold onto their jobs and, more and more, overt censorship through hiring committees, tenure committees (where they exist), publishing venues, and various political groupings set loose on campuses to terrorize faculty—and students—if they persist in teaching and discussing truth from the perspective of those at the bottom of society.

EDUCATION AS LIBERATION: TAKING IT TO THE STREETS

On the one hand fewer workers must be trained—in traditional blue collar as well as white collar, professional, and technical jobs. As important, if not more so, the ideological function of higher education—to search for knowledge and understanding—is increasingly dangerous when that search is calling into question the viability of the economic, political, and social structures of the last five hundred-plus years of capitalist world hegemony. Now that the world is on a trajectory of revolutionary transformation, this knowledge and understanding contain fighting words and ideas, theories and findings. And the ruling corporate class has no intention of allowing faculty the tenure and academic freedom, the well stocked and staffed institutions of higher education to educate the people. Nor will it fund students to acquire this critical and transformative understanding of the world. Within this context, the attack on higher education makes sense from the point of view of the ruling class.

Today we live in a new world—the reforms we fought for have been eliminated and the root causes of our social problems stand more exposed than ever and in greater need than ever of being addressed. The challenge is ours. If we are truly educators, as I trust we are—then I am sure we will work in our communities to create a new learning environment with the teachers, the youth, and those who have already been discarded by this brutal system. This process must inform our research and communications among ourselves as we organize those scholars and students who will, in unity with our communities, develop the popular education and action necessary to win. Our right for a liberatory research and education agenda must be against the same forces that have created untold poverty and misery among working class peoples in the United States—Native Americans, African Americans, Latina/os, Asian Americans, and European Americans—and throughout the world. We will get only what we are organized to take. Together we can make it happen!

NOTES

1. These figures are for the entire academic year for in-state students.
2. The board figures beginning in 1990 are for twenty meals a week rather than meals served seven days a week previously. Also, these figures do not include the cost of books, supplies, and travel—estimated at about $1,000.

REFERENCES

Ambrosio, Tara-Jen and Vincent Schiraldi. 1997. *From Classrooms to Cell Blocks: A National Perspective*. Washington, D.C.: The Justice Policy Institute.

Aronowirtz, Stanley and W. DiFazio. 1994. *The Jobless Future: Sci-Tech and the Dogma of Work*. Minneapolis: University of Minnesota Press.

Beck, Allen J. 1995. "Prisoners in 1994" in Bureau of Justice Statistics Bulletin (August) p. 1. Washington, D.C.: U.S. Department of Justice.

Carter, Deborah and Reginald Wilson. 1995 *Minorities in Higher Education: 1994—13th Annual Report*. Washington, D.C.: American Council on Education.

——. 1996. *Minorities in Higher Education: 1995–1996—14th Annual Report*. Washington, D.C.: American Council on Education.

Chait, Richard. 1995. "The Future of Academic Tenure" in *AGB Priorities* (Spring): 1–12.

Common Agenda Coalition & National Priorities Project (CAC & NPP). 1995. *Creating a Common Agenda: Strategies for Our Communities*. Washington, D.C.: Common Agenda Coalition.

Ewen, Lyna, W. Katz-Fishman, and G. Slaughter. 1990. *Murder of the Mind*. Atlanta, GA: Project South.

Greenberg, Daniel S. 1995. "Surplus in Science," *The Washington Post*, 12 December, A25.

Joint Center for Political and Economic Studies (JCPES). 1995. "Political Trend Letter" in *Focus* (October/November). Washington, D.C.: JCPES.

Katz-Fishman, Walda and Jerome Scott. 1994. "Diversity and Equality: Race and Class in America," *Sociological Forum* 9, no. 4 (November): 569–81.

Kominiski and Adams. 1992. [Cited in 1996 draft dissertation by Paula Snyder, Department of Sociology and Anthropology, Howard University].

Kuumba, M. Bahati, Jerome Scott, and Walda Katz-Fishman. 1995. "Liberation Research and Project South: Weapons in the Hands of the Oppressed," in *Selected Proceedings of the First National Conference on Urban Issues—Crossing Boundaries: Collaborative Solutions to Urban Problems*, edited by D. Koritz, et al., SUNY College at Buffalo–Center for Multidisciplinary Applied Research in Urban Issues.

Mauer, Marc and Tracy Huling. 1995. *Young Black Americans and the Criminal Justice System: Five Years Later*. Washington, D.C.: The Sentencing Project.

Mills, Mike. 1996. "Reorganized AT&T to Cut 40,000 Jobs." *The Washington Post*, 3 January, A1, A21.

Mishel, Lawrence and J. Bernstein. 1995. *The State of Working America. 1994–1995*. New York: M. E. Sharpe.

Peery, Nelson. 1993. *Entering an Epoch of Social Revolution*. Chicago: Workers Press.

Rifkin, Jeremy. 1995. *The End of Work: The Decline of the Global Labor Force and the Dawn of the Post-Market Era*. New York: Tarcher/Putnam.

Soley, Lawrence C. 1995. *Leasing the Ivory Tower: The Corporate Takeover of Academia*. Boston: South End Press.

U.S. Bureau of the Census. 1994. *Statistical Abstract of the United States: 1994* (14th edition). Washington, D.C.

Washington Post. 1995. "Nation's Prison Population Soars Above 1 Million." 10 August, A25.

Woodson, Carter G. 1990 (1933). *The Mis-education of the Negro*. Trenton, NJ: Africa World Press.

EDITOR'S NOTE

Things have changed since Walda Katz-Fishman's article was written in 1995, but not for the better. Some might argue that we have a three-tier system. Poor African American males go to prison, poor students go to community college, and the elite go to Ivy League colleges as always.

First, African American males and the criminal justice system: Crime rates are down, yet more people are in jail. There are almost 1.5 million people in state and federal prisons (the highest in the industrialized world). The federal prison population has increased almost 8 percent per year since 1995 and state prison populations have increased over 3 percent each year. It is telling that due to the unparalleled rates of incarceration in the twentieth and twenty-first centuries—the criminal justice system is one of the few industries that has experienced growth, especially in terms of the job market.

For African American males, it is beyond a crisis. In New York, for example, African American males make up 51 percent of the state prison population and 91 percent of New York City prisoners. If parole and probation are factored in there are twice as many African American males under the jurisdiction of the criminal justice system than are enrolled in any form of higher education in New York State, including community colleges.[1] African Americans are only 13 percent of illegal drug users in the United States, but make up 35 percent of drug arrests, 55 percent of drug possession convictions, and 74 percent of those incarcerated for drug possession.[2] In essence, African American males are sentenced to a different kind of education than the rest of their contemporaries, one that guarantees a large proportion will not only leave prison with fewer life chances than when they entered, but that they will be disenfranchised in the process.

Second, low-income students and higher education: More people understand the relationship between attending college and upward mobility. However, in state after state, it is the same scenario: spending cuts for higher education and that translates to fewer dollars for student aid. For example, in Michigan the average tuition at the state's fifteen public universities has increased more than 67 percent in the last decade while state funding has increased 12 percent. Wayne State University reported a 20 percent cut in state aid and had to cut professors, academic advisors, deans, and groundskeepers. The university has lost over a hundred faculty members in the medical school in the last three years. Not only did Michigan State have to eliminate nine academic programs and cut five hundred jobs, it also had to change the terms of its employee health insurance. In all, the university had to cut $66 million from its budget. Over the last twenty years, state funding for public institutions in Michigan has declined from 62 percent of university budgets to 40 percent.[3] Michigan's plight has been repeated in public universities all over the nation.

The declining financial support of higher education has the greatest impact on low-income students. For low-income students, community college is what they can afford, when a bachelor's degree is what they need. Pell Grants are a federal subsidy intended to assist with college costs for students who have a financial need. "In 1973, 40.5 percent of the students receiving federal Pell Grants . . . attended four-year public schools. In 2001, that portion was only 31 percent."[4] Now, students who lack financial means are going to community colleges, in part, because tuition hikes at two-year schools have been less than at four-year institutions (53 percent and 85 percent respectively) in the last decade.[5] Without benefit of a bachelor degree, low-income students will miss out on the opportunity for greater social and economic mobility.

Even when students receive a Pell Grant, it covers only about 39 percent of the cost compared to 84 percent in 1973.[6] The College Board reports that more public universities are admitting fewer low-income students and offering more assistance to "merit" students.[7]

As a result, low-income students, without financial assistance, are much less likely to receive a bachelor degree by age twenty-four (only about 4.5 percent will do so). On the other hand, 51.4 percent of students whose families have income between $85,000 and $90,000 will finish by age twenty-four.[8]

Third, elite students and college education: While the struggle to receive a college education has been heightened for low-income students who attend public institutions, Ivy League colleges received five to twenty times the median amount of grant money to provide for the everyday needs of poor students even though they have huge endowments—Harvard's and Yale's endowments are in excess of $10 billion and Princeton's is almost $9 billion.[9]

Ivy League schools receive between $169 and $211 for each student who applies for financial aid, while the median amount for colleges is $14.38. Stanford has fewer low-income students than California State at Fresno, but receives seven times as much aid in one program, twenty-eight times in another program, and one hundred times in still another program.

For every Pell dollar one of its students received in 2001–2003, Harvard received $0.98, MIT received $1.09, Princeton, $1.42, while City University of New York received $0.04. For work-study-program students, Yale received $592.75, Duke, $600.28, Columbia, $677.93, while nearly one hundred colleges received less than $20.00. The median amount was $87.67.

Other educational concerns: Not only are spiraling costs and lack of funding a concern for young people and their families, but sagging standardized test scores at early ages are problematic, too. Only 15 percent of fourth graders from low-income households achieved a proficiency reading level in 2003 and only 41 percent of nonpoor fourth graders did.[10]

No wonder then, that of the 1.2 million students who took the ACT test, only one in four met college readiness standards. That means that only 26 percent of those completing the test scored well enough to expect they will earn at least a C in science, and less than half of students' scores were high enough to expect they could earn at least a C in math.[11]

ACT scores are consistent with a report that fifteen-year-old students in the United States rank near the bottom of industrialized countries in math skills.[12] Is there a relationship between students' less than dazzling performance on the ACT and their financial ability to attend a four-year institution? Is it possible that students from low-income households are not achieving in school because they see the handwriting on the wall, just like Lemert's Hallway Hangers (in the first reading)?

It is ironic that U.S. student rankings are low vis-à-vis students in other industrialized countries considering that nationally student math standardized test scores have slightly improved. However, there is some evidence that the rise in student test scores is not due to increased knowledge on the part of students. According to the research of Tom Loveless, of the Brookings Institute, the higher math test scores occur because the eighth grade achievement tests do not include fractions and percentages.[13] The fact that 17 percent of students at public four-year institutions require remedial math before they begin work on a degree substantiates Loveless' findings.[14]

The current administration wants to cut as many as nineteen education programs, including The Javits Gifted and Talented Education Program that funds projects like the one that identifies and assists bright kids in the poorest school districts and the bilingual Spanish and English school honors courses.[15] Other programs to be cut include Parental Information and Resource Centers, Arts in Education, Elementary and Secondary School Counseling, National Writing Project, to name a few. One Education Department official indicated that war and homeland security needs prohibit the continued funding of the nineteen programs.[16]

Even Microsoft's Bill Gates expressed concern: "I am terrified for our work force of tomorrow. . . . In math and science. . . . By 12th grade U.S. students are scoring near the bottom of all industrialized nations. . . . In 2001, India graduated almost a million more students from college than the U.S. did. China graduates two times as many students with bachelor's degrees and they have six times as many graduates majoring in engineering."[17] We used to make up for the gap in engineers by importing them, but people can now stay home and compete with the United States.[18]

It has been argued that the educational system reproduces the class system. Does Katz-Fishman's reading and the editor's note provide a sense of that? And now that China and India are primed to compete toe-to-toe with the United States, does it appear that the United States is up for the challenge?

NOTES

1. Michael I. Niman, "Incarceration Nation: The US is the World's Leading Jailer, *Buffalo Beat*, 4 January 2000.

2. Ibid.

3. Maryanne George, "Higher Education, Higher Bills," *Detroit Free Press*, 9 August 2005

4. Jane Bryant Quinn, "Colleges' New Tuition Crisis," *Newsweek*, 2 February 2004, 49.

5. Ibid.

6. Ibid.

7. Ibid.

8. Ibid.

9. "Rich Colleges Receiving Richest Share of U.S. Aid, *The New York Times*, 9 November 2003, 1, 18.

10. Bob Herbert, "Left Behind, Way Behind," *The New York Times*, 29 August 2005, A19.

11. Tamar Lewin, "Many Going to College Aren't Ready, Report Finds," *The New York Times*, 17 August 2005, A13.

12. June Kronholz, "Economic Time Bomb: U.S. Teens Are Among Worst at Math," *The Wall Street Journal*, 7 December 2004, B1.

13. Ibid

14. Ibid.

15. Shailagh Murray, "Bright, Poor—and Out of Luck," *The Washington Post National Weekly Edition*, 25–31 July 2005, 15.

16. Ibid.

17. Thomas L. Friedman, "It's a Flat World, After All," *The New York Times*, 3 April 2005, 33–37.

18. Ibid.

Epilogue

Social scientists, for the most part, go about the business of researching and teaching in an unbiased, objective manner. Further, sociology 101 teaches us that sociology is not about presenting what *should* be, but what *is*. Through the words of the distinguished scholars assembled in this text, you have read what *is*. You have been given information about the differential treatment members of minority groups experience in a variety of situations and under varying conditions. It is for you to decide if this is the way it *should* be. It is for you to decide whether discriminating against members of minority groups or excluding white males is the best way to organize a society. It is for you to decide whether denying people jobs, promotions, or neighborhoods in which to live because of the shape or the color of their skin is the sign of a just society. If you feel disturbed by some or all of what you have read, then it is for you to change what *is* and decide what *should* be.

When I step into the classroom at the beginning of each semester my goal is to make students think out of the box for the fifteen weeks we spend together. Through this text you have been a student in my classroom. By reading the selections you have been exposed to another view, another angle from which to think about old issues. If you have begun to think out of the box, I hope it will not end with the reading of the final entry. Many, many former students tell me that once they stepped out of the box, it's impossible to get back inside. May you pursue a life outside of the box!

Index

About the Editor

Barbara A. Arrighi is associate professor of sociology at Northern Kentucky University. Professor Arrighi's research and teaching have focused on gender, work, and family.